The Founding Fathers and
the Place of Religion in America

❖

The Founding Fathers and

the Place of Religion in America

❖

Frank Lambert

PRINCETON UNIVERSITY PRESS

PRINCETON AND OXFORD

Copyright © 2003 by Frank Lambert
Requests for permission to reproduce material from this work
should be sent to Permissions, Princeton University Press
Published by Princeton University Press, 41 William Street,
Princeton, New Jersey 08540
In the United Kingdom: Princeton University Press,
3 Market Place, Woodstock, Oxfordshire OX20 1SY
All Rights Reserved

Library of Congress Cataloging-in-Publication Data

Lambert, Frank, 1943–
The founding fathers and the place of religion in America / Frank Lambert.
p. cm.
Includes bibliographical references and index.
ISBN 0-691-08829-2 (alk. paper)
1. Church and state—United States—History—18th century.
2. Freedom of religion—United States—History—18th century.
3. United States—Religion—To 1800. I. Title.
BR516.L29 2003
322′.1′0973—dc21   2002024346

British Library Cataloging-in-Publication Data is available

This book has been composed in Dante

Printed on acid-free paper.∞

www.pupress.princeton.edu

Printed in the United States of America

1   3   5   7   9   10   8   6   4   2

FOR BETH

❖

❖ Contents ❖

❖ *Acknowledgments* ❖

WHILE I have benefited from the good offices of many people in writing this book, foremost in directly shaping this book is my editor, Thomas LeBien. I am indebted to him for his vision and imagination in the early conception of the project and his knowledge and encouragement in seeing it to completion. The book is better because of his work. I also profited from the critical reading of the manuscript by two scholars, Leigh E. Schmidt and Patrick Griffin, whose insightful comments sharpened my argument. I am once again indebted to Senior Editor Lauren Lepow for her skillful editing, in places making the obscure clear and at others the pedestrian graceful. I, of course, am responsible for remaining flaws and errors.

More removed from the actual writing of the book, but nevertheless a powerful influence, is Tim Breen of Northwestern University. Our friendship extends over fifteen years and has progressed from that of mentor-student to that of colleagues. As an outstanding scholar and teacher, Tim has inspired me through his exemplary record of excellence. And he has on many occasions imparted trenchant conceptual insights, often sketched on a napkin, that have stimulated my own thinking. He aided the writing of this book more directly by inviting me to teach his classes while he was at Oxford University as the Harmsworth Professor. I was able to test ideas on church-state relations before some delightful, tough critics, undergraduates in a capstone course for history majors and graduate students in a reading seminar.

I owe much to the bright undergraduate and graduate students at Purdue and Northwestern Universities who helped shape this work by participating in classes and seminars on the place of religion in America. Through lively discussion and thoughtful papers, they challenged me to reevaluate assumptions and consider alternative frameworks.

I also have the good fortune of having a wonderful, supportive family. My wife, Beth, unfailingly encourages my scholarship, enduring periods of preoccupied silence followed by animated volubility. Our sons, Talley and William, both businessmen with history majors, provide real or feigned interest and, upon occasion, direct research assistance, locating and retrieving archival materials. Punctuating the writing of this book have been two weddings and a birth, bringing to our family two delightful daughters-in-law, Caroline and Paige, and a wonderful grandson, William Reid.

The Founding Fathers and

the Place of Religion in America

❖

❖ Introduction ❖

I N 1639, a group of New England Puritans drafted a constitution af-
firming their faith in God and their intention to organize a Christian
Nation. Delegates from the towns of Windsor, Hartford, and Wethers-
field drew up the Fundamental Orders of Connecticut, which made clear
that their government rested on divine authority and pursued godly purposes. The opening lines express the framers' trust in God and their dependence on his guidance: "Forasmuch as it hath pleased the All-mighty
God by the wise disposition of his divyne providence so to Order and
dispose of things, ... [and] well knowing where a people are gathered
togather the word of God requires that to mayntayne the peace and vnion
of such a people there should be an orderly and decent Government
established according to God, to order and dispose of the affayres of the
people." Moreover, the aim of the government so instituted was religious:
"to mayntayne and presearue the liberty and purity of the gospell of our
Lord Jesus which we now professe, as also the disciplyne of the Churches,
which according to the truth of the said gospell is now practised amongst
vs."[1] Like their neighbors in Massachusetts Bay, the Connecticut Puritans
determined to plant a "Christian Common-wealth," what Governor John
Winthrop hoped would become a "City upon a Hill" that would inspire
believers everywhere as a model Christian Nation.[2]

Those Puritan Fathers exemplify two of the most enduring views of
colonial America: America as a haven of religious freedom, and America
as a Christian Nation. First, the Puritan settlers had fled England, where
Archbishop William Laud had persecuted them because they refused to
subscribe to religious beliefs and practices that they deemed to be unscriptural. Now in the American wilderness, they were free to worship
according to the dictates of their consciences, governed only by the rule
of God's word. And, second, those Puritan Fathers organized a Christian
State. They established their Congregational churches as the official reli-

1

gion of Connecticut, supported by tax revenues and defended by the coercive arm of government. The churches defined "heretics," and the state punished them, even to the point of executing those found guilty of "direct, express, presumptuous, or high-minded blasphemy." Moreover, citizenship in the state was directly tied to one's religious faith. The authors of the Fundamental Orders meant for only godly Christians to rule, an intention embodied in the oath of the governor, which committed the chief magistrate to govern "according to the rule of the word of God."[3]

One hundred and fifty years later, George Washington took another oath, swearing to "faithfully execute the office of the President of the United States" and pledging to the best of his ability to "preserve, protect and defend the Constitution of the United States." The constitution that he swore to uphold was the work of another group of America's progenitors, commonly known as the "Founding Fathers," who in 1787 drafted a constitution for the new nation. But unlike the work of the Puritan Fathers, the federal constitution made no reference whatever to God or divine providence, citing as its sole authority "the people of the United States." Further, its stated purposes were secular, political ends: "to form a more perfect Union, establish Justice, insure domestic Tranquility, provide for the common defence, promote the general Welfare, and secure the Blessings of Liberty." Instead of building a "Christian Commonwealth," the supreme law of the land established a secular state. The opening clause of its first amendment introduced the radical notion that the state had no voice concerning matters of conscience: "Congress shall make no law respecting an establishment of religion or prohibiting the free exercise thereof."[4] In debating the language of that amendment, the first House of Representatives rejected a Senate proposal that would have made possible the establishment of the Christian religion or of some aspect of Christian orthodoxy.[5] There would be no Church of the United States. Nor would America represent itself to the world as a Christian Republic.

Just as 1639 represents a defining moment in Americans' religious heritage, so does 1787. While the Puritan Fathers gave us the symbols of America as haven of religious freedom and America as a Christian Nation, the Founding Fathers provided enduring legacies that define the place and role of religion in American society. Their bequests were the ideas of separation of church and state and the free exercise of religion extended to people of all faiths or no faith. Their achievement can be understood only against the backdrop of the American Revolution. Clearly, they were architects of a political revolution, throwing off constitutional monarchy for a democratic republic. But they were also framers of a religious revolution, rejecting the idea of an established or official religion, which was the organizing principle informing church-state relations in the vast majority of countries, as indeed it had been in most of the American colonies. Never before had there been such a total separation of religious and political institutions. But the ban on establishment was not the Founders' only legacy in church-state matters. Regarding religion as a natural right that the governed never surrendered to government, they prohibited any interference in citizens' rights to the free exercise of religion.

These two defining moments in American history, 1639 and 1787, frame the central question of this book: How did the Puritan Fathers erecting their "City upon a Hill" transform into the Founding Fathers drawing a distinct line between church and state? The answer lies in the changing meaning of freedom in the concept of freedom of religion. To the Puritans who fled persecution, Massachusetts Bay represented the freedom to practice without interference the one true faith, which they based solely on the Bible, correctly interpreted. Thus religious freedom in the "City upon a Hill" meant freedom from error, with church and state, though separate, working together to support and protect the one true faith. Those who believed differently were free to go elsewhere and sometimes compelled to do so. The Founding Fathers had a radically different conception of religious freedom. Influenced by the Enlightenment, they had great confidence in the individual's ability to understand the world and its most fundamental laws through the exercise of his or her reason. To them, true religion was not something handed down by a church or contained in the Bible but rather was to be found through free rational inquiry. Drawing on radical Whig ideology, a body of thought whose principal concern was expanded liberties, the framers sought to secure their idea of religious freedom by barring any alliance between church and state.

The radical change in the meaning of religious freedom greatly concerned many in 1787. William Williams of Connecticut was appalled when he first read a draft of the proposed United States Constitution.

The merchant and delegate to the Connecticut Ratifying Convention expected to see in the document's preface language similar to that found in the Fundamental Orders, some acknowledgment that the new republic rested on a Christian foundation and depended upon divine providence. Instead he saw no hint of the nation's religious heritage: no mention of God, no appeal to divine guidance, no pledge to build a godly society. Williams thought that the Preamble ought at least to express *"a firm belief of the being and perfections of the one living and true God, the creator and supreme Governour of the world."* To Williams, the period between 1639 and 1787 represented decline, at least in the important matters of personal piety and public morality. He wanted the United States Constitution to include a religious test for officeholders that would "require an explicit acknowledgment of the being of a God, his perfections and his providence."[6] After all, the Connecticut Constitution, as well as those of most of the states, called for such a test.

Unlike Williams, James Madison applauded the new federal constitution for its contribution to religious life in the new republic. To him, it safeguarded religious freedom for all citizens by eliminating the government's voice in ecclesiastical matters. He regarded religion as a "natural right" that the governed never surrender to their governors. Further, he thought that "true" religion would triumph by its own merits if its advocates were free to pursue it without coercion. To Madison, "the separation between Religion & Govt in the Constitution of the United States" was the surest guarantee of "the sacred principle of religious liberty."[7] History was filled with examples of unholy alliances between church and state as religious and political leaders sought to curry each other's favor for their own selfish ends. Indeed, the Puritan Fathers themselves had fled England when Charles I's strict enforcement of religious conformity violated the Puritans' liberty of conscience. While Williams was primarily worried about America as a "Christian Nation," Madison was more concerned about America as a haven of religious liberty.[8]

The same questions that Williams and Madison raised in the late eighteenth century continue to interest Americans today, sometimes expressed with great passion. During the last two decades of the twentieth century and continuing into the twenty-first, Americans have engaged in a culture war that informs much of the country's political discourse in the new millennium. On one side of the debate are those who insist that

America has been since its conception a "Christian Nation," and that somewhere along the way, as such it has lost its bearings. They blame "liberals" for not only turning their backs on the country's religious heritage but openly attacking those who embrace "traditional" Christian values.[9] To support their claims, these conservatives often conflate the planters—such as the New England Puritans and the Chesapeake Anglicans—and the Founders into one set of forefathers who came to America to plant "true" Christianity and to practice it in freedom. Further, they insist that the Founders never intended a separation of church and state, arguing that at most the First Amendment aimed at preventing Congress from favoring any single sect. In searching the historical record, these partisans seek or invent a "usable past" that supports their positions. For example, in asserting that early America was a Christian Nation, they gloss over the fact that many Americans, especially Native Americans and African Americans, were non-Christians, and they fail to recognize the deep-seated differences among Christians, so deep that in some instances one sect questioned whether another was Christian at all.

Partisans on the other side of the culture war also consult the nation's Founders for a "usable past" of their own. They, too, tend to conflate the two sets of progenitors by making both the Founding and the Planting Fathers impassioned champions of a religious freedom that extended liberty of conscience to all. They often conceive of religion as strictly a private matter between individuals and God; in their view, the fight for religious freedom has always been that of individuals insisting on practicing their faith as they deem they should. These liberals in the culture war forget that many of the champions of religious liberty and separation of church and state during the late eighteenth century were fighting for the right to express their beliefs *publicly.* None were more insistent on keeping government out of religion than were the Baptists, whose experience in England and in the colonies had been that of persecution by states favoring an established church. Yet Baptist leaders Isaac Backus and John Leland fought for the right to a form of public worship that many of the rational Founders would later roundly criticize. Thus at the center of the culture war remains the question of how to reconcile the notion of America as a Christian Nation with that of America as a haven of religious freedom where the beliefs of a diverse and pluralistic population are respected.

Each side of the cultural debate finds ample scholarly support for its position. Much of the work produced by legal scholars and constitutional historians focuses on the First Amendment and the Founders' "original intent" concerning the dividing line between church and state. Those who subscribe to Thomas Jefferson's metaphor of a wall separating church and state adopt a separationist perspective, while those who endorse the view that the Founders never intended such a division subscribe to an accommodationist interpretation. Separationists accept Justice Hugo Black's logic in *Everson v. Board of Education* (1947). His understanding of the establishment clause gave no voice whatever to any state or federal government in religious matters. "Neither a state nor the Federal Government can set up a church," he wrote, adding that "neither can pass laws which aid one religion, aid all religions, or prefer one religion over another."[10] Historians, social scientists, and lawyers have weighed in on the separationist side.[11] In this model, Jefferson is the Founder of choice, and the Virginia struggle for religious liberty is normative.[12] Moreover, religious freedom is interpreted as "the absence of government constraint upon individuals in matters of religion." That is, the individual, rather than society, is the focus, reflecting a radical Protestant as well as Enlightenment perspective.[13]

Accommodationists oppose such a restrictive reading of church-state relations and charge separationists with assigning the federal government an antireligious position.[14] They believe that the Founders recognized the importance of religion in society and intended for the government to support religious instruction and practice as long as it favored no particular sect. Rather than interpreting the establishment clause as aimed toward protecting individual religious liberty, accommodationists argue that the Founders wished to protect "the various religious practices of the states, including preferential establishments in some of them." Further, instead of regarding government's position negatively, as the absence of interference with free exercise, they view it as a positive role in promoting the blessings of religion. Chief Justice William Rehnquist provided the legal basis for the accommodationist interpretation in *Wallace v. Jaffree* (1985): "Nothing in the Establishment Clause requires government to be strictly neutral between religion and irreligion, nor does that Clause prohibit Congress or the States from pursuing legitimate secular ends through non-discriminatory sectarian means."[15]

The separationist and accommodationist interpretations provide clear, powerful analytical categories for partisans debating church-state relations in the twenty-first century. However, as tools for investigating the Founders' deliberations and actions, they suffer from a presentist perspective that fails to consider adequately the historical context of late-eighteenth-century America. Indeed, they tell us more about the present debate than they do about the founding era. Each reads a consensus back into the deliberations over framing and ratifying the Constitution that obscures the highly contingent terms in which the Founders searched for a way to define the place of religion in the new republic. Separationists portray the Founders as embracing a radical Enlightenment philosophy that viewed religion solely as an issue of individual freedom with no consideration for religion's value in providing society with a moral ground. Accommodationists depict the Founders as agreeing on a broad, catholic view of Christianity, one that all Americans could support, thereby glossing over the bitter differences that separated Protestants from Catholics and divided Protestants into countless sects. Both view the issue as one involving only a few men, the Founders, paying little heed to the constituents who sometimes dictated that the lawmakers adopt positions counter to their personal preferences. And, too often, each side presents the other in caricature, with separationists seeing accommodationists as opposed to religious freedom, and accommodationists viewing separationists as opposed to religion. Both are teleological in that they depict a straight line running from their particular version of the Founders' views to those of their own advocates.

This book attempts to capture some of the contingent nature of the Founders' deliberations regarding the place of religion by paying close attention to historical context and striving to consider events as they unfolded. It explores the options available to the Founders, the history of church-state relations that they pondered, and the constraints that they were under. It investigates the choices that the delegates to the Constitutional and Ratifying Conventions considered. By 1787 each of the thirteen states had, often through bitter and divisive debate, decided the place of religion, and the Founders were aware of the many proposals suggested as well as those passed. The book also examines how they interpreted the interaction between religion and politics in European, English, and colonial American history. Most were well read in history and law and brought that knowledge to bear on their proceedings. Further, this study looks at the cultural and political boundaries that circumscribed the Founders' decisions and actions. They operated within a Revolutionary moment that made Americans wary of any real or perceived threat to their "natural" liberties, including that of liberty of conscience. Moreover, they faced the daunting task of trying to forge a "more perfect union" out of thirteen disparate states, each with numerous interests or factions, including many different religious sects.

In this investigation, the "place" of religion has two meanings. First, it defines a space within which religion operates. For the Planting Fathers, that was a church-state sphere wherein an established church or official religion enjoyed government protection and support. For William Penn and Roger Williams, founders of Pennsylvania and Rhode Island, respectively, religion functioned freely outside state supervision, within unregulated, voluntary congregations. The second connotation of the place of religion is that of significance, or the importance of religion to civil society. All of the Planting Fathers and some of the Founding Fathers believed that religious instruction in moral behavior was essential for a virtuous citizenry. Other Founders disagreed, viewing religion as more a divisive than a uniting force.

This book argues that in deciding the place of religion in the new republic, the Founding Fathers, rather than designing a church-state framework of their own, endorsed the emerging free marketplace of religion.[16] Forty years before the American Revolution, a religious revolution swept through the colonies in a spiritual revival known as the Great Awakening, and thousands of evangelical Dissenters embraced the radical notion that individual experience, not church dogma or government statute, was authoritative in religious matters. Salvation, they argued, occurred through the outpouring of God's grace in what they called a spiritual "New Birth." Thus empowered, converted men and women, called New Lights, challenged both church and state authority in matters of faith. Many left their own congregations and started Separate Churches or joined with such radical sects as Baptists. They insisted that religion was strictly voluntary, and that no government could compel an individual to subscribe to any belief or practice. The result was a new place for religion, a religious marketplace in which individual men and women chose among voluntary, competing sects.

The best description of the transformation of the place of religion in America comes from an unlikely source. In his *Wealth of Nations*, published in the same year as the Declaration of Independence, Adam Smith devoted a section to church-state relations and their change over time. A political economist, Smith explained religious organizations and exchanges in the same terms he used to describe commerce. In his view, established churches, such as those put in place by the Planting Fathers, were operationally similar to the great trading monopolies of the day. "The clergy of every established church constitute a great incorporation," he wrote. Supported by the state and protected from competition, "they can act in concert, and pursue their interest upon one plan and with one spirit, as much as if they were under the direction of one man." He added that "where there is . . . but one sect tolerated in the society," religious teachers give full vent to their "interest and zeal," including the propagation of fear, prejudice, and superstition, and thus can become "dangerous and troublesome."[17] Smith's description fit the regulated religious economy of Connecticut and, indeed, of most of the English colonies planted in North America. In describing religion in early Virginia, Thomas Jefferson depicted a Smithian monopoly. The original charter, he pointed out, contained an "express Proviso that their laws 'should not be against the true Christian faith, now professed in the Church of England.' " The laws establishing the church required all inhabitants to be assessed the parish levy "whether they were or not members of the established church."[18]

Extending his advocacy of free trade to the exchange of religious ideas, Adam Smith believed that religion would prosper in a free and open religious market where men and women could choose among contending faiths. In a society without an established religion, there would be "no doubt . . . a great multitude of religious sects." Faced with competition on all sides, "each teacher would no doubt [feel] himself under the necessity of making the utmost exertion and of using every art both to preserve and to increase the number of his disciples." But just as competition would make religious teachers more industrious, it would check fanaticism. He argued that religious "zeal must be altogether innocent where the society is divided into two or three hundred, or perhaps into as many thousand small sects, of which no one could be considerable enough to disturb the public tranquility. The teachers of each sect, seeing themselves surrounded on all sides with more adversaries than friends, would be obliged to [exercise] . . . moderation." Finally, a competitive religious market would offer inhabitants choice. "If politics had never called in the aid of religion," Smith reasoned, "it would probably have dealt equally and impartially with all the different sects, and have allowed every man to choose his own priest and his own religion as he thought proper."[19] Smith argued that such a religious market was not some fanciful notion, declaring, "It has been established in Pennsylvania," where no church enjoyed state privilege and numerous sects competed for the allegiance of men and women.[20]

Adam Smith's notions about the wisdom of free choice in a competitive religious market appealed to the Founders, who confronted the challenge of creating a union in a diverse, pluralistic society. James Madison worried about forging a republican union in a vast country consisting of many local factions, all insisting on protecting their own interests or, worse still, imposing their views on others. In reading writers of the Scottish Enlightenment, including Adam Smith, he came to see that if some means could be found whereby the various factions could check each other's ambitions to dominate by advancing their own interests, then diversity and pluralism would not undermine union and would indeed promote liberty.

Few of the Founding Fathers, including Madison, agreed with New Light beliefs and practices, but most endorsed their ideas of religious freedom. The New Lights were too enthusiastic and emotional for the Founders, whose sensibilities ran more toward Enlightenment rationalism. But the point of agreement was emphasis on individual choice. Like the Great Awakening, the Enlightenment placed the individual at the center of the search for truth, encouraging men and women to question all traditional authority and conduct their own investigations, relying solely on their own reason and observation. Even those Founders who leaned toward traditional religious authority recognized that the new religious marketplace offered a possible solution to the problem confronting them in the late 1780s: how to avoid disunion through sectarian strife.

The first attempts to fix the legal place of religion occurred in 1776 in state constitutional conventions, often in heated, contentious exchanges. Some delegates fought for a continuation of the religious settlement put in place by the Planting Fathers. They argued that the establishment of the "true" religion, the faith of their fathers, had served society well and should be continued. Dissenters objected, calling for constitutional recognition of the free marketplace of religion as the best guarantee of freedom of conscience. At the end of the first round of constitution making, only the three Puritan states of Massachusetts, Connecticut, and New Hampshire preserved a religious establishment, and those came under sustained attack by Dissenters until they were dissolved in the nineteenth century. The Founding Fathers faced an even more difficult challenge in 1787 as they considered the place of religion in the federal constitution. Their first response was silence. That is, wanting to avoid any religious rancor that would threaten union, they delegated no power concerning religion to the federal government. The effect of that choice was to allow the emerging religious marketplace to function, subject only to restraints that the New England states imposed. But delegates to the Ratifying Conventions wanted explicit assurance that the federal government would neither establish a religion nor interfere with free exercise. The result was the First Amendment clause prohibiting establishment and guaranteeing free exercise. In proposing language for that amendment, Madison called for a ban on any establishment, state or federal. Some in the Senate, however, wanted language that would allow for nonsectarian government support of religion. The compromise was, in effect, an endorsement of a marketplace of religion operating free of government involvement.

By their actions, the Founding Fathers made clear that their primary concern was religious freedom, not the advancement of a state religion. Individuals, not the government, would define religious faith and practice in the United States. Thus the Founders ensured that in no official sense would America be a Christian Republic. Ten years after the Constitutional Convention ended its work, the country assured the world that the United States was a secular state, and that its negotiations would adhere to the rule of law, not the dictates of the Christian faith. The assurances were contained in the Treaty of Tripoli of 1797 and were intended to allay the fears of the Muslim state by insisting that religion would not govern how the treaty was interpreted and enforced.[21] John Adams and the Senate made clear that the pact was between two sovereign states, not between two religious powers.[22]

Like markets in goods, the religious market never operated in its pure form free of any government influence. Even Adam Smith thought that on occasion state intervention was necessary to mitigate worrisome

11

trends in the religious marketplace. He fretted that some enthusiastic sects might become "unsocial or disagreeably rigorous" in their morals. As a remedy, Smith proposed "the study of science and philosophy, which the state might render almost universal among all people of middling or more than middling rank and fortune." Further, he advocated a state-imposed probationary period, "to be undergone by every person before he was permitted to exercise any liberal profession, or before he could be received as a candidate for any honourable office of trust or profit." While agreeing with the American Founders that there should be no religious test, Smith favored a science test of sorts, requiring ministers, along with lawyers and other professionals, to demonstrate a certain knowledge of science and philosophy before becoming practitioners. He thought that such knowledge would have a moderating influence on the teachings of the more narrow, enthusiastic sectarians.[23]

Almost from the beginning, Americans have sought various ways to regulate the religious marketplace. Some Founders believed that religion was too important in a republic to leave in the hands of voluntary associations of believers, and they sought state promotion of Christianity. They wanted some religious presence in the public realm. Though they failed in an attempt to provide publicly funded religion in the Northwest Territory (1785), they were able to secure the place of chaplains in the military and to permit state-declared days of thanksgiving and prayer. Throughout the nineteenth century and continuing to the present, various groups, dissatisfied with the effectiveness of the religious marketplace in promoting particular teachings and behavior, have advocated government intervention to permit state-sponsored religious practices, such as prayers in public schools. The lines in the ensuing debates have been drawn, as they were during the early republic, between those who want no interference with the free marketplace of ideas and those who desire some sort of state regulation.

While the Founding Fathers are at the center of this study, Dissenters are also an important focus. According to one historian, the distinguishing characteristic of American religious history is Dissent. Dissenters played a major role in settling British North America and placed their stamp on its culture.[24] British and Loyalist observers cited Dissent as a major factor in the American Revolution. Edmund Burke said that American Dissenters represented a "refinement on the principle of resistance," and that they, long accustomed to challenging ecclesiastical power, led the attack on political power in 1776.[25] Burke's comment can be extended to the constitutional fight over the place of religion in America. Dissenters, including those evangelical dissenters who now opposed the heirs of the Puritan Dissenters, insisted on complete religious freedom. In the fight for a free religious marketplace, Whigs and Dissenters made common cause.

This examination, or reexamination, of how America's founding fathers—both seventeenth-century planters and eighteenth-century republicans—defined the place and role of religion in the nation and state is organized in three parts. Part One, "Religious Regulation," explores the Founders' British and colonial heritage and the religious regulations flowing from it. During colonization, most English planters were virulently anti-Catholic, and unregulated religion was unthinkable because it would allow papists to gain a foothold in what the adventurers conceived to be a Protestant land. Moreover, many planters were passionate sectarians, stressing fundamental differences that separated Protestants. New England Puritans could not imagine allowing Anglicans to practice their unbiblical faith in their midst, and Chesapeake Anglicans were equally adamant in stamping out the Puritan heresy. During the settlement period, British immigrants to North America could find sufficient land to pursue their particular brand of Protestantism without interference from those with different beliefs. With the notable exceptions of Rhode Island and Pennsylvania, religious regulation, if not monopoly, was the goal in most colonies, although economic and social changes made that an elusive aim.

Part Two, "Religious Competition," examines a profound shift in the way that many colonists understood religious faith and religious freedom. It explores those people and forces that challenged religious regulation and promoted religious competition. Influenced by an exploding population, a flood of immigration, and an expanding commercial market, coupled with the widespread acceptance of new ideas empowering individuals, religion in America grew much more competitive and pluralistic. Churches could not accommodate all the change, and religious regulations came under great strain as newcomers brought their new ideas and ways into a given colony, challenging existing laws and structures. The established clergy complained about the unwelcome competition from itinerant preachers who invaded their parishes and wooed their parishioners. Laymen and -women, however, exulted in the expanded religious choice. They delighted in being able to consider competing claims; they expressed a new sense of power in choosing the message or style that most appealed to them. By the American Revolution, an unlikely alliance emerged to fight for complete liberty of conscience. Enlightened politicians, including most of the Founders, and awakened evangelicals, consisting of tens of thousands of dissenters, joined forces in challenging establishment laws restricting freedom of religious choice.

Part Three, "Religious Freedom," explores that brand of freedom in the birth of the republic and depicts its triumph more in terms of the workings of the free marketplace of religion than as the design of enlightened statesmen. Conflict arose between those who desired some sort of religious establishment and those who wanted no state interference with religion at all. For the delegates at the Constitutional Convention in 1787, religion was a divisive issue that threatened the union they were trying to forge. Fractured by pluralism and enflamed by sectarianism, Americans were unlikely to agree upon any federal establishment, no matter how broadly stated. Thus the delegates opted to avoid conflict by making no mention whatever of religion in the proposed Constitution except in the ban against all religious tests. Thereby, they gave legal standing to the free religious marketplace. Similarly, in those few states that retained establishment provisions, dissenters pressured lawmakers to follow the federal model and permit religion to operate in a free, competitive marketplace, a goal finally realized in 1833 with disestablishment in Massachusetts. Though state constitutions continued to impose various religious tests throughout the nineteenth century, Americans had moved beyond religious regulation to religious freedom.

While providing analysis of key events that shaped church-state relations and individuals who were central to major struggles involving religion and politics, this is by no means an exhaustive study of religion in America. Such an effort would take into consideration a myriad of sects and individuals whose actions shaped the practice of religion, and would require volumes. This book focuses primarily on those individuals and groups that shaped the writing and revision of laws and constitutions defining the place and role of religion in a colony, a state, or the nation as a whole. For the most part, the sources come from religious and political

leaders, but this does not mean that ordinary men and women who sometimes followed them and sometimes challenged them do not play key
roles. From the beginning, leaders in America lacked the institutional
underpinning that gave their English counterparts stature and authority.
There were, for example, no resident bishops, no peerage, and no standing army. Leaders had to persuade. Sometimes followers dictated events
by taking a different path from that of their leaders. Indeed, our story
ends with tens of thousands of nameless men and women caught up in
a great evangelical revival that changed the course of religion in America
as envisioned by such enlightened men as Thomas Jefferson and James
Madison, who were confident that all Americans would soon embrace a
deistic or rationalist perspective.

An epilogue notes some of the unintended consequences of the Founders' religious settlement. For one, the alliance between enlightened leaders and their evangelical supporters soon unraveled. Jefferson had been
confident that his religious views would prevail, and that, in a generation
or two, all Americans would embrace a rationalist Unitarianism. However, he underestimated the extent and fervor of revealed religion, and
he lived to witness a great revival of religion that took the country by
storm. Jefferson also failed to anticipate the democratization of American
religion wherein ordinary men and women applied the Revolution's legacies of popular sovereignty and egalitarianism to the religious marketplace. As a result, scores of new sects sprang up, rendering the term
"dissenter" meaningless in a society without an official church. In the
nineteenth and twentieth centuries, such freedom promoted vigorous
debates aimed at defining America's religious character. As contestants
in the current culture war turn to the Founders for historical validation
of their respective positions, they confront the reality of a dual legacy: if
John Winthrop's monopolistic "City upon a Hill" is to prevail, it must
triumph in James Madison's free marketplace of ideas.

PART ONE

Religious Regulation

❖

THE SO-CALLED Elizabethan Settlement defined religious faith
and freedom in England on the eve of American colonization.
When she ascended to the throne in 1558, Elizabeth I was determined to end the religious strife that had plagued the reigns of the two
previous Tudor monarchs as the country first tilted toward an "unabash-
edly Protestant" church under Edward VI and then lurched back into the
Catholic fold under Mary I. Persecution of Catholics and Protestants in
turn threatened to spark the kinds of religious wars that ravaged France
in the sixteenth and Germany in the seventeenth century. Moving with
a speed that underscored the importance she attached to the matter,
within six months of her coronation Elizabeth pushed her settlement
through Parliament. Like her father, Henry VIII, she opted for a middle
way, "a Protestant Creed decently dressed in the time-honored vestments
of Catholicism."[1] She established the Church of England once again as
the kingdom's official religion, and she secured passage of the Act of
Uniformity, requiring all subjects to support the church in public worship
while allowing for liberty of conscience in private beliefs. Though successful in bringing religious peace, the Elizabethan Settlement left many dissatisfied. Catholic recusants and Protestant dissenters could not subscribe
to the church as the one "true" faith, and eventually many sought refuge
in America in order to practice their faith in freedom.

The planting of English colonies in North America defied a single religious settlement. Other European countries colonizing the New World had planted their national churches in American soil. Spain's devout monarchs, for instance, had established the Catholic Church in New Spain. But the nature of English colonization precluded the direct transference of the Church of England. While encouraging colonization, Elizabeth, and the Stuart monarchs who succeeded her, relied upon private entrepreneurs and investors to finance and manage colonizing expeditions. Accordingly, a number of joint stock companies and individual proprietors undertook the task of planting colonies on the North America mainland, thirteen in all between 1607 and 1732. The religious character of each colony, then, was determined by the adventurers who sponsored it and the settlers they recruited to populate it, not by the crown.

The first two English colonies illustrate the diverse religious transplantations. In 1607, the Virginia Company of London transplanted the Church of England in the Chesapeake, and in 1629, the Massachusetts Bay Company planted Puritanism in New England. In each case, the planters were free to define faith as they saw fit and to determine the place and role of religion within their colonies. Virginians gave the church official status, supporting it with tax revenues and protecting it by punishing dissenters and heretics. Similarly, Massachusetts Puritans made the Congregational churches the established religion. In both colonies, settlers were convinced that they had planted the one "true" religion. America's spaciousness made the rival claims possible, providing Churchmen and Dissenters alike sufficient space to practice their respective religions separately, making possible a much broader religious liberty than what England afforded. Moreover, vast tracts of land meant that dissidents within Virginia or Massachusetts could find a spot elsewhere and establish religious settlements of their own choosing.

Like their queen, the American colonists stood in the Reformation tradition of religious freedom. Apart from the Anabaptists and a few other radical sects, Protestant confessions fought, not for each individual to worship as he or she pleased, but for each Christian church to worship according to its lights. Catholics denounced individual religious freedom as the "most culpable indifference." And Theodore Beza, the Calvinist theologian, stigmatized religious liberty as "a most diabolical dogma because it means that every one should be left to go to hell in his own

18

way."[2] Most Protestants believed that unfettered religious freedom led to a licentiousness wherein all beliefs and practices were deemed equal. Thus Anglicans and Puritans alike had no intention of planting mixed, and therefore corrupt, religious seeds in America, vowing instead to keep their respective colonies pure and untainted by divergent views.

Experimentation, as well as diversity, characterized religious settlement as immigrants took advantage of their newfound freedom to put into practice their most cherished religious ideals. Puritans sought to make Massachusetts Bay a "Christian Common-wealth" that conformed its every practice and institution to scriptural precepts, while Pennsylvania Quakers conducted a "Holy Experiment," inspired by a dream of Protestants of many sects living together in harmony. Though these efforts arose out of religious convictions first conceived in the Old World, settlers found new possibilities in the New World for defining religious faith and freedom.

❖ 1 ❖

English Heritage

I N THE SPRING of 1607, 104 Englishmen aboard the *Susan Constant*, *Godspeed*, and *Discovery* sailed into Chesapeake Bay. Their transatlantic voyage had been grueling; for about a third of their original number even fatal. Sent by the Virginia Company of London, the enervated survivors faced the daunting task of establishing a productive, profitable plantation in a part of the New World that showed no immediate signs of easy riches, nothing resembling the mountains of South American silver that filled Spanish galleons. Thus in the midst of a wilderness that in the next few years would prove to be both deadly and barren, the small band of Englishmen turned to religion. Constructing a makeshift chapel from what materials were at hand, they gathered for public worship, giving thanks for their safe arrival and asking for divine guidance. Captain John Smith described it:

> wee did hang an awning (which is an old saile) to three or foure trees to shadow us from the Sunne, our walls were rales of wood, our seats unhewed trees, till we cut plankes, our Pulpit a bar of wood nailed to two neighbouring trees, in foule weather we shifted into an old rotten tent, for we had few better, and this came by the way of adventure for new; this was our Church, till wee built a homely thing like a barne, set upon Cratchets, covered with rafts, sedge, and earth, so was also the walls.

In their unfamiliar surroundings, the settlers found solace in the familiar prayer book of the Church of England, whether or not a minister was present to lead them. Smith summarized services during the first few years: "wee had daily Common Prayer morning and evening, every Sunday two Sermons, and every three moneths the holy Communion, till our Minister died, but our Prayers daily, with an Homily on Sundaies; we continued two or three yeares after till more Preachers came, and surely God did most mercifully heare us."[1]

Those early religious services represented something more than religious fervor or fear. Indeed, in their religious observances the settlers were acting on royal authority. The previous November, King James I had directed the Virginia Company's president and council to ensure that the "true Word and Service of God . . . be preached, planted and used according to the rites and Doctrines of the Church of England."[2] To be sure, Smith and those first settlers accepted the preeminence of the Church of England on conviction as well, believing that it represented the "true" faith, a reasonable middle ground between Roman Catholic superstition on the one hand and Puritan fanaticism on the other. Prior to his American sojourn, Smith had traveled extensively in Europe and recorded his observations and experiences in his diary. While in Rome, he ridiculed what to him were strange and superstitious rituals at Saint Peter's Cathedral:

> Pope Clement the eight, with many Cardinalls, [did] creepe up the holy Stayres, which they say are those our Saviour Christ went up to Pontius Pilate, where bloud falling from his head, being pricked with his crowne of thornes, the drops are marked with nailes of steele, upon them none dare goe but in that manner, saying so many *Ave-Maries* and *Pater-nosters*, as is their dovotion, and to kisse the nailes of steele.[3]

Smith's description barely conceals his contempt for a faith that relies upon such a rendering of divine history.

Smith had equal contempt for radical Protestants, whom he alternately referred to as Puritans and precisionists, a derogatory term for those who split theological hairs in justifying the correctness of their own views while lambasting the errors of others. In 1631 when he published his observations of New England, he called the Separatist colony at Plymouth a "fooles Paradise." He said that religion was their only governor, and that what they called humility was self-pride.[4] The Puritans in neighboring Massachusetts Smith found more to his liking because they at least claimed to remain a part of the Church of England, although he commented that they were "more precise than needs." Separatists or not, all Puritans, he suspected, were not "so good as they should be"; even among Christ's apostles one was a traitor, and therefore one should not be surprised to find some "dissemblers" among the Puritans as well.[5] When some Puritans came to Virginia, they were quickly identified as disturbers of the peace and treated accordingly.

Smith's brief account of public worship and religious attitudes in the earliest days of English colonization begins a story of religion in America that runs from 1607, the first settlers' planting of the one "true" religion in the New World, to 1787, the birth of the United States, with its radical constitutional separation of church and state. It also poses the central paradox of religion in America and the theme of this book: the simultaneous belief in the superiority of one faith as the foundation of a moral nation and the desire in a free society for unfettered religious liberty. Before we can understand how early Americans struggled with church-state issues and resolved the question of religious freedom, we must first examine the assumptions the settlers brought with them. John Smith's modest service on the banks of the James River and his certainty of its importance to the success of his enterprise, as well as his suspicion of the religious beliefs and practices of his neighboring colonists, capture a long history of a struggle between church and state that developed into a passionately held conviction that religious freedom was essential to the practice of the one true faith.

THE CROWN AND THE CHURCH

England staked its claim to a New World empire under the aegis of a king viewed by his subjects as a latter-day Constantine. Just as the Roman emperor had been the champion of Christianity in the Old World, King James I was making certain that Reformed Christianity overspread the New World. Anglican minister William Symonds assured a group of departing settlers of their sovereign's noble character and high purpose. "Our most sacred Sovereign, in whom is the spirit of his great ancestor Constantine, the pacifier of the world and planter of the Gospel in places most remote, desireth to present this land a pure virgin to Christ."[6] In planting Protestant Christianity in North America, English men and women would enjoy the blessings and support of both church and state.

The note of harmony in Symonds's pronouncement belied the stormy past of church-state relations in Europe. Henry VIII's 1537 decree pushing the pope aside and declaring himself head of the Church of England was one more chapter in a centuries-long struggle between king and pope over supremacy in English ecclesiastical matters. Dating back to the earliest acceptance of their faith by the Roman Empire, Christians had wrestled with the question of the proper relationship between church and state. The Bible was ambiguous and even contradictory in its admonitions. For example, exactly what should Christians "render unto Caesar" and what should they "render unto God"? And how exactly was one to live "*in* the world" without being "*of* the world"? They sought their daily bread in the mundane world of commerce, but they believed that earthly riches were corruptible and transitory compared to the pure and eternal treasures to be found in the Kingdom of God. The founder of their faith had warned them that they could not serve both "God" and "mammon." Yet the Apostle Paul had instructed them to "be subject to the governing authorities," an admonition difficult to heed when those governing authorities were persecuting Christians.[7]

In the early fifth century, Augustine of Hippo addressed the problem of Christians' dual citizenship. In 426, he published the *City of God*, a systematic treatise explaining to Christians and their critics the Christian promise of a future, eternal "City of God" and the reality of a present, transitory "earthly city." He began the work in 413 shortly after Alaric and the Visigoths sacked Rome, thereby destroying the Romans' boast that their capital was the "eternal" city. Augustine distinguished between the heavenly and earthly cities on the basis of their inhabitants and their priorities. He wrote: "Certainly, this is the great difference that distinguishes the two cities of which we are speaking. The one is a fellowship of godly men, and the other of the ungodly; . . . In the one city, love of God has been given pride of place, and, in the other, love of self."[8] His message was clear: Christians should strive to become citizens of the everlasting City of God, which is reserved for the godly alone.

Augustine explained that in the earthly city, God uses godly and ungodly rulers to advance his work. He believed that the hand of providence directed all human affairs, and that even those deemed evil in this world may, under divine direction, have salutary results. An evil emperor may persecute Christians and thereby teach them to rely only on God. A good emperor may aid the spread of Christianity. Augustine insisted that God gave power to the persecutor of Christians, Emperor Nero, just as he did to the protector of Christians, Emperor Constantine. While men cannot understand this, "all these things are ruled and governed as it pleases the one true God."[9] Having made the point that God overrules all emperors, Augustine, nevertheless, praised "the Christian emperor" who "did not seek the favour of demons, but worshipped the true God Himself." It was under Constantine's rule that "God granted it that he should found a city to be a companion of Rome in empire," that is, a Christian state.[10]

Sixteenth-century Protestants viewed Constantine as a godly ruler who mightily advanced the cause of Christianity, first, by stopping the persecution of Christians in the Roman Empire and, second, by rooting out heresies that threatened to undermine the early church. Expressing sentiments probably shared by most English Protestants, Henry Bullinger, Protestant minister at Zurich and friend of many Protestant English exiled during the reign of the Catholic Mary Tudor, praised Constantine for calling a council of bishops at Nicaea (325) "to establish true and sincere doctrine in the church of Christ, with a settled purpose utterly to root out all false and heretical phantasies and opinions." When the bishops failed to adhere to biblical precepts in settling the question of the nature and persons of the godhead, Constantine, Bullinger noted, insisted that they consult holy Scripture, "which must instruct us in the understanding of God's holy law."[11] In other words, not only was Constantine the protector of early Christianity; he was a proto-Protestant who insisted on the rule of Scripture in deciding doctrine.

Later Protestants, however, reevaluated Constantine's place in church-state relations, recognizing that the emperor exacted a demanding price for favoring Christianity. Writing in 1781, Baptist minister and American defender of religious freedom Isaac Backus noted that Constantine's support of Christianity came at a great cost. Backus contended that whatever good Constantine did for the church, he negated it by making Christianity an instrument of state power and control. The American minister asserted that "Constantine the Great appeared to profess the Christian religion and acted as head of the church for twenty-four years without paying so much regard to the authority of Christ as ever to be baptized till a few days before his death." Nonetheless, as emperor and self-professed champion of Christianity, he "adopted as a maxim that errors in religion, when maintained and adhered to after proper admonition, were punishable with civil penalties and corporal tortures." As a result, "nature and grace, law and Gospel, church and state, were *confounded* together."[12] From that beginning, Backus maintained, politics and religion were inextricably bound throughout Christendom to the detriment of the Christian faith.

After the fall of the Roman Empire in the fifth century, the question of church-state relations vexed European rulers, some of whom attempted to strengthen their temporal power through divine anointing. When the Frankish sovereign Charles the Great, also called Charlemagne, extended his power over all of western Europe in the eighth century, he built a strong alliance with the papacy. He renewed and expanded the church's territory in Italy; he treated the pope as "the chief prelate in his realm"; and he imposed Christianity on the inhabitants of the lands he conquered, thus extending Christianity through all of Europe. As an expression of his gratitude, Leo III placed the Roman imperial crown on Charlemagne's head as the ruler knelt in Saint Peter's Cathedral on Christmas Day, 800, a clear symbol of the close ties between pope and emperor. Both emperor and pope viewed such ties between church and state as mutually beneficial. For Charlemagne and his successors, God's consecration gave a "theocratic stamp" to the empire and elevated their personal status. For Leo III and future popes, it put the sword in the service of the Cross in the great cause of extending Christianity.[13]

The mutually advantageous separation of allied temporal and spiritual powers, however, blurred as the Middle Ages unfolded. One problem was the decline of a central authority as Europe fractured into thousands of tiny fiefdoms under the immediate control of powerful local lords. In such an environment, emperor and pope often found it difficult to exert their overlordship. In addition to wielding secular powers, the nobility also held sway over religious matters. For example, "the private oratory . . . became the village church, and the right of presentation was vested in the secular patron." The clergy, especially the greater clergy such as abbots and bishops, were themselves feudal lords, exercising temporal as well as spiritual power. While they were religious figures, they were also landholders in their own right and vassals of the king.[14]

Two fundamentally different models of church-state relations emerged in the Holy Roman Empire and came into open conflict in the eleventh century. The most vexing question was that of investiture: who, emperor or pope, had the power to induct the clergy into office? Emperors claimed that the clergy were vassals within the feudal system and therefore should be inducted by the secular head of state. Popes countered that priests were church officials and should thus be presented by the first bishop of the church. For pope and emperor, however, the matter was far more profound than the question of who was to place clerical robes on those designated for church offices. It was a conflict of authority, a question of sovereignty.

The papal interpretation insisted that priests were part of a hierarchy through which the sacraments were administered and over which there could be no secular control. While willing to concede that, in matters of landholding and feudal obligations, the clergy came under secular authority, popes were unwilling to grant to the emperor power to invest the clergy with staff and ring, the symbols of spiritual authority. In 1095, Urban II went so far as to deny the emperor any authority including that over purely secular matters, but popes were unable to make good on such a bold claim and had to settle for a division of authority between spiritual and temporal powers.[15]

On the other side of the question, emperors insisted that they exercised power by divine right, and therefore claimed that they were more than mere laymen. Anointed by God, emperors saw themselves as holding a priestly office and thus "ruled in things spiritual as well as in things temporal by the ecclesiastics and nobility under him." Popes could not and did not accept such an interpretation and denied that the emperor's coronation invested him with priestly powers. Emperors, like popes, had to back away from such extreme claims and settle for a division of power that recognized the church as the supreme spiritual authority.[16] On both sides it was a division repeatedly tested and tried.

The most dramatic moment in the Investiture Controversy came at the zenith of papal authority in church-state relations. The Tuscan Hildebrand was elected pope in 1073 and took the name Gregory VII. He brought to the papacy the most extreme interpretation of church power, maintaining that the papacy constituted a "divinely universal sovereignty, which all must obey, and to which all earthly sovereigns are responsible, not only for their spiritual welfare, but for their temporal good government." He believed that only the pope could dismiss bishops, and that the pope could depose emperors. Further, he thought that the pontiff himself was above being judged by any earthly power.[17] With this exalted view of world leadership, however impractical it would prove to be, Gregory VII confronted Henry IV, emperor of the Holy Roman Empire.

For his part, Henry IV was equally convinced that the emperor and not the pope was sovereign over temporal and religious affairs. In 1075, he precipitated a confrontation when he defied Hildebrand's decree against lay investiture by making an appointment to the archbishopric of Milan. Then Henry called a council at Worms in 1076; the German bishops there assembled delivered a stinging denunciation of Hildebrand, rejecting his authority as pope. Hildebrand's reply was "the boldest assertion of papal authority that had ever been made." He excommunicated Henry, denied him any authority over Germany and Italy, and released his subjects from their oaths of allegiance to the emperor. In what degenerated into a medieval street brawl, Henry retorted with a fiery letter calling Hildebrand no pope but a "false monk" and challenged him to "come down, to be damned throughout all eternity."[18]

Henry blinked first in the showdown. Weakened by considerable political opposition in Germany, the emperor faced the prospect of losing his throne as subjects refused to rally behind an excommunicated ruler. Thus he appealed to Hildebrand to lift the excommunication decree, which the pope repeatedly refused to do. Finally, in a dramatic step to save his crown, Henry crossed the Alps in the dead of winter and presented himself at the castle gate at Canossa where Hildebrand had sought refuge. On three successive days, the emperor stood barefoot at the castle gate, a penitent seeking papal absolution. With his advisers pleading for him to lift the excommunication, Hildebrand finally absolved Henry. Ironically, the pope's action strengthened the ruler's political position by denying his opponents an important tool for turning his subjects against the emperor. More important, the episode led to compromise in the struggle between the emperor and the pope for dominance.

In 1122, with Calixtus II on the papal throne and Henry V wearing the emperor's crown, pope and emperor agreed to a division of power. In the compromise, the king "renounced investiture with ring and staff, i.e., with the symbols of spiritual authority." And the pope "granted [the emperor] the right of investiture with the temporal possessions of the office by the touch of the royal sceptre."[19] While the accord did not end the power struggle between the heads of church and state over control of religious affairs, it did recognize a division of authority between spiritual and temporal realms.

The twelfth century also witnessed a dramatic church-state confrontation in England. The protagonists were Henry II, who became king of England in 1154, and Thomas Becket, who became archbishop of Canterbury in 1161. At first, these two strong-willed men were warm personal friends and colleagues at court. Illustrating the close ties between the temporal and the spiritual, Becket, while an archdeacon at Canterbury, became Henry's chancellor, an appointment that made him one of the kingdom's most powerful political figures. Loyal to the monarch, who was fourteen years his junior, Becket "served as Henry's chief envoy, led at least one military expedition, and assisted in creating order out of the confusion that had marked the twenty years of disputed rule that preceded Henry's reign."[20]

When Theobald, archbishop of Canterbury, died in 1161, Henry appointed Becket to succeed him. The decision was primarily political. The monarch wanted someone sympathetic to royal interests in the highest church office, primarily to curb the growing independence of the ecclesiastical courts that had usurped the power of the king's courts. Henry's aim was to build a more powerful state, which, in his thinking, meant one dominated by the crown, not by secular and clerical nobles.[21] In many respects, the church represented a "state within a state" in that it enjoyed rights and privileges, ironically granted through royal franchises, that gave it considerable independence. The church had its own system of courts; a clergyman possessed "benefit of clergy," which in effect made "his first crime free"; and the church could defy royal power by granting sanctuary to fugitives and by staying the king's writ. Perhaps most worrisome to Henry was the clergy's insistence that the church was subject to "the international monarchy of the pope at Rome," and that her faithful children could appeal to Rome when they deemed their spiritual rights to have been infringed. The church's ultimate power over the crown was that of excommunication, which had proven so effective in concluding the Investiture Controversy of 1075. Excommunication likewise threatened Henry.[22]

Determined to make the church submissive to royal rule, Henry in 1164 convened a meeting of ecclesiastical and secular leaders at Clarendon in Wiltshire. Archbishop Becket headed the church delegation that, at first, accepted Henry's version of which powers customarily belonged to the state and which to the church. The resulting constitutions of Clarendon is both a list of outstanding disputes between crown and church and the royal resolution of them. The sixteen articles addressed various aspects of Henry's three major concerns over the church's encroachment on royal prerogatives. First, it banned all appeals to the pope at Rome that thereby bypassed the king. Article 4 declared that "Archbishops, bishops, and parsons of the kingdom are not permitted to go out of the kingdom without the licence of the lord king." Second, the constitutions attempted to prevent the church's use of excommunication as a countermeasure against the king and his supporters. Article 7 baldly stated that "no one who holds of the king in chief, nor any of his demesne ministers, shall be excommunicated." Third, Henry made clear that royal and ecclesiastical courts were not on equal footing. Article 3 is one of several statements giving royal courts jurisdiction over clergy. "Clergymen charged and accused of anything shall," it reads, "on being summoned by a justice of the king, come into his court, to be responsible there for whatever it may seem to the king's court they should there be responsible for."[23] When Becket withdrew his support of the constitutions of Clarendon, a rift opened between him and Henry, symbolizing the widening breach between church and state. Becket's subsequent murder in Canterbury Cathedral in 1170 made him a martyr and forced Henry to relinquish some of the power he had taken from the church; nonetheless, in England the crown thenceforth ruled supreme.

Popes recognized that their power over the English church was minimal. Pope Martin V (1417–1431) conceded, "It is not the pope but the king of England who governs the church in his dominions." His successor, Eugenius IV (1431–1447), "bitterly added that in his day there was only one Englishman . . . at the papal court and he quite correctly claimed that hard-headed Englishmen no longer went to Rome because there was nothing to be gained from going there."[24] More than a hundred years later and after the English monarch Henry VIII had made the Church of England independent of Rome, Queen Elizabeth I offered a decidedly Protestant interpretation of church-state relations in England, contending that Christianity in Britain predated the arrival of papal emissaries. She explained to her critics that "papists" were the intruders:

> whereas you hit us and our subjects in the teeth that the Romish Church first planted the Catholic [faith] within our realm, the records and chronicles of our realm testify the contrary; and your own Romish idolatry maketh you liars; witness the ancient monument of Gildas unto which both foreign and domestic have gone in pilgrimage there to offer. This author testifieth Joseph of Arimathea to be the first preacher of the word of God within our realms. Long after that, when Austin [Augustine] came from Rome, this our realm had bishops and priests therein, as is well known to the learned of our realm by woeful experience, how your church entered therein by blood; they being martyrs for Christ and put to death because they denied Rome's usurped authority.[25]

While English Protestants agreed with Elizabeth's historical perspective, they recognized that she and other Protestant monarchs, like their Catholic counterparts, could retard as well as advance the cause of Christ. Both Churchmen and Dissenters addressed the proper role of magistrates in their respective creeds. The Church of England's Thirty-nine Articles (1571) made it clear that while the crown was head of temporal affairs, the church presided over spiritual matters. Article 37 states, "Where we attribute to the Queen's Majesty the chief government, . . . , we give not to our princes the ministering either of God's word or of sacraments." Similarly, Presbyterians proclaimed in the Westminster Confession (1643) that God "hath ordained civil magistrates, to be, under Him, over the people, for His glory, and the public good." However, it emphatically limited governmental power: "The civil magistrate may not assume to himself the administration of the Word and sacraments, or the power of the keys of the kingdom of heaven."[26]

THE AGE OF FAITH

Sixteenth-century England was an Age of Faith, and one took his or her faith seriously. Hundreds died for their beliefs, and thousands of others suffered various deprivations. All, Protestant and Catholics alike, deemed religion to be the centerpiece of a moral society. The leading promoter of American settlement thought that it was essential to colonization. Richard Hakluyt counseled the Virginia Company to take along "one or twoo preachers." He spelled out the benefits that would accrue: "that God may be honoured, the people instructed, mutinies the better avoided, and obedience the better used."[27] While his sentiments found widespread support, there was much disagreement over which preachers should be sent and what they should teach.

Colonies in the New World were divided along rigid religious lines because on the eve of European colonization, the Old World was ablaze in religious wars, pitting Christian against Christian. When, on October 31, 1517, Martin Luther tacked his Ninety-five Theses on the door of the castle church in Wittenberg, he had no idea that his criticism of the Holy Roman Church would plunge Europe into a religious civil war. His goal was to reform the church through academic debate; he hoped that his list of grievances would bring church practices back in line with biblical principles. But neither Luther nor anyone else could have foreseen the depth and intensity of resentment that had built up against the church or the opportunism that political leaders would manifest amid the religious unrest. At least initially, however, England was spared. Indeed, if the English had colonized the New World in 1517, or in 1492 as the Spanish had, they would have planted Catholic colonies.

For a thousand years before the Protestant Reformation swept through England, the Holy Roman Church had provided spiritual nurture and solace to the English in what was an Age of Faith. Men and women placed their trust in the authority of the church and its sacraments for saving their souls. From birth to death, the church offered its blessings to each individual. The seven sacraments were visible signs of God's grace as administered by the one, holy, and catholic church. Through baptism, confirmation, the Eucharist, penance, extreme unction, ordination, and matrimony, individuals found "true union with Christ."[28] Life in medieval and early modern Europe was precarious, as witnessed by the devastating Black Death of the fourteenth century that caused a severe drop in population. Science had not yet emerged to detect and counterattack the bacteria transmitted by fleas from infected rats, and thus people were helpless in face of a disease they did not understand. But the church offered refuge and hope. As long as one remained within its secure fold, even death could not separate him or her from the grace of God, which extended beyond the grave to eternal life.

At times, however, parishioners lodged grievances against the church, especially when its teachings and practices seemed remote from daily experience. One such time occurred in England after the Black Death in the fourteenth century. John Wycliffe, an Oxford scholar, drew up a list of propositions condemning certain church practices. In particular, he criticized the church hierarchy, with its many levels of intermediaries, as an ineffective means of conveying God's grace to individuals. Rather, he believed that the Bible, not the clergy, was the sole rule of faith, and that its truths needed no intermediary interpretation. Among his teachings, he held that "it is not laid down in the Gospel that Christ ordained the Mass," that any "priest may preach the word of God apart from the authority of the Apostolic See or a Catholic bishop," and that the "excommunication of the Pope or of any prelate is not to be feared, because it is the censure of antichrist." His conclusion that the "Roman Church is the synagogue of Satan" brought about swift condemnation by a church council convened to deal with heresy.[29]

Thousands of English men and women agreed with Wycliffe's assessment of the Roman Church and mounted a protest that soon had a political as well as a theological agenda. Indeed, Wycliffe's criticism tapped into a deep well of social resentment among the rising gentry and merchants angered by the great nobles' monopoly of political power. The Lollards, as the protesters were known, were centered in the south of England and in London, the most populous and politically influential part of the kingdom. They leveled their attacks on clerical wealth and power. The church was by far England's single largest landholder, and the Lollards believed that the clergy were more concerned with adding to their own wealth than with promoting the welfare of their parishioners. They particularly resented the mortuary fee, a payment the clergy demanded of a grieving family upon the burial of a beloved parent or child. King Henry IV, however, had little sympathy for the Lollards, viewing them as social levelers as well as religious firebrands. Accordingly, he put down the insurrection by force and directed Parliament to condemn the protestants, England's first official persecution of heretics.[30]

A century after the Lollard protest ended, a cataclysmic upheaval known as the Protestant Reformation shattered forever the unity of the Church of Rome. Again, clerical wealth and power were at issue. In the view of many Catholics, the clergy seemed to extract more and more money from the faithful while providing fewer and fewer spiritual services. The sale of indulgences, in particular, struck Luther as doctrinally unsound while striking many Catholics as extortion. The necessity of funds for constructing Saint Peter's Cathedral in Rome prompted the sale of indulgences, which were fees for remission of sins that had condemned departed souls to Purgatory. A graded schedule of rates determined how much a family must pay to purchase remission for their loved ones. Kings and bishops paid twenty-five Rhenish gold guilders, while poor citizens paid a half guilder. The archbishop of Mainz lauded the graded scale as evidence of the church's mercy and concern for the less fortunate, declaring that "the kingdom of heaven should be open to the poor as much as the rich." Luther saw the sale of indulgences as an act of greed, not mercy. He ridiculed the practice in his theses: "Those who assert that a soul straightway flies out (of purgatory) as a coin tinkles in the collection-box, are preaching an invention of man"; "It is sure that when a coin tinkles greed and avarice are increased." To him, Christ's merit of grace was an infinite treasury that never diminished. The faithful need not pay anything.[31]

Soon reformers all over Europe called for radical reforms that no pope could accept. Indeed, Luther in Germany, John Calvin in France, and Ulrich Zwingli in Switzerland rejected the authority of the pope, and the episcopacy altogether, as unscriptural. The Bible, they insisted—not any human institution, including the Church at Rome—was the supreme authority in matters of faith. Moreover, they taught the "priesthood of all believers," meaning that each individual had the means of salvation at his or her disposal. Salvation came through faith alone, they argued, and not through works directed by the church, such as acts of penance. In other words, ordinary people had free and direct access to the throne of God; they were empowered to seek forgiveness and grace without having to go through any intermediary and without making any payment for the privilege. Anger mingled with joy, however, and many protesters expressed pent-up resentment through attacks on church buildings and on the clergy, stripping away all the costly inventions that had stood between them and what they now understood to be the "true" faith of the Bible.

Currents of anticlericalism ran through England as well. While many bishops and priests performed their offices with diligence and compassion, many others gave laymen and -women reason to think that the church was more concerned about temporal than about heavenly matters. Whether the Church of England was in as deplorable condition as its critics made out is beside the point; the fact is, widespread opinion that it was corrupt constituted the greater reality that shaped events. Without question, the church was filled with abuses. Many parish clergymen were poor and ignorant, unable even to read the Latin of the Mass. At the same time, the higher clergy were "wealthy and worldly." The church owned about one-third of the land in England, and resident abbots and priors lived "the life of the rural gentry with whom they consorted, administering their estates, hunting, dining, and occasionally drinking."[32] English bishops and cardinals wielded great political power at court. Indeed, on the eve of the English Reformation, Cardinal Wolsey was the most powerful man in England, outside of King Henry VIII himself.

For all their grievances against the church, the English initially remained loyal to Rome, in large part because Henry VIII and leading scholars defended the Holy Roman Church. Scholars were divided but far from enthusiastic about Martin Luther's theses. Most of the Oxbridge humanists, such as John Colet and Thomas More, while advocating reform of the church, refused to join the Protestants. Humanism was the "new learning" of the day and widespread at the universities, beginning as a challenge to a prevailing curriculum dominated by such outstanding teachers as Duns Scotus and William Ockham, who based their systematic discussion of Christian doctrine on the authority of the church fathers and Aristotle. Like the Scholasticism it challenged, humanism also appealed to authority—granted, to pagan, pre-Christian classics, but nevertheless to authority—and was as uncritical as the system its advocates hoped to replace. The scholars considering Luther's works were not critical-thinking scientists who insisted on examination of a question independent of traditional assumptions or authority, Christian or pagan. The leading humanist was Erasmus of Rotterdam, who produced an edition of the New Testament from the original Greek that called into question the scriptural authority of the priesthood and the papacy. While the "new learning" of humanism abounded in England, it did not bring on the English Reformation.[33]

It was not until the 1530s, almost twenty years after Luther initiated the debate, that England joined the Reformation ranks, and the motivation at first was more political than theological. Henry VIII had fixed his desire upon Anne Boleyn and appealed to Pope Clement VII for an annulment of his marriage to Catherine of Aragon. Henry expected approval. He had proven himself a loyal son of the church when he won the title Defender of the Faith by affixing his name to a 1521 book attacking Luther and defending the pope. Thus when the pope denied his request, Henry launched a furious attack that ended in a complete break with Rome. In 1533, he pushed through Parliament the Act of Restraint of Appeals, which forbade English subjects to appeal to Rome. The following year, Parliament endorsed the Supremacy Act, which declared "that the king our sovereign lord . . . shall be taken, accepted, and reputed the only supreme head in earth of the Church of England."[34] With those acts of state, England joined the Protestant camp. Henry's personal and political desire for a divorce precipitated the break with Rome, and it is hard to conceive of an English Reformation without his blessings and leadership. Nonetheless, the fact that the separation was so swift and complete indicates that Henry's actions struck a responsive chord in a population eager to rid itself of a church that too often failed to meet its parishioners' needs.

Although there was much disagreement among the English over particular articles of faith and ecclesiastical practices, there was general agreement over what separated English Protestants from Catholics. Like their counterparts elsewhere, the English protesters insisted that the Bible, not the church, was the supreme authority, and that faith alone was essential to salvation. The Church at Rome held that the church itself had been given authority over all matters of faith, and that such good works as payment of indulgences determined the state of one's soul. The Thirty-nine Articles made clear what the source of authority was in the Church of England: "it is not lawful for the Church to ordain anything contrary to God's word written, neither may it so expound one place of Scripture, that it be repugnant to another. Wherefore, although the Church be a witness and a keeper of Holy Writ: yet, as it ought not to decree anything against the same, so besides the same ought it not to enforce anything to be believed for necessity of salvation." While Dissenters from the Church of England differed over matters of organization and practice, they agreed that Scripture alone was sufficient in leading one to saving faith. In language very similar to that of the Anglicans,

Presbyterians expressed their views in the Westminster Confession of Faith: "The authority of the Holy Scripture . . . dependeth not on the testimony of any man or Church; but wholly upon God."[35]

By the time the English undertook colonizing efforts in North America in the late sixteenth century, the difference between Catholics and Protestants had become far more than a matter of theological dispute. English Protestants ceased to regard Catholics as brothers and sisters who had a different interpretation of the Christian faith. Rather, they considered the Catholic Church to be outside the Christian pale altogether, referring to it as a pagan and superstitious faith. In 1609, Anglican minister William Symonds urged prospective settlers to carry to America "no traitors, nor Papists that depend on the Great Whore." By referring to Catholics as "Papists," he suggested that they were not faithful followers of Christ but unthinking slaves of the pope. And by calling the church the "Great Whore," he indicated that it had prostituted itself for earthly rewards by accepting monetary payments for bestowing its favors on its ignorant members.[36]

English anti-Catholic sentiments were hardened by events at home and abroad. Henry VIII's daughter Mary was a devout Catholic who wished to reverse England's Reformation. Accordingly, when she acceded to the throne in 1553, she strove mightily to restore the religion of Rome in her country. Born of a Spanish mother and married to Philip II, king of Spain (1556–1598), Mary had strong ties to the nation that had emerged as the most powerful champion of the Catholic Church. Swiftly she undid the parliamentary acts that had established the Protestant Church of England, and removed from office those religious leaders who refused to acquiesce, perhaps a third of all clergymen. Hundreds of Protestants were executed on the Smithfield pyres, and thousands fled to Geneva and other centers of Protestantism, where their faith deepened. When they returned from exile after Mary's death in 1558, many brought with them a determination to rid the Church of England of the last vestiges of Catholicism.

The martyrs of the Marian persecution more sharply defined English Protestants by giving them their own heroes of the faith and by intensifying their hatred of Catholics. Moreover, John Foxe's *Book of Martyrs* became an influential part of the American settlers' English heritage. The account of Reverend John Rogers's martyrdom reprinted in the *New En-*

gland Primer inspired and indoctrinated generations of New England schoolchildren. Rogers was a reader at Saint Paul's Cathedral when, under Queen Mary, "the Gospel and true religion were banished, and the Antichrist of Rome, with his superstition and idolatry, introduced." Rogers was not opposed to close ties between church and state as long as the ruler subscribed to and upheld the "true" faith. He stated his case in a sermon at Saint Paul's shortly after Mary's accession, expressing his hope of "displacing the papists, and putting good ministers into churches." He dreamed of living to see "the alteration of this religion, and the gospel to be freely preached again." He was called to account for his heretical and seditious sermon and, when he refused to recant, was imprisoned at Newgate. At any time Rogers could have saved himself, but "when once called to answer in Christ's cause, he stoutly defended it, and hazarded his life for that purpose." He faced death with courage and grace, praying for, rather than condemning, the guard who escorted him to Smithfield.[37] The lesson to the children was clear: their faith was worth dying for, and they, like Rogers and other martyrs, must be willing to offer this ultimate sacrifice.

Under Queen Elizabeth's reign (1558–1603), Protestantism once again became the official state religion, and England emerged as the leading Protestant power, challenging Catholic Spain. Shortly after being crowned, she made clear her intention to rid England of the papal influence reintroduced by her half sister. She told her chief advisers, "Our realm and subjects have been long wanderers, walking astray, whilst they were under the tuition of Romish pastors, who advised them to own a wolf for their head (in lieu of a careful shepherd) whose inventions, heresies and schisms be so numerous, that the flock of Christ have fed on poisonous shrubs for want of wholesome pastures."[38] When Philip II attempted to make England Catholic by force, Elizabeth defeated the Spanish Armada (1588) in a glorious naval battle in the English Channel. The English forces were aided by a "Protestant Wind" that destroyed many of the enemy's surviving vessels by dashing them against Britain's rocky coast as they tried to escape back to Spain.

Thus religion in Tudor England was far more than personal piety; it was power politics.[39] And planting the Protestant faith in America was motivated by more than evangelical zeal; it was an instrument for checking Spain's expanding power. When English settlers first sailed for

America in 1584, they carried with them a faith worked out over fifty years of religious turbulence, both for individual believers and for the kingdom of England. They went to the New World as emissaries of Christ and subjects of their king. In 1492, Columbus had purported to represent the one and holy catholic church, and thus he claimed America for *the* Christian faith. With the Christian church splintered into warring branches, English settlers vowed to make their settlements strongholds of the "true" church, Protestant Christianity.

The Act of Uniformity, Religious Liberty, and Dissent

A simple game of ball could set off a religious dispute in England on the eve of American colonization. One of the issues that most concerned Puritans was the profanation of the Sabbath. Strictly adhering to the scriptural commandment to "keep the Sabbath holy," Puritans forbade participation in recreational activities and sporting events on that day. Their proscription caught James I's attention on one occasion when the king, returning from Scotland, was passing through Lancashire: there he "found that his subjects were debarred from lawful recreations upon Sundays after evening prayers ended and, upon holy days." James deemed the ban to have harmful social implications, as "he prudently considered that if these times were taken from them, the meaner sort, who labor hard all the week, should have no recreations at all to refresh their spirits." Consequently, in 1618, he issued a royal decree prohibiting Puritan bans against sports and recreation. He rebuked the "Puritans and precise people" for "the prohibiting and unlawful punishing of our good people for using their lawful recreations and honest exercises upon Sunday and other holy days, after the afternoon sermon or service." He noted that Lancashire was "much infected" by two types of people, namely, "papists and Puritans," who insisted on placing their own narrow interpretations and interests above those of the kingdom. By linking Puritans with Catholics and regarding the influence of both as infestations, James made his low opinion of the Puritans clear to all his subjects. In spelling out what he deemed to be lawful behavior on the Sabbath, James offended Puritan sensibilities. He specifically approved of "May-games, Whitsun-ales, and

Morris-dances, and the setting up of Maypoles," all activities that Puritans regarded as pagan.[40]

Whether or not people should be allowed to play games on the Sabbath was an issue of religious liberty. In the dispute, it became clear that the Puritans had a very different interpretation of religious freedom from that of the crown. In 1571, Elizabeth I had pushed through Parliament the Act of Uniformity, which called for "one uniform order of common service and prayer, and of the administration of sacraments, rites, and ceremonies in the Church of England, which was set forth in one book, intituled: The Book of Common Prayer."[41] The queen believed that the Act of Uniformity did not violate individuals' freedom of conscience. First, uniformity had to do with public observance of religion, not private beliefs. She was concerned about peace in her realm and believed that religious squabbling between sects could tear apart her kingdom as it had France. Second, the Thirty-nine Articles stated that "it is not lawful for the Church to ordain anything contrary to God's word written." To Elizabeth, this meant that the public practice of religion would conform to Scripture. Surely, she thought, all Protestants could subscribe to common worship based on the Bible. Moreover, the Act of Uniformity did not prevent individuals, including Puritans, from believing as their conscience directed them so long as they did not undermine the Church of England and the peace of the realm. In Elizabeth's judgment, however, Puritans wished to impose their private views on the public practice of religion. Of the Puritans she wrote in 1583: "I see many overbold with God Almighty making too many subtle scannings of His blessed will, as lawyers do with human testaments. The presumption is so great, as I may not suffer it." Further, Elizabeth saw the Puritans as undermining royal rule under the guise of freedom of conscience. She warned, "I must pronounce them dangerous to a kingly rule: to have every man according to his own censure, to make a doom of a validity and privity of his Prince's government with a common veil and cover of God's word, whose followers must not be judged, but by private men's exposition."[42] In other words, she feared that if private judgments were allowed full reign without the cloak of uniformity, the result would be religious and civil anarchy.

Dissenters had a very different understanding of religious liberty. They believed that freedom was deliverance from bondage, and that Christ had delivered them "from this present evil world, bondage to Satan, and dominion of sin." More than that, "under the new testament, the liberty of Christians is further enlarged, in their freedom from the yoke of the ceremonial law, to which the Jewish Church was subject; and in greater boldness of access to the throne of grace." That is, Dissenters believed that they were freed from all human "yokes," including that of the Church of England. No church could bind Christians in all things because "God alone is Lord of the conscience, and hath left it free from the doctrines and commandments of men, which are in any thing contrary to His Word; or beside it, in matters of faith or worship."[43]

Puritans believed that the Church of England was filled with practices "contrary to [God's] Word," that human invention rather than divine instruction shaped its organization and worship. They wanted to "purify" the church of everything not explicitly sanctioned by Scripture. They objected to the very structure and hierarchy, finding no biblical justification for bishops and priests. They opposed many of the ceremonial accoutrements, including priests' vestments, altars, and the sign of the cross. And they attacked the method of selecting ministers, believing that too many clergymen received their posts through preferment rather than through divine calling.

Unlike another group of Dissenters, Puritans wanted to change the church from within. Separatists thought that the church was corrupt beyond reform, and thus separated themselves from it. Puritans, however— even those who eventually emigrated to New England—pledged their determination to work for change from within. Their hopes for real reform came with the accession of James VI of Scotland to the throne of England. Upon Elizabeth's death in 1603, Puritans hoped that the new monarch would be more sympathetic to their views. They knew that James came from Scotland, whose Reformation under the leadership of John Knox had been more thoroughgoing than that in England. Knox had spent time in John Calvin's Geneva and led Scots in organizing their church along Reformed lines. The result was a church built on a presbyterian structure and a belief in strict predestination, wherein God alone dispenses saving grace without regard to human works. Thus it was with great optimism that a committee of Puritan divines petitioned the new king to hear "our particular grievances" suffered under the Tudors. At a conference held at Hampton Court, the ministers set forth their complaints. They informed him that the Book of Common Prayer continued many papist practices not sanctioned by Scripture and in violation of Reformation principles, including "interrogatories administered to infants," the presence of the cross in baptism, the use of the ring in marriage, "popish opinions" taught and defended, and noncanonical books of the Bible read in services. Moreover, they insisted that the ministry needed a thorough cleansing, with those who "cannot preach" being removed from office and nonresident clergymen disallowed to continue holding their sinecures. They also prayed for religious toleration: that persons of faith should "be no more suspended, silenced, disgraced, [and] imprisoned for men's traditions." Men and women ought to be allowed to worship as their consciences dictated as long as their practices were "prejudicial to none but to those that seek their own quiet, credit and profit in the world."[44]

The Puritan ministers were not advocating doing away with a state church. Rather they wished to restructure the Church of England according to their interpretation of biblical teachings, insisting that only those elements supported by the Bible should be retained within the church. That meant no bishops, which prompted James's aphorism "No Bishop, no King." However, the petitioners assured James I that they did not "desire a disorderly innovation, but a due and godly reformation." They insisted that far from being radicals, as some accused them of being, they were loyal subjects who simply wanted to make certain that the church was ordered along scriptural lines.

King James's response to their petition was hardly what the Puritans wanted or expected. First, he informed them that he had not called "this assembly for any Innovation," and affirmed his belief that "the government Ecclesiastical, as now it is," has worked well, "both for the increase of the Gospell, and with a most happy and glorious peace." He rejected the notion that matters of ceremony were "to be left in Christian Liberty, to every man, as hee received more and more light, from the illumination of God's spirit." Puritans had charged, for example, that the wearing of the surplice was a practice borrowed from heathens, but King James retorted that he did not see it that way, that it "had beene, for comelinesse, and for order sake." James vowed that he would not allow private views to disrupt public order. The church might not have been perfect, but it rested on sound Reformation principles, and he would not tolerate private actions tearing it apart. "I will none of that," he declared; "I will have one doctrine, and one discipline, one Religion in substance, and in ceremonie." Some bishops at the conference thought that the Puritans were splitting theological hairs, prompting someone to recall a characterization of Puritans that circulated at Cambridge University: "A Puritane is a Protestant frayed out of his wits." Such name-calling indicated the Churchmen's frustration, and it also suggested that neither side was willing or able to accept the validity of the other's position. At any rate, King James had had enough. As he rose from his chair to go to his inner chamber, he aimed this parting shot at the Puritans: "I shall make them conforme themselves, or I will harry them out of the land, or else do worse."[45]

As it turned out, it was James's successor, Charles I, who harried some Puritans out of the land. To the Puritans, Charles and his archbishop, William Laud, veered dangerously close to the Roman Church. In fact, both were sincere in their devotion to the Protestant Church of England and insisted on religious uniformity within the realm. Most Dissenters stayed in England, continuing to push for reforms. Depending upon one's position in the dispute between Churchmen and Puritans, the latter were either "stiff-necked" obstructionists or faithful servants of Christ who were unwilling to compromise their faith for anyone, including bishop and king. When the Puritans triumphed in the English civil war in the 1640s, their military commander and Protector, Oliver Cromwell, discovered that Puritans were unwilling to compromise and thus not easy to govern.[46] To Scottish Presbyterians who insisted on their view of church organization, he responded in frustration, "I beseech you, in the bowels of Christ, think it possible you may be mistaken."[47] Convinced that they interpreted Scripture aright, Puritans rarely imagined that they might be mistaken. They were anxious about living according to Scripture, but they were confident in making the Bible their sole authority.

In 1629, a group of Puritans concluded that to be faithful to their convictions, they must leave England. One of their leaders, John Winthrop, wrote that "this land growes wearye of her Inhabitants," explaining that an economic and spiritual depression made life exceedingly difficult. While he did not wish to abandon his country and his church by removing to America, he drew comfort that such a move could benefit both. He reminded his followers of the benefits that had accrued from an earlier move away from established religion: "It was a good service to the Churche of the Jewes that Joseph and Marye forsooke them, that their mesiah might be preserved for them against tymes of better service."[48] Similarly, he hoped, Puritans would establish in New England a model commonwealth built solely on the word of God.

Thus a central part of America's English heritage was a spirited Dissent that provided lively competition for the established church. With the Puritan migration to the New World, the English plantations were inhabited by both Churchmen and Dissenters. Both brought with them fundamental beliefs shaped by decades of struggle in England. The ocean that separated the Old and New Worlds also constituted a highway connecting the two. As colonists sailed to America, they took with them cultural baggage that would greatly influence the societies they built. Religion was no exception. When John Smith and his fellow travelers worshiped, they were faithful to their English heritage. First, they believed that their religion was an important pillar of society, and that the Church of England represented the "true" religion. Accordingly, they brought with them copies of the Book of Common Prayer to direct their services. Second, while their worship was no doubt sincere and heartfelt, it was also undertaken in obedience to royal instructions. Third, they subscribed to the Act of Uniformity and believed that in outward religious expressions, all English subjects should conform to the established church. John Smith viewed the Separatists who founded the Plymouth Colony in 1620 as a dangerous sect. He said that they "liked their own conceits" and disregarded "any knowledge of any but themselves." Smith called Plymouth a "fooles Paradise" where, with "onely Religion [as] their governour," the Pilgrims "would have no Superiours."[49]

Winthrop and his fellow Puritans also constructed their Holy Commonwealth from ideas forged in England. They, too, believed that religion was the mainstay of society, but of course they believed that their churches, "communities of saints," constituted the "true" church. Second, they thought that the state had an important role to play in religion, protecting it against infidels, papists, and heretics and promoting its advancement through taxation for hiring ministers and building meetinghouses. Third, they insisted on religious uniformity within Massachusetts Bay. Indeed, their notion of religious liberty was freedom from error, which justified their removing those who would not conform to their practices. Winthrop had little regard for Virginia, which was "weakly provided" with righteousness.[50]

Whatever their theological differences, the Protestant immigrants held one shared conviction: religious freedom was essential for a people desiring to define and practice the one true faith. From their past, the various English transplants brought with them a keen appreciation of the tensions running between church and state. Dissenters were more concerned about how state power could subvert faith, while Churchmen were more worried about how sectarian strife could undermine civil order. But both also looked to the future, and they had an equally keen anticipation that the New World would afford them the freedom to organize society around their own religious assumptions.

❖ 2 ❖

Transplanting the Church of England
in the Chesapeake

K ING JAMES chartered Virginia as a Christian mission. When he incorporated the Virginia Company in 1606, he declared that it would bring glory in propagating "Christian religion to such people, as yet live in darkness and miserable ignorance of the true knowledge and worship of God." The gentlemen of the company, though seeking profits there, agreed that "true" religion must be planted in the Chesapeake, and instructed their colonial governors to establish the Church of England in the wilderness. In 1612, William Strachey, gentleman and resident secretary of the company, pronounced in his preface to the colony's *Lawes* that the mission was a success: Virginia had indeed become a "Christian Colonie."[1] John Rolfe went further, portraying Virginians as a chosen people. Best known for his role in promoting Virginia's tobacco cultivation, Rolfe saw the early settlers in theological terms, on one occasion referring to them as a "peculiar people, marked and chosen by the finger of God."[2]

Strachey's claim that Virginia was a "Christian Colonie" has registered only the faintest historiographical blip. Most historians portray early Virginia planters as primarily interested in the pursuit of profit, not in the practice of piety.[3] The notable exception is Perry Miller's study of early Virginia literature. Noted for his exploration of the "New England Mind," Miller claims that in their writings the "planters and promoters present themselves as only secondarily merchants and exploiters, only secondarily

Englishmen; in their own conception of themselves, they are first and foremost Christians, and above all militant Protestants." While admitting that the Virginians did not always order their lives according to the religious principles they professed, Miller, nevertheless, argued that their "desire for profits or for estates" did not obliterate their determination to conquer the wilderness for the "glory of God." He concluded with a bold assertion: "Religion, in short, was the really energizing power in this settlement, as in others."[4]

Miller's attempt to save early Virginians' historiographical souls failed. For one thing, evidence from the early period soon told a very different story, portraying a Virginia filled with avarice and exploitation. Captain John Smith, for ten months president of the colony, suggested that talk of a Christian colony belied reality and was a mere public relations ploy. He wrote that officers of the Virginia Company were hypocritical, making "Religion their colour, when all their aime was nothing but present profit."[5]

Colonial historians have found it easy to ignore or downplay religion in early Virginia, in part because they have been drawn to the mountains of sermons, religious diaries, and church histories left by New England Puritans. While both Anglicans and Puritans were Protestants, their Protestantisms were strikingly different. In short, the Puritans were a much noisier crowd. They were Dissenters who maintained an ongoing, vociferous protest against the Church of England. By contrast, Anglicans were Churchmen who quietly embraced the national church. Puritans were evangelicals, whose primary mission was the salvation of souls, often a wrenching, emotional experience that came "only by an anguished 'conviction' of personal wickedness followed by the joyful release of 'conversion.'" Anglicans, on the other hand, were less anxious about their souls, emphasizing instead "the importance of men and women living upright lives by exercising reason and learning self-restraint."[6] Historians have been far more drawn to the noisy Puritans, who aimed at nothing less than perfection in a society organized around scriptural tenets.

So much attention has centered on the New England Puritans that some tend to see them as *the* spiritual fathers of all Anglo-Americans. Yet Virginia's religious transplantation is an important part of the colonial landscape and heritage; it must be understood on its own terms, not simply judged by evangelicals' standards. And that leads us back to Strachey's claim and Smith's counterclaim regarding Virginia as a "Christian Colonie." One need not conclude that Strachey was a publicist or Smith a perfectionist. Indeed, the underlying assumption of this chapter is that Virginian gentlemen, first those investors in London who set policy and then the planter-gentry that emerged as a ruling elite in the 1640s, were motivated by both profits and piety. The question is how they ordered their society to realize these twin aims that often clashed in the pursuit. As Protestants, they embraced the concept of original sin and believed that church and state must exercise control over men's passions. As members of the Church of England, they followed prescribed patterns of worship, and as devotees of the latitudinarian branch, they preferred moderation in all things religious. Popularized by Archbishop John Tillotson's sermons, latitudinarianism stressed the common core of teachings that all Christians could embrace, and downplayed the doctrinal hairsplitting that fueled sectarianism. As loyal English subjects, they accepted the Act of Uniformity and insisted that religious liberty extended only to private sentiments, not to public religious expressions. Finally, as frontiersmen, they had to adapt their inherited culture, including religion, to a new environment, one that strained, and at times broke, traditional institutional bonds.[7]

"Nursing Fathers" of the Church

The gentlemen who planted religion in Virginia acted as "Nursing Fathers" of the church. That metaphor had a long and enduring history, stretching back to Virginians' forebears and forward to their descendants. In the sixteenth century, reformers like John Calvin urged European rulers to nurture Protestant Christianity just as the prophet Isaiah had assigned a prominent role to civil authorities in the restoration of Israel following that nation's return from Assyrian bondage. "Kings shall be your foster fathers, and their queens your nursing mothers," he reassured the people of Judah.[8] Similarly, John Jewel, bishop of Salisbury (1522–1571), saluted Queen Elizabeth as nurse of the Church of England.[9] The metaphor would appear yet again after the American Revolution, when petitioners from Amherst County, Virginia, pleaded with Virginia's assemblymen to play their traditional role as "Nursing Fathers" of the church.[10] But by as early as the opening of the seventeenth century, Virginia's planters had faced and become familiar with the awesome responsibility of tending an embryonic church struggling in a hostile environment.

It proved to be a difficult task during Virginia's stormy beginning. In fact, one storm almost rendered Virginia just one more of England's short-lived experiments in North America. While sailing to Virginia in 1609 to bring relief to the struggling and starving colonists, the ship *Sea Venture* foundered off the Bermuda islands, and its crew was given up for dead. When the long-awaited supply vessel failed to appear, despairing Virginians decided to abandon the colony and return to England. Virginia would go the way of earlier attempts to plant colonies in North America, a failed effort because settlers, unable to produce their own foodstuff, lived from supply ship to supply ship. Then, on the day before their planned departure, Lord De La Warr appeared at the mouth of the James with the relieving fleet. Miraculously, the crew of the *Sea Venture* had not only survived the shipwreck but managed to construct new ships and journey on to Virginia. This episode inspired William Shakespeare's *The Tempest*, but it did even more for the besieged colonists. To them, it was a miracle, and ministers on both sides of the Atlantic heralded it as such. Writing from Virginia, Alexander Whitaker concluded that "the finger of God hath been the onely true worker heere."[11] And William Crashaw in London agreed: "If euer the hand of God appeared in action of man, it was heere most euident: for when man had forsaken this businesse, God tooke it in hand."[12] Miracles occurred in the Protestant world. God was sovereign, and he guided human affairs in ways that sometimes defied human reason. The wreck of the *Sea Venture* and the relief of the colony confirmed the colonists' faith that God could and would suspend the laws of nature for his followers.

Though saved from immediate failure, the struggling colony's future remained shaky. Jamestown's "seasoning time" continued to test Virginians' faith, and it exposed a worrisome gap between the moral foundation envisioned by king and clergy and actual settler behavior. During its first several years, Virginia's survival hung by a thread. Though ravaged by deadly disease and a devastating Indian attack, the settlers were their own worst enemies, bickering with each other, carping instead of working, and neglecting public worship. Within two years, the church at Jamestown, which had replaced Smith's original lean-to made of sail and wood, stood in disrepair, a visual symbol of the precarious state of religion in the struggling colony. When Strachey arrived with the new governor, Thomas Gates, in 1609, he described the fortified town, paying particular attention to the church. Within the palisades ran a street with houses, a marketplace, a storehouse, a military post, and a "pretty chapel." Strachey noted, however, that the church was dilapidated and unfrequented, signifying the colony's physical and moral decline. Believing that religion and morality must be supported if the society were to survive, Gates immediately gave orders that the church be repaired; Strachey reported that, as he wrote, many hands were about the task. The structure was sixty feet long and twenty-four wide and after its renovation would have a "chancel in it of cedar and a communion table of black walnut; all the pews and pulpit were of cedar, with fair broad windows . . . to shut and open, as the weather shall occasion." The idea was to brighten the building by ensuring that it would "be very light within," and Gates ordered that it "be kept passing sweet and trimmed up with divers flowers."[13]

More important, the new governor led a revitalization of religious exercises. Strachey stated that "there was a sermon every Thursday and two sermons every Sunday, [with] the two preachers taking their weekly turns." Every morning, "at the ringing of a bell . . . about ten o'clock, each man addressed himself to prayers, and so at four of the clock before supper."[14] Gates hoped that with three weekly services and prayers twice daily, Virginians would find the moral strength to survive their battles with disease, poverty, Indian attacks, and, above all, their own human foibles.

Gates viewed the church as an instrument of the state, a primary, and he hoped effective, means of restoring order in Virginia. Accordingly, he turned Sunday services into an elaborate ritual that would visually display his authority and that of the London gentlemen whose instructions he followed. Again, Strachey is our eyewitness:

> Every Sunday, when the Lord Governour went to church, he was accompanied with all the Councillors, Captains, other officers, and all the gentlemen, and with a guard of fifty Halberdiers in his Lordship's livery, fair red cloaks, on each side and behind him. The Lord Governour sat in the choir, in a green velvet chair, with a velvet cushion before him on which he knelt, and the council, captains, and officers sat on each side of him, each in their place.[15]

The ceremony reminded all present that God ordained an obedient society where some are called to lead and others to obey.

When, with his miraculously resurrected crew, the new governor, Lord De La Warr, arrived in 1610, he did more than rely upon the newly spruced-up church and divine services to promote religion and morality. He and his council promulgated a series of laws mandating and regulating the teaching and practice of religion, and the preamble underscores the importance that the Company of Virginia attached to religion and its role in the colony. First, Virginia's leaders in America should do no less in supporting religion than the king did in England: "Whereas his Majestie . . . hath in his owne Realmes, a principall care of true Religion, and reverence to God, and hath alwaies strictly commaunded his Generals and Governours . . . to let their waies be like his . . . for the glorie of God."[16] De La Warr imposed martial law on Virginians and made religion a strategic part of gaining and exercising social and political control.

Signifying the importance attached to religion, the first laws that De La Warr promulgated addressed religious and moral needs, reminding Virginians that the primary duty of a good citizen was to worship and obey God. Phrased in military language, the law read:

Since we owe our highest and supreme duty, our greatest, and all our allegeance to him from whom all power and authoritie is derived, and flowes as from the first and onely fountaine, and being especiall souldiers emprest in this sacred cause, we must alone expect our successe from him, who is onely the blesser of all good attempts, the King of kings, the commaunder of commaunders, and Lord of Hostes, I do strictly commaund and charge all Captaines and Officers, of what qualitie or nature soever, whether commanders in the field or in towne, or townes, forts or fortresses, to have a care that the Almightie God be duly and daily served, and that they call upon their people to heare Sermons, as that also they diligently frequent Morning and Evening praier themselves by their owne exemplar and daily life, and duty herein, encouraging others thereunto, and that such, who shall often and willfully absent themselves be duly punished according to the martiall law in that case provided.[17]

That "God be duly and daily served" was now a civil duty, backed by the full power of the state, which promised to "duly punish" those who refused to comply.

Additional laws also made religious observance a civil duty. To ensure respect for the "Chain of Being," or, under martial law, the "Chain of Command," settlers were forbidden to "speak impiously or maliciously, against the holy and blessed Trinitie, or any of the three persons, that is to say, against God the Father, God the Son, and God the holy Ghost, or against the knowne articles of the Christian faith, upon paine of death." Closely linked to blasphemy was the sin of treason. If citizens were allowed to curse their heavenly ruler, they were dangerously close to denouncing their earthly ruler. Thus De La Warr followed the proscription of impious speech with a command that "No man shall use any traiterous words against his Majesties person or royall authority, upon paine of death."[18]

Having protected God and king, the governor next shielded from attack the two other pillars of authority: the Bible and the church. The former was defended in the negative: "No man shall speake any word, or do any act, which may tend to the derision . . . of God's holy word, upon paine of death"; the latter in the positive: "Everie man and woman duly twice a day upon the first tolling of the Bell shall upon the working daies repaire unto the church to hear divine Service." Moreover, Virginians were to arrive at church fully prepared by private devotions: each inhabitant was to "duly sanctifie and observe the same, both himselfe and his familie, by preparing themselves at home with private prayer, that they may be the better fitted for the publique, according to the commandements of God, and the Orders of our church."[19] Thus the state insisted that the practice of piety begin at home.

Martial law in early Virginia brought church-state relations into their closest alignment. Deemed important in saving the colony, religion became an instrument of public policy. From the perspective of individual residents, correct religious practice was no longer a private, voluntary matter of conscience; it was now a civil duty. Accordingly, the clergy acted as officers of the state. Virginia lawmakers directed ministers in how they were to discharge their clerical duties. By statute, ministers were directed to preach "one sermon every Sunday in the yeare," unless they were indisposed, at which times the churchwardens would present the sermon. In addition, the law required ministers every Sunday a half hour before evening service to "examine, catechise, and instruct the youth and ignorant persons of his parish in the ten commandments, the articles of the beliefe and the Lords prayer." Parish priests also had the statutory obligation to administer Holy Communion "thrice in the yeare, whereof the feast of Easter to be one." Having laid out the minister's duties as preacher, teacher, and priest, the legislators spelled out his pastoral responsibilities. Upon learning that someone was "dangerouslie sicke" in his parish, for instance, the minister must "resort unto him or her to instruct and comfort them in theire distresse."[20] Thus the state insinuated itself into church operations down to when and how ministers must discharge their duties.

However, religious reality did not always follow religious prescription. With the discovery that tobacco was the means to great riches, private avarice undermined public morality. As early as 1620, Jamestown had become "the first American boom town" with all of the opportunities and temptations that such places represent. The hope for quick wealth led some to think of Virginia "not as a place of Habitacion but onely of a short sojourninge." The quest for profits overshadowed the practice of piety at every level of society. Large, unscrupulous planters "engrossed the commodities most in demand, to resell at monopoly prices." Small, struggling yeomen who did not strike it rich squandered their crops on the "liquor and luxuries that show up in boom towns."[21] When the Virginia Company surrendered control to the crown in 1624, the colony was not only financially but morally bankrupt.

By midcentury, a new set of gentlemen rulers nursed the church. Virginia was no longer under martial law and had developed the social, political, and economic structures that enabled it to survive and even flourish. Although its cultivation came too late for the colony's original investors to recoup their losses, tobacco proved to be the road to riches for some, and tobacco quickly came to define colonial society. A labor-intensive crop, tobacco enriched only those planters who could afford sufficient numbers of servants and/or slaves to make a large enough crop to withstand falling prices in the tobacco market. As a result, a small planter elite emerged at the top of society's pyramid, under which spread a large number of struggling freemen and indentured servants, and at the very bottom of which were slaves, whose relative numbers remained small until toward the end of the seventeenth century. The great planters occupied the chief political posts, thanks to royal appointments and deferential politics. In 1624, the Virginia Company, finding the venture financially disastrous, surrendered its charter to the crown, and Virginia became a royal colony with an appointed governor and council and a representative House of Burgesses as its provincial government. At the county level, freemen deferred to their wealthier and better-educated neighbors and elected them as justices of the peace who exercised judicial and administrative powers. As long as elected officials "treated" voters with respect and, perhaps more important, food and beverage at election time, incumbents were reelected to office and sent to the House of Burgesses at Williamsburg.

As they did in politics, the leading planters wielded enormous power over parish churches. The same men who passed legislation requiring Virginians to support their churches and ministers and regulating church government and teachings became the rulers of parish churches. Without bishops and courts to run the church's affairs, the Church of England in Virginia relied upon the vestry, a body of laymen in each parish, to manage its operations. The leading men in each parish, the same men who held county and provincial political offices, constituted the local vestry, and in 1658, the burgesses passed legislation settling ecclesiastical power in the hands of the vestries. In other words, with no Hildebrand challenging them, lawmakers empowered themselves to exercise authority over local church matters. The statute directed that "all matters concerning the vestrey, their agreements with their ministers, touching the churchwardens, the poore and other things concerninge the parishes or parishioners respectively be referred to their owne ordering and disposeing from time to time as they shall think fitt."[22] Indeed, becoming a vestryman was as much a political and social position as an ecclesiastical one. William Byrd II proudly recalled his rise to political power by listing the various offices that served as stepping-stones to high office. He began with his election to the vestry, which recognized him as a leader in Henrico County. From there he was named commander-in-chief of the county militia and was on a trajectory that would give him influence and power outside the county, eventuating in a seat on the governor's council. Membership in the vestry also conferred or perhaps recognized social standing. Seating in Virginia parish churches, like that in New England Puritan meetinghouses, mirrored the community's social hierarchy. Accordingly, Byrd ended up in "the best pew in the church," an indication that he was "the social sun of parish society."[23]

As it had during the period of martial law, the state continued to concern itself with the moral conduct of its citizens, relying for enforcement primarily on vestrymen, who acted as officers of both the church and the state. Illustrative is a law enacted in 1658 that regulated Sunday behavior. In language reminiscent of the Puritan restrictions that James I had repealed in 1618, the act read in part, "That the Lord's day be kept holy, and that no journeys be made except in case of emergent necessitie on that day, that no goods bee laden in boates nor shooteing in gunns or the like tending to the prophanation of that day, which duty is to be taken care of by the ministers and officers of the severall churches."[24] Other laws attempted to promote moral behavior by "suppressing the odious sinnes of drunkenesse, blasphemous swearing and curseing, [and] scandalous liveing in adultery and ffornication."[25]

Illustrating the close ties between church and state at the local level, court cases indicate that clergymen applied to the county government for aid and adjudication over such matters as payment of clerical salaries, church construction, and the performance of church officials. William Cotton, minister of Accomack, frequently appeared in the county court demanding that he and his parish receive full benefit from the provincial establishment laws. In 1635, he presented the county court with a writ from the legislature at James City "for the building of a parsonage house upon the Glybe land." Because his church members did not provide him with a house, he took the matter to court. The county judges, however, deemed that this was a matter that belonged to the parish vestry, and because no vestry had yet been named, the judges appointed eleven citizens as vestrymen. Thus court-appointed gentlemen executed the legislature's orders to provide the rector with adequate housing.[26]

It was one thing to legislate morality but something else again to enforce it. County court records teem with cases of ecclesiastical disputes and immoral behavior. In fact, ministers could not even count on being paid. Cotton again illustrates the point: on February 19, 1634, in the Accomack County Court, he filed a complaint charging the churchwardens with negligence in levying and collecting the duty. Answering for the wardens, John Major said that they had dutifully levied the tax, but that one, Mr. Obedience Robins, whose name gave an ironical twist to the proceedings, refused to pay. The provost marshall, Walter Scott, testified that when he took a warrant to Robins to collect the tithe, Robins "tore the same" in front of him.[27] The record does not explain why Robins felt so strongly about the tithe, but it does suggest that the state was prepared to enforce the law through its judicial process. The court ordered that Robins be levied double the quantity of corn and tobacco for being in default. Cotton was also a party in a slander case heard by the same court. The legislature had passed a law against defaming ministers, but that did not stop some laymen from speaking their minds against clergymen. According to Cotton's complaint, one Henry Charelton had said that "if he had mr. Cotton without the Church yeard he would have kickt him over the Pallyzados calling of him black cotted raskoll." For his unholy attack on Cotton, Charelton was sentenced to sitting in the stocks "three severall sabouth days in the tyme of Dyvine servis and their aske mr. Cotton forgiveness."[28]

Virginians considered some behaviors to be offenses against both church and state and involved both institutions in punishing violators. In a case that illustrates the dual nature of moral conduct, the Accomack County judges heard testimony by one Francis Millicent, who claimed that Elias and Jane Hartrey said that one "John Foster was in bed with Mary Jolly," an indentured servant, in the Hartreys' house, and that the Hartreys feared that such conduct on their premises would cause people to consider their home a "Bawdy house." When the Hartreys testified in court that they never made such a statement and furthermore never saw "any dishonesty by Mary Jolly," the judges concluded that Millicent had "unjustly and wrongfully scandelized and defamed Mary Jolly." They sentenced him to "be whipt and have thirty lashes." But that was not all. Millicent had to "aske the said Mary Jolly forgivenes publiquely in the Congregation the first Sabbath that she is able to come to Church."[29] Millicent had violated the colony's defamation laws, but he had also violated the biblical commandment against bearing false witness. Therefore, he had to make amends before God and the congregation as well as before the crown's officials.

Reports on how well Virginia gentlemen nursed the church were mixed.[30] In 1656, planter John Hammond published *Leah and Rachel*, a highly favorable account of the Chesapeake written to counter critical reports on Virginia and Maryland, and aimed at attracting new settlers. While earlier reports had depicted Virginia as a lawless, godless land, Hammond argued that that was no longer the case. He claimed that lawmakers had intervened to reverse the "general neglect and licentiousnesses there" by passing laws "tending to the glory of God, [and] the severe suppression of vices." Moreover, the inhabitants began to "provide [for] and send home for Gospel Ministers, and largely contributed for their maintenance." With the arrival of more ministers, Hammond contended, "then began the Gospel to flourish." The result of the introduction of wholesome laws and competent, dedicated ministers was a country now "full of sober, modest persons, both men and women, and many that truly fear God and follow that perfect rule of our blessed Saviour, to do as they would be done by."[31]

Five years later, an emissary from the bishop of London submitted a very different account of religion in Virginia. Reverend Roger Green accompanied Reverend Phillip Mallory on a fact-finding mission to assess the needs of the church. Green's report was very critical of the state's support of religion, placing most of the blame on the immense power held by local vestries. He reported that "not above a fifth part" of Virginia's fifty parishes were supplied with ministers. In addition, the planters who controlled the vestries neglected to "build Churches, Houses of God amongst them," and they failed to assure the "maintenance of the Ministry of Gods publick Worship, Word, and Sacraments." Green indicted lawmakers for not providing schools. The lack of schools, he argued, created a "very numerous generation of Christian Children born in Virginia . . . unserviceable for any great Employments either in Church or State [and] likewise it obstructs the hopefullest way they have, for the Conversion of the Heathen."[32] To Green, the religious establishment in Virginia was a failure because the planters who ran the legislature and the vestries refused to spend necessary funds for churches, ministers, and schools.

In 1671, Governor William Berkeley defended the state's support of religion and shifted the blame to the poor-quality ministers and some troublemaking Dissenters. In response to an inquiry by the Lords Commissioners of Foreign Plantations, Berkeley claimed that the church in Virginia operated just as did the church in England in "instructing the people" and providing for ministers. He said that in Virginia "the same course . . . is taken [as] in England out of towns; every man according to his ability instructing his children." Further, he reported that "we have fforty eight parishes, and our ministers are well paid," thereby neatly dodging the issue of vacancies. He then gratuitously offered his dim view of the quality of the ministers, suggesting that they would "be better if they would pray oftener and preach less." But, he explained, "like all other commodities, so of this, the worst are sent us, and we had few that we could boast of." Berkeley closed by declaring that the government had succeeded in checking the influence of Dissenters. "I thank God," he wrote, "there are no free schools nor printing, and I hope we shall not have these hundred years; for learning has brought disobedience, and heresy, and sects into the world, and printing has divulged them, and libels against the best government. God keep us from both!"[33] He believed in the establishment of a state church and religious uniformity because he feared that religious pluralism bred animosities and divisions antithetical to a well-ordered society.

A Gentleman's Religion

Not only did Virginia's leading gentlemen nurse the church; they shaped it to reflect their religious taste and bolster their social standing. From their arrival for services each Sunday to their departure at the close of worship, their prominence was made manifest. They came in finer carriages or on better horses than did their lesser neighbors, and they expected and received deferential treatment, for everyone else depended on them to some degree. The minister himself knew that the vestrymen had put him in his position, and he knew that they could remove him. Some in attendance were the great planters' servants or tenants. Others were yeomen farmers who had borrowed money from their wealthy neighbors in order to plant a crop. All knew that they might someday appear before the county court, where the gentlemen sat as justices of the peace. The leading planters brought secular concerns to the church grounds for discussion before services, thereby reinforcing on sacred soil their social, political, and economic preeminence. Philip Fithian, a critic of the church for its lack of piety, observed that "before service," gentlemen engaged in considerable display and exchange, "giving & receiving letters of business, reading Advertisements, consulting about the price of Tobacco, Grain & c. & settling either the lineage, Age, or qualities of favourite Horses." On one occasion Peyton Skipworth's agent arrived with one of the baronet's prize stallions "so that the people might look the proud creature over with a view to having him cover their mares."[34]

Once parishioners entered the church building, they were reminded at every turn of the greatness of God and the high rank of Virginia's first gentlemen. In his description of Christ Church, Lancaster County, historian Rhys Isaac observed that the "architectural plan maximized the visibility to the assembled community of a numerous emulative gentry"; they sat in "great oak-walled pews reserved for magistrates and leading families" located at the front of the sanctuary. The service itself buttressed the church's authority and commitment to order and continuity. Services in the Virginia wilderness followed the same prescribed and repetitive pattern as did public worship in the great churches of England, following year after year the readings and rituals contained in the Book of Common Prayer. The liturgy forestalled any "creative individualism" on the part of schismatics and dissenters that might threaten the gentry's hegemony. And, as one last expression of the deference shown the leading families, when the entire parish exited the church, "women and humbler men waited to leave until the gentlemen had gone."[35]

Seventeenth-century conceptions of an English gentleman as well as Protestant principles shaped the character of religion in Virginia. According to one historian who has analyzed the reading preferences of the "First Gentlemen of Virginia," "the virtues of the gentleman owed more to Aristotle than to Christian writings, though, from the middle of the seventeenth century onward, the religious note grew stronger." Gentlemen in the Chesapeake, like those in England, aspired to the classical Greek concept of the golden mean, aiming in all aspects of human endeavor for moderation, temperance, self-control, and proportion. They subscribed to the latitudinarian approach to religion that had emerged in the Church of England, a somewhat tolerant perspective that had little patience for doctrinal hairsplitting. They believed that the church's articles of faith and prayer book were adequate guides to worship and behavior, an attitude that made them far less spiritually "anxious" than New England Puritans. For the latter, anxiety meant concern over election, an individual's fear that perhaps he was not among those predestined for salvation. In the absence of certainty, a Puritan constantly looked for signs that would indicate divine favor or, more worrisome, divine disfavor. The steady diet of Calvinist doctrine imbibed at church services, held usually two days a week and supplemented by daily devotionals, reminded the Puritan that he was a sinner who, but for the grace of God, deserved eternal damnation, fostering what William James called religion of the "twice-born." One brooded over his life in general and himself in particular. In *The Pilgrim's Progress*, a seventeenth-century evangelical classic, the Puritan John Bunyan presented himself as one "beset by doubts, fears, and insistent ideas." He often expressed self-contempt and despair: "Nay, thought I, now I grow worse and worse; now I am farther from conversion than ever I was before. If now I should have burned at the stake, I could not believe that Christ had love for me."[36]

By contrast, latitudinarian Anglicans had a very different outlook, one far more sanguine about their spiritual condition. They operated out of a perspective that James called religion of the "once-born," seeing God, not as a harsh judge ready to condemn sinners, but as "the animating Spirit of a beautiful harmonious world." Such a benign view of the divine leads to a cheerful view of humans. The once-born "are not distressed by their own imperfections . . . [and do] not shrink from God."[37] With such a theological underpinning, religion becomes a reasonable proposition aimed toward the happiness of men and women.

Latitudinarians focused more on the moral requirements of Christianity than on doctrinal injunctions. Indeed, they believed that there were few "essential doctrines," and that those were clearly laid out in the Scriptures in plain language. Moreover, they contended that Christian precepts reinforced the tenets of natural law; in other words, "natural" religion and "revealed" religion were compatible. What had been made known to humankind through unaided reason had been made explicit through divine revelation. Both had as their end the desire for human happiness, and latitudinarians subscribed to the notion that the Christian's duty to embrace moral behavior was consistent with the individual's natural inclination toward enlightened self-interest. According to Archbishop John Tillotson, one of the most popular spokespersons for seventeenth-century latitudinarians, "religion and happiness, our duty and our interest, are really but one and the same thing considered under several notions."[38]

At the personal level, latitudinarians emphasized a good, loving, benevolent God who above all wished his followers to engage in "good works." Evangelical dissenters also believed in good works, but to them, works followed an infusion of grace and had nothing to do with salvation. To latitudinarians, good works were those practices that happy, grateful children gladly followed as an expression of gratitude and well-being. Rather than turning inward and engaging in agonizing soul-searching for assurance of personal salvation, latitudinarians assumed that they were secure in their faith, and, therefore, they focused on external performance of duties such as praying, religious instruction, church attendance, and care of the needy.

A comparison between two contemporary diarists, Samuell Sewall of Boston and William Byrd of Westover in Virginia, serves to illustrate the difference in religious concerns, outlooks, language, and security between a New England Puritan and a Virginia Anglican in the early eighteenth century. Sewall, who reached prominence in Massachusetts as chief justice, was born in 1652 and began keeping a diary in 1674 at the age of twenty-two. His diary has been a treasured source for historians trying to understand New England society, politics, and culture. It also reveals much of Sewall's spiritual life. For example, in 1678–1679, he records great anxiety over his "unfitness and want of Grace" even though he was a church member in good standing who had successfully undergone a months-long examination into his religious fitness. His March 16, 1678/79, entry reflects his thoughts after he had taken communion:

I never experienced more unbelief. I feared at least that I did not believe there was such an one as Jesus Xt., and yet was afraid that because I came to the ordinance without belief, that for the abuse of Xt. I should be stricken dead; yet I had some earnest desires that Xt. would, before the ordinance were done, though it were when he was just going away, give me some glimpse of himself; but I perceived none.[39]

The striking contrast between Sewall's and Byrd's spiritual concerns is evident in diary entries that allow us to follow them to their respective churches on the same Sundays. Typical entries that will serve to illustrate the two different styles are those for November 6, 1709. First, Sewall's:

Lord's day; Mr. Rowland Cotton preach'd in the forenoon; Mr. Corwin in the Afternoon. Mr. Pemberton had propounded hanah Butler to renew her Baptismal Covenant; and now mention'd it, and said she had sin'd scandulously against the 7th Comandment; read her Confession immediately, and by the silential vote restored her. I think it is inconvenient, when persons have so fallen, not to give the Church some previous notice of it; that the Brethren may have Oportunity to enquire into the Repentance. An ignorant Consent is no Consent. And I understood Mr. Pemberton that he would not go in that way again. Once before he did it, saying he know not of it when the party was propounded.[40]

Clearly Sewall was deeply engaged in the drama of baptismal renewal at the meetinghouse that day. He described in detail what transpired and offered his commentary. Adultery was a serious matter to Puritans, serious enough for the congregation to have removed Hannah Butler from its fellowship. But Sewall, ever anxious about how he stood before God, expressed his concern about voting on her restoration without having had ample time and information to assess her repentance. He believed that he would be held accountable for all his actions, including that of restoring fellowship to a fallen woman, and he wanted solid justification for all that he did.

On that same Sunday, William Byrd attended the church of Abingdon Parish near Williamsburg, where he sat as a member of the court. His entry reads as follows:

About 11 o'clock we rode to the church of Abingdon Parish which is the best church I have seen in the country. We heard a sermon of Parson Smith. After church we returned to Mr. Burwell's and Mr. Berkeley and his wife with us.[41]

In this typical description of his experiences at church, Byrd tells us more about the building, "the best church" *building* he had seen in Virginia, than about what transpired during the service. Nothing about the sermon topic or his reaction to the discourse. There is no hint of an anxious soul standing before a divine judge.

Another comparison serves to illustrate the difference between Sewall's and Byrd's approaches to religion. On April 5, 1709, Sewall wrote that he "went to Roxbury Lecture." What is noteworthy about that brief entry is that it is for a Tuesday. Many Puritan congregations offered a regularly scheduled lecture during the week, supplementing Sunday services. It was an opportunity for additional biblical and doctrinal instruction. While Samuel Sewall was in church that evening, William Byrd "played at billiards" and then "read to the ladies Dr. Lister's *Journey to Paris*." He did close his entry, as he did most days, by noting that "I said my prayers." The point is not that Sewall was "more religious" than Byrd. Rather it is that the two men belonged to different Protestant traditions that instilled in them widely varying concerns about the states of their souls.

The two men's respective reading preferences further illustrate how they viewed the Christian faith. On October 23, 1717, the opening day of the General Court in Boston, Judge Sewall gave each of the deputies a copy of Joseph Alleine's *Alarum to the Unconverted* (1692). A favorite among Puritans, this work was also published under the title *The Sure Guide to Heaven*.[42] As both titles suggest, the book deals with individual salvation and the sinner's utter dependence upon God's grace. Sewall wanted to give the deputies something of substance, of eternal value, and he chose this popular book on redemption. No doubt he knew that the best-seller would be received as a valuable gift.

Byrd's interest in religious literature took a very different turn. He showed little interest in the fine distinctions of theological discussions, preferring instead those books that dealt with moral behavior. He frequently read from Archbishop Tillotson's sermons and from *The Whole Duty of Man* (1658). The latter was very popular among latitudinarians in Virginia, with its emphasis on "good works." The person usually cited as the author, Richard Allestree, intended the book "to be a short plain Direction to the very meanest Readers, to behave themselves so in this World, that they may be happy for ever in the next." Rather than depicting a wrathful God demanding rigid compliance with harsh commandments, Allestree pictures a loving Father who sends his son to "enable us to do what God requires of us." One way Christ assisted men and women was to change the law given to Adam, which prohibited the committing of the "least Sin, upon Pain of Damnation, and requiring of us only a honest and hearty Endeavour to do what we are able, and where we fail, accepting of sincerely Repentance." In other words, according to

The Whole Duty of Man, God recognized that the terms of the first covenant were too unreasonable, and he replaced it with a second covenant that could be kept through a good-faith effort.[43] Thus while Sewall read anxiety-provoking works that led one to worry about the state of one's soul and to fret about how to get to heaven, Byrd read comforting books that assured the reader of God's having lowered the bar for salvation to an attainable level.

One last comparison between Sewall and Byrd illustrates how each man interpreted events through his theological lens. On July 13, 1709, Sewall recorded in his diary details of a fire that had forced him and his family to evacuate their house the previous evening. After describing the flames and smoke that filled a closet adjoining his bedroom, he reflected on why the fire occurred in the first place, and why he and his family escaped unharmed. Although there was no indication that he had caused the fire or contributed to its breaking out in any way, Sewall was quick to search for spiritual meaning in the event. He asked "the Lord [to] teach me what I know not; and wherein I have done amiss [and] help me to doe so no more." Thus his first thoughts were those of sin and punishment. Then he thanked God for his "Parental Pity" in enabling the Sewall family to discover and extinguish the flames before anyone was burned.[44] The entire episode, then, was a sermon, and Sewall sought to understand the divine message within it.

While Sewall wondered about the spiritual meaning embedded in a potential disaster, Byrd displayed little anxiety about the state of his soul. Even when he committed what he knew to be sins, he assumed that God forgave him. While in Williamsburg in October 1711, Byrd reported that he and some of his friends met an Indian girl who "had got drunk and made us good sport." Afterward he went to his quarters where, he recorded, "I neglected to say my prayers and had good health, good thoughts, and good humor, thank God Almighty." On another evening on the town, Byrd and his buddies drank a "bowl of punch of French brandy" and then "talked very lewdly and were almost drunk." He stayed out until four o'clock in the morning and then went to his lodging, "where I committed uncleanness, for which I humbly beg God Almighty's pardon." Byrd's entry indicates that he lived by a moral code, that his behavior often violated that code, but that he readily assumed God's forgiveness.[45] At no time does Byrd appear as one worried about his spiritual well-being, even when he is aware of his shortcomings.

If Byrd and others of the gentry were not anxious about religious matters, the Virginia clergy were. Throughout the seventeenth century they labored under a number of problems, many of which stemmed from the lay control of parish churches. First, there was no resident bishop to oversee ecclesiastical affairs as in England. Virginia came under the supervision of the bishop of London, but from such a distance he was unable to exercise effective control. Real power lay with the civil government and with the local vestries. The governor had the power to induct ministers into vacant posts, but in reality positions went unfilled unless the vestry presented a candidate for the slot. According to one account of the state of religion in 1660, "Four-fifths of the parishes were vacant at that time because of the sheer impossibility of securing a supply of ministers from England: consequently, the vestries of the respective parishes were compelled to employ laymen as readers to hold services, and do what they could by baptizing dying children and performing such other ministrations as they were permitted to perform."[46] When Charles II returned to England in 1660, Virginia clergymen petitioned for a resident bishop. The bishop of London reported that those requests were followed by a "great Alarm" sounded by Virginia gentlemen, who protested such an appointment through "Petitions and Addresses with all violence imaginable."[47] Unwilling to provoke further disorder in the realm, the archbishop decided against naming a bishop for America.

Recognizing, however, that some supervision was necessary, in 1689 the bishop of London issued a commission to James Blair to become Virginia's commissary. This was a partial step on the bishop's part, no doubt a reflection of his reluctance to again upset Virginia's gentlemen and one that was preordained to fail. Under English canon law, a commissary was a lesser church official, and thus Blair was charged with bringing discipline to the church in Virginia without being given the power to do the job. Blair wasted no time in trying to put the church on a more orderly footing, and in doing so, he immediately incurred the disfavor of the gentlemen-vestrymen. On July 23, 1690, Blair called a convention of all clergymen that met in Jamestown to discuss two proposals. First, the convention proposed establishing a college in Virginia to train much-needed ministers. Second, the clergymen approved a plan to establish "a series of ecclesiastical courts for the trial of both clerical and lay offenders against the moral law." The latter proposal clearly threatened the hegemony of the gentlemen, who had theretofore exercised effective control over both church and state. Consequently, the measure calling for ecclesiastical courts never surfaced from the deep recesses of the House of Burgesses where it was buried.[48] Blair discovered that those who had power were most reluctant to relinquish it.

By 1697, a number of church-state issues had created sufficient tension between Blair and prominent laymen to warrant an extraordinary conference held at Lambeth Palace in London. Blair had asked the archbishop of Canterbury to convene the meeting, and it was attended by some of Virginia's leading men, including planters William Byrd II and Benjamin Harrison, and John Povey, the colony's agent. Blair wished to bring before the archbishop and the bishop of London some of his complaints against Governor Edmund Andros regarding in particular the College of William and Mary and in general what Blair described as the "bad circumstances of the Clergy." Much of the conference consisted of Blair's attacks on Virginia's religious settlement and on Andros's administration, and Byrd's defenses and counterattacks on clerical conduct. In heated exchanges, the two disputed facts and each other's interpretations of those facts. Blair claimed that before Andros he had never heard of a minister's being turned out of office against the minister's will, "purely by a vote of the Vestry." Byrd countered that the governor and the assembly were "favorable to the Clergy" and had revised laws in favor of the clergy. The archbishop was less concerned about specific instances of clerical abuse than he was about the structure that placed ministers' fates in the hands of laymen. Upon hearing how the vestry and governor controlled clerical appointments, the archbishop replied, "This seems to me a very strange way they have there that their Ministers are not inducted, but may be removed like domestic Servants by a Vote of the Vestry." He asked, "Who would be a Minister in that Country?"[49]

Consequently, in 1707, the bishop of London submitted to the archbishop of Canterbury a proposal for an "American suffragan" necessitated by "Disorders" that he feared would lead to "an entire discouragement of the Clergy."[50] He believed that it was time to send someone who could recruit and train ministers, fill vacancies, and maintain discipline within the clergy. He thought that a suffragan, who was an assistant to a bishop, might be less objectionable than a bishop to Americans. He was wrong on that point, and the archbishop decided not to risk provoking the gentlemen who jealously guarded their leadership of the church.

Gentlemen and clergy agreed on one key point. Both wanted to protect the church from Dissenters, papists, and infidels. Ministers preached against religious outsiders, and planters maintained a literary arsenal against them. Ralph Wormesley's library contained cautionary books about Catholics, such as Thomas James's *A Manuductio; or, Introduction unto Divinity, Containing a Confutation of Papists by Papists* (1625). And he possessed a number of Anglican sermons and treatises as antidotes to Dissenting thought.[51]

Religious Outsiders

The gentlemen who ran Virginia's government, both those residing in England and those in the colony itself, subscribed to the idea of religious uniformity. To them, the absence of uniformity was religious pluralism, which would only lead to endless quarreling among contentious sects and would result in civil disorder, if not civil war. For evidence of that belief, they had only to observe what was happening in England as Puritans and Churchmen waged continuous warfare, first in Parliament and then on battlefields during the English civil war. Virginians closely followed the unholy clashes of Protestant against Protestant as various sects insisted that their particular understanding and practice of Christianity constituted the only "true" church. As early as 1632, the Virginia General Assembly passed a law "that there be a uniformitie throughout this colony both in substance and circumstance to the cannons & constitutions of the church of England as neere as may bee and that every person yeild readie obedience unto them uppon penaltie of the paynes and fortfeitures in that case appoynted."[52] In the lawmakers' thinking, such a law did not violate liberty of conscience. Persons were free to believe according to their understanding of Scripture. But they were not at liberty to promote beliefs and practices in public that would undermine the one established faith. Gentlemen also believed that major issues concerning Christian doctrine had been decided by the Church of England, and that they had been collectively and publicly settled by those whose education and circumstances best enabled them to address such matters. While individuals might hold different views in private, public religious expression was set until another learned body should revise it.

Ralph Wormesley's library indicates that the gentleman planters who promoted uniform religion were prepared to defend it against enemies both within and without the church. The first line of defense was legislation. In particular, Virginians sought to protect themselves against the evil influence of "popish recusants." Proscribed from the free practice of their religion in England, Catholics in colonial America were fair game for discrimination. Virginians moved swiftly in 1640 to rid themselves of "popish" influence. First, an act prohibited Catholics from holding any public office unless they "had taken the oath of allegiance and supremacy," meaning that they subscribed to the authority and teachings of the Church of England. Second, by law "popish priests" arriving in the colony should be deported forthwith.[53]

Cecil Calvert, Lord Baltimore, encountered firsthand the Virginians' hostility toward Catholics. Robert Beverley, planter and author of *The History and Present State of Virginia* (1705), recorded an account of Baltimore's reception. He wrote that Calvert, a Catholic, "thought for the more quiet Exercise of his Religion to retire, with his Family, into that new World. For this Purpose he went to *Virginia*, to try how he liked the Place." His reception was anything but hospitable: "But the People there look'd upon him with an evil Eye, on Account of his Religion, for which alone he sought this Retreat; and by their ill Treatment, discouraged him from settling in that Country."[54] While Virginia was represented by its gentleman planters as a "Christian Colonie," its doors were open only to the Protestant branch of the Christian faith.

Moreover, the early Virginians sought to protect their society from the evil influence of "radical" Protestant sects that did not recognize the church's authority. Quakers replaced Catholics as the greatest immediate threat to religious uniformity and tranquillity. In England and the colonies, Quakers were particularly noisome to ecclesiastical and civil authorities because the only sovereign they submitted to was the "Light Within," that is, their own consciences. Such a sect could not be tolerated in a hierarchical society. Thus, citing unlawful assemblies of "an unreasonable and turbulent sort of people, commonly called Quakers," the legislators enacted a law for suppressing that sect. Claiming that the Quakers published "lies, miracles, false visions, prophecies and doctrines," the lawmakers concluded that the nonconformists were attempting to "destroy religion, lawes, comunities and all bonds of civil societie." Accordingly, ships' captains were forbidden to bring Quakers into the colony. In addition, those who did manage to slip into Virginia were to be "imprisoned without baile" until they "with all speed . . . depart the collonie and not to returne again." Those who returned a third time would be treated as felons.[55]

Puritans also posed a threat to Virginia's uniformity, especially in the 1640s when the Puritan Parliament was openly opposing the king and church in England. Though there were not large numbers of Puritans in Virginia, those present were bold enough to ask their Massachusetts brethren to send them three ministers. As one historian has observed, the date of the request, 1642, the "very year that civil war started in England," suggests that the Puritans' motives were more than religious. "It is exceedingly difficult to see in this action any other motive than the political one of bringing representatives of the strongly organized Puritan government in New England as official messengers to discover such Puritan sentiment as they might find in Virginia and organize it into a body to join with New England and their co-religionists in England in their war against the king." The swift action of the Virginia legislature to enact a law against nonconformist ministers suggests that the lawmakers viewed the Puritan ministers as political "fifth columnists" interested in political advantage, not as evangelical missionaries primarily concerned about men's souls.[56]

In opposing Catholics and Dissenters, Virginia Anglicans expressed their view that religious liberty did not preclude the state's maintaining order, and that the Act of Uniformity was essential. Individuals were free to hold any view that their consciences dictated as long as those views did not in any way undermine the authority of the state and its established church. Quakers, for instance, held the dangerous belief that all men, including slaves, had a spark of the divine and were equals under God. Clearly such sentiments could not be allowed in a slaveholding colony. In other words, it was acceptable to believe but not to express the belief.

Non-Christians presented Virginians with a special problem. On the one hand, their charter cited the conversion of natives to Christianity as one of the justifications for settlement. On the other hand, Virginians regarded both slaves and Indians as pagans who could be exploited and need not be accorded the rights due Christians. Virginians regarded Indians, for example, as "savages" and "infidels." The epithet "savage" had a special and ignoble meaning in English political history because it was first used against another group of outsiders, the Irish. Indeed, there was a direct link between the fight against Irish Catholics in the seventeenth century and that against Native Americans. After Oliver Cromwell and his New Model Army had defeated Royalist forces and turned England into a republic, he personally led a military mission to subdue the Irish. In fighting of a savagery unmatched by that of the American Indians, Cromwell's forces killed perhaps as many as one-third of the Irish, justifying the slaughter in part because of their victims' religion. After the Restoration, many Oliverian soldiers emigrated to Virginia, where they fought Indians with and without government sanction.

Early Virginians dismissed Native American religion as "Superstitious and Idolatrous," the same adjectives Protestants had long used in describing the Holy Roman Church. Robert Beverley acknowledged that natives had "Conceptions of God, and another World," but deemed them to be "unworthy" notions. Upon querying one Indian about native ideas of God, Beverley learned that "they believ'd God was universally beneficent, that his Dwelling was in the Heavens above, and that the Influences of his Goodness reach'd to the Earth beneath." Rather than seeing a close affinity with the Christian view, Beverley pointed out that Indians also believed in an Evil Spirit that they worshiped instead of God. For Virginians, then, the matter was simple: Indians must be converted to the Christian faith, the only true religion. The question was how best to bring about their conversion.

Beverley believed that the early Virginians had missed an opportunity to convert natives through intermarriage. He argued that the marriage between Pocahontas, daughter of the Powhatan chief, and John Rolfe, an English gentleman, provided a model that should have been followed. Instead of the vicious warfare that characterized relations with Indians, intermarriage would have resulted in many, if not most, of the Indians' being "converted to Christianity."[57] By the early 1700s, Virginians viewed education, not marriage, as the best means of converting the natives. The idea was to concentrate on Indian youth, believing that they were more malleable and therefore more easily converted. Consequently, the legislature appropriated funds for the College of William and Mary to educate a number of the "chief rulers' children." James Blair gave this sanguine report to the General Assembly in 1711: "I doubt not but whilst by kind and Gentle means we endeavour to Change the Savage nature of their youth, they will imbibe, with the English Language, the true principles of our excellent Church, from whence will arise two of the greatest benefits, the salvation of many poor souls, & withal, the best of securities, to our persons & Estates, for once make them good Christians & you may confide in 'em."[58] Blair's expectations turned out to be overly optimistic. When the natives, not surprisingly, refused to turn their sons over for the proposed benevolent brainwashing, the Virginians could concede neither that the Indians might prefer their own religion, nor that they might be suspicious of why white men wanted to convert them.

In the end, little came of the Virginians' missionary work among native Americans. Guns, not Bibles, became the primary means of dealing with Indians. The legislature mandated that every head of family "shall bring with them to church on Sundays one fixed and serviceable gun with sufficient powder and shott." After the 1622 Indian attack that killed almost one-half of the settlers, the survivors did not want to be caught off guard again, even when worshiping the Prince of Peace. Those who failed to comply with the mandate incurred a fine of ten pounds of tobacco levied by the churchwardens.[59]

Planters also considered their slaves to be religious outsiders. Unlike native Americans, however, slaves were under the direct control of their masters. As a result, whether or not slaves were introduced to Christianity depended largely upon individual slaveholders. Neither the church nor the state undertook the mission of Christianizing slaves. Many slave-owners believed that English law did not allow them to hold another Christian in bondage, and, not wanting to jeopardize their legal claim to ownership, made no effort to convert their slaves. Further, some slaveholders thought that conversion would spoil their slaves, that is, fill their heads with notions of brotherhood, redemption, and equality. On the other hand, there were those who argued that such Christian principles as honesty and obedience would be valuable for their bondsmen. As the number of slaves began to rise in the 1660s, the legislature decided to clarify the status of slaves who became Christian. In self-serving language, the law's preamble announced that it was "by the charity and piety of their owners" that some slaves "were made partakers of the blessed sacrament of baptisme." Then, in no uncertain terms, the act declared that "the conferring of baptisme doth not alter the condition of the person as to his bondage or ffreedome." Returning to its praise of masters, it explained that "diverse masters, ffreed from this doubt, may more carefully endeavour the propagation of christianity by permitting children, though slaves, or those of greater growth if capable to be admitted to that sacrament."[60]

Virginia's gentlemen offered their slaves what Frederick Douglass called "slaveholders'" Christianity. Typically, those slaves whose masters allowed them to attend services sat together in the back or in the balcony. After the regular service was concluded, they stayed for a special sermon directed at them. As Douglass noted two hundred years later, its message was transparent. Rather than preaching the good news of emancipation and redemption, ministers admonished slaves to be subservient and obedient, and to accept their lot in this life while hoping for a better life to come. This "slaveholding religion," Douglass declared, had nothing to do with "the Christianity of Christ." Instead, this "hypocritical" Christianity was a clear case of "stealing the livery of the court of heaven to serve the devil in."[61]

Despite the slaveholding oligarchy's attempts to regulate religion, there was the ever present fear that a religious underground among slaves would subvert the "true" faith and public order. Francis Le Jau, missionary in neighboring Carolina, warned about the dangers of teaching slaves to read the Bible, describing how some literate slaves placed their own construction on Scripture. He indicated that his best student was armed with insurrectionary notions that could stir up his fellow slaves by identifying current sins, presumably of whites as well as blacks, with those described in the Bible as punishable in the final judgment.[62]

Fearing the dangers of a free marketplace of religion where individuals of all classes and races choose their own interpretations, Virginia's "Nursing Fathers" regarded the church more as an instrument of social control than as a vehicle of personal salvation. Without question, they had constructed an institution that throughout the seventeenth century enabled them to pursue both profits and piety with a minimum of conflict. In the eighteenth century, however, they would face stiff competition from evangelical outsiders who dared to challenge, and even criticize, the gentry's claims of presiding over a "Christian Colonie."

❖ 3 ❖

Puritan Fathers and the "Christian Common-wealth"

B EST KNOWN for his role in promoting Virginia tobacco, John Rolfe
sometimes interpreted the early Chesapeake settlement in theological terms, on one occasion calling it the work of a "peculiar
people, marked and chosen by the finger of God." But religion and religious concerns expressed by inhabitants *in* a colony do not make it a
religious colony. Virginians did not order their social, political, and economic institutions according to scriptural precepts. The Puritans who
settled Massachusetts Bay did. Theirs was a religious colony, defined,
not by occasional pious utterances, however sincerely spoken, but by
"pervasive religiosity."[1]

From its inception, Massachusetts was an exceptional place whose very
founding was unique among all the English colonies. When Cotton
Mather wrote *Magnalia Christi Americana* in the early eighteenth century,
he wished to explain why his forefathers had decided to plant colonies in
North America. To sum up their motivation, he quoted one of the company's investors, a Captain Weymouth, who recorded his observations
about English colonization in America. Referring to all the settlements,
Weymouth declared that "one main end of all these undertakings, was
to plant the gospel in these dark regions of America." Mather accepted
Weymouth's statement, adding that the question was "how well the most
of the English plantations have answered this *main end*." He then made
his own bold declaration concerning Massachusetts Bay Colony: "I am

now to tell mankind, that as for *one* of these English plantations, this was not only a *main end*, but the *sole end* upon which it was erected." Far from being just another English colony that sought piety as well as profits, Massachusetts was "the spot of *earth*, which the God of heaven *spied out* for the seat of such *evangelical*, and *ecclesiastical*, and very remarkable transactions." Here was a place, he maintained, "that our blessed Jesus intended a *resting place*."[2]

When the *Arbella* led the small fleet of vessels into Salem harbor on June 12, 1630, she brought a people with a divine mission and a royal charter. The Puritans viewed themselves as a chosen people, an American Israel, who had entered into a covenant with God to plant a Holy Commonwealth in the New England wilderness. Their leader, John Winthrop, was aware of the band's distinctive nature. The law of the gospel, he reminded his fellow passengers aboard the *Arbella*, "teacheth us to put a difference betweene Christians and others." Accordingly, the Puritans must acknowledge that they were "a Company professing [themselves] fellow members of Christ," organize a new society wherein they should account themselves "knitt together by this bond of love," and keep their communities free of all who were outside the gospel covenant.[3]

This was to be no ordinary commonwealth. Winthrop recognized that "the worke and ende we aime at . . . are extraordinary," and, therefore, he argued, "wee must not content our selves with usual ordinary means." "The end," Winthrop declared, "is to improve our lives to doe more service to the Lord [and to] comforte and encrease the body of christe whereof we are members, that our selves and posterity may be the better reserved from the Common corruptions of this evill world to serve the Lord and worke out our Salvation under the power and purity of his holy Ordinances." In other words, the Holy Commonwealth must seal itself from the evil world in order to maintain purity. Citizenship in this commonwealth would be far more exacting than what the Puritans had previously experienced. "Whatsoever wee did or ought to have done when we lived in England," he wrote, "the same must wee do and more alsoe where wee goe." Set apart from the evil world, they would also differ from most other Christians. "That which the most in theire Churches maintaine as a truthe in profession only," Winthrop stated, "wee must bring into familiar and constant practise."[4] The Puritans of Massachusetts

Bay would set about to order their lives in a way that fostered the practice of piety in all that they did.

Though the Puritans viewed their mission as divine, they recognized the need for political power to bring it to a successful end. While the churches would organize themselves according to biblical principles, they would require a supportive state to protect them from undesirable elements whose teachings and behavior might taint the Holy Commonwealth. There had to be a coercive power sympathetic to the Puritan goal. Fortunately, they had a royal charter in their possession that granted sufficient power to the Massachusetts Bay Company to make and execute laws for their purposes. Unwittingly, whoever drafted the charter in King Charles I's court failed to include a clause requiring the company to maintain its headquarters in London, where crown officials could provide close supervision. Virginia's charter had such a requirement, and royal officials kept a close eye on that colony's struggles until they rescinded its charter in 1624 and made Virginia a royal province. Winthrop, a lawyer, recognized the Puritans' good fortune in having their patent in hand. They were free to frame their government and society as they wished, certain that they could successfully argue that their laws conformed to those of England. With no king or bishops or bureaucrats present, with transatlantic messages requiring months to make the circuit between Boston and London, and with the crown distracted by parliamentary challenges at home, the Puritan Fathers were confident that they had a relatively free hand to build their Christian utopia.

The Holy Commonwealth was not intended for everyone, not even for all Christians. Of course, Catholics or "papists" were unwelcome, but so were other Protestants, including Anglicans, Quakers, and Baptists. To Puritans, intolerance in the name of Christian purity was not only defensible but mandatory for a covenanted people. In Massachusetts, religious freedom was defined as freedom from error. Such a stance soon earned them bad press in England. Rather than extending toleration to those of different religious convictions, the Puritans persecuted dissenters in their midst just as they had been persecuted as English Dissenters. One divine, Nathaniel Ward, pastor at Aggawam, wrote a spirited apology in 1647 defending the Puritans' practices toward those who disagreed with them. He took issue with "unfriendly reports" representing the Puritan emigrants as being "wild opinionists, [who] swarmed into a remote wilderness to find elbow-roome for our phanatic Doctrines and practises." Rather, they were serious and pious Christians who sought a place where they could live and worship as they wished. Ward said that those of a different mind could do the same. In what amounted to both a promise and a threat, he wrote, "all Familists, Antinomians, Anabaptists, and other Enthusiasts shall have free Liberty to keepe away from us, and such as will come to be gone as fast as they can, the sooner the better."[5] Such an attitude would eventually contribute to the end of the Holy Commonwealth. In 1684, King James II rescinded the Massachusetts Bay charter in part because of complaints from good Protestant English subjects who were not allowed to worship in the colony according to the dictates of their consciences. But for a span of fifty years, Massachusetts Puritans set about creating, often by coercion, their promised land in the wilderness.

"THE RELIGIOUS DESIGN OF [THE PURITAN] FATHERS"

While in England, the Puritans developed a set of assumptions about religion, its practice, and its place in society; the wilds of New England provided the freedom for Puritans to build a community on those assumptions. In Massachusetts Bay, instead of being Dissenters from the established religion, Puritans established their Congregational churches as the official religion. This meant that the state mandated towns to build meetinghouses, hire "orthodox" ministers, and pay taxes to support those churches. And while Puritans pleaded for religious freedom in England, in New England they denied any such liberty to those whose faith did not conform to Congregational Puritanism.[6] Writing at the end of the seventeenth century, the Lord Bishop of Salisbury noted the relation between religious freedom and political power. "Every party cries out for Liberty & toleration," he said, "till they get to be uppermost, and then will allow none. Witness those of N[ew] E[ngland] where they have sufficiently proved the Truth of the Doctrine & have showed their tenderness to dissenters in the plainest manner by Acting such Cruelties, which are hardly to be paralleled in Heathen persecutions."[7] New England Puritans used their newfound power to seal their churches and communities from heretical influences.

Without question, Winthrop and his band of Puritans removed to New England for religious reasons. To be sure, they also pursued profits. After all, good Puritans were industrious and thrifty, virtues that were bound to produce plenty in an abundant land. But the primary motive was religious. In 1629, the emigrants set down the "Reasons to be considered for justifying the undertakers of the intended Plantation in New England, and for encouraging such whose hearts God shall move to join with them in it." First, there was a missionary reason: "It will be a service to the Church of great consequence to carry the Gospel into those parts of the world, to help on the fullness of the coming of the Gentiles, and to raise a bulwark against the kingdom of AnteChrist, which the Jesuits labor to rear up in those parts." The Puritans saw themselves as advancing the work of Protestant "Gentiles," a designation that conveyed the sect's strong animus against both Catholics and Jews. In other words, the Puritans would be planting "true religion" in New England. Second, the Puritans were fleeing the church's desolation in Europe, brought on by Christians' own sins, and seeking refuge in the wilderness, a place of biblical purpose where the faithful members of God's church could "go and provide tabernacles and food for her when she be restored." With corruption at every turn in their homeland behind them and an uncorrupted wilderness before them, the Puritan emigrants had an opportunity to start anew. Such an undertaking would be only for the Christian warrior who was willing to give up all and endure great privation in order to build the new church.[8] But the promised rewards were great. If the Puritans were faithful, then they could indeed erect a "City upon a Hill."

Determined to establish a community based solely on biblical principles, the New England Puritans set about the task of constructing institutions that supported that lofty aim. Every aspect of life must reflect the overarching goal of living as the primitive Christians had sought to live: residing in the world without being of the world. The godly family was the basic social institution, a microcosm of the entire community, with a loving patriarch at its head making sure that each member was brought up in the fear of the Lord and pursued a calling with industry and purpose. While the family practiced piety through daily devotions, the local church was the center of public worship, providing instruction for a body of believers bound to each other and to God in a sacred covenant. Indeed, the Puritans insisted that everyone must reside in a village or town in order to attend services at the centrally located meetinghouse. Compared to the rituals of the Church of England, Puritan services were simple affairs, featuring a sermon that "opened" the word of God in what was called the "plain Style." Because of the importance of the word, educational institutions were mainstays of the "New England Way." Though parents had the responsibility of teaching their children to read, communities maintained schoolmasters who taught basic skills and inculcated moral principles. And Harvard College prepared young men for the ministry.

Winthrop considered the Puritans to be a new chosen people, an American Israel. That lofty notion carried great promise and somber warning. In stating the "case between God and us," he declared,

> we are entered into covenant with Him for this work. We have taken out a commission. The Lord has given us leave to draw our own articles; we have promised to base our actions on these ends, and we have asked Him for favor and blessing. Now if the Lord shall please to hear us, and bring us in peace to the place we desire, then He has ratified this covenant and sealed our commission, and will expect strict performance of the articles contained in it. But if we neglect to observe these articles, . . . the Lord will surely break out in wrath against us and be revenged of such a perjured people, and He will make us know the price of the breach of such a covenant.[9]

As a lawyer, Winthrop understood the concept of consideration in contracts or covenants. Each party to the agreement granted certain rights to the other in exchange for something deemed valuable. In this case, God extended his protection and blessing to the Puritan settlers of Massachusetts Bay. But, in return, he expected obedience and faithfulness. Moreover, the God of Winthrop's covenant was the wrathful deity that Moses described as promising the Chosen People of Israel that they would "surely perish" if they were seduced by "pleasures and profits." In other words, the covenant was conditional: God's Elect could expect "covenant-mercies [only] on condition of covenant-duties."[10]

In order to become a full member of a church and thereby qualify as a citizen of Massachusetts Bay, one first had to assure his or her fellow parishioners that he or she had indeed entered into a covenant of grace with God. Demonstrating one's "election" required a public confession of faith before those who had already qualified as "visible saints," the

Puritan designation for church members. Accordingly, one gave an account of a "conversion experience" wherein God had wrought his work of grace within the individual's heart. To outsiders, insistence on conversion contradicted belief in election. If God had already chosen one to be saved, why did that person need to "believe" to undergo conversion? New England Puritans, however, saw no contradiction. They insisted that an individual could do nothing to effect his or her own salvation. But they also maintained that God had modified his covenant of grace to give true believers assurance of their election. If one *believed* that he or she was saved—that is, made a genuine confession of faith—then that *belief* was evidence of divine grace within one's life.[11]

To Puritans, covenant was more than an individual matter. They subscribed to the view that there was a social covenant binding them together in a society under God's providential care. John Eliot, a Puritan minister, testified that visible saints are eager to "enter into covenant with the Lord to become his people, even in their Civil Society, as well as in their Church Society."[12] Thus covenants bound Puritans together, not just in the meetinghouse, but in the statehouse and countinghouse as well. In the Holy Commonwealth, Puritan divines, guided by Scripture, not the marketplace and its laws, established rules governing economic exchange. Such a statement is surprising given the fact that New England Puritans lived in a world increasingly shaped by the rhythms of commercial capitalism. Indeed, the very founding of the colony was part of England's search for new markets and new supplies of raw materials. Moreover, with its rocky soil preventing the establishment of large-scale agriculture such as that underway in Virginia, Massachusetts Bay depended on trade in the Atlantic market. In order to thrive, New England merchants had to compete in a mercantile world where such impersonal forces as prices, demand, and supply were set within a complex web of exchange with nodes far removed from British North America. And New Englanders enjoyed success in the marketplace. Cotton Mather spoke for most Puritans in linking religious faithfulness with economic prosperity. He observed that as the first generation of settlers *"proceeded* in the evangelical service and worship of our Lord Jesus Christ, so they *prospered* in their secular concernments."[13] But Puritans must always remember that they were part of a moral economy where the goal was "fair prices" and "just wages," not maximum profits.[14]

The Puritan Fathers intended their towns to be "Christian, Utopian, Closed, Corporate" communities. Christian because Christian love unified the inhabitants. Utopian because theirs was a conscious effort to live in perfect conformity with the dictates of Scripture. Closed because "membership was selected while outsiders were treated with suspicion or rejected altogether." And Corporate because they demanded that members give up some of their individual freedom to the community in exchange for holiness, peace, and order.[15] Maintaining such communities proved to be a difficult challenge. First, as the towns grew, and as second- and third-generation farmers had to travel several miles to reach their farmland, some of them wished to withdraw and form their own towns closer to their land. Some of the Founders viewed this geographic separation as spiritual decline, a moving away from the forefathers' mission. They may have misread the moment: when their sons and grandsons did establish new communities, they replicated those they had left, making them closed, covenanted, and Christian as well.[16]

Ironically, the threat to the utopian communities often came from among those who stayed in the original towns. Anne Hutchinson is the best known because of her celebrated case before the General Court. The wife of a merchant, she became disturbed over a theological issue: the covenant of grace versus the covenant of law. She insisted that with Christ's sacrifice, the former negated the latter, and that Christians were saved by grace alone and freed from the obligation of doing "good works." She accused most ministers, except her own pastor John Cotton, of preaching only the covenant of works. When she attracted a large following, officials grew alarmed at the disunity that ensued and summoned her to court on the charge of heresy. Specifically, she was charged with antinomianism, the belief that Christians did not have to obey commandments and laws. At her trial, she defended her position by declaring that she had received a direct revelation from God. Winthrop saw the matter as a question of authority: "the ground work of her revelations is the immediate revelation of the spirit and not by the ministry of the word." If she were allowed to prevail, everyone could make similar claims, each citing private revelations as his or her guide, with the result being social chaos. Winthrop judged Hutchinson's revelation to be the reason for all the "tumults and troubles," all the "mischief," that disturbed the peace and unity of the Holy Commonwealth. To protect the covenanted community, Hutchinson must be "cut off from us," and thus the court ordered her banishment.[17]

Merchants who placed profit ahead of community also found themselves in court for violating the civil covenant. Robert Keayne's case of 1639 illustrates the tension between scriptural precepts and market demand. At his Boston shop, Keayne sold general merchandise at prices some of his customers thought exorbitant. In particular he sold nails at prices yielding from 50 to 100 percent profit. The court fined him £100 for his oppressive business practices, finding his guilt aggravated by his being "an ancient professor of the gospel" who had "come over for conscience' sake, and for the advancement of the gospel here." For such a man of the church to engage in avaricious behavior would hardly signal to the world that New England was a "City upon a Hill." However, the court considered mitigating circumstances, such as the absence of a specific law regulating prices and the fact that "he was not alone in this fault, . . . [that] all men through the country, in sale of cattle, corn, labor, etc., were guilty of, the widespread practice of the like excess in prices." In most societies, including that of Virginia, the court's judgment would have ended the matter. But in the "Christian Common-wealth," Keayne had to face church censures. His pastor, John Cotton, both at the request of the magistrates and out of his own conviction, preached a sermon arguing that morality, not the market, must determine economic exchange, and setting forth rules governing pricing.[18]

A great many of the children and grandchildren of the Puritan Founders, however, either could not or would not adhere to the demanding terms of the covenant. By 1662, ministers, fearing that subsequent generations were less zealous than their forebears in nurturing the faith, called a special synod to deal with declining church membership. Desiring to keep people within the church, the synod concocted a Half-Way Covenant whereby those who did not qualify on their own as "visible saints" could gain church membership through a grandfather clause. It allowed children of baptized but unconverted members to be baptized and become members themselves.[19] No doubt a reflection of their sincere concern over the state of their churches, the ministers' solution had practical consequences too. Because "Half-Way" members were in the church, they were bound by its teachings, and the Holy Commonwealth remained intact. In defending the covenanted community, ministers knew that they could continue to foster and count on a close working relationship between church and state.

"SHIELDS UNTO THE CHURCHES OF NEW-ENGLAND"[20]

Puritan churches were independent, voluntary associations of believers. A group of individuals "gathered" a church through a process of intense self-evaluation aimed at ensuring that they themselves were of the Elect, and then they determined who else in the community qualified as members. These laypersons possessed full authority to shape the church and its affairs: they hired and fired ministers and teachers; they drafted a church covenant; and they worshiped according to their own lights. Democratic churches, however, did not mean that the state was democratic. In fact, John Winthrop had a very low opinion of democracy. "A democracy is," he declared, "among most civil nations, accounted the meanest, and worst of all forms of government." Further, he could find no "warrant in Scripture for it; there was no such government in Israel."[21] He preferred what he called a "mixed aristocracy" wherein magistrates exercise power through a divine calling. God granted to some men special powers of judgment and authority to direct the affairs of state. John Cotton agreed: "Democracy, I do not conceive, that ever God did ordain as a fit government, either for Church or commonwealth." He thought that Christian "gentlemen of the country" were best suited to preserve what he called "well-ordered liberty," which he defined as "authority in magistrates, liberty in people, purity in the Church."[22] Though there were dissenting opinions, and while town meetings gave people a voice in local affairs, most Puritans in early Massachusetts Bay were willing to defer to their magistrates.

In constructing their Holy Commonwealth, New England Puritans drew a clear line between civil and religious authority. Because of the persecution they had suffered in England, they denied government any power over church matters. In England, for example, the monarch could appoint and remove church officials. In New England, the governor and General Court had no similar power. Similarly, the clergy in Massachusetts Bay were to play no official role in political affairs. In England the great bishops sat in the House of Lords. In New England, ministers were barred from holding public office. But though they played no official role in the state, ministers exerted tremendous indirect influence on political affairs. First, they preached the necessity of choosing godly men as government officials. And second, they frequently acted as advisers to the court and legislature, most often interpreting the scriptural passages that lay behind the colony's laws. Unlike Hildebrand—who censured Henry IV, whom he viewed as a rival—Puritan divines in Massachusetts supported the magistrates, whom they regarded as "Shields unto the Church."

Massachusetts Puritans did not wish to erect a theocracy wherein the clergy ruled. According to one scholar, "of all the governments in the Western world at the time, that of early Massachusetts gave the clergy least authority." Authority for running the state "rested firmly in the hands of laymen."[23] Moreover, the clergy and their churches could not remove government officials from office. They could excommunicate officials from their congregations, but excommunication did not alter the status of the official within the government, a marked contrast with the church's influence in English civil affairs. As historian Edmund Morgan explained, "In England excommunications carried heavy civil disabilities, in Massachusetts none. The right to vote and hold office was not revoked by loss of church membership."[24]

The Puritans believed that the church had a responsibility to support good government. The best service the church could render the government was to prepare "fit instruments both to rule and to choose rulers." Therefore, New England Puritans determined that "none are admitted freemen of this Commonwealth but such as are first admitted members of some church or other in this country." And because local congregations decided who was and was not a church member, the churches conferred citizenship. John Cotton insisted that Massachusetts be governed by civil law and not by the church. "Magistrates are neither chosen to office in the Church nor do govern by directions from the Church," he wrote to counter critics who claimed otherwise, "but by civil laws, and those enacted in General Courts and executed in courts of justice by the governors and assistants." Aside from preparing its members to be moral persons suited to vote and rule, the church "hath nothing to do" with government.[25]

While the state had no voice in church affairs and the church none in state matters, church and state nevertheless supported each other in the

Holy Commonwealth. According to the Cambridge Platform of 1648, "church government stands in no opposition to civil government . . . nor any way entrenches upon the authority of civil magistrates in their jurisdictions." Rather, the church makes good government possible by encouraging a "more hearty and conscionable obedience" among its members. Likewise, "as it is unlawful for church officers to meddle with the sword of the magistrate, so it is unlawful for the magistrate to meddle with the work proper to church officials." Magistrates are not to be policemen of the heart, having no jurisdiction over such matters as "hardness of the heart, erroneous opinions not vented." They did, however, have jurisdiction over behavior proscribed by the churches, including "idolatry, blasphemy, heresy, venting corrupt and pernicious opinions that destroy the foundation, open contempt of the word preached, profanation of the Lord's Day, disturbing the peaceable administration and exercise of the worship and holy things of God."[26]

Perhaps the state's most important function in regard to the church was to use its coercive power as "guardian of the [colony's] divine commission." If Massachusetts was to be a "City upon a Hill," the state must punish those who preached heresies and uttered blasphemies. The state did not, however, function as an arm of the church in punishing heretics and blasphemers. Rather, it considered those offenses as it would any other threat to civil order and harmony and dealt with them through the offices of magistrates and juries.[27]

For government to support the Puritans' religious mission, it must be run by Christian men. To the minister John Davenport and most Puritans, the central issues were those of suffrage and officeholding. If the election of magistrates rested solely with the Elect—that is, church members— and if they selected only church members for office, then Christians would hold the reins of power in what the Puritans regarded as a "Christian Common-wealth." Davenport distinguished between Christians' political rights in a "Commonwealth already settled and one yet settled." He argued that when the Apostle Paul exhorted Roman Christians to be subject to higher powers, he "considered the Civil State as settled." But if Paul had been directing them to lay the "Foundation of a Christian Common-wealth, he would not have advised them to chuse such Governours as were out of the Church." Indeed, the apostle qualified a similar admonition of civil obedience in his epistle to the Christians at Corinth, reproving them for "carrying *their differences before Heathen magistrates to be judged by them*, though he press[ed] them to be *subject to their power*." But the Puritans of New England found themselves in a far better position than had the Christians at Rome or Corinth; they were in a land where the civil state was not yet settled. To Davenport, the message was clear: "they should rather chuse such as are Members of the Church for that purpose then [*sic*] others that are not of that estate."[28]

Davenport defended his argument that only members of the churches should hold public office by citing prevailing practice in other lands or, as he called it, "the Consent of all Nations." He noted that in England, "none are intrusted with managing of Publick Affairs" but members of the Church of England. He said that in Holland, known for its broad religious toleration, "Grave Maurice removed all Arminians from office and chose only those of the Dutch Church." And of course, he pointed out that in "Popish Countreys and Plantations, they observe it strictly, to intrust none with the managing of Publick Civil Affairs but such as are *Catholics*." Similar church-state patterns were found in non-Christian lands. Turkey permitted only those "devoted to Mahomet" to serve as officers of the state. And in America, the "very Indians that Worship the Devil" are the ones who govern their tribes. Davenport concluded "that it seems to be a Principle imprinted in the minds and hearts of all men in the equity of it, That such a Form of Government as best serveth to Establish their Religion, should by the consent of all be Established in the Civil State."[29] In other words, in Christian New England, only members of the true church, the Congregational churches, should hold public office.

Thomas Walley, pastor at Barnstable in Massachusetts Bay, set forth the duties of Christian magistrates in a Christian land. In the Election Sermon of 1669, he told the civil officials that "God hath called you to be Healers to a poor sick Country: that word in Scripture that is rendered to *govern*, is divers times rendered to *heal*." By using the term "healer," Walley meant to emphasize the state of spiritual decline that he saw prevalent in New England. He contended that "when the people by their sin have brought all things into Confusion, and their ruine almost present, then they shall be desirous of healing Rulers." In his opinion, New Englanders were in such a condition and needed godly rulers who could facilitate healing. Walley saw the state as having a direct responsibility for ensuring religious instruction, meaning that the magistrates should make certain that only orthodox ministers were installed.[30] Underlying his argument are two tenets widely held in seventeenth-century New England. First, that the greatest fear any society should have is that of God's wrath directed toward disobedient followers. Second, that the linchpin of a free and harmonious commonwealth is God's law, most clearly expressed in the Ten Commandments. To the Puritans, the Old Testament bore witness to God's terrible judgment visited upon his covenanted people of Israel when they disobeyed his laws. The application was clear: the new chosen people faced the same sort of divine retribution if they strayed.

Twenty years after Winthrop called for a "City upon a Hill," New England Puritans viewed their work as unfinished. Failure to erect the Christian utopia could not be attributed to the "wrong" sorts' having come to Massachusetts in the Great Migration that brought some thirty thousand English men and women between 1630 and 1650. William Stoughton thought quite the opposite, exclaiming of the immigrants that they were "choice grains" bound to God in a covenant relationship, a Chosen People. Peter Bulkeley, pastor at Concord, reminded his congregation in 1651 that they were no ordinary people. Echoing Winthrop, Bulkeley declared, "we are as a city set upon a hill, in the open view of all the earth, the eyes of the world are upon us, because we profess ourselves to be a people in covenant with God." Lest his audience think that such a city could be erected solely because its inhabitants had been chosen or predestined, Bulkeley asserted that predestination did not excuse those selected by God from right living, although right living might not win God's favor. In other words, if the Puritans were to enjoy a "city set upon a hill," they must work for it. "There is no people but will strive to excel in something," he continued; "What can we excel in, if not in holiness?"[31] Through God's grace and their hard work, Bulkeley argued, the Puritans of Massachusetts could create a Christian nation.

Many believed that the church and state should work together to bring Indians within the "Christian Common-wealth." The Puritan policy toward natives was that of civilization and conversion, a policy that gained acceptance after costly wars: the war of extermination against the Pequots in 1637 and a war of attrition against the Narragansetts. In 1645, the General Court noted the "paucity of converts and warned 'the reverend elders' that more positive steps were about to be taken." The following year, Puritan divine John Eliot preached his first sermon to the Indians, and the legislature immediately passed a series of laws to support his missionary efforts. The magistrates forbade natives to worship their own gods, appointed two ministers to preach to the Indians, and purchased lands "for the incuragment of the Indians to live in an orderly way amongst us." Between 1651 and 1674, Eliot established fourteen "praying towns" modeled on the utopian idea of a "Christian Common-wealth" governed according to the Bible. There young Indians would acquire the manners and culture of the English and be introduced to the true word of God. Few, however, were willing to give up their own religion and culture, and many returned to their own people. After King Philip's War (1675–1676), the legislature turned the remaining four "praying towns" into reservations, home to a few Indians who were not killed in the war or sold into slavery. In places where ministers and magistrates had hoped Indians would embrace the gospel, natives found themselves "physically restricted."[32]

Not all Puritans, however, thought the state should create a "Christian Common-wealth" for English settlers or Native Americans. Roger Williams, pastor at Salem, asserted, "The civil state of the nations, being merely and essentially civil, cannot (Christianly) be called 'Christian states.' " And he thought that Massachusetts Bay was not an exception. Williams differentiated between spiritual and civil power. The true Christian church was a spiritual power, he argued, consisting of true Christians who were scattered throughout the world, not gathered into a single state that could be called "Christian." He said that the New Testament made no claims for Christ's "forming or reforming" his church to coincide with "the civil and worldly powers." Conversely, the state or "civil sword" has no right or power to "act either in restraining the souls of people from worship, etc., or in constraining them to worship."[33] In support of that contention, Puritans often cited Christian martyrs who, despite the state's condemning them to death by fire for worshiping according to their consciences instead of adhering to prescribed forms, sang God's praises even as the flames consumed them.

In separating spiritual and civil powers, Williams denied to the state any power over spiritual beliefs, non-Christian as well as Christian. All people, he contended, are answerable only to God for their beliefs and not to human institutions, including the churches and polities of Mass-

achusetts Bay. Some people did not attend or support Puritan congregations because of "an utter dislike of all Protestant worship and a
high esteem of their own Catholic faith." In other words, if Massachusetts Puritans established a "Christian Nation," it would be decidedly
Protestant in nature and, therefore, unacceptable to other Christians
whose consciences convinced them that Catholicism was closer to the
true or spiritual Christian church. Moreover, a so-called Christian Nation
violated non-Christians' liberty of conscience. He wrote that "Papists
[whom many Protestants regarded as non-Christians] and Jews . . . ought
freely and impartially to be permitted their several respective worships, their ministers of worships, and what way of maintaining them
they freely choose."[34]

Banned from Massachusetts Bay for defying church and civil authorities, Roger Williams thought that the separation between church and
state should be strengthened. While on a visit to London in 1651, he
wrote a stinging denunciation of English laws forcing citizens to pay
tithes supporting clergymen in the Church of England, even if the tax-
payer did not subscribe to the church's tenets. He began his argument
by differentiating between a "civil" and a "Christian" state. The former
is strictly civil and secular, while the latter is a *"Spiritual State* of the *Church
of Christ Jesus"* that transcends any polity. The civil state, he claimed,
cannot prevent Christians from being good Christians, nor can it coerce
persons into becoming Christians, and he held that it was "against the
testimony of *Christ Jesus* for the civill state to impose upon the soules of
the People a *Religion*, a *Worship*, a *Ministry, Oaths* . . . , *Tithes, Times, Days,
Marryings*, and *Buryings* in holy *ground*."[35]

Having said what the state should not do in religious matters, Williams
asked, "What is then the express duty of the civil magistrate as to Christ
Jesus, His Gospel and Kingdom?" He answered that the first task of the
government was to remove "the Civill *Bars, Obstructions, Hindrances* in
taking off those *Yoaks* that pinch the very *soules* and *consciences* of men,
such as yet are the *payments of Tithes* and the *Maintenance of Ministers* they
have no faith in." Whether imposed by the crown in England or the
General Court in Massachusetts Bay, laws establishing religion—that is,
supporting *a* particular religious profession—were to Williams violations
of gospel freedom. Thus the first duty of government in religious affairs
is a negative one: to remove all constraints to freedom of conscience,

including those imposed by government itself. The second duty followed: the state should grant "a free and absolute *permission* of the *consciences* of all men in what is meerly spiritual." Anticipating the objection that an absolute freedom of religion would propagate "horrible opinions" and religious errors, Williams differentiated between opinions "savouring of *Impiety,* and [those] of *Incivility.*" He argued that "*Christ Jesus* never cald for the Sword of *Steel* to help the Sword of the *Spirit,*" and, therefore, he saw no role for government in monitoring religious opinions. He believed that the truth would eventually prevail in a free exchange of ideas. On the other hand, Williams considered opinions and practices of incivility to be "the proper *Object* of the *Civill Sword.*"[36]

Williams's outspoken opposition to church-state relations in Massachusetts resulted in his banishment. He purchased a tract of land from the Narragansetts and founded the colony of Rhode Island, where he attempted to put the principles of separation of church and state and religious liberty into practice.[37] According to one scholar, Rhode Island represented the first time a people "guarded jealously the rights of conscience by ignoring any power in the body politic to interfere with those matters that alone concern man and his Maker."[38] Massachusetts officials thought otherwise, and they bade Williams good riddance, believing that he was a schismatic who threatened religious uniformity.

"A WELL-BOUNDED TOLERATION"

Those who exiled Williams thought his views of religious freedom were wrongheaded and dangerous. To Nathaniel Ward, intolerance was a virtue. The Ipswich pastor thought that some things were so evil that good Christians were obliged to despise and oppose them. He said that he "naturally" detested four things: "the standing of the Apocrypha in the Bible; foreigners dwelling in my country, to crowd our native subjects into the corners of the earth; alchemized coins; and tolerations of diverse religions, or of one religion in segregant shapes." He regarded anyone who tolerated "diverse religions" as "either an atheist, or a heretic, or a hypocrite, or at best a captive to some lust." Ward called "poly-piety . . . the greatest impiety in the world." On the other hand, "true religion is *ignis probationis*, which does *congregare homogenea segregare heterogenea*

89

[ordeal by fire, which draws together the like and separates the unlike]."[39] If fire, a product of nature, burns away impurities, so should laws, a human construct, rid a society of heterodoxy.

Ward argued that Scripture warned against religious toleration. He claimed that "God does no where in His Word tolerate Christian states, to give tolerations to such adversaries of His truth, if they have power in their hands to suppress them." Rather, God ordained that religion derived its power from purity and simplicity, and that any mixture of religious impurities is "pernicious." Ward remembered with horror having lived in a city "where a Papist preached in one church, a Lutheran in another, a Calvinist in a third; a Lutheran one part of the day, a Calvinist the other, in the same pulpit; the religion of that place was but motley and meager, their affections leopardlike."[40] Thus he was alarmed to learn that West Indian planters had drafted a law permitting religious toleration, making it actionable to "disturb any man in his religion, or to discommend it, whatever it be." In his mind, Ward saw that law as the "ruin of true religion." Such toleration by so-called Christians was nothing short of the devil's work. Ward claimed that a "universal toleration of all hellish errors" would transform "Christ's academy" into the "devil's university," where a heretic is free "to go to hell . . . and carry as many after him as he can."[41]

Ward's notion that religious liberty was defined in terms of religious purity was a persistent theme of Election Sermons in Massachusetts Bay. Magistrates were reminded of their duty to rid the commonwealth of those who held erroneous views. In a typical charge, Thomas Walley admonished the elected officials in 1669 to "Let it be your great care, That the great Truths of God, *the Faith once committed to the Saints*, may be preserved: *Buy the Truth, and sell it not.*"[42]

It was in the context of discussing the threats of religious error that Walley addressed the subject of religious toleration. His statement is representative of the many offered by Puritan divines who argued that Christians must recognize the limits of what they could and should allow to prevail in their midst. He stated that "it would not consist with love to God and Jesus Christ to tolerate that which would blaspheme the Name of God, or damn the Souls of men." While blasphemy must not be permitted, on the other hand, "neither would it consist with our profession to Christ and Saints," Walley asserted, "to trouble those that peaceably differ from the generalty of God's people in lesser things." He added that "those that are like to live in Heaven with us at last, we should endeavour they might live peaceably with us here." Having staked out what must be extirpated and what must be accepted, Walley offered this guideline: "A *well-bounded Toleration* were very desireable in all Christian Common-wealths . . . but it must be *such a Toleration* that God may not be publickly blasphemed, nor Idolatry practised." He summed up his sentiments on toleration by declaring that no error should be tolerated that disturbs the "Peace and Order in Church or State."[43] The best solution was an established church and enforced religious uniformity.

Massachusetts Puritans regarded their faith as the true expression of "primitive" or New Testament Christianity, and hence they deemed any other sect as unnecessary and dangerous. Of all the Protestant churches, theirs avoided unscriptural errors, steering a middle course between the extremes of papism on one side and enthusiasm on the other. While there were few Catholics in Massachusetts, papism, according to the Puritans, infiltrated through the Church of England, as evidenced by the Anglican liturgy, which looked suspiciously like that of the Church of Rome. And enthusiasm, or faith based on claims of direct communication with God instead of correct interpretation of the Bible, was embodied in Quakerism, which the Puritans considered to be hatched by human innovation, not divine inspiration. Regarding both as heresies that threatened the "Christian Common-wealth," Puritans believed that both must be extirpated.

Increase Mather was one of many Puritan divines who linked the Church of England and Catholicism. Mather argued that the proof of the connection lay in the fact that Catholics saw no difference between the Roman and English liturgies. He related that "a Jesuit being asked how hee liked the Service at [Saint] Pauls, gave this Answer, I have nothing against it, but that it is done by your Priests." Mather asked his Puritan readers, "How then can wee Joyn in Prayers taken out of the Idolatrous Mass Book and offer them to the Holy God?"[44]

To Mather and other Massachusetts Puritans, papists, whether Roman or Anglican, were misguided in many of their beliefs and practices because they did not make Scripture the sole basis of their faith. Both were hierarchical churches that gave authority to the utterances of "church fathers," thus claiming church tradition to be on equal footing with biblical teachings.

Posing a comparable threat to the Puritans were Dissenters, especially Quakers and Baptists.[45] Far from viewing the Friends as another Protestant sect that differed in lesser matters, Puritan divines saw them as dangerous blasphemers of a "destructive nature . . . to Religion, the Churches, and the State." In one of many attacks against Quakers, John Norton, pastor at Boston, delivered a scathing polemic in 1659. The cover of his printed discourse bears an important designation that gave his comments civil as well as ecclesiastical authority. Beneath his name and title is the phrase "by the Order of the General Court," meaning that Norton's appointment as "Teacher of the Church of Christ at Boston" emanated from the province's highest governmental body. Armed with such a commanding presence, Norton proceeded to blast the Quakers, who were, he claimed, deluded by "Satan, or any Jesuitical, or other malignant and serpentine agents, who make use of the *mystery of iniquity* . . . [to] abuse their ignorant, and selfe conceited proselytes." He called them "Pests" whose only virtue might be that of "messengers of Divine Wrath" similar to the plagues God visited on the Egyptians to convince Pharaoh to release the Children of Israel.[46]

Mary Dyer was a particularly irritating "pest" whose persistent spreading of heresy ended in her execution. Mary's sin was preaching her faith as a Quaker. She insisted that the source of religious authority was the "Light Within," that spark of the divine spirit residing within every human being. That view alone was dangerous because it undermined the authority of the Puritan clergy, who insisted that the Bible, rightly interpreted, represented the true ground of religion. Mary had no use for Calvinism and said so. Moreover, she refused to observe the Lord's Supper and Holy Baptism, the Puritans' two sacraments. The magistrates twice banished her from the colony for heresy, and twice she returned and resumed her preaching. The magistrates once again forced her into exile, warning her that if she returned, she would be executed. She did, and she was. In fact, between 1659 and 1661, Massachusetts hanged four Quakers who refused to stop preaching their faith.

Norton believed that the civil authorities had a major role in protecting the people of Massachusetts from dangerous heresies like Quakerism. Magistrates must defend religion, but only *true* religion, and they could best do that by promoting its regular exercise. "All experience proveth," Norton claimed, "that the bitter root of heresie, hath never prevailed, where Doctrine, Catechism, and Discipline have been upheld in their purity and vigour." And "as God hath armed the Magistrate with Civil Power for the defence of Religion, so hath he animated him unto the regular and seasonable exercise thereof." Magistrates had the obligation to mount a "Regular Defense of Religion" that included the following: vindicating "the name and trueth of God from the dishonour done thereunto by Heresie, and Blasphemie"; working to "cure the offender"; putting away "evil" from the Chosen People; preventing the "infection, and spreading contagion of an evil example"; and preventing the "wrath of God and continuing the state still in the enjoyment of the protection and benediction of the covenant."[47]

Norton recognized that some would object to such vigorous action by the state as an infringement on liberty of conscience. He defended what he called the "Interposal of Authority in matters of Religion" as being necessary for the churches to exercise their authority to deal with any of their members "for holding forth, or teaching of false doctrine."[48] Norton distinguished between "Liberty of Conscience" and "Liberty of Errour." He defined liberty of conscience as "a freedom from all impediment in respect of man, as to the following of the dictates of Conscience, in acting according to Rule." But, Norton pointed out, liberty of error, or "liberty of the error of conscience, is falsely called liberty of Conscience, being indeed opposite thereunto." The liberty of error is the liberty to blaspheme, to seduce others to tell lies "in the name of the Lord." With such a distinction, Norton made clear that Massachusetts should not defend liberty of error, which was akin to protecting licentiousness. However, he was careful to define the limits of magistrates' authority in punishing religious error. "The object subjected to the Coercive Power of the Magistrate, must be some Act of the outward man," he declared. "Tis not *matter of judgment*," he added, "but *matter of fact*, which Civil-power dealeth with." Norton clarified the matter thus: "Whilst a man keepeth his heterodoxy to himself, he is doubtlesse out of reach of the Magistrates in that respect." Actions that would bring punishment on the heterodox included "teaching his errors as truths," "causing irregular separation from Church-communion," and "sowing seeds of discord, or mutiny in the Common-wealth."[49]

Norton offered a more precise definition of the Puritans' "well-bounded Toleration" by differentiating between two ways of practicing heresy: "Quiet and alone" and "Turbulent, i.e., Incorrigible." Everyone in Massachusetts had the right to believe whatever he or she wished in private. But when their beliefs were "accompanied with soliciting the people to apostacy from the Faith of Christ," then they were subject to punishment by the civil government. At first, Norton declared, Quakers were treated as those holding a private heresy, but their recent aggressive behavior in disturbing the peace of church and commonwealth forced the magistrates to punish them, "up to and including banishment." Clearly Quakerism was a heterodoxy that must be exterminated to keep religion pure.[50]

In 1654, a devout Puritan, Edward Johnson, published a history of New England defending the Holy Commonwealth against charges of religious bigotry. He reminded readers that the primary mission of the settlers was to establish a society "to keepe the truths of Christ pure and unspotted." He also took cognizance of the colony's many critics, especially those who charged the Massachusetts government with persecuting "the people and churches of Christ." On the contrary, Johnson argued, the civil authority had supported true religious liberty by expelling "all such beasts of prey (who will not be reclaimed), that here might be none left to hurt or destroy in all God's holy mountain." He understood that many persons thought that "all sorts of sectaries (that acknowledge a Christ) should be tolerated by civil government, except Papist[s]." But he declared that the government of Massachusetts Bay "has hitherto and is for future time resolved to practice otherwise." To ensure the purity of faith, only "men truly fearing God, wise and learned in the truths of Christ," can hold office. And they must be "zealous for the maintenance of the truths of Christ."[51]

In his apology for the "New England Way," Johnson defended the state's role in promoting religious purity. One legitimate governmental function was to employ civil censures to encourage men and women to "not only professe the truth, but also hate every false way." Johnson said that the state does not "compell men to believe by the power of the Sword, but to indeavor all may answer their profession, whether in Church Covenant or otherwise." If the threat of force encourages people to live according to the covenant, then the end justifies the means. He denied that government attempted to "exercise civill power to bring all under their obedience to a uniformity in every poynt of Religion." Rather,

the state attempts to keep inhabitants "in the unity of the spirit, and the bond of peace." Johnson assured his readers that the government of Massachusetts Bay had never "mixed their civill powers with the authority peculiarly given by Christ to his Churches and Officers of them, but from time to time have laboured to uphold their privileges, and only communion one with another."[52]

Johnson reminded Puritans of their unique mission and explained that that high calling required a vigilant and vigorous state. "The upholding of the truths of Christ is, the chiefe cause why many have hitherto come," he noted. Further, those faithful believe that "the downfall of Antichrist is at hand, and then the Kingdom[s] of the earth shall become the Kingdome of our Lord Christ in a more peculiar manner, than now they are." Thus, expecting to extinguish the enemy of Christ and usher in the Kingdom of God, the Puritans have a right, Johnson declared, to a state that supports the church. "Surely godly civill government shall have a great share in that work," he wrote. Magistrates in Massachusetts are "conscious of ruling for Christ," and Christian voters of a "sound judgment vote for [none] but those who earnestly contend for the faith." He warned that the "increase of Trade, and Traffique may be a great inducement to some" to vote on the basis of economic rather than religious considerations.[53]

Johnson concluded his apology by looking at the laws the state enacted and enforced to promote religious purity. He assured readers that these were drawn up "to the end that they might be most agreeable with the rule of Scripture." Lawmakers printed the laws for all to see, "that none may plead ignorance, and that all who intend to transport themselves hither, may know this is no place of licentious liberty, nor will this people suffer any to trample down the Vineyard of the Lord, but with diligent execution will cut off from the city of the Lord the wicked doers." The Puritans of Massachusetts did not intend to promote or permit religious liberty if that meant allowing persons to believe as they wished and not according to the "Word of God." Furthermore, Johnson warned, "let not any ill-affected persons find fault with [the laws] because they suit not with their own humour, or because [lawmakers] meddle with matters of religion." Those critics of the New England Puritans should not be surprised that any who "seek to jostle them out of their own right, . . . meet with all the opposition a people put to their greatest straits can make."

According to Johnson, it would be more surprising and unreasonable for a people who had risked so much to establish a society based on God's word to have been less vigorous in defense of their mission. If a people is so bold as to "pray unto the Lord for the speedy accomplishment of His Word in the overthrow of the Antichrist," they cannot then coddle "sinful opinions and damnable errors that oppose the truths of Christ."[54] Spiritual war called for martial law.

Not all Massachusetts Puritans accepted Johnson's view of religious intolerance. In particular, Boston's leading merchants grew restive under a regime that pursued a policy of exclusivity. According to one historian, by 1660 the merchants' "involvement in the world of Atlantic commerce committed them to interests and attitudes incompatible with life in the Bible Commonwealth." They found themselves at odds with their ministers: "The health of Puritanism required isolation and the most rigorous selection of newcomers; the well-being of trade demanded the free movement of people and goods and a rising population." It was just that notion that prompted Edward Johnson's warning against religious toleration in support of expanded trade or any other cause. He reminded merchants that "whereas [God] had purposely pickt out this People for a patterne of purity and soundnesse of Doctrine, as well as Discipline, that all such may finde a refuge among you, and let not any Merchants, Inkeepers, Taverners and Men of Trade in hope of gaine, fling open the gates so wide, as that by letting in all sorts you mar the worke of Christ intended."[55]

By the middle of the 1670s, however, Johnson's fears of toleration's ushering in spiritual declension seemed to have been prophetic. John Hull, treasurer of the colony and a concerned Puritan, noted in his diary for 1674: "This Summer, the Anabaptists that were wont to meet at Noddle's Island meet at Boston on the Lord's Day. . . . Some Quakers are also come and seated at Boston. Some of the magistrates will not permit any punishment to be inflicted on heretics as such." Increase Mather, one of the Puritan patriarchs, called the magistrates' inaction a "Sinfull Toleration." He warned that "the *Toleration of all Religions* and Perswasions, is the way to have no Religion at all."[56] In other words, if "pure" religion is the goal, any admixture of that which is impure will destroy that purpose.

The "City upon a Hill" was a utopian vision that failed in part because of internal stresses evident from the beginning, and from external pressures in the latter part of the seventeenth century. Certainly dissenters

from within such as Anne Hutchinson and Roger Williams exposed weaknesses within the body politic, but for the most part the ministers and magistrates were able to contain those kinds of differences. What was more difficult, however, was to maintain a level of holiness sufficient to leaven the whole colony. Within two decades of its founding, Massachusetts's collective holiness rested on a minority of its population. Fewer and fewer men and women were willing or able to claim that they were saints and thereby qualified to become church members. Indeed, by 1647, because of the dwindling numbers, the General Court dropped the requirement that voters must be church members. A society founded on a social contract and resting on broad participation in public affairs could ill afford a narrow electorate. Thus it was that by 1662, with small numbers of the second and third generations proving that they should be numbered among the Elect, the Puritan divines conceived of the "Half-Way Covenant," whereby the children of baptized but unconverted church members could become "Half-Way" members until their own conversion made them full members. Such a contrivance was aimed at maintaining the facade of a "Christian, Utopian, Closed, Corporate" community when evidence to the contrary was mounting.

Illustrating the decline of the ideal Christian community is the sorry story of the Salem witch trials in 1692. Torn asunder by economic, social, and political divisions, residents clustered into two warring factions: those of the stagnant agricultural Salem village in the west and those of the growing commercial Salem town of the east. Rather than acting as "loving mediators," both ministers and magistrates contributed to the spiral of violence that erupted when minister Samuel Parris of the Village Church gave credence to some little girls' accusations of witchcraft. Ever ready to take up his pen, Cotton Mather in nearby Boston provided theological explanation for the malefic presence of witches and their satanic overlord. And judges of the Court of Oyer and Terminer moved quickly to sentence nineteen men and women to death as convicted witches. Moreover, they ordered the sheriff to seize the felons' estates under the law of "escheat and forfeiture."[57] While scholars are divided over whether the trials represented departures from customary rules of evidence, certainly some of the judges themselves and a subsequent legislature came to view the proceedings as a "Prosecution . . . of persons of known and good Reputation."[58] As some scholars have concluded, Salem represents an important shift in the character of Puritan New England, from that of a confident band of believers whose institutions of church and state promoted unity around the one "true" faith to that of fearful factions enlisting those same institutions for partisan ends. "The central issue at Salem," wrote two colonial historians, "was not witchcraft, but violence, fanaticism, and fear. Never before in the colony had the concern about evil spirits reached epidemic proportions."[59]

Those striving to shore up the "City upon a Hill" also had to contend with external forces. Dissenters in Massachusetts had long complained to English officials that the Puritan majority violated their religious rights. While English Dissenters could worship as they chose within their own churches, New English dissenters could not. What particularly galled the court at Whitehall was that the Massachusetts Puritans disallowed Anglicans from erecting churches or holding services within the colony. Edward Randolph was a special agent for the crown who investigated accusations that Massachusetts violated English law. His indictment charged that the government officials "doe not allow liberty of conscience nor the Exercise of Religion professed by the Church of England, constraining all persons to be present at their [i.e., Puritan] meetings."[60] This meant that the crown's own church was not tolerated, the crown that had granted Massachusetts's charter in the first place. Accordingly, Charles II decided that he would not tolerate a colony that would not tolerate Anglicans or Catholics or others. Therefore, in 1684, he rescinded the Massachusetts charter, and the Holy Commonwealth officially came to an end. A year later, James II was king, and he further diminished Massachusetts's power by making it part of a new administrative entity known as the Dominion of New England, placing all the New England colonies plus New York and New Jersey under one royal governor. When Sir Edmund Andros arrived in Boston as governor, he wasted no time in demonstrating that Puritan rule was over. He suspended the General Court as an independent, representative body; he levied taxes without legislative authority; he questioned the legality of all land patents not issued by the king; and he instituted religious toleration, specifically granting Anglicans a place to worship in Boston.

Not surprisingly, the Puritans rose up against Andros and his arbitrary rule and quickly forced him out of Boston in what is known as the Glorious Revolution. What is surprising, however, is the language they used in justifying their actions. One would expect Puritans to defend their rights as they always had, by appealing to the authority of Scripture; instead they turned not to the law of Moses or the law of Christ, but to the civil law, insisting on their English "liberties and privileges." In language that American Patriots would invoke almost a hundred years later, Puritans signaled a revolutionary shift in their understanding of religion and politics. Formerly, the foundation of "civil power had been godliness, and Puritan freemen made certain that 'visible saints' controlled the . . . government." But now, "property—more than godliness—served as the basis for political leadership and participation." And Puritans dropped "scriptural rhetoric" as they laid claim to their English rights of "Liberty and Property."[61]

Sixty-two years after John Winthrop first sailed into Boston harbor, another Puritan leader arrived from London. On May 14, 1692, Increase Mather returned to Boston from his unsuccessful attempt to get the old charter restored. As he and the new royal governor, Sir William Phips, approached Boston, Mather must have thought about the difference between his arrival and that of Winthrop aboard the *Arbella* in 1630. Winthrop had come with the old charter in hand to establish a Holy Commonwealth. Mather returned from London after failing to win the Puritan case for restoring the old charter. The new charter that Mather and his fellow Puritans had to accept contained a guarantee of religious liberty to all Protestants. The charter expressed a fundamental principle that would play an important part in defining the place and role of religion in America. Though a royal charter, it did not impose religious uniformity by requiring all subjects to pay homage and taxes to the Church of England. Rather, it tacitly recognized that religion was a private pursuit, and that a free people allowed to follow the dictates of their consciences would arrive at different conceptions of what was and was not Christian. The new charter did not, however, settle the issue. The people of Massachusetts would continue to struggle over the meaning of religious liberty and how to secure it. While some clung to the notion that it was freedom to exclude those with erroneous views, others embraced the idea that it was liberty of conscience.

A "Holy Experiment" in Religious Pluralism

IKE MASSACHUSETTS' "Christian Common-wealth," Pennsylvania's "Holy Experiment" was conceived as a religious utopia, and the two undertakings shared much in common. Persecuted in England, Puritans and Quakers alike sought freedom in America, and each erected a community that gave full expression to its most cherished beliefs. For the Puritans, that meant exclusion, establishing a colony of "visible saints" bound together in covenanted relationships. Citizenship and officeholding were restricted to those who could demonstrate Divine Election. For the Quakers, it meant inclusion, erecting a colony open to all peace-loving Christians, a brotherhood of goodwill. Believing that all people had within them a spark of the divine, William Penn, the founder of the New World's experiment in Quaker friendship, envisioned a colony where Christianity itself was regarded as the one true religion, a place where a common Christian faith transcended sectarian differences.

Like John Winthrop, Penn wished to establish a colony that gave full expression to religious liberty, but his concept of freedom was the polar opposite. Winthrop sought a homogeneous society of orthodox Christians freed from religious error. Those who were not Puritans, including, and particularly, Quakers, were not welcome unless they kept their beliefs and practices to themselves. Penn embraced heterogeneity. Wishing only that settlers be good men and women and believers in the Christian faith, he openly recruited sectarians of all sorts from England and Europe, including Protestants of every stripe and even Roman Catholics. In Pennsylvania, no Christian believer would be excluded from citizenship or officeholding because of his faith. His "Holy Experiment," wherein Christians of all faiths would live together in bonds of love and peace, rested on two assumptions. First, that holy or pious people would populate Pennsylvania. And, second, that these settlers would put public good above private interest.

Unlike Massachusetts Bay, then, Pennsylvania represented a bold departure from church-state relations in England. Many of the elements that made up the New England "Christian Common-wealth" were transferred from England: a strict religious uniformity, a legal religious establishment, and a circumscribed religious toleration. To be sure, Puritan churches replaced the Church of England as the established church, but, nonetheless, Massachusetts had an official, state religion, financed by tax revenues and defended by the judicial system. Pennsylvania, on the other hand, imposed no religious uniformity, established no sect as a state church, and extended genuine religious liberty to all Christians. Penn hoped that his colony would resolve the paradox of pursuing the one true faith in a free society by making that faith coextensive with Christianity as a whole and recognizing freedom of conscience for all.[1]

In the end, Penn's "Holy Experiment" failed. His utopia, wherein Pennsylvanians would transcend narrow sectarianism and embrace a common Christianity, was besieged and eventually undermined by the force of people's feelings about matters of theology, church organization, and religious practice. Differences mattered, and religious tensions and resentments spilled over into the political arena; elected representatives carried their religious beliefs with them into the legislative assembly, where narrowly held, sectarian tenets shaped public policy. The Quaker Party had the upper hand in the Assembly, and from its adherents' perspective, the state was certainly "Christian." But to non-Quakers the state was heavy-handed and favored the sect in power, hardly a "Christian" state in any sense that all Christians could wholeheartedly embrace. Throughout the first half of the eighteenth century, political factionalism, drawn in part along sectarian lines, intensified; by the 1750s, political factions bore sectarian names: the "Quaker Party," the "Anglican Party," and the "Presbyterian Party."

The "Holy Experiment"

William Penn intended to establish a colony whose liberal godliness would be an example for all Protestants everywhere. He related his dream in a letter to James Harrison, a Quaker whom Penn later appointed to a judgeship in his new colony:

> For my country, I eyed the Lord, in obtaining it; and more was I drawn inward to look to him, and to owe it to his hand and power, than to any other way; I have so obtained it, and desire to keep it; that I may not be unworthy of his love; but do that, which may answer his kind Providence and serve his truth and people: that an example may be set up to the nations: there may be room there, though not here, for such an holy experiment.[2]

Though he had received in 1681 from Charles II a charter granting him authority over his new colony, Penn recognized God as the true granter. Unlike the Puritans of Massachusetts, he looked to the "Light Within" for his colonizing inspiration rather than to Holy Scripture as interpreted by persons "called" to the ministry. Like the Puritans, however, Penn conceived of his colony as a sacred or holy place, inhabited by holy people. The "Holy Experiment," like the "Holy Commonwealth," rested on a spiritual base.[3]

To understand the contours of early Pennsylvania, we must first examine the dominant influences that shaped William Penn's conception of his "Holy Experiment": his Quaker faith and economic self-interest. First, Penn was a Quaker who had been repeatedly imprisoned for his faith. Arising in England in the late 1640s under the leadership of George Fox, Quakerism was one of the most radical expressions of Protestant Christianity. Friends, as devotees called themselves, opposed all attempts, whether by church or by state, to restrict the individual's freedom of conscience. Sovereignty, in their view, rested solely with God, not with human institutions and creeds. Further, they believed that God was Light, the source of all truth and understanding, and that there was within each person a divine presence that guided moral behavior. While everyone on earth had the Light, not all realized it, let alone allowed its power to direct their lives. This central belief promoted an egalitarian view, and

Quakers refused to recognize artificial distinctions among individuals, whether created by class, religion, ethnicity, or politics. Freedom of conscience, they argued, was a God-given right extended to all, laws of uniformity notwithstanding. To church and state officials in England, Quakers were obstinate and "stiff-necked," refusing to recognize, for instance, the church's definition of the Christian faith as set forth in the Thirty-nine Articles, and denying the state any authority to administer oaths to its citizens. Viewed as a defiant and therefore dangerous sect that threatened the peace of the kingdom, Quakers were arrested, punished, and, sometimes, executed.[4]

Economic self-interest was the second factor that contributed to Penn's liberal notions of religious freedom. Having accumulated large debts, he needed revenues from Pennsylvania to stay out of English prison. Penn wished to extract enough wealth through quitrents on land to shore up his faltering finances, hard-hit by "failing estates in Ireland and England." But it would be a gross error to identify cupidity as his prime, let alone sole, motivation. He put his desire for revenue from colonization this way: "Though I desire to extend religious freedom, yet I want some recompense for my trouble."[5] In other words, his venture was for profit as well as piety, and he saw the two as compatible. The fastest way to generate income from his colony was to attract productive people quickly. Accordingly, Penn traveled throughout England and western Europe passing out advertisements for his new American colony that offered land and religious liberty. For persecuted Protestants, the latter was a particularly powerful lure.[6]

Penn had not always been an advocate of universal religious liberty. Indeed, as a zealous convert, he was convinced that Quakerism was the true, and only true, faith, and that all others were heretical. In 1668, he published a pamphlet entitled *Truth Exalted*, which he billed as a "short, but sure, Testimony against all those Religions, Faiths, and Worships that have been formed and followed in the darkness of Apostacy." By contrast, he added, it would also bear witness to "that Glorious Light which is now risen, and shines forth in the Life and Doctrine of the despised Quakers, as the alone good old way of Life and Salvation." In brief, his thesis was that only Quakers followed the beliefs and practices of primitive Christianity—that is, those set forth by Christ. Tainted by original sin and corruption of Adam's apostasy, all other Christian groups had fallen away from Christ's original and perfect model. Quakerism stood alone as the key to "Life and Salvation."[7]

Having painted all sects with the same condemnatory brush, Penn specified defects in particular religious groups. Addressing Catholics as "you Papists," Penn asserted that the Church of Rome had substituted the "Doctrine of the Precepts of Men" for the will of God. In attacking Protestants, Penn found it convenient to divide them into Anglicans and Separatists, by which he meant Dissenters. He excoriated Anglicans for violating the Elizabethan tradition of religious toleration when they persecuted the Quakers during the Restoration period. He added that Anglicans continued a strong attachment to Catholicism with their "Mass-Book [i.e., the Book of Common Prayer] and Popish Canons." As for Dissenters who exercised power following the civil war, Penn found them to be great hypocrites who were "fighters for Liberty of Conscience when opprest; but the greatest Oppressors, when in power." Finally, he took swipes at Jews, "who crucified the Lord of Life," and the universities, which had become "signal places for idleness, looseness, prophaneness, prodigality, and gross ignorance." He summarized his diatribe by contrasting all others to the Quakers. " 'O ye Idolatrous, Superstitious, Carnal, Proud, Wanton, Unclean, Mocking and Persecuting Princes, Priests, and People,' now is the time to repent and turn to the truth revealed to the Quakers."[8]

Two years after writing *Truth Exalted*, Penn singled out Catholics for another bitter attack. While in Ireland he came across a 1656 publication entitled *An Explanation of the Roman Catholic Belief*. Written in a moderate tone by an English Catholic, Christopher Davenport, the tract, Penn feared, would prove seductive to those who did not understand Catholicism as well as he. In 1670, Penn published a rejoinder, using Scripture and logic to dismantle Davenport's claims one by one. He attacked such "Papist" beliefs as "prayer to saints, justification of merits, Holy Eucharist, prayer in Latin, obedience to civil magistrates, and the ecclesiastical hierarchy." Penn suggested that Protestants could not trust Catholics because "it is one of their most sacred Maxims, Not to keep Faith with Hereticks." He reminded his readers (i.e., Protestants) that the Catholic Church was responsible for "the great Deluge of Blood brought upon the European World." In conclusion, Penn asked if it were not "the Design of Popery [to] be an utter destruction of all true and solid Religion?"[9]

Just two months after Penn wrote his attack on Catholicism, he published a strong defense of religious liberty. What changed his perspective was Anglican persecution that targeted Quakers, Dissenters, and Catholics alike. After visiting Quakers who were victims of a new wave of imprisonment in both England and Ireland, he wrote in his diary on March 19, 1670, "I sett about a book against persecutions Call'd the Great Case of L[iberty] of C[onscience] Debated and Defended." Parliament had just passed the second Conventicle Act, which fined those who attended or preached at Dissenting services. Addressing his remarks for the "KINGS Consideration," Penn asked the crown to act in religious matters in a way pleasing to God, and not according to "some one angry Party of men." Within a year of publishing the work in Ireland, Penn returned to England and reprinted it in London. By the time the piece was ready for press, Penn was arrested and imprisoned at Newgate. Arrested under the Conventicle Act for preaching on a Sunday morning, Penn insisted that he was "being persecuted for worshipping God." After being released following a short stay, he was again arrested for participating in a Friends' meeting near Spitalfield, this time cited for violating the Five Mile Act, which forbade those who preached at conventicles to live within five miles of an incorporated town.[10]

From the Tower of London, he rewrote the preface to his work on liberty of conscience, signing it, "From a Prisoner for Conscience Sake, W.P." In the pamphlet, Penn called for toleration instead of persecution and argued that the present restrictions against freedom of worship violated freedoms guaranteed to all citizens by "English birthright." He pledged that he would endure persecution as long as the government refused to recognize the sanctity of liberty of conscience. He argued that "Christian principles" included toleration, and he lamented England's substituting tyranny of the established church for the papal authority the country had overthrown. Dissenters, he declared, were like Socrates, who had died for what he considered to be the truth; England, he added, was like the Greek state that, following its condemnation of Socrates, suffered its own downfall. Having made his case from Scripture, reason, nature, and history, Penn concluded by asking, "Now upon the whole, we ask, What can be more equal, what more reasonable than Liberty of Conscience, so correspondent with the Reverence due to God, and Respect to the Nature, Practice, Promotion, and Rewards of the Christian Religion."[11] Thenceforward, Penn became an outspoken champion of religious liberty.

When he received his American land grant from Charles II, Penn systematized his views of church-state relations in general and how they would be expressed in Pennsylvania. He prefaced his first *Frame of Government* in 1682 with a discourse on the place and nature of government and its relation to the divine plan outlined in Holy Scripture. He began by declaring that God at the time of creation decided to govern the earth through a deputy. With the "precept of divine love and truth, in his bosom," man would live under a rule that required no "coercive or compulsive means." But, alas, Adam's lust and disobedience against holy law undermined the Creator's plan. Unable to trust men to govern aright, God introduced the Law. Penn cited passages from the New Testament indicating that the Law resulted from human weakness and disobedience. He noted that "the Apostle teaches in divers of his epistles: 'The law,' says he, 'was added because of transgressions.' In another place, 'Knowing that the law was not made for the righteous man; but for the disobedient and ungodly.' " Having instituted Law to govern his creatures, God then made men and women subject to that Law. Again, Penn cited the apostle, who "opens and carries the matter of government a little further: 'Let every soul be subject to the higher powers; for there is no power but of *God*. The powers that be are ordained of *God*: whosoever therefore resisteth the power, resisteth the ordinance of *God*.' " To Penn, the New Testament settled the matter of the "divine right of government beyond exception, and that for two ends: first, to terrify evildoers; secondly, to cherish those that do well." Moreover, he concluded, because God was both author and object of "pure religion" and supreme lawgiver, then "government [was] a part of religion itself, a thing sacred in its institution and end."[12] In his utopian view, godly legislators would make the state an extension of religion.

Godly people, Penn explained, had nothing to fear from government. He asserted that "rulers are not a terror to good works, but to evil," and asked, "wilt thou then not be afraid of the power? Do that which is good, and thou shalt have praise of the same." In his "Holy Experiment," governors were to be considered "minister[s] of God to thee for good." In that light, citizens, including Quakers, who had resisted government in England, were to be "subject, not only for wrath, but for conscience' sake." Good government could not remove the cause of evil—only Christ could do that—but Penn maintained that it might crush "the effects of evil." But, he added, government is hard only to "evildoers." Otherwise, it is capable of "goodness, and charity." Speaking to those who "think there is no other use of government than correction, which is the coarsest part of it," Penn wrote that "daily experience tells us that the care and regulation of many other affairs, more soft, and daily necessary, make up much of the greatest part of government."[13]

In explaining the particular *Frame of Government* he designed for his colony, Penn observed that most enlightened people agree on the ends of government but disagree on the means. All believe that happiness is the central aim. But, he added, just as people differ over theology, they differ over politics. Penn lamented that "men side with their passions against their reason, and their sinister interests have so strong a bias upon their minds that they lean to them against the good of the things they know."[14] Penn's experiment in government rested in large part on his belief that good people mattered more than good laws. He claimed to be no devotee of monarchy or aristocracy or democracy; good government, he felt, transcended all three. He declared that *Any government is free to the people under it* (whatever be the frame) *where the laws rule, and the people are a party to those laws*, and more than this is tyranny, oligarchy, or confusion." It would not be the constitution that would make good government in Pennsylvania, but good governors. Penn put it this way: "Let men be good, and the government cannot be bad; if it be ill, they will cure it. But, if men be bad, let the government be ever so good, they will endeavor to warp and spoil it to their turn." He elaborated,

I know some say, "Let us have good laws, and no matter for the men that execute them"; but let them consider that, though good laws do well, good men do better, for good laws may want good men and be abolished or evaded by ill men; but good men will never want good laws nor suffer ill ones. It is true, good laws have some awe upon ill ministers, but that is where they have not power to escape or abolish them, and the people are generally wise and good, but a loose and depraved people (which is the question) love laws and an administration like themselves. That, therefore, which makes a good constitution, must keep it, viz.: men of wisdom and virtue.[15]

Penn concluded his preface by stating his view that God-fearing people in the "Holy Experiment" must obey laws in order to live free. Government must be an even exchange: the people freely offered "their just obedience," and magistrates respected the people's freedom through honorable, "just administration." Restating the relation between freedom and power, Penn averred that "liberty without obedience is confusion, and obedience without liberty is slavery." To put such a formula into practice would require both a good constitution and able magistrates. But above all, what Penn was counting on were sanctified immigrants, obedient citizens and faithful magistrates, men and women rising above the self-centeredness of the "Old Adam" to live together as the "New Adam" in one body politic. Only "holy" people could make the "Holy Experiment" work.[16]

Penn's notion of religious liberty extended to all theists. His *Frame of Government* (1682) pledged "That all persons living in this province, who confess and acknowledge the one Almighty and eternal God, to be the Creator, Upholder and Ruler of the world; and that hold themselves obliged in conscience to live peaceably and justly in civil society, shall, in no ways, be molested or prejudiced for their religious persuasion, or practice, in matters of faith and worship." Further, the state would not establish any religion, nor would it levy taxes to support religion. No one would be "compelled, at any time, to frequent or maintain any religious worship, place or ministry whatever." In Pennsylvania, religion was put on a voluntary basis, with persons free to associate with the sect of their choosing and with churches expected to finance their own operations. All believers were welcomed; only atheists were excluded. Moreover, no Christian would be barred from political power because of his or her religion. But he did impose a religious test on officeholders, specifying that only those who "shall be such as possess faith in Jesus Christ, and that are not convicted of ill fame, or unsober and dishonest conversation," shall qualify, thereby excluding Jews and other non-Christians.[17]

In his 1701 revision of the *Frame of Government*, Penn made an even stronger and more explicit guarantee of religious liberty, while retaining the religious test. Anglicans in the colony had complained that the Quaker-dominated legislature had restricted religious liberty by lengthening the residency requirement for Anglicans to vote or hold office. Penn declared that "Almighty God [was] the only Lord of Conscience," and that no one would suffer loss of civil liberties because of his "conscientious Persuasion or Practice." He amended the religious test to include all Christians regardless of sectarian differences: "all Persons who also profess to believe in Jesus Christ, the Saviour of the World, shall be capable (notwithstanding their other Persuasions and Practices in Point of Conscience and Religion) to serve this Government in any Capacity."[18]

"A GREAT MIXT MULTITUDE"[19]

Penn's "Holy Experiment" looked good on paper, and it was especially appealing to persecuted Protestants. Penn and his agents advertised abundant land and religious liberty throughout the British Isles and western Europe, targeting in particular those Protestant sects that dissented from established religion. In England and Wales, they included Quakers and Baptists; in France, the Huguenots; and in Germany, various Pietist and Reformed groups that were out of favor with Lutheran or Catholic princes.

And they came, planting in Pennsylvania the seeds of a religious pluralism that made the colony distinctive within the Atlantic world. Those settling in Pennsylvania had never seen anything like the colony's religious pluralism. Accustomed to a state religion or to a dominant church, they were unaccustomed to the sectarian medley they encountered. One Swedish Lutheran minister was astounded, commenting that "Because there is freedom of conscience, here they have gathered together, of every opinion and belief." He claimed that "even in the same family or house, 4 or 5 may be found [each] professing a different religion: . . . parents and children, owners and servants, yes even man and wife, may each have his religion."[20] Such a sight would have been unthinkable in Massachusetts Bay or in Virginia, or, for that matter, anywhere else in the world. The "great mixt multitude" represented a remarkable variety of religious expression. It included the great rivals in the Protestant Reformation, as well as the protagonists in Europe's bloody wars of religion that came in its aftermath. It included both England's persecutors and persecuted in the struggle for power before, during, and after the civil war. And it included, though in small numbers, non-Christians.

Adam Smith argued that Pennsylvania made his conception of a free religious market more than an abstraction. He contended that William Penn had created what Independents had dreamed of toward the end of the English civil war: a "plan of ecclesiastical government, or more properly no ecclesiastical government." Smith believed that "if it had been established [in England], though of a very unphilosophical origin, it would probably by this time have been productive of the most philosophical good temper and moderation with regard to every sort of religious principle." By that, he meant that there would be freedom of conscience, where everyone could pursue his or her notion of the "one true religion," and where all ideas would have free play. Such a scheme, he concluded, "has been established in Pennsylvania, where, though the Quakers happen to be the most numerous, the law in reality favours no one sect more than the other, and it is there said to have been productive of this philosophical good temper and moderation."[21]

Immigrants came to Pennsylvania for economic as well as religious freedom, but as one early settler observed, the two were closely linked. Gabriel Thomas arrived in the colony in 1682 and flourished there until 1697, when he wrote an account of life in Pennsylvania. He noted that because the state did not support and finance an official church, the residents "pay no Tithes, and their Taxes are inconsiderable." Thomas continued, "the Place is free for all Persuasions, in a Sober and Civil way; for the Church of England and the Quakers bear equal Share in the Government." Though his statement ignored political factionalism based in part on religious differences, Thomas was correct. The charter of 1696 extended civil liberties to all Christians except Catholics. Thomas concluded by offering his insight into the connection between trade and free religion: "there is no Persecution for Religion, nor ever like to be; 'tis this that knocks all Commerce on the Head, together with high Imposts, strict Laws, and cramping Orders."[22] Thomas sounded very much like modern capitalists decrying high taxes and government regulations. Unlike modern businessmen who take freedom of religion for granted, however, Thomas understood that Pennsylvania was exceptional and fortunate in that regard, much to the advantage of the free flow of commerce.

There was also a free flow of religious ideas, and sometimes competition resulted in schism. Quakers found themselves in an unusual position in Pennsylvania: that of no longer being a Dissenting sect. In fact, during the colony's formative decades, Quakers were in the majority, and until the middle of the eighteenth century, they continued to exercise effective control of the legislative assembly. Freedom from persecution, however, did not exempt them from internal disputes. Within ten years of the colony's founding, two rival groups of Quakers were locked in a struggle whence emerged a splinter group that one historian has called the first American denomination, adding yet another sect to the pluralistic society.[23] At the center of the "Keithian Schism" of the early 1690s was a fundamental disagreement reaching to the heart of the "Holy Experiment." William Penn had avoided defining "true" religion in a narrow, sectarian way. Now Quakers were doing just that as they bitterly disputed what it meant to be a Quaker.

Ironically, the very nature of Quakerism made controversy endemic to the sect. Believing that God made his will known to individuals through direct revelation, Quakers were constantly differing over conflicting opinions about divine will. But unlike differences expressed between devotees, the Keithian Schism involved the entire colony and exposed Quakers as contentious religious fanatics rather than peace-loving Christians. The instigator was an educated Scottish Quaker who arrived in Philadelphia in 1689 as master of the new Friends school. In addition to his pedagogical duties, George Keith was very active among Friends, attending meetings, preaching on occasion, and writing books and tracts. One of the themes he developed was the necessity of a creed for Quakers. Throughout the colonies Quakers had come under attack for the lack of a specific set of beliefs that defined the faith of all Friends. The absence of agreed-upon articles of faith resulted in a wide range of beliefs espoused by individuals, many of which were heretical, according to their critics. Wishing to end such criticism, Keith drew up a set of rules and regulations governing the Friends' faith and practice and presented it to the Yearly Meeting. The Yearly Meeting was the Quaker gathering of delegates from Pennsylvania, Delaware, and the Jerseys to consult on various issues arising from the regional Monthly Meetings and from individual congregations. In a congregational, democratic organization, however, the Yearly Meeting's authority was limited. There was no permanent hierarchy or staff, and the gathering did not impose control from above. Rather, the delegates took action only when there was a sense of the whole group, a consensus, that the proposed measure was indeed the will of God. Thus when Keith introduced his plan to impose order and discipline on all Quakers, the Yearly Meeting quickly rejected it on grounds that a creed was "unQuakerly."[24]

Keith broke from the Yearly Meeting and with his followers formed what were known as the Christian Quakers: when the regular Quakers rejected his proposals, which included some fundamental tenets of Christianity, Keith had questioned whether they were indeed Christians. The Christian Quakers looked very much like other sects, complete with a creed and clergy. The Keithian controversy, however, was much more than a theological division. It had immediate political implications. Keith and his adherents opposed the Quaker politicians who still dominated the government. In 1692 the Keithians, supported by about one-fourth of all Quaker delegates, held their own separate Yearly Meeting. After the session, Keith published twelve questions aimed at the "regular" Quakers, eight of which were doctrinal in nature and four political. When William Bradford printed the document without the government's permission, he touched off a political storm that threatened to wreck Penn's "Holy Experiment." Insisting that his questions were all religious, Keith criticized Quaker officeholders, calling the deputy governor Thomas Lloyd an "Impudent Man, telling him he was not fit to be a Governor, and that his Name would stink." He labeled members of the Council "Impudent Rascals" and tarred the magistrates as well. The Quaker government responded swiftly, though the officials were careful to say that their criticism was aimed at Keith's "civil transgressions," not his religious views, and that their quarrel with him had nothing to do with religious differences. They ordered Keith to stop publishing pamphlets "that have a tendancy to Sedition, and Disturbance of the Peace, as also to the Subversion of the Present Government."[25] Keith did not cease, and charges and countercharges ensued, ending in indictments and court cases; Pennsylvania was exposed to the world as a place where, notwithstanding Penn's intentions, religious differences among Quakers resulted in political rancor and turmoil.

Religious pluralism also meant interfaith competition. With no state interference, churches and sects enjoyed free exercise of religion, which included the freedom to proselytize—that is, to seek converts from among each other's members. But competition did not preclude cooperation. In the early 1690s, Philadelphia Baptists and Presbyterians, both subscribing to Reformed or Calvinist theology, shared the same building for worship and listened to each other's ministers preach on alternate Sundays. However, the arrangement soon fell apart. When a New England–trained Presbyterian preacher, Jedidiah Andrews, came to town in 1697, "there appeared some scruples" among Presbyterians about sharing a meetinghouse and pastors. Attempting to salvage the joint venture, Baptists proposed that preachers at common assemblies be selected from a list of "approved ministers who are fitly qualified and sound in the faith and of holy lives to preach and pray" to members of both groups. When the Presbyterians showed no interest in working out an agreement, the Baptists decided to meet separately.[26]

The arrival of Anglicans accelerated religious competition. Frustrated in their efforts elsewhere, especially in New England, Anglicans viewed Pennsylvania as an opportunity to build a strong base for their missionary activities. In addition to targeting "pagan" Indians, Anglicans sought to bring Dissenters back into the Church of England. Backed by royal officials, the bishop of London, and the Society for the Propagation of the Gospel in Foreign Parts (SPG), the church was well situated by 1700 to offer stiff competition to the majority Quakers. Thwarted in Puritan New England and restrained by Virginia vestrymen, Anglican priests took full advantage of Pennsylvania's religious liberty to seek converts, in effect launching a massive missionary effort to undercut the Pennsylvanian privilege that permitted it. In their view, pluralism was not a virtue. Rather, it led to confusion and contentiousness as sects squabbled over minor matters rather than united within one church whose teachings were consistent with Holy Scripture.

The SPG's founder, Thomas Bray, was optimistic about the church's efforts to win converts. In a report on his visit to the colony in 1700, Bray heaped praise on Penn's experiment that had attracted so many godly people. He declared that in Pennsylvania "if in any part of the Christian World, a very good proportion of the People are excellently dispos'd to receive the Truth," which to him was best preserved in the Church of England. Bray was pleased to report that the Keithites had left their sectarian narrowness and were "so very well affected . . . to the Interest of our Church that, in the late Election of Assembly-Men, . . . they had almost carried it for the Church-men." He was also encouraged by the close relations that prevailed between Lutherans and Anglicans, noting that the two congregations of Lutherans lived "in very good Accord with our Minister, and his Church."[27] Lutherans, like Anglicans, disapproved of the sectarianism, but they were not as optimistic as Bray about the bridging of differences. One frustrated Swedish Lutheran minister thought that "here there are fanatics almost without number." He complained that it was very difficult to plant a church because sects including *"Anabaptists, Calvinists, Presbyterians, Sabbatarians* and *Latitudinarians"* were each "diligent in propagating the teachings of their principles."[28] Thus religious competition bifurcated as sectarians tried to win converts, while Churchmen tried to woo back sectarians.

While religious groups sometimes engaged in lively competition, no group suffered from persecution as did their counterparts in other colonies and in Europe. No one was banished because he or she expressed opinions the magistrates deemed dangerous to public order and harmony. And when itinerant preachers drifted into the Pennsylvania back-country, nervous ministers did not petition the legislature demanding that outsiders secure licenses to preach. For the most part, sectarians lived in peace among themselves. Where religious groups did clash, however, was in the political arena. When Quakers as the majority party sought to legislate their own religious and moral convictions, other Protestants sought to check their influence. The separation of church and state in Pennsylvania did not preclude religion's being hotly debated in politics. The colony had one of the most fractious political arenas, and the major factions were identified with specific religious affiliations.[29]

RELIGION, POLITICS, AND THE FAILURE
OF THE "HOLY EXPERIMENT"

William Penn had assumed that holy people, regardless of ethnic background or religious persuasion, would make good laws and live harmoniously. Accordingly, he lectured his Council on putting aside sectarian interests for the common good. "Though you are not of one Judgement in Religion," he admonished, "you are of one ffamily in Civilis, and should Aime at ye publick good."[30] Recognizing the dangers of one sect's attempting to impose its views on the commonwealth, Penn determined to use Pennsylvania's religious pluralism to his advantage and thus filled his early government with appointees from diverse religious backgrounds, explaining that such appointments would "Ballance factions, not . . . Irritate nor give Strength to them." He was convinced that a "union in civils," meaning a union of different sects, would strengthen the province, especially in times of danger, by giving all groups a voice in determining policy.[31]

Not all of his fellow Quakers agreed. Having endured persecution in England and hazarded dangers in settling in a wilderness, many were reluctant to cede power to others. They wanted to make laws that conformed to their beliefs, and now that they had the opportunity to do just that, Penn invited persons of different beliefs to share power. Other Quakers, however, agreed with Penn. Thus there arose a "great discontent" between those Quakers who wished to distribute power liberally and those who wished to keep it within their hands. Robert Turner, one of Penn's supporters who shared his views on religious liberty, described the unrest: "our ffriends for this severull years—in ye province: I observe doe not put up or opposse [i.e., nominate]—Either dutch—sweed. ffeene [Finn] or any other person not of our perswation: Baptist Endpendent-Presbitterian—or church of England man—(but what wee did force this Election) wch gives occasion of mutteringe & discuntent—& workes a gainst our good & Quiet." Turner feared that if Quakers did not "strive for all," they could "losse all," meaning that if they did not grant full liberty to all religious sects, they could lose that liberty themselves.[32]

While Quakers and the many other sects coexisted in relative harmony, respecting each other's rights of conscience, they clashed over public policy. Until the middle of the eighteenth century, Quakers had a majority in the legislative assembly and thus wielded considerable political power. In fact, non-Quakers came to view the Friends as the "Quaker Party," suggesting just how close a link existed between religion and politics. Penn's vision of a "Christian" polity collapsed when his coreligionists made it a "Quaker" polity. Quakers took with them into the statehouse two cherished convictions that aroused vociferous opposition. First, Friends refused on religious principle to take any civil oath, arguing that they should and would swear fealty only to God. Thus they enacted laws exempting members of their faith from taking oaths as citizens, office-holders, jurors, witnesses, and the like. Rather, they would simply make an "affirmation" of their loyalty to the English monarchy as sovereign of the civil power. Second, as pacifists, Quaker lawmakers refused to take military measures against hostile natives and their French patrons. Whitehall respected the Quakers' pacifism and did not force them to field an army but mandated that Pennsylvania at least raise funds to support New York's militia. Even then, the Quakers demurred. To non-Quakers, in refusing to provide basic protection for Pennsylvania citizens, the Quaker Party had subjected all to mortal danger in the name of sectarian beliefs.

The very character of Quaker religion undermined the Friends' ability to govern well. Two sets of conflicting values gave their governance a bipolar appearance. On the one hand, they embraced restraint, community, control, and hierarchy. On the other, they valued freedom, equality, individualism, and nonconformity. One scholar pointed out that the first set of traits was centripetal and contributed to harmony and order, while the second was centrifugal and led to conflict and sectarianism. Penn had hoped that the communitarian ideals would prevail, and that the Quakers would "sublimate their individualistic and antiauthoritarian tendencies and join hands in the work of building a constructed society." After he saw the Quaker majority in action during the 1680s, Penn's hopes faded. He called them "governmentish," "brutal," and susceptible to "scurby quarrels that break out to the disgrace of the Province." One of Penn's confidants feared that "stinging waves of pestiferous apostates and runagandoes" would lead to the infant government's downfall. Quakers quickly split into two parties that divided government. A Proprietary Party, also known as the Quaker Party, dominated the Assembly and opposed the Anti-Proprietary Party, led by Philadelphia merchants and outlying large landholders who controlled the Council. Though nonreligious factors contributed to the strife, religion played a major role. Some of the Quakers in the Council were drifting away from the Society of Friends and supporting the Church of England. Convinced that the Quakers could not govern effectively, Penn in 1688 brought in a "transplanted Massachusetts Puritan," John Blackwell, as deputy governor. Unfortunately, Blackwell's authoritarian style led to even more unrest.[33]

Sometimes economic self-interest undermined unity among Pennsylvania Friends. The conviction that the Divine Light dwelled within each individual, including African slaves, predisposed Quakers toward abolitionist sentiments, and some voiced their opposition to slavery, beginning a nascent abolitionist movement. However, Quaker merchants and landowners, like other early American settlers, faced a severe labor shortage that could not be satisfied entirely by indentured servants. Consequently, many Friends overrode their theologically based opposition to slavery and "avidly sought slave labor when their manpower requirements could not be otherwise met." Indeed, abolitionism among Pennsylvania Quakers became widespread only after "white indentured laborers became available in sufficient numbers to supply their needs."[34] Like Massachusetts Puritans, Pennsylvania Quakers found it difficult to refrain from being of the world while living in it.

While Quakers differed on the question of slavery, they were not divided over the place of women in religious and civil society. Unlike Puritans, who viewed women as "weak vessels" who had succumbed to temptation and sin in the Garden of Eden, Quakers ascribed no similar liability to women's character. According to one scholar, "sex bias had no place in [the Quakers'] conversion experience; there was nothing inherent in the female to prevent her spiritual rebirth, to hinder the work of the Divine Light." Women took an active part in proselytizing, acting as missionaries who conveyed the "truth" of the Divine Light throughout America. Indeed, as recounted in chapter 3, it was a female Quaker missionary, Mary Dyer, who had caused the Puritans so much consternation in Massachusetts Bay. By 1740, Quaker women, who had long held "women's meetings" aimed at disciplining women and controlling membership in their society, assumed full partnership in the Yearly Meeting, the Quakers' annual governing conference. Thenceforth, women were included in every "part of the Friends' meeting structure and hierarchy." Though females did not take an active role in public affairs as voters or officeholders, they, nonetheless, exerted considerable political influence. As "moral custodians" with particular responsibility for keeping their families tied to the Friends' Society, pious, active women no doubt wielded considerable influence among their husbands, fathers, brothers, and sons by reminding them of religious principles to which the menfolk must adhere in formulating law.[35]

Quakers faced considerable opposition from the many non-Quaker sects in Pennsylvania. Of all non-Quakers, Anglicans expressed the most resentment toward the rule of "Dissenters and apostates." Accustomed to privileges associated with religious establishment, Anglicans in Pennsylvania found themselves on the outside of a regime dominated by a despised group of enthusiastic dissenters who had little regard for the church's traditions and conventions. Moreover, many no doubt shared Blackwell's view that Quakers held "Principles un-suitable to civill Governmt & Polity." Some of the complaints leveled against Quaker rule included their beliefs and practices regarding "oaths and affirmations," their leniency with respect to smuggling and piracy, and their "innovations" in political and social affairs. In their minds, Penn's notion of religious liberty was in fact religious licence.[36]

History made Pennsylvania Quakers in their own turn wary of growing Anglican influence. As members of the Church of England steadily drifted into the colony during the 1690s, the Quaker majority viewed them as a threat. In 1695, Anglicans built Christ Church in Philadelphia, and soon thereafter a number of Quaker merchants began to attend services there. Causing additional anxiety was the fact that Governor William Markham and both Robert Quary and John Moore of the vice-admiralty court were Anglicans. While Quakers held onto their majority in the Assembly, clearly Anglicans had influence disproportionate to their numbers in the province. To restrict Anglican political sway, the Quaker government in 1696 enacted stricter property requirements and lengthened the residency requirement for voters. In short, faced with non-Quaker incursions, Quakers rejected Penn's ideal of all Christians working together in harmony to govern a pluralistic society in godly harmony.[37]

When Penn took title to the lands granted him, he and the Quakers inherited a political division based in part on religion. The three counties below the Delaware were sparsely settled by people of English, Dutch, and Swedish descent who were primarily Churchmen, that is, Anglicans, Lutherans, and Calvinists. When the Quakers moved into the three counties north of the Delaware, political and economic tensions developed between the two regions. Those in the Lower Counties, as they were called, resented the Quaker-dominated legislature, which favored Philadelphia and the Quaker merchants in the commercial rivalry between the two regions. Eventually the conflict was resolved through separation, with Delaware getting its own charter in 1701. Citizens there enjoyed liberty of conscience and gradually became an Anglican colony, with the Swedes transferring their allegiance to the Church of England.

The Anglicans who remained in Pennsylvania grew to be the Quakers' severest critics. Though initially constituting a small minority, members of the Church of England enjoyed considerable clout from their royal patronage. As early as 1699, Penn considered the Anglicans to be a political faction bent on overthrowing his proprietary government. His secretary James Logan described the Anglican party as "the faction that had long contended to overthrow the settled constitution of the government." There was more than a grain of truth to the charge. Led by two of Christ Church's most prominent vestrymen, the Anglicans complained that the Quaker legislature had passed laws offensive to Anglicans. In a complaint to the Board of Trade, Robert Quary and John Moore detailed what they considered to be "offensive": "laws banning rough games, cock fights, state plays; laws . . . regulating marriages and granting religious liberty in the latitudinarian tradition of Friends; and a law which allowed attestations or affirmations in place of oaths for provincial officials, judges, and juries." Quary and Moore termed Quaker rule an "uneasy and intolerable yoak and burthen" and characterized the recent legislation as "contrary to our religious rights and consciences."[38] Thus in Pennsylvania, Anglicans made the same charge against the state as Quakers had made earlier in England. To them, Penn's guarantees of religious liberty notwithstanding, Quaker Pennsylvania was in effect legislating uniformity.

Military affairs drew the greatest criticism of Quaker government from non-Quakers, especially Anglicans, who tended to view Quakers as strictly pacifist. Indeed, Friends contended that warfare was sinful, "but they recognized the validity of other men's conscientious belief in its propriety." Nevertheless, their pacifism and the inadequate defenses it fostered resulted in Penn's temporarily losing his charter in 1692 during King William's War. For two years New York's Benjamin Fletcher acted as governor of Pennsylvania to ensure that it complied with imperial calls for arms. When Fletcher presented the Pennsylvania Assembly with a royal order to provide men and material for the war effort, the response fell short of the governor's requests. An angry Fletcher interpreted the Assembly's inaction as a case of narrow sectarian principles' preempting sound public policy. He wrote that the assemblymen had "so much self conceit they will rather dye than resist with Carnall weapons." Fletcher couched his next plea for defensive measures in language that respected

Quaker beliefs. He assured the assemblymen that he was not asking Pennsylvanians to carry arms or to "levy Money to make War," but was seeking only supplies for Indian allies, a request, he argued, similar to the biblical injunction to "feed the Hungry, and clothe the Naked." But the Quaker lawmakers rejected even that request. They capitulated only when Penn made a special plea for the assemblymen to aid the "poor Indians" whose crops and food stores had been destroyed in the war.[39]

As Queen Anne's War (1702–1713) kept alive hostilities between the French and the English, Penn sought some formula under which Quaker assemblymen could maintain their pacifism yet provide funds for the war effort. He believed that Quakers could grant funds "especially, since Money be given under the Style off Peace & Safety, or to defray the exegences of the governmt." But some Quakers disagreed. In 1709, Governor Charles Gookin, recognizing that Quakers were obliged "by their Principles, not to make use of Arms," requested £4,000 from the Assembly. The assemblymen refused, explaining that "the raising Money to hire Men to fight (or kill one another) is Matter of Conscience to us, and against our religious Principles." Even London Quakers thought that their brethren across the Atlantic were being too scrupulous, questioning "how Ffriends could be wholly exempted from their proportion's of the Charge if layed upon them by publick Taxation (any more than We are here in England)."[40]

Defense was the issue that eventually brought down Quaker rule. The eighteenth century witnessed a constant struggle to maintain a balance of power among European states, and every crisis that threatened that balance opened a colonial American theater of war. With each outbreak of hostilities, Pennsylvania Quakers put religious principle above public policy. In 1739, at the beginning of the War of the Austrian Succession, once again the Quaker-dominated Assembly voted against defense appropriations. Governor George Thomas fired back a response that questioned both their views and their attitudes. He reminded them that the French and their Indian allies controlled extensive land bordering Pennsylvania and had easy access to the English colony. Further, he noted Pennsylvania's strategic location at the midpoint of the North American English coastline. Thomas questioned their providential view of public affairs. "I agree with you," he wrote, "that good Men may hope for the Protection of the Supreme Being, but History, both sacred and prophane, shews us that Goodness has not generally served to protect them from the rage of Enemies." He claimed that a majority of Pennsylvanians agreed with petitioners who called for putting the country into a "Posture of Defense." As the impasse dragged on, Thomas pointed out that the Quakers were withholding basic government services in the name of religious liberty. "I believe," he concluded, "this is the first Instance of a Number of [Quakers] having made use of Liberty of Conscience for tying up the Hands of His Majesty's Subjects for defending a valuable Part of Dominions, situate almost in the Center of those in North America."[41]

When William Penn died in 1718, he had already judged his "Holy Experiment" a failure. It had been a noble attempt to unite Christians of all faiths in a single state where each sect enjoyed freedom of conscience, yet where all believers could join together under their common Christianity. Instead, what had resulted was political factionalism often drawn along sectarian lines.

With Georgia's settlement in 1732, Britain's colonization of mainland North America came to an end. Founders in each of the thirteen colonies had planted what they considered to be the one true religion, and they all deemed their provinces to be havens of religious liberty. Virginia had transplanted the Church of England to American soil, its founders believing that a religious uniformity centered on the established church would promote a moral, orderly society without violating dissenters' rights to believe as they wished—as long as they did so in private and did nothing to undermine the church. Other colonies in the Chesapeake and Lower South also made the Church of England the established church, although it was much weaker in Georgia than in the Carolinas. The demand for immigrants in that buffer colony forced its trustees to guarantee religious liberty to sectarians across the Christian spectrum, as well as to Jewish settlers.

Massachusetts had also opted for religious uniformity, but it had established the Congregational or Puritan churches as the official religion in a society that defined religious liberty as freedom from heresy. Connecticut and New Hampshire became Puritan colonies too, but Rhode Island, founded by dissenters exiled from Massachusetts, welcomed all Protestants and refused to establish any church or sect. In part because of what Anglicans and others termed religious persecution, Massachusetts Bay

Colony lost its original charter in 1684, the event marking the official end of the "Holy Commonwealth." The new royal charter guaranteed religious liberty to all Protestants, although the Puritans were strong enough to continue their establishment.

Unlike regions to the north and south, the Middle Colonies had begun as pluralistic societies that rendered establishments impractical. Though New York eventually made the Church of England its official church, the establishment laws were weak and religious liberty was guaranteed for dissenters. Pennsylvania had embarked on a "Holy Experiment" that accepted pluralism as the many faces of a common Christianity and the foundation of a society where sectarians would cooperate with each other for the public good. That experiment failed because one sect, the ruling Quaker Party, maintained a legislative majority and was unwilling to sacrifice deeply held tenets to accommodate Christians who deemed those beliefs to be nonessential to the faith and harmful to society. Freedom of conscience, then, enabled the majority sect to impose its will on society in much the same manner as an established church.

What was common throughout the colonies was religious localism. That is, regardless of the religious settlement, churches operated within fixed boundaries under the jurisdiction of a local governing body. There prevailed in all the colonies some form of the parish system, whereby ministers and their congregations worshiped with little or no outside competition or interference. Pennsylvania notwithstanding, most Americans functioned, in Adam Smith's terms, in a regulated religious market. Changes in the first two-thirds of the eighteenth century, however, would challenge the religious world as defined and instituted by Americans' spiritual forefathers. The population would double and then double again. New waves of immigrants would make the colonies even more diverse and pluralistic. New ways of spreading the gospel would break down conventional parish boundaries and introduce religious competition as itinerant preachers entered communities, offering men and women an alternative to what was available at the local church. New ideas would challenge many of the notions that the Founders had cherished, including Christianity's most basic assumptions. In short, the world of 1763 would in many respects be one "turned upside down," forcing Americans to reconsider their original assumptions about church-state relations and freedom of religion.

PART TWO

Religious Competition

❖

B Y THE MIDDLE of the eighteenth century, population growth, resulting from robust immigration, a "consumer revolution," and geographic expansion, strained the original planters' religious settlements, testing prevailing definitions of faith and freedom and the institutions that preserved them. America and Americans were on the move: men and women crossing the Atlantic from Germany, Scotland, and Northern Ireland and then migrating down the backcountry; new goods arriving in colonial seaports and then being transshipped to stores and shops mushrooming throughout the settlements, including on the frontier; and new ideas arriving from Europe and England and circulating throughout British North America. Religious establishments and parish boundaries, which had served reasonably well to preserve orthodoxy, now failed to contain new arrivals and their dissenting notions. Regulated church-state arrangements gave way to an emerging free market of ideas characterized by greater religious competition for settled ministers and expanded religious choice for their parishioners.

Since 1700, population had doubled and redoubled, pushing settlement beyond the boundaries of existing parishes and into frontier regions without adequate numbers of qualified ministers. Tens of thousands of immigrants arrived, many—such as Ulster Presbyterians from Northern Ireland and Pietists from Germany—bringing notions that challenged religious establishments and adding more sects to an already pluralistic society. In addition, new Enlightenment ideas that questioned traditional authority, including that of the Bible itself, soon became standard texts at Harvard, Yale, and William and Mary. And when clergymen tried to reassert their authority, they encountered a new, broad definition of religious freedom espoused by Radical Whigs that questioned any interference with an individual's rights of conscience. At every level, from local parishes to colonial governments, the old institutions that had protected the planters' conception of the one "true" religion began to crack.

The original planters had vowed to keep divergent ideas out of their settlements, a task that became ever more difficult with a growing population pushing against town borders and an expanding commerce bringing hawkers and peddlers with their new goods and ideas. In the end, defenders of local institutions and traditions failed, as many within their communities eagerly embraced the newcomers and their wares. Insistent upon exercising choice, consumers, whether considering manufactured goods or religious notions, demanded the right to choose for themselves. The result was a new, more expansive definition of religious freedom, one characterized by religious competition among the sects. The world of the settled ministry was turned upside down. No longer able to count on a monopoly within their parishes, clergymen had to woo individuals who were now empowered to decide religious matters for themselves.

The most publicized and visible assault came, ironically, in the person of a fervent evangelical itinerant preacher who greatly admired the "good old Puritans" who had first brought the true gospel to the American wilderness. George Whitefield's 1739 arrival touched off a revival that spilled outside churches and into the streets and marketplaces as huge crowds rushed to hear the young, dynamic "Divine Dramatist," whose performances in the pulpit moved audiences of thousands to tears and shocked many of the settled ministry. Whitefield and scores of like-minded itinerants traveled throughout the colonies preaching their message of the "one thing needful," a religious New Birth. Believing that they had a mission to preach the gospel to everyone, the itinerants disregarded parish boundaries. And these religious entrepreneurs borrowed extensively from the same consumer market whose products they often decried, employing such commercial techniques as advertising to generate advance publicity for their preaching tours. When unsympathetic or hostile local pastors refused to invite them into their churches, the travel-ing preachers simply stepped up on their portable pulpits and preached in the churchyard or from the courthouse steps, telling their listeners that true religion obtained in a personal conversion experience, not in the church or the clergy. Parishioners found such a message empowering. Itinerants provided local people with a choice, and many exercised that choice by removing their ministers or leaving their congregations and forming new ones. Ministers, hardly surprisingly, saw the itinerants as unwanted competitors.

The eighteenth century exposed the weaknesses of the planters' reli-gious settlements or, rather, revealed them as inadequate for the times. First, colonial religious establishments depended on a homogeneous pop-ulation and ample unsettled land to absorb dissidents, conditions difficult to maintain in a period of population growth and commercial expansion. Second, the laws and institutions designed to maintain religious unifor-mity by silencing critics and shutting out dissenters broke down under the pressure of itinerancy. Defenders of established churches attempted to safeguard their prerogatives by passing laws requiring itinerants to obtain licenses, but their efforts were as futile as, in the biblical metaphor, an attempt to contain new wine in old wineskins.

From every part of society, people with new ideas about faith and freedom sought change, which led to clashes between those advocating an expansive religious freedom and those supporting religious uniformity. Pro-revival evangelicals, or New Lights, became more vocal in their oppo-sition to laws requiring them to pay taxes for the support of a church they did not regard as the true faith. Lawyers invoked Whig ideas to check the clergy's efforts to reassert their authority over such matters as higher education or parish governance. Professors filled their students with Enlightenment ideas, leading some of the brightest minds to view the law rather than the ministry as the surer path to an orderly, rational, and virtuous society. Individuals challenging existing religious settle-ments did not agree on what constituted the "one" true faith, but they did agree that they ought to have the freedom to define that faith for themselves.

❖ 5 ❖

"Trafficking for the Lord" and the
Expansion of Religious Choice

ATE in the colonial period, Virginia attorney general Peyton Randolph feared that the religious system that had helped bring peace and order to the colony was succumbing to a sectarian assault. The cause of his concern was a group of evangelical dissenters in western Virginia who, having broken away from the Church of England in the early 1740s, invited Presbyterian itinerant preachers from Pennsylvania and New Jersey to come lead their worship. When Samuel Davies and other ministers answered the call, they ignored parish boundaries and preached at times and places of their own choosing. Moreover, they disregarded the Book of Common Prayer and even vilified the established religion. In his assessment of the matter, Randolph warned that "it will give great Encouragement to fall off f[ro]m the established Church if they [the preachers] are permitted to range and raise Contributions over the whole Country." Randolph contended that the parish system was one of Virginia's traditional pillars of an orderly society, and that itinerancy undermined that stability by sowing "Dissentions & Confusion among the People."[1] Randolph's judgment endorsed the status quo: a highly regulated parish system that promoted religious uniformity by keeping out undesirable teachings.

Gilbert Tennent, a kindred spirit and colleague of Davies from Pennsylvania, stated the case for an open religious market and religious competition. Tennent defended itinerants' actions as an effective means of spreading the gospel in a regulated religious system. He explained that he and his fellow evangelicals resorted to invading parishes only when the "settled ministry" failed to proclaim the "one thing needful," the necessity of a spiritual "New Birth." Therefore, he encouraged men and women to ignore parish boundaries in the "Getting of Grace and Growing in it," and reminded his readers that church members had every right and even responsibility to find someone who could show them the way to salvation. He urged his listeners to recognize that they had a choice, that there was a growing variety of printed and preached sermons from which they could choose. According to Tennent, one sermon does not fit all: "at one time we cannot hear all, neither doth the Explication and Application of all, equally suit such a Person, in such a Time, or Condition, or equally quicken, and subserve the Encrease of Knowledge."[2] Believing that he was preaching scriptural truth, and that God had mandated that he reach the whole world, Tennent was willing to challenge prevailing regulations and those who enforced them.

The event that evoked such different assessments from Randolph and Tennent was the so-called Great Awakening, an evangelical revival that swept through the English mainland colonies in the 1740s. It is beyond the scope of this study to examine that event in any systematic and comprehensive way.[3] Rather, the focus here is to consider the revival as introducing a new, competitive religious market that offered choice to men and women accustomed to a religious monopoly. Such economic language is justified because revival leaders themselves, as well as their critics, frequently described their mission with tropes drawn from the marketplace. Boston pastor Benjamin Colman considered the message of the "New Birth" to be "Holy Merchandize," and another minister, Thomas Foxcroft, welcomed the "Imported Divinity" that evangelist George Whitefield brought from England. Whitefield conceived of his mission to the colonies as one of "trafficking for the Lord."[4] Opponents also viewed the revival in market terms, denouncing itinerants as unlicensed peddlers whose ramblings should be regulated. One disapproving commentator reasoned that there was "a very wholesome law in the province to discourage Pedlars in Trade," and that there ought to be one "for the discouragement of Pedlars in Divinity also."[5]

By the time the revival had run its course, it had indeed *turn'd the World upside down.*[6] The Great Awakening increased religious competition, undermined establishment laws, and gave individuals greater choice in religious beliefs, practices, and styles. No longer could a parish minister count on a monopoly within his own parish lines. Empowered by the assurance that they had undergone a "New Birth" experience, individuals on occasion voted their pastors out of office or separated themselves from his church and formed their own congregations. In short, a freer, more liberal religious marketplace emerged in which claims to one true religion were hotly contested. Though defenders of the established churches in some cases secured laws restricting itinerants' activities, the measures were largely ineffective. Buoyed by large popular followings, itinerants gave persons more choice in the religious marketplace. And laymen and -women expressed great independence in choosing, often going in directions of which the itinerants themselves disapproved.

REGULATED PARISHES

In 1720, most Americans lived in colonies with an established church. Approximately 85 percent of the almost half a million inhabitants of British North America lived in provinces where either the Church of England or the Congregational churches constituted the official church. The Anglican Church was established in Virginia, Maryland, Delaware, North Carolina, and South Carolina; it was also loosely established in New York, although a Dutch Reformed preponderance weakened its hold there. Congregational churches were established in Massachusetts, Connecticut, and New Hampshire. While Pennsylvania had no official church, the Quakers had sufficient numbers to control the legislative assembly. New Jersey and Rhode Island were similar to Pennsylvania in that there numerous sects coexisted, albeit not harmoniously.

Most persons, then, lived within the kind of regulated religious system that Peyton Randolph advocated. Whatever their polity, nearly all churches at the local level enjoyed a virtual monopoly. Each of the three major branches of Protestant Christianity—Anglicans, Presbyterians, and Congregationalists—operated within the parish system, which ensured that their borders were safeguarded against harmful outside influences such as heretics, schismatics, and proselytizers. No preacher could come within parish boundaries without permission.

The roots of the parish system reach back to medieval Europe. The Church of Rome enjoyed a virtual monopoly in western Europe and was determined to maintain that position. In the first chapter of Benedict's Rule for monks set down in the sixth century, "bad" monks are inveighed against, the worst being the "gyrovagues" who roamed about from place to place without settling down. At the diocesan level, priests had to have special permission to enter another bishop's diocese. They even devised formulaic coded letters that authorized priests to move into another diocese. Of course, many just wandered about "illegally," as we know from court cases and repeated attempts to keep them under supervision. In one instance in 847, a woman named Thiota preached the impending end of the world as she traveled from Constance to Mainz. Made to appear before the bishop of Mainz, she admitted that her motive was financial, not theological. Coached by a priest, she had hoped to make some money from her prophecies. For her offense, "she was publicly flogged by the judgment of the synod and ignominiously stripped of the ministry of preaching which she had unreasonably taken up and presumed against the custom of the church; thus shamed, she finally put an end to her prophesying." The cumulative record indicates that there was quite a bit of boundary breaking in the Middle Ages, with the issue being fiscal as well as doctrinal. Itinerant preachers represented competition for local preachers. What has survived in the legislation and legal cases are the attempts of bishops to safeguard the parishes they supervised.[7]

Similarly, ministers in the American colonies sought to make their parishes Protestant sanctuaries. Every denomination and sect devised a system regulating access to the ministry, usually through educational requirements and ordination. And each group subscribed to a specific set of doctrines, often embodied in a creed or confession of faith that defined orthodoxy. Worship in parish churches, then, proceeded under the leadership of an ordained minister charged with maintaining particular theological emphases and traditions. For Congregationalists and Presbyterians, services centered on a sermon or the spoken "Word of God." While each individual was expected to read the Bible, they recognized that some were ordained by God to "open" or explain its meaning. Thus men and women gathered for worship at fixed times to listen to their pastor preach a sermon that examined a chosen biblical text, elucidated the doctrines contained therein, and applied the lessons to the parishioners' lives. Almost any entry of Samuel Sewall's diary for a Sabbath or Lecture-Day illustrates the set pattern: an educated, ordained minister preaching on a passage from the word of God and expounding its doctrinal significance. On January 30, 1717/18, for instance, Cotton Mather preached a sermon on Psalms 41:4, which suggested the title, "Heal my Soul." The doctrine drawn from this "excellent Sermon" was that "He only is a Blessed Man whose mind God Heals."[8] Sewall's brief diary entry reveals the major features of Congregational worship: the very fact that Sewall cited the Scripture text and its doctrine in his diary suggests that the sermon was intended as spiritual nourishment to enrich parishioners in their daily lives.

When Anglicans gathered for Sunday worship, they, too, followed a predictable order of worship. Rather than being centered on the sermon, though, their services followed the liturgical calendar contained in the Book of Common Prayer. No matter where a member of the Church of England worshiped on a given Sunday, he or she knew what to expect. When William Byrd traveled, he often stopped at churches in neighboring parishes for worship. On Sunday, November 6, 1709, for instance, while away from home, at "about 11 o'clock . . . [he] rode to the church of Abingdon Parish" where he and his fellow worshipers followed the prescribed liturgy for the day, the same one he would have observed had he been in his own parish church.[9]

Thus both Sewall and Byrd, and most other Americans, worshiped within well-regulated local parishes. They met at fixed times and sat in assigned pews. Their services followed the familiar patterns that their particular church or sect deemed authoritative. And they were protected from heretics and schismatics who might threaten their orderly worship.

A parish minister derived his own authority from his ability to interpret the Bible correctly, and he strengthened his authority by being part of a ministerial united front. As long as a denomination's pastors were in general agreement on key doctrines, there was little chance for an outsider to make inroads with parishioners by exploiting differences. Churches could accommodate minor disagreements without causing serious breaches. If unchecked, however, serious doctrinal strife such as the antinomian crisis in early Boston could lead to internal splits and expose the church to external ridicule. As seventeenth-century London minister Edward Elton put it: "When teachers meete together in one truth . . . it doth free the teachers from the note and blemish of lightnesse and new-fangled giddinesse." But if "we follow factions, some hold of one and some of another, we shall be brought to that exigent, that we must either confesse Christ to be divided (a thing impossible) or our selves to be no members of Christ, and that we are carnall."[10]

To a political economist, colonial religion before 1740 constituted a highly regulated market. Adam Smith claimed that the clergy of the established church had one "great interest": to "maintain their authority with the people." That authority depended on "the supposed certainty and importance of the whole doctrine which they inculcate, and upon the supposed necessity of adopting every part of it with the most implicit faith, in order to avoid eternal misery." Carrying the weight of defending the "true" religion, then, the clergy tended their parish boundaries with great determination. They could brook no disagreement.[11] In New England and in the southern colonies, the clergy had state assistance in keeping out undesirables. In the Middle Colonies, denominations themselves assumed responsibility for maintaining their own parishes. Presbyterian synods, for instance, examined ministerial candidates and resolved doctrinal disputes.

Ministers understood that parish lines were permeable and required eternal vigilance to keep out heterodoxy. The insidious nature of sin demanded constant care, especially at a time when colonists were becoming more and more immersed in the Atlantic market. Commerce was a process that could render both great good and great harm to the church.[12] On the one hand, it could plant religion in regions throughout the world. Indeed, trading companies had founded many of the American colonies, and it was trade that continued to carry the Protestant faith ever westward into the North American interior. On the other hand, commerce brought evils that tempted believers to seek treasures of this world instead of those of the next. Ministers constantly warned of the seductive nature of luxury goods and the sinful pride they promoted. Trade also brought to America heterodox ideas and, worse still, non-Christians.

Trade presented a dilemma for colonial ministers trying to regulate religion. Many parishioners, especially influential merchants in the seaports, believed that an exclusionary religious system was bad for business. Their suppliers, financiers, customers, and agents were people of all faiths, and when those people immigrated to America or visited on business trips, they should be allowed to worship as they chose.[13] That presented a problem for ministers who wished to keep their parishes free of undesirable or rival faiths. Sometimes merchants and ministers clashed over whether persons of different regions and religions would be allowed to worship within their parish. In 1656, when a small group of Jews in New Amsterdam petitioned the Dutch West Indies Company for the right to conduct private worship services in their homes, ministers of the Protestant Dutch Reformed Church opposed the plea, arguing that the next step would be public worship in a synagogue, and that would pose dangers for Christians. The divines explained their opposition: "that the wolves may be warded off from the tender lambs of Christ." The colony's director-general, Peter Stuyvesant, a staunch anti-Semite, rejected the Jews' appeal for "the free and public exercise of their abominable religion." Jewish merchants in Amsterdam took up the cause of their New World brothers and reminded the directors of the company that Dutch authorities allowed Jewish religious services "in quietness" both in Holland and in the other Dutch colonies. Influenced by the Amsterdam merchants, the directors voted to allow Jews to worship, but only "within the privacy of their own homes."[14]

After the English assumed control of New Amsterdam and renamed it New York, the Jewish toehold grew more secure, not because the English were more tolerant of Judaism than the Dutch had been, but because the need for productive settlers overrode religious biases. Whitehall's concern was stimulating trade, not preserving parish boundaries. Accordingly, in 1740 Parliament passed a law enabling Jews in the American colonies to become citizens, because "the increase of people is a means of advancing the wealth and strength of any nation or country." In 1756, Lord Chancellor Philip Hardwicke reacted to objections against making Jews citizens by declaring, "Even with respect to the Jews, the discouraging of them to go and settle in our American colonies would be a great loss, if not the ruin of, the trade of every one [of the colonies]."[15]

From New England Congregationalists' perspective, Anglicans represented a far greater threat than did the tiny Jewish minorities in Newport, New York, Philadelphia, and Charleston. Eager to make gains among colonial Dissenters, the Church of England had initiated a bold and innovative strategy at the beginning of the eighteenth century. They decided to compete head-on with Dissenters in every part of the colonies, including the Puritan strongholds of New England. Such an effort required capital, and concerned church leaders, aided by enterprising laymen, raised huge sums through a device borrowed from the world of commerce: the joint stock company. Through selling subscriptions to individuals, the organizers formed two associations that would become the engines of their competition with the American dissenters. First, they founded the Society for the Propagation of Religion in Foreign Parts (SPG), which sent missionaries into every region of British North America much as English mercantile houses sent salesmen to peddle their wares. A second company, the Society for Promoting Christian Knowledge (SPCK), printed thousands of books for distribution in the colonies in hopes that ideas on the printed page could penetrate Dissenters' parishes even if missionaries could not.

Alarmed by Anglican successes in wooing away members and starting new churches, Dissenters retaliated by using every means at hand to secure their parish lines. One effective weapon was taxation. In 1713, Anglicans in Braintree, Massachusetts, petitioned Governor Joseph Dudley, protesting the disadvantage they faced in building and supporting a local church there. The petitioners complained that "those few who are of the Church of England Communion are rated and taxed most extravagantly to support the dissenting Clergy." It was the Congregationalists whom the Anglicans were describing as "dissenting," a valid use of the term in England but not in New England. In Massachusetts, Congregationalists were not dissenters; the Anglicans were. Paying taxes to support the established church put them under a "very great hardship" because they faced large expenses in building and maintaining their own church and supporting their minister.[16] Dudley denied their request for relief.[17]

In England, of course, Anglicans were accustomed to having all the government protection accorded an established church. But in colonies where there was no establishment at all or dissenting churches were established, American clergy of the Church of England were outsiders and were forced to seek protection from the mother country. In 1713, a group of New Jersey clergymen asked the archbishop of Canterbury to appoint a resident bishop to protect them. They complained that the lack of qualified ministers slowed their progress toward raising "the true and Orthodox Worship of God" in their colony in "Conformity to our pure and Apostolick Church." The problem was that in recent years agents of the "evil Spirit" had undermined their efforts to advance the cause of "true" religion. They could see no other solution for enjoying peace within their own parishes but the "Speedy Sending a Bishop into these parts to protect us & Stand in the Gap against any Person who may Encourage or countenance any Lawless designs against the Church."[18] In the case of those clergymen, the necessity of a regulated religious market was underscored by what appeared to be a not only unregulated but lawless environment.

Despite such attempts by religious outsiders to circumvent the colonial parish system, it proved effective in maintaining religious monopolies where a particular church was established. Agriculture dominated, and agricultural life favored the parish system by fixing people in a particular location. While there was some population movement, New Englanders could regulate its flow into towns, "warning out" those deemed undesirable, especially religious heretics. The bigger problem in Massachusetts was keeping sons and grandsons of orthodox men and women within the covenanted community. As they moved farther away from the towns of their births, it became increasingly important to ensure that they perpetuated the parish system by safeguarding the "pure" church within secure boundaries. In the Chesapeake and the Carolinas, the great planters acted as gatekeepers in their role as vestrymen, making certain that only those ministers who conformed to the faith and practice of the Church of England, and who upheld the harmony of the social order, were invested with a living. Occasional challenges notwithstanding, until 1740, ministers were secure within their own jurisdictions, confident that they alone enjoyed government protection and support for religion, that they were the sole arbiters of orthodoxy, that their parishioners would hear no other preacher, and that laymen and -women would conform to their teachings.

Then, with the arrival of George Whitefield in 1739, parish boundaries crumbled all over the colonies. One observer called the English evangelist and the religion that he brought an "imported Divinity," likening Whitefield and the revival he sparked to the latest London fashions. Thus it was by commerce that colonial America's regulated religious market was thrown into disarray, as local pastors, known as the "settled ministry," found themselves suddenly besieged by uninvited itinerant preachers who wooed their parishioners with an altogether different "brand"[19] of religion.

There was historical precedent for commerce's corrosive effect on fixed religious structures. Colonial ministers in the eighteenth century hoped that commerce would again be an engine for change, but for the good, praying that it would bring to America's shores a revival of the one true religion. Writing early in the 1700s, Cotton Mather believed that America was at the intersection of great changes in religion and commerce. He pointed out that the center of trade was shifting from the Mediterranean to the Atlantic and from Europe to America. He further believed that trade had brought the Protestant Reformation to America, and that Americans would complete the work that the reformers had begun in the sixteenth century. Just as God in times past had scattered gospel seeds via trade, he would, Mather proclaimed, revive Christianity in a similar way. "By Navigation there will be brought the Word of a glorious Christ unto a Multitude afar off," he wrote, "and as the *Ships cover the Sea*, the Earth (and thou America too) shall be filled with the Knowledge of the glorious God."[20] Though Cotton Mather did not live to witness it, navigation did bring a great revival to America, but he might not have been entirely pleased. On October 30, 1739, the *Elizabeth* dropped anchor off the Delaware coast, bringing George Whitefield, whose "trafficking for the Lord" would trample on every religious regulation imposed by civil and religious authorities.

"A SETT OF RAMBLING FELLOWS"

In the 1740s, colonial ministers everywhere feared a new threat to the parish system. Virginia clergymen saw itinerants invading their parishes despite establishment laws designed to keep unwanted competitors at bay. One of the wandering preachers was Samuel Davies, an itinerant preacher from New Jersey. He had come to Hanover County, Virginia, at the request of a group of evangelicals who had read some of Whitefield's sermons and now sought preachers who could deliver discourses of that same evangelical ilk. The settled ministry in western Virginia deeply resented a Christian preacher's invading their parishes. According to one clergyman, if Davies had come into a country where the Church of England was "in the same state of corruption as the Romish Church was at the time of the Reformation," then the clergy would have supported his missionary activities. But that was not the case at all. At least in their estimation, Protestant Christianity was well served by Virginia's parish ministers. The ministers could interpret Davies presence only as that of a proselytizer who was interested not in bringing people into the Christian fold but in enticing them into his own Presbyterian sect. The bishop of London agreed with that assessment, maintaining that the Act of Toleration did not protect an itinerant preacher who traveled "over many Counties to make Converts in a Country . . . where till very lately there was not a Dissenter from the Church of England."[21]

The bishop's interpretation notwithstanding, Davies and the other itinerants who soon followed him continued their aggressive pursuit of converts within Anglican parishes, putting the settled ministry on the defensive. After Davies and John Todd had invaded his parish, James Maury could only warn his colleague whose county was next on the itinerants' well-publicized preaching tour. "It seems not improper to inform You," Maury wrote, "that the revd Davies & Todd have lately been guilty of what I think Intrusions upon me, in having preached each of them a Sermon at a Tavern in my Parish." The unthinkable had happened: competition in the heart of what Maury had considered to be his exclusive jurisdiction. He observed that neither of the itinerants had "obtained any properly authenticated License to exercise their Function," an ecclesiastical regulation that had theretofore protected the clergy's monopoly. Maury closed by reporting that Davies and Todd had promised upon leaving "to range upon our Frontiers," the district where the Church of England's hold was tenuous.[22]

Within a new "religious economy," the Virginia clergymen and their counterparts throughout the colonies suddenly faced stiff religious competition. The itinerants assumed that religious affiliation was a matter of choice, not compulsion, and that "religious organizations must compete for members." Indeed, the itinerants, who borrowed heavily from merchants of consumer goods, understood that "religious economies are like commercial economies in that they consist of a market made up of a set of current and potential customers and a set of firms seeking to serve that market." Davies and Todd, for instance, assumed that their "potential customers" included members of the Church of England. If they could be effective in propagating their message by adapting commercial techniques, then they were willing to be religious entrepreneurs. In market terminology, churches succeed or fail depending on organization, sales representatives, product, and marketing techniques. Or, in churchly language, "the relative success of religious bodies . . . depend[s] upon their polity, their clergy, their religious doctrines, and their evangelization techniques." The itinerants succeeded in attracting tens of thousands of colonists through new "evangelization techniques" specifically designed to convey their message to an audience both inside and outside existing parish boundaries.[23]

A consumer revolution in the English Atlantic provided evangelicals with new models for defining their audiences and new techniques of conveying the gospel to them. Eager to expand sales, London merchants in the early 1700s began to conceive of the marketplace as much larger than any they had previously known. First, they paid attention to a much broader social spectrum, designing and pricing merchandise such as textile goods to meet the demand of the "middling" and "lesser" sorts as well as that of the "better" sorts, the group that they had previously targeted. Second, they expanded the geographical boundaries of the market, reaching across the Atlantic to Americans, whose numbers would climb to one million by midcentury. Innovative merchants developed selling strategies such as newspaper advertising to appeal to potential customers long before a salesman ever had face-to-face contact with the buyer. One of the most effective means of advertising was to plant in the newspaper what appeared to be a story but in fact was a florid account "puffing" the virtues of the product being sold. Josiah Wedgwood became a master of extolling his pottery in this fashion.[24] Rather than assuming that buyers would seek them out and come to them for merchandise, merchants now pursued consumers wherever they were.

George Whitefield was the first evangelical to adapt these new merchandising strategies to the preaching of the gospel. To him, God's grace was a "heavenly cargo" far more precious than earthly baubles and thus should be "sold" in the widest possible market. He and his fellow evangelist John Wesley both conceived of their field of labor in global terms. Each on separate occasions referred to the "Whole World as My Parish," an expansive notion similar to that of the merchants' transatlantic vision. With that understanding, Whitefield and Wesley refused to recognize existing parish boundaries as defining areas off-limits to them. In order to penetrate parish lines, evangelicals on both sides of the Atlantic devised two means. First, they engaged in aggressive advertising that went far beyond what ministers had ever done before. Whereas settled ministers in London would place an announcement in the public newspapers giving the time and place for a special sermon, evangelicals hyped their upcoming revival services by reporting in detail the exciting results of their previous meeting. They reported record crowds, sometimes embellishing attendance figures, indicated how much money had been raised, and gave some sort of qualitative assessment of the sermon's effect on the audience. When Whitefield announced his intention to go to America to preach the same sermons that had attracted crowds estimated as high as fifty thousand in London's Moorfields, he spoke to an already captivated audience. Advance publicity begun months before he arrived in a particular location served to build anticipation to a fever pitch. Second, evangelicals penetrated parish lines by sending itinerant preachers all over the Anglo-American world. Where they found a sympathetic parish minister, they preached from his pulpit. Where parish ministers opposed them, they preached wherever they found space within the parish: in market squares, from courthouse steps, at racecourses, in public parks, and even in taverns.

Such bold new practices disregarded the customary regulated religious market in America and caused great distress among the settled ministry. Reverend Patrick Henry found the itinerants' advertising particularly disturbing, in large part because it was so effective. In a letter to a fellow clergyman, Henry warned about Davies's advertised plans for June 1747: "Mr. Davies is to preach at Goochland Court-house next Thursday, from whence he is to travel as far as Roanoke, preaching at certain appointed places in his way." Henry based his report on advance publicity he had seen posted about the countryside: "circular Letters and Advertisements are dispersed all over the upper parts of this Colony, that the People may have notice of the times & places of meeting. My informer has one of the circular Letters, and the Advertisement at Goochland Court-house has, I believe, been seen by hundreds."[25] Henry was aware that through advertising, itinerants bypassed parish ministers and invited parishioners to consider an alternative worship experience. He knew that such tactics threatened to forever change the theretofore largely exclusive relationship he had enjoyed with his people. In short, he now faced competition within his own parish.

If Henry and fellow minister James Maury were concerned over the success of the itinerants' advertising, they were dismayed at the success of their preaching and ideas. Maury noted that "Disaffection in the People to regular Pastors of unblemished Morals & unquestionable Abilities, together with many other unhappy Effects, have usually attended the Ministry of Itinerants & Enthusiasts in the Colony." Patrick Henry described similar effects within his parish at Hanover: "these Itinerants . . . screw up the People to the greatest heights of religious Phrenzy, and then leave them in that wild state, for perhaps ten or twelve months, till another Enthusiast comes among them, to repeat the same thing over again."[26] Henry was one of the Anglican ministers who led the fight for statutory regulation of what was rapidly becoming a free market of ideas, a prospect that, in his judgment, meant chaos.

Where itinerants could not go, evangelical publications could. Although George Whitefield did not visit the westernmost parts of Virginia, his printed sermons did. One of the Scottish factors who bought tobacco from Hanover County farmers left a volume of the celebrated evangelist's sermons with some of his clients. Dissatisfied with the religious fare offered at Saint Paul's Church, a small group began meeting, first in homes, and then in "reading rooms" they constructed for the express purpose of reading Whitefield's and other evangelicals' works. Thus "printed sermons did the work of an itinerant with no minister present at all—only a group of literate laymen who experienced New Birth while reading them."[27]

Disturbed by the evangelicals' success, the clergy turned to civil magistrates for help. To shore up parish boundaries and curtail religious competition, the settled ministry invoked existing establishment laws and promoted additional ones to stop itinerants and their subversive sermons, whether preached or printed. As phrased by Virginia's governor William Gooch, the struggle between the settled ministry and the invading itinerants was one of the "rights of society" versus "freedom of speech." The former, Gooch argued, compelled him to "put an immediate stop to the devices and intrigues of these associated schismatics," as he called the itinerants and their followers. Itinerants disrupted social and religious order, attempting to draw "weak brethren" from the church by "railing against our religious establishment."[28]

Similarly, Connecticut ministers viewed itinerants as disrupting civil and religious order and moved swiftly to strengthen parish boundaries there. In 1742 the Assembly passed an act requiring itinerants to acquire state licenses and to refrain from going "into parishes immediately under the care of other ministers." The law's preamble claimed that prior to the arrival of the itinerants, the people of Connecticut had "enjoyed great peace and quietness" under the regulations contained within the Saybrook Platform (1708). The work of a synod that the General Court had convened for the purpose of "religious reformation," the Saybrook Platform called for a more regulated and tightly ordered religious market in Connecticut.[29] It was that good order that itinerants shattered, thus necessitating "An Act for regulating Abuses and correcting Disorders in Ecclesiastical Affairs." Confident that the existing religion taught within parish lines was adequate, the legislators sought to ensure that the people were not disturbed by those proclaiming a different "brand" of the gospel.

Two years later, itinerants continued to cross parish lines in Connecticut in direct violation of the law. One preacher who challenged the law was Benjamin Pomeroy, who maintained that the measure violated reason and the word of God. He declared that the state was guilty of religious persecution, and accused the magistrates of being "on the devil's side and enemies to the kingdom of Christ." He believed that he preached the true gospel, and that the New Testament commanded him to do so throughout the world, regardless of artificial boundaries such as parish lines. For his persistence, the Assembly indicted him, found him guilty, and fined him fifty pounds.[30] Pomeroy's insistence on a free and open religious marketplace met the legislators' equally determined resistance to any weakening of the regulated market they had constructed. For the moment, the state prevailed.

Even in Pennsylvania, where there was no establishment law to regulate religion, itinerants faced censure from the churches themselves. By 1716, Presbyterians had become so numerous in the Middle Colonies that they formed a synod overseeing the three presbyteries of Philadelphia, New Castle, and Long Island. That body attempted to strengthen both doctrinal purity and Presbyterian discipline among its member churches. But in 1738, a group of Pennsylvania evangelicals from Northern Ireland led a challenge that split the synod. William Tennent, three of his sons, and a handful of others began to insist on an "experimental" form of evangelicalism. By that term, they meant that "a definite experience of regeneration followed by assurance of salvation was the indispensable mark of a Christian." They believed that many of their ministerial colleagues had not themselves undergone a conversion experience and hence were unable to guide their parishioners toward a "New Birth." To train ministers in experimental evangelicalism, Tennent founded a seminary of his own, derisively referred to by his critics within the synod as the "Log College" because of its crude structure. Tennent and his followers split with the synod when a special committee demanded that ministers without university degrees must submit to a special examination of their doctrinal understanding. The Log College men refused to submit to such high-handed treatment and separated themselves from the body, eventually forming their own synod at New Brunswick.[31] The result was greater religious competition, this time within a single denomination.

Throughout the colonies in the 1740s, New Light itinerants and Old Light settled ministers who opposed them were locked in a competitive struggle. They contested each other's definition of "true" religion, while they vied for the loyalties of laymen and -women. At least initially, the advantage belonged to the newcomers. "Teachers of new religions," Adam Smith reasoned, pursued converts with industry and zeal, in part because of conviction and in part because of self-interest: they depended on voluntary contributions for their sustenance. On the other hand, clergymen of established systems were less able to make "any vigorous exertion" to defend their positions because, "reposing themselves upon their benefices, [they] had neglected to keep up the fervour of faith and devotion in the great body of the people." When new sects attacked the Church of England, the clergy were always quick to call upon the civil magistrates to defend its privileges. But, Smith concluded, the sects gained converts despite persecution because the "arts of popularity, all the arts of gaining proselytes, are constantly on the side of [the church's] adversaries."[32] It is debatable whether Smith's analysis would hold for all periods of history, but it did fit the American religious market in the mid–eighteenth century.

In the specific instance of the American colonies, Benjamin Franklin thought that the itinerant preachers had a competitive edge over the settled ministry. Facing their parishioners at regularly scheduled services, the latter had to compose one or two new sermons each week. The itinerants could preach the same sermons over and over to different audiences, improving their performance by "frequent Repetitions." According to the astute Franklin, "This is an Advantage itinerant Preachers have over those who are stationary: as the latter cannot well improve their Delivery of a Sermon by so many Rehearsals."[33] The ultimate judges of the competition between the revivalist itinerants and their critics were laymen and -women who listened to competing sermons and read competing books, and often reached conclusions that went well beyond what religious leaders desired.

To Charles Woodmason, Anglican minister along the South Carolina frontier, evangelical itinerants represented, at best, competition for the established church and, at worst, chaos. But for the men and women in the backcountry, they represented choice. Like the chapmen, tinkers, and hawkers peddling wares that made the settlers' lives easier or brighter, itinerant preachers brought colorful messages of hope, comfort, and encouragement and no doubt provided some with a moment of diversion. A merchant before he became a minister, Woodmason recognized that on the frontier he was operating in an unregulated religious market, and his success depended upon his wooing souls for the church. He knew that his listeners would weigh his claims against those of the many dissenters they heard, and would choose to follow the one who most appealed to them.[34] Woodmason saw the competition as formidable and unscrupulous. He reported that the "Synods of Pennsylvania and New England send out a Sett of Rambling fellows yearly," and he charged that "among this Medley of Religions—True Genuine Christianity is not to be found," claiming instead that the newcomers make "double the Profits I can make." He wrote, "If there is a Shilling to be got by a Wedding or Funeral, these Independent fellows will endeavor to pocket it," adding that "they beat any Medicinal Mountebank." He reported that whenever he gave notice "to be at such a place at such a Time [for preaching services], three or four of these Fellows [New Lights] are constantly at my Heels—They either get there before me, and hold forth—or after I have finish'd, or the next Day, or for days together." And the itinerants had success. Woodmason commented on how rapidly New Light Baptists advanced their cause in the backcountry. Referring to laymen and -women in the Carolina interior, he observed that "twelve months past most of these People were very zealous Members of our Church and many of them Communicants." But, he added, the New Lights have had "Success" and have made "rapid Progress."[35]

Though opposed to their practices, Woodmason admitted that the dissenters were an industrious lot, unlike Anglican parish ministers back in the eastern counties. Of the settled ministry, he observed, "none yet among them ever went out of his Parish, nay not even round his Parish to baptize." He said that he had "seen in Charlestown, Children brought to the font to be baptized, and the Minister put them off till another Day, because he was going to Dinner, or Tea, or Company." Woodmason saw a direct link between the clergy's lack of industry and what he observed on the frontier: "I must freely say, that it has been owing to the Inattention and Indolence of the Clergy, that the Sectaries have gain'd so much ground here."[36] He also believed that the vestry-controlled parish system was too rigid to respond to the fluid society along the fast-growing frontier. Within the Anglican polity, "ev'ry Minister has a Particular and distinc[t] Charge. He has a Circle assigned Him, in which He is to move and not stir out of. He cannot leave his Church for one Sunday without leave of the Vestry . . . under Pain of a Fine."[37] By contrast, dissenting itinerants went wherever they were in demand. Concurring with Woodmason's assessment, Thomas Jefferson noted that the Dissenting teachers' industry in propagating their views contrasted sharply with the established clergy's "inactivity." As a result, "the zeal and industry of sectarian preachers [gave them] an open and undisputed field."[38]

As revivalist itinerants and their opponents competed for souls, they swapped charges that the other side did not practice "true" Christianity. Opponents charged the roving evangelicals with being "enthusiasts," a pejorative term for those who based their religious claims on dubious assertions of direct divine revelation. In the view of defenders of orthodoxy, whether Congregational, Anglican, or Presbyterian, enthusiasts elevated their private judgments above Scripture. Revivalists countered that many, if not most, of the settled ministry were "unconverted" and, in the words of George Whitefield, knew "no more of true Christianity than did Mahomet."[39] Through such heated exchanges, rival religious leaders offered laymen and -women clear choices and a newfound power. By their choosing, they could determine the shape of a given congregation, presbytery, synod, or even entire sect or denomination.

"AS THO' THEY HAD THEIR RELIGION TO CHUSE"

The Great Awakening represented more than new religious competition introduced by innovating preachers. It also recognized the individual's primacy in the drama of salvation. One experienced the New Birth within himself or herself, outside of creeds or confessions or articles of faith. Emboldened by such personal experiences, thousands of men and women for the first time recognized that they, not their churches nor their pastors, could decide religious matters for themselves. While Protestants had always preached salvation by faith alone and the priesthood of the believer, the revivals drew out the "individualistic logic of Protestantism . . . further than ever before." The Awakening's central message encouraged people to "trust only in 'self-examination' and their own private judgments, even though 'your Neigbours growl against you and reproach you.' " Some New Lights went so far as to assert the "absolute Necessity for every Person to act singly . . . as if there was no another human Creature upon Earth."[40] One result was a loosening of the traditional bonds between individuals and the church, especially the established churches that opposed the Great Awakening.

The revivals reversed the roles of ministers and parishioners. For decades, dissenting ministers had preached "jeremiads," sermons lamenting the present generation's falling away from their forefathers' deep piety. They excoriated the laity for their lack of religious fervor. Evangelical itinerants agreed that religious decline was evident, but they blamed the clergy, not the laity. They claimed that few pastors had consistently and fervently preached the necessity of the "New Birth," and further, that many ministers themselves had never undergone a conversion experience. After their own conversions, many laymen and -women began to question their pastor's "brand" of religion and chose a competitor's offering.

Upon occasion the choice was made in dramatic confrontations between parish minister and revival itinerant. On Sunday, July 26, 1741, parishioners at Stonington, Connecticut, walked toward the meeting-house for morning worship as they and their ancestors had on each Sabbath since the town's founding in 1649. Their minister for the past thirty-seven years, Nathaniel Eells, was an orthodox, Harvard-educated pastor whose stated goal was "to promote the true Religion of the Holy Jesus, and hand it uncorrupt to succeeding Generations."[41] But as they approached the church on this particular Lord's Day, the townspeople divided; some filed into the meetinghouse as usual, while others veered off toward a spot on the village green "under the Trees" where an itinerant evangelist, John Davenport, was about to preach. A farmer, Joshua Hempstead, described in his diary what happened next. Out of curiosity aroused by extensive newspaper coverage, Hempstead had ridden from his nearby home in New London and joined the "great Number of hearers" standing expectantly around Davenport.[42] What struck him more than anything else about the unusual proceedings was that on this Sunday the people of Stonington had a choice between two different versions of the word of God.

While we do not have a record of Eells's sermon that day, we do know from his writings how he regarded the spiritual empiricism by which New Lights made one's conversion experience authoritative. He feared that "some in our Land look upon what are called *secret Impulses* upon their Minds, without due Regard to the *written Word*, [as] the Rule of their Conduct." He thought that the revival was in fact reviving the heresy of Antinomianism that had threatened the Puritan community a hundred years earlier. In a dramatic courtroom confrontation in 1636, Anne Hutchinson had claimed an immediate revelation as sufficient authority for disregarding certain biblical dictates.[43] Eells, as John Winthrop had before him, insisted that personal experiences must conform "to the pure Doctrines of the Gospel" and withstand "Arguments fetched from *Scripture* and *Reason*."[44]

We do know from Hempstead what Davenport preached that day. Directing his sermon at Eells's parishioners, Davenport assumed that most of the members had never undergone a spiritual conversion, thereby suggesting that the pastor's preaching had been misdirected and ineffective. Like other New Light preachers, Davenport first tried to shake the sense of security that church members had developed by virtue of being part of a covenanted community. He warned them that only the indwelling Spirit could save them through a divine act of regeneration, a New Birth. Having made them aware of their spiritual peril, Davenport then proceeded to provide assurance that conversion could come instantaneously, and that the convert could know for certain that he or she had been redeemed. The itinerant did not blame his audience for their lost condition; rather, he blamed Eells. While New Englanders were familiar with jeremiads, they were unaccustomed to attacks on their ministers. For an outsider to criticize an ordained minister who had been called by a gathered congregation to preach the word of God was to question the authority and integrity of the Congregational polity that had prevailed since the Puritan Fathers had settled the region. Nonetheless, Davenport pressed his case and was in Hempstead's opinion "Severe in Judging & Condemning Mr. Eells." The itinerant's message and manner appealed to some while repelling others, thus presenting the people of Stonington with a clear choice that Sunday. Hempstead witnessed the choices exercised: "many of the People in [Davenport's] Assembly withdrew into the meetinghouse where Mr. Eells preacht to them as he was wont to do & ye Rest Stayed by Mr. Davenport until ye Exercise was over."[45]

After listening to Davenport on several other occasions, Joshua Hempstead chose to remain within his New London congregation. In addition to hearing Davenport preach that day in Stonington, Hempstead continued to attend the itinerant's preaching services in and around New London, probably at the urging of one of his sons. However, his assessment of the evangelist's message and methods grew more negative. On Sunday, February 27, 1743, he attended one of Davenport's meetings and commented on the sermon: "it was Scarcely worth the hearing," and he complained, "the praying was without form or Comelyness. It was difficult to distinguish between his praying & preaching for it was all Confused Medley." Hempstead dismissed the sermon: "he had no Text nor Bible visable, no Doctrine, uses, nor Improvement nor anything else that was Regular."[46] In other words, when judged against the "plain style" sermons that Hempstead was accustomed to and preferred, Davenport's sermon fell short. Hempstead also disapproved of New Light exhorters after hearing a number at a meeting at New London in late 1742. Before the minister arrived for services, two young men, "Newlight Exhorters begun their meeting and 2 or 3 Women followed both at once and there was such medley that no one could understand Either part."[47] Preferring order to enthusiasm, Hempstead remained an Old Light, although at least one of his sons was a New Light.

Another Connecticut farmer, Nathan Cole from Kensington, gave a more positive assessment of the New Lights and made a different choice. His response to George Whitefield's preaching at Middletown stands in stark contrast to Hempstead's reaction to Davenport, and the difference has more to do with the individuals than with the itinerants. Hempstead listened with a critical ear that weighed Davenport's performance against a traditional standard and found Davenport wanting. Cole, on the other hand, described a powerful emotional, almost mystical experience in hearing Whitefield. Upon looking up at Whitefield standing above him on the scaffold built for the occasion, Cole said the evangelist "looked as if he was Cloathed with Authority from the Great God." Then when he preached, his words gave the farmer "a heart wound," because he began to think that he was not one of God's Elect. Indeed, when he went home that day, Cole was miserable. He wrote, "I was loaded with the guilt of Sin, I saw I was undone for ever; I carried Such a weight of Sin in my breast or mind, that it seemed to me as if I should sink into the ground every step." But later, "in the twinkling of an Eye, as quick as A flash of lightning" God appeared to him offering grace and forgiveness, and Cole said, "my burden was fallen off my mind; I was set free."[48] As a result of his conversion, Cole separated from the Congregational Church, became a lay exhorter who helped organize a Separate church in Kensington, and eventually joined the Baptist church.

One scholar has aptly called the Great Awakening and the religious competition it fostered the "Triumph of the Laity."[49] By exposing parishioners to a new message and new messengers, the revival gave laymen and -women new choices. Depending upon their preferences, Congregationalists could choose between Old Lights, advocates of the status quo, and New Lights, devotees of the new evangelicalism. Presbyterians could opt for Old Sides or New Sides. Alternatively, Protestants could leave the mainline denominations and join one of the splinter groups the revival spawned—say, a Separate or Baptist congregation or the fast-growing Methodist Church. With religion more voluntary than ever, ministers, many for the first time, had to woo members, and that in great part meant understanding that laypeople had specific beliefs and particular preferences regarding preaching and worship styles that could be ignored only at great peril.

The revival empowered those who experienced the New Birth, regardless of their gender, race, or class. Some converts became lay exhorters, delivering to public gatherings extemporaneous messages that often criticized "unconverted" ministers for not preaching the "one thing needful."

Opponents found particularly offensive the evangelical practice of encouraging "women, yea, girls to speak in the assemblies for religious
worship." Women, as well as slaves and lower-sort men, justified their
preaching by insisting that they were "moved by the Spirit" when they
urged others to rely only on God's grace for their salvation. Some women
went beyond exhorting in their own congregations and became "public
evangelists" who traveled from town to town as itinerant preachers. By
daring to preach from pulpits as well as from pews, some defied social
and religious traditions in their "diatribes against the temptations of
sin."[50] Such behavior offended the sensibilities of Old Light critic Charles
Chauncey, who cited the scriptural commandment "Let your women
keep silence in the churches" as sufficient condemnation of "FEMALE EX-
HORTERS."[51] Ebenezer Frothingham, pastor of a Separate Church at Weth-
ersfield in Connecticut, defended lay exhorting as justified by biblical law
even though it was opposed by human legislation. He accused the
"Courts of civil Justice" that upheld the ordained ministers' monopoly of
following the work of "Men's crafty Wisdom." Rather than recognizing
that God's Spirit knows no class boundaries, the judges determined that
"the poor Man is non-suited" to proclaim the word of God. According
to Frothingham, opponents of exhorters might prevail in corrupt courts
that upheld the established church, but the oppressors would one day
face "an impartial Court of eternal Equity and Righteousness."[52]

But, to critics, this new unregulated market in faith was chaotic, particularly where the revival had made significant inroads. Charles Woodmason was appalled at the religious scene in the Carolina backcountry in
the 1760s. The New Lights had made many converts along the frontier,
as itinerants found the men and women there to be receptive to their
extemporaneous sermons and the emotional services they conducted.
Woodmason could not understand why men and women preferred the
New Lights' "Wild Extempore Jargon, nauseaus to any Chaste or refin'd
Ear," to "our Solemn, Grave and Serious Sett Forms." Woodmason observed in horror one revival meeting at which the laity engaged in a
"thousand" extravagancies: singing, ranting, dancing, crying, laughing,
rejoicing, and so forth. For him such behavior represented a shocking
"Abuse of sacred Ordinances."[53]

Accustomed to a state church that controlled access to the ministry,
Woodmason was taken aback by the authority the laity accorded unedu-

cated, unordained preachers and lay exhorters. Each of the mainline de-nominations—the Congregationalists, the Anglicans, the Lutherans, and the Presbyterians—enforced strict guidelines concerning ordination, ad-mitting to the ministry only those deemed to qualify. But on the frontier, unlearned exhorters dared to proclaim the gospel to their audiences. He ridiculed "Ignorant Wretches" who disputed "Abstruse Theological Question[s]—Speculative Points—Abstracted Notions, and Scholastic Subtelties, such as the greatest Metaph[ys]icians and Learned Scholars never yet could define, or agree on."[54] Hand-wringing and sour grapes notwithstanding, clearly the huge crowds that flocked to the New Light services, as contrasted with the tiny gatherings at Anglican worship, sug-gested that the New Lights appealed much more to backcountry taste.

As an ordained Anglican priest, Woodmason believed that society was best served by a single established church that embodied and safeguarded "true" Christianity. The Bible, rightly interpreted by qualified teachers, was the sure guide to religious truth. What he saw on the frontier was a multitude of sects, with each congregation claiming that its beliefs and practices were preferable to all others. Woodmason described the prolif-eration of religious groups: they "Divide and Sub divide, Split into Par-ties—Rail at and excommunicate one another—Turn out of Meeting, and receive into another."[55] Rather than turning to a church hierarchy and its canon law scholars for guidance, frontier congregations based their claims to truth on individual experience. And the laity had the last word.

In contrast to Woodmason's denunciation of expanding choice in the backcountry, Baptist minister John Leland applauded the arrival of dis-senters on the Virginia frontier. He recorded that "west of the Blue Ridge, a number of Presbyterians emigrated from Pennsylvania, and did not chuse to worship in the Episcopal mode, but set up their own form of worship." Religious choice came at a high cost to the Presbyterians be-cause under Virginia law, they "were obliged to pay to the Episcopal Clergymen, as much as if they had been Episcopalian." Then, in the mid-1760s, Baptists began to spread throughout Virginia, their proliferation in part resulting from the work of ministers from northern states and in part rising from within "the South."[56] Baptists insisted on the right of each person to make his or her religious choices without any state coercion. According to Leland, "every man must give an account of himself to God, and therefore every man ought to be at liberty to serve God in that way that he can best reconcile it to his conscience." A free religious market-place was the Baptists' ideal. There, "religion is a matter between God and individuals: religious opinions of men not being the objects of civil government, nor any way under its control."[57]

Virginia Anglicans found themselves the object of successive waves of invading dissenters, each appealing to the "lower" and "middling" sorts with unconventional tactics. Presbyterian itinerants arrived in the mid-1740s at the invitation of the Hanover dissenters who had left Saint Paul Parish. Then, in the 1760s, Baptists came, followed in the 1770s by the Methodists. In each instance, the newcomers found men and women seeking spiritual nourishment unavailable in the gentry-controlled Anglican churches, where services were formal and appealed primarily to the literate planters who dominated the vestries. By contrast, the Dis-senting preachers whose sermons they read and heard appealed to the heart as well as to the head and insisted that religion was more than following a liturgy of little relevance to the parishioners' lives. Instead, New Lights talked about a "New Birth," a life-changing experience wherein one could know that he or she was saved. Moreover, New Lights called for a deeper commitment to practical piety, meaning that one's faith should be expressed in daily matters, infusing the most mundane chores with significance.

For more than one hundred years, religious instruction had proceeded from the "upper ranks, in whom knowledge was vested for safekeeping, to the lower, who were to receive it deferentially." But with Presbyterians, Baptists, and Methodists stirring up people to make their own choices regarding matters of faith, the traditional religious monopoly was re-placed by a competitive scramble for converts, with a variety of persons from all social ranks claiming that their religious views represented truth. One guardian of the old order, Robert Carter Nicholas, speculated about the outcome of such a licentious approach to religion: "Suppose . . . every Man was allowed . . . *Freedom of Judgment* . . . let all Men, think and speak and preach as they will, or rather, as they *can*; instead of that Uniformity of Doctrine which our Church has formerly been blessed with, what a Babel of Religions should we have amongst us?" He could not fathom the notion that individuals, regardless of education, would be allowed to make their own choices concerning religion. Surely, he thought, they ought to recognize that they can "rely with greater Safety upon the glorious Luminaries of our Church" for guidance rather than upon their own "private Preacher."[58] Thousands of Virginians, however, did in fact prefer their own "private Preachers." Consider the outdoor service in 1771 when two thousand Baptists gathered by a stream for a baptismal ceremony. An eyewitness described the emotional scene: "The multitude stood round weeping, but when we sang *Come we that love the lord* & they were so affected that they lifted up their hands and faces towards heaven and discovered such cheerful countenances in the midst of flowing tears as I had never seen before."[59] The appeal of such "heart-religion" weakened Virginia's religious establishment. If not in the eyes of the law, churches were in fact becoming voluntary associations whose membership and finances depended upon attracting new members, rather than resting upon any privileged position granted by the government.

The Great Awakening's greatest threat to Virginia's ruling class was its appeal to slaves. While the Anglican liturgy bore little resemblance to West African religious practices, the highly emotional Methodist and Baptist revivals gave blacks their "first experience with an emotional dimension of white religiosity." As one scholar of African American Christianity observed, "for the first time, [slaves] saw whites responding to a religious demand with the totality of their being and participating in religious trances, shouts, mourning, and rebirth," echoing themes rooted deeply in their own culture. When blacks turned out to revival services "in great numbers," slaveholders grew alarmed.[60] They could ill afford to have non-slaveholding whites and their own slaves embracing a religion that made individual choice its hallmark. Such a stance undermined church-state authority and threatened society itself.

Religious choice did not, however, mean that every person chose to embrace the evangelical message. Not every Virginian who heard or read New Light sermons opted to follow the evangelicals; some chose to remain within the Church of England. One couple, Jacob Moon and his wife, were appalled to learn that their friend and Anglican minister Devereux Jarratt had converted to Methodism. They scoffed at his "sudden fondness of 'the new light cant.' " The Moons insisted that "being Church people [Anglicans], . . . they . . . could listen to nothing but what came through that channel." While that statement suggests that the couple blindly followed the church's dictates, their decision to stay with the church was more than unquestioning loyalty; it was a considered choice.

It was in the Moons' house that Jarratt had found the volume of Whitefield's sermons that so influenced his faith and ministry. Noting the presence of the book in their home, one scholar concluded that "evidently the Moons had explored their religious options and decided to hold fast to their Anglican faith."[61] More important than the different choices that Jarratt and the Moons made is the fact that each considered religious options, and each selected the one that he or she deemed more personally suitable.

Despite several itinerants' attempts to preach the necessity of the New Birth to them, few Native Americans chose to become evangelicals. The most notable successes came from the preaching of Eleazor Wheelock, pastor at Lebanon, Connecticut, who undertook to instruct Indians in experimental Christianity. To further his evangelizing efforts, Wheelock organized an Indian School for educating young natives, but within a few years it attracted more English boys than natives. A small number of Indians, however, not only experienced the New Birth but became preachers themselves. Samson Occam, a Mohegan, was the best known, traveling throughout Long Island and New England preaching the New Light gospel. Most Indians, though, made a very different choice, opting to renew their commitment to their own religious traditions in what one historian has called the Indians' "Great Awakening." Fearing that many natives had sold their souls in their desire to purchase European goods, Indian spiritual leaders called on their people to repent and return to the faith of their fathers.[62]

By the end of the colonial period, the American religious landscape was dramatically different from that envisioned by the original planters. Consider Massachusetts. In the mid–seventeenth century, Congregationalists were able to preserve the purity of the "City upon a Hill" by accommodating those members who voiced minor disagreements with accepted beliefs and practices and removing those who persisted in major attacks on orthodox teachings and teachers. By the mid–eighteenth century, however, Boston was beginning to resemble pluralistic Philadelphia. In 1747, Timothy Cutler reported that "our religious congregations in this Town are 3 of them Episcopal, pretty large also, 10 large Independent congregations and 3 small congregations, one French, upon the Genevan model, one of Anabaptists, and another of Quakers." In addition, there were two more congregations derived from "the late humour of separation, one of independents and the other of Anabaptists." He thought that "Papists may be many but they are too conceal'd for me to give much account of them."[63] The Puritan ideal of religious uniformity was shattered. The hope had been for a single, truly reformed church, consisting of saints obedient to biblical precepts that governed their faith and practice. Now there was a "Medley of Religions."

When the revival first swept through the colonies, Church of England clergymen were caught off guard, ill-equipped to compete with the itinerants' no-holds-barred approach. Timothy Cutler's reports indicated that he and other parish priests were unprepared for the lay involvement in perpetuating the revival. After Whitefield had departed, the "popular fury" continued unabated, as "many illiterate Tradesmen are helping it forward, pretending a Call to the public exercise of their Gifts of Praying and Preaching."[64] Cutler reported in late 1743 that two Separate congregations had formed in Boston, the result of a decision by five hundred laymen and -women that their former ministers were not preaching the "true" word of God that the New Lights had introduced. He said that such splintering resulted from the "enthusiasm of the times." One group formed a Baptist congregation, "ordained an illiterate man for their teacher and at present meet in a private house, [and] several have already received immersion from him." The other group constituted themselves as a "separate independent Congregation." Cutler said they had "accommodated a barn for the purpose of their meeting, which is opened when a strolling exhorter comes among us, otherwise they meet in a private house."[65] Though Cutler ridiculed the new congregations' accommodations and teachers, he knew that they were part of a new religious market that had new rules or, from his perspective, no rules. Most disturbing was their disregard for the authority of the church and its ordained ministers.

Cutler and his colleagues slowly adapted and eventually found ways to compete. When the revival first erupted in New England in late 1740, they found themselves on the defensive. Itinerants, mass preaching services, and scores of religious books and pamphlets overwhelmed them. But then the clergy began to fight back. Cutler wrote the SPG in London, requesting books and pamphlets to counter those of the evangelicals.[66] Most important for the Anglicans, they discovered their competitive advantage and exploited it successfully. Cutler presented the church as an island of order in a stormy sea of enthusiastic disorder. He appealed to

"Sober People" to reflect on the popular fury that abounded and come to the Church of England. In early 1742, he expressed his confidence that "my Congregation with others of the Church, will be gainers in the long Run." By 1747, he could report some success. He reported that on a bitterly cold Christmas day his congregation "was crowded with Dissenters, I believe above three times in Number more than my own People." He attributed their coming to a preference for "quiet and order."[67] Cutler knew that the church would never appeal to the masses in New England, but he was confident that it would find a secure and important niche in the new competitive religious environment.

The Great Awakening represented more than competition for the settled ministry; it also had powerful political implications. The large number of New Lights swelled the ranks of dissenters who challenged traditional church-state relations, especially the establishment of the Congregational churches. In Connecticut, the most outspoken new dissenters were the Separates, representing perhaps as many as forty new congregations that had split from Old Light churches, numbering among their members some of the colony's most influential people. Many Separates left the Congregational fold altogether and became Baptists, erecting about sixty parishes by the end of the eighteenth century. Anglicans, also considered dissenters in Connecticut, benefited from their neighbors' disenchantment with all the squabbling over whether or not a revival had occurred, and if so, what it meant. All of the new groups—Separates, Baptists, Anglicans—"changed the relationship of dissenters to the Establishment." Before the Awakening, one who withdrew from the established church was stigmatized. Afterward, most parishes contained many individuals, prominent citizens among them, who were dissenters, and dissent thereby became more respectable.[68] As Separates and Baptists formed their own associations and Anglicans petitioned for a bishop, dissenters took on the character of denominations within the Protestant faith. However, those outside the establishment protested against what to them appeared to be state favoritism shown to the standing order, especially the requirement that all pay taxes to support the Congregational churches.

Dissenter protests against paying the church rate proved effective. Baptists who did not "believe in enforced religious contributions" were exempted from paying them, and Anglicans could apply their taxes to support their own ministers. However, the state continued to regulate the practice of religion in ways that dissenters found irksome. For instance, Anglicans objected to the provision that they could redirect their church tax revenues only if they lived close enough to a minister " 'conveniently' to attend worship." New Lights continued to oppose legislation regulating the activity of itinerants, forbidding anyone to preach outside his parish unless invited by another pastor. New Lights interpreted such interference by the civil authority as intent to "crush the work of God."[69]

The New Lights sparked a debate in Connecticut over fundamental church-state relations including the legitimacy of establishment. The magistrates defended their support of the standing order by asserting that as " 'nursing Fathers to the Church,' [they] were to promote godliness out of regard for the best interest of the people and to maintain order in the community." They predicted that the absence of state support would lead to collapse of religion, and one person predicted that "there would not be ('tis probable) one regular visible Church left subsisting in this Land *Fifty* Years hence." The New Light opposition to establishment was divided into a moderate and a radical wing. The Separates voiced the radical position on any civil support of religion by arguing that the Christian church stood solely on "the Revelation of Jesus Christ, and the Gospel Plan of Salvation," while society was bound by "the moral Law, and the Rule of Equity and Righteousness." Civil authorities had no jurisdiction in matters of faith because "Christ alone was governor of the church and judge of those who disobeyed the Gospel." Magistrates should confine themselves to punishing those who breach the moral and civil laws that bind men and women into a peaceful society. Moderate New Lights made a similar argument, though with less extreme language. One of their leaders, Solomon Williams, insisted that Christ "never directed any secular Force to be used either to maintain, or advance" his kingdom. Indeed, he added, civil force in religious matters only made "Men Hypocrites" and impeded the work of evangelism. "Compelled by the civil government to observe the external acts of religion," he reasoned, "men ceased to seek for the new birth."[70]

As a result of New Light political protest, the Connecticut establishment weakened between 1750 and 1765. In 1750, the legislature sympathized with New Light views and dropped the measure requiring itinerant preachers to be licensed. It also began to exempt Separate congregations from paying ecclesiastical taxes. Though the radical New Lights continued to push for a complete separation of church and state, the moderates welcomed the more tolerant climate within Connecticut, where, by 1765, the establishment "was neither an agency of social control nor a symbol of community coherence, but only the religion of the majority." With growing numbers of dissenters, the religious landscape took on the character of a free market with competing sects seeking new members through persuasion, not coercion. The result was mixed. On the one hand, the lively and spirited competition offered more choice to men and women, who could select among several different churches and choose the one that best suited their tastes and needs. On the other hand, increased competition was divisive, further fragmenting any sense of Christian community and unity. When ministers criticized each other, often in harsh tones, they lost some of the respect they had once enjoyed. As one lay critic stated, "Nothing sinks the Reputation of the Ministry more . . . than for them to revile and reproach each other. No wonder in that Case, if we of the Laity have a low Opinion of you, when you seem to have so very low an Opinion of yourselves." After 1765, the civil authority "was the sole institution binding society. The state was the symbol of social coherence, as once the Established churches had been."[71] Though Connecticut society boasted more churches and more religious services than ever before, the provincial government was more secular. While religious regulations remained on the law books, growing numbers of men and women insisted on making their own religious choices.

The Great Awakening was short-lived. It was over by the late 1740s, with the notable exception of Virginia, where it persisted into the 1760s and 1770s and exerted its most direct influence on the American Revolution. For individuals, the revival offered a "new 'liberal' sense of self by challenging ordinary Christians to make critical choices from among contending preachers, each of whom claimed to speak the word of truth." To many who chose the New Birth, that choice became an individual right to be exercised and defended, despite establishment laws regulating dissent. Accustomed to ministers operating within local religious monopolies, Connecticut Old Light Isaac Stiles denounced the "intrusion of choice into spiritual matters." He was appalled by New Light behavior, their acting "as tho' they had their Religion to chuse."[72] In choosing "their

Religion," New Lights exposed the difficulty of regulating religion in a pluralistic society where civil and religious authority was weak, certainly compared to that in England and Europe. While itinerants did not eradicate the parish system or overturn establishment laws, they introduced highly effective means for the growing number of sects to compete for souls. Ironically, within this more competitive marketplace of ideas intended to foster the spread of "true" religion, some very influential Americans embraced another set of ideas imported from Europe, a new, more secular view of the world that questioned Christianity itself.

❖ 6 ❖

Deists Enter the Religious Marketplace

A S A LEADING PRINTER and newspaper publisher, Benjamin Franklin played a major role in promoting the Great Awakening, all the while rejecting its message of the New Birth. He published several editions of George Whitefield's sermons and journals, making them bestsellers in colonial America. He gave the revival front-page coverage in his *Pennsylvania Gazette* and dispatched stories to the five other newspapers, from Boston to Charleston, in which he had a financial interest. But he had no use for the evangelical message. Franklin was a freethinker who preferred to follow the dictates of his own reason, not church dogma. Specifically, he found "the Eternal Decrees of God, Election, Reprobation" to be "unintelligible" and "doubtful." Those beliefs were at the heart of the Reformed wing of the Protestant faith and central to Whitefield's message. Despite their religious differences, Whitefield and Franklin became friends through their business relationship, and Whitefield sometimes stayed at Franklin's house when he was in Philadelphia. The evangelist constantly tried to get his printer to embrace the message of the New Birth, but to no avail. On one occasion when Franklin invited Whitefield to stay at his home, the itinerant replied that if Franklin "made that kind Offer for Christ's sake, [he] should not miss of a Reward." Franklin responded, *"Don't let me be mistaken; it was not for Christ's sake, but for your own."*[1]

Franklin subscribed to Deism, a religious perspective spawned by the Enlightenment, a European philosophy that emphasized reason over revelation as the best guide for human progress, and nature over Scripture as the clearest window onto God. Like Whitefield's revival, the deistic movement was a British import that appealed to many of the best-educated Americans. To Franklin and others, Deism offered a religious choice to those who could no longer follow the "corruptions" and "superstitions" of Christianity, especially the Calvinist brand that prevailed in America.

George Whitefield made clear what decision he hoped Americans would make when faced with that choice: his wish was that men and women would return to the faith of the Puritan Fathers. As he sailed toward the colonies on his first preaching journey in 1739, he identified his mission with that of such seventeenth-century New England Puritan divines as "the venerable [John] Cotton, [John] Norton, and [John] Elliot, and that great cloud of witnesses, which first crossed the Western ocean for the sake of the gospel, and faith once delivered to the saints."[2]

It soon became apparent, however, that some Americans were choosing Deism, the faith of the Enlightenment, rather than the faith of the Puritan Fathers. Jonathan Edwards, the revival's foremost theologian, singled out Deists as a particularly dangerous group, describing them as men and women who had

> Wholly cast off the Christian religion, and are professed infidels. They are not like the Heretics, Arians, Socinians, and others, who own the Scriptures to be the word of God, and hold the Christian religion to be the true religion, but only deny these and these fundamental doctrines of the Christian religion: they deny the whole Christian religion. Indeed they own the being of a God; but they deny that Christ was the son of God, and say he was a mere cheat; and so they say all the prophets and apostles were; and they deny the whole Scripture. They deny that any of it is the word of God. They deny any revealed religion, or any word of God at all; and say that God has given mankind no other light to walk by but their own reason.[3]

For Edwards, a doctrinal dispute among Christians was one thing—a thing that might even be termed heresy—but the Deist denial of Christian fundamentals was an altogether different and far more dangerous challenge. Deism represented a new kind of religious competition and a far greater peril than the customary sectarian rivalry. It offered an alternative to revealed religion.

Edwards would have been appalled had he lived long enough to see that many of the leading Founding Fathers who shaped the new republic of the United States of America were Deists. Coming of age in the years following the Great Awakening, and educated for the most part in the two decades preceding the American Revolution, these men all held in high regard works produced by the English Enlightenment's trinity of Francis Bacon, Isaac Newton, and John Locke, whose works were full of optimism that human beings through their own reason and observation could unlock the laws of nature and thereby control it for human good. Among the Founders who rejected the faith of their Puritan Fathers for the Enlightenment were Franklin, Thomas Jefferson, Thomas Paine, John Adams, Alexander Hamilton, James Madison, and John Jay, all of whom, with the exception of Franklin and Paine, attended college during the period 1755–1775. Indicative of their high regard for the Enlightenment was Jefferson's commissioning artist John Trumbull to paint the likenesses of Bacon, Locke, and Newton. He considered them to be "the three greatest men that have ever lived, without any exception, and as having laid the foundation of those superstructures which have been raised in the Physical and Moral Sciences." To give them the place of honor in his home, he wished to arrange their likenesses on "the same canvas, that they may not be confounded at all with the herd of other great men."[4] Jefferson and the other Founders relied heavily upon Enlightenment ideas to shape their views of religion and politics and the place and role of each in the new republic.

The significance of the Enlightenment and Deism for the birth of the American republic, and especially the relationship between church and state within it, can hardly be overstated. In brief, the United States was conceived not in an Age of Faith such as that of the Puritan Fathers but in an Age of Reason, a name given to the eighteenth century by the title of Thomas Paine's harsh critique of Christianity. Thus the Founding Fathers viewed issues of religion and politics through a prism that was very critical of Christianity's abuses, especially those perpetrated when political and religious leaders forged alliances in the joint names of Caesar and God to impose their will on the people. The Founders thought that people should be free to seek religious truth guided only by reason and the dictates of their consciences, and they determined that a secular state, supporting no religion but protecting all, best served that end. Under their guidance, America would not become a Christian republic in the sense that countries in the Mideast would become Islamic republics.

THE NEW LEARNING

Ezra Stiles attended Yale just one generation after his father Isaac, but the two men found very different intellectual worlds in New Haven. Ezra discovered in the Yale Library a whole new universe of ideas that undermined his confidence in his father's way of thinking. The New Learning was Newtonian science, a radically different way of viewing the universe, its creator, and human understanding. Reflecting on his father's education, Ezra wrote that "Newtonian Science had not passed the Atlantic then; and after its Arrival he [Isaac] had no Taste or Genius for more than a superficial Knowledge of it." Rather, he asserted, his father had read "the old Logic, Philosophy, and Metaphysics," though, insofar as he himself judged it to be "unintelligible," Ezra questioned how much of it his father could have understood. The fact is that Newton's works, along with those of other Enlightenment writers, had been on the Yale Library bookshelves when Isaac Stiles was a student. Through a donation by colonial agent and Yale benefactor Jeremiah Dummer (1681–1739), a collection of such books arrived in 1714, but "Yale was slow to absorb the new learning."[5] By contrast, Ezra Stiles and his generation of college students, which included many of the Founding Fathers, were quick to imbibe it. The result was a thorough critique of religious and moral thought in general and of Christianity in particular.[6]

For Ezra Stiles, the Yale Library was an intellectual window opening onto a new, exciting, wide world that both elucidated and challenged old beliefs. At the age of fifteen, this minister's son from North Haven, Connecticut, arrived at the New Haven college in 1742 secure in his Puritan beliefs. After all, they were anchored in truths revealed in Holy Scripture and manifested in nature. Four years before entering Yale, the boy had "calculated that God had made the world 5,700 years before. Looking at the great cliff of East Rock as he rode into New Haven, he could be sure the Deluge had washed over it exactly 4,032 years ago in the time of Noah." While his religious heritage gave him the confidence to decipher such mysteries as the age of the earth, it also engendered a degree of arrogance, perhaps no more or less than that of many other teenagers who see with clarity their parents' limitations. Writing sixteen years after his graduation from college, Ezra dismissed his father's scholarship: "He read much, but digested almost nothing." Stiles wrote, "His mind was stored with rich and valuable Ideas, but classed in no Order, like good Books thrown in Confusion in a Library Room."[7]

Ezra Stiles's characterization of his father's mind as disorderly was misleading and probably inaccurate. It was not true that Isaac Stiles failed to order ideas within a logical framework; rather, it is clear that he subscribed to a classification method that was very different from that preferred by his son. When the elder Stiles attended Yale in the early 1720s, Puritan orthodoxy was arranged in an orderly set of notions developed by French philosopher and logician Petrus Ramus (1515–1572). The Ramist system's underlying notion was that "everything in the world represents some idea in the mind of God." Ramists sought to discover those ideas, and Yale students like Samuel Johnson (1696–1772) kept notebooks meticulously classifying all knowledge into "innumerable divisions and subdivisions," which managed to "put the mind of God in 1,267 propositions." As has been noted, "the arrogance of such a system escaped its advocates."[8] Certainly it eluded Isaac Stiles. Graduating eight years after Johnson, the elder Stiles did not go to similar lengths in classifying the mind of God, but he expressed his views with similar dogmatic certainty. His son's generation would challenge that certainty.

During the Great Awakening, Yale was a revival center. By the end of the eighteenth century, however, it had become a seat of free thought in general and Deism in particular. Briefly enamored with Deism, Ezra Stiles for one returned to a tolerant, orthodox Calvinism, growing concerned about the new faith's erosion of Christianity, especially among college students. In 1759, he expressed alarm at how the New Learning had invaded America's colleges and how "Deism has got such Head in this Age of Licentious Liberty." The Enlightenment and Deism continued to pervade the academy at the end of the century. Writing from the perspective of the Second Great Awakening in the early nineteenth century, Lyman Beecher, minister and member of Yale's class of 1793, recalled that when he was a student, the "college was in a most ungodly state. . . .

That was the day of the infidelity of the Tom Paine school. Boys that dressed flax in the barn, as I used to, read Tom Paine and believed him. . . . Most of the class before me were infidels, and called each other Voltaire, Rousseau, D'Alembert."[9]

To appreciate the New Learning, one must first understand the "Old Learning." While from the beginning Harvard provided instruction in the arts, sciences, and literature and prepared students for law and medicine as well as the ministry, the emphasis was on theological education. It was a Puritan institution; as such, its tutors and professors taught students the received "truths" of Puritan divines. Scripture contained truth, but its messages were often hidden or obscure, and someone with a divine calling must "open" the Bible's proper meaning. A central goal of education for the Puritan Fathers, then, was to instruct students in biblical interpretation.

Another component of the "Old Learning" was instruction in right methodology, orthodox doctrine, and correct ecclesiastical polity. Biblical study alone was insufficient to build the "City upon a Hill." One must also study the doctrinal teachings of the giants of the faith who had systematically set forth the Bible's great truths. Puritans believed that God had given to some individuals the gift of discerning his word, and, therefore, they considered the great teachers to be authorities on matters of faith. Their "champions of the truth" inspired them to ask: "What worthy Ministers did that first age of the Reformed Churches yeeld? as *Luther, Calvin, Martin Bucer, Cranmer, Hooper, Ridley, Latymer,* &c. What a wonderfull measure of heavenly light did they of a sudden bring into the Church? and that out of the middest of darknesse and Popery."[10] However indebted the Puritans were to sixteenth-century reformers for ideas and inspiration, they maintained that it was not those mortals but God's word itself that was the "same schoolmaster" of true Christians of all ages. Their primary task as ministers, then, was that of expounding the word, and how to do that properly was the heart of the curriculum at Harvard and Yale in their formative years.[11]

To serve the truth, the Old Learning was dedicated to honing an intellectual sword that would slay all opposing claims, especially those advanced by papists. While Calvin's thought on such doctrines as the sovereignty of God, predestination, and limited atonement provided raw material for Puritan learning, it was insufficient. What was lacking was what English Puritan Richard Baxter called "method." He believed that "truth should be long studied and diligently elaborated, 'till it be concocted into a clear methodical understanding, and the Scheme or Analysis of it have left upon the soul its proper image, by an orderly and deep impression.' " Harvard and Yale students pored over Samuel Willard's *A Compleat Body*, New England's greatest effort in "method," in order to "organize and classify all doctrines methodically before they endeavored to write sermons." Other texts at Harvard and Yale that offered systematic, methodical exposition of all knowledge included William Ames's *Medulla Sacrae Theologiae* and John Wollebius's *The Abridgement of Christian Divinity*. Early in the eighteenth century, Cotton Mather recommended a new systematic work, Petro van Mastricht's *Theoretico-Practica Theologia*; within its thirteen hundred pages "the whole of Christian theology and morality, theory and practice, is laid out with a minuteness and precision that bring a hundred years of methodizing to a stupendous fulfillment."[12]

Thus, under the Old Learning, students recognized the absolute authority of the Bible as the sole repository of truth. Further, they accepted the need for a rigorous method to discern that truth. Answers to all life's great questions could be found in a methodical search of God's word. They were, then, totally dedicated to perpetuating the great traditions of their faith, believing that those traditions were ultimately rooted in the Covenant of Grace itself.

On the other hand, the "New Learning" taught students to doubt all authority, including that of the Bible and religious teachers. It introduced students to truths that lay outside the Scriptures and presented new methods for finding them. Each of Jefferson's "trinity" made a contribution that opened a new intellectual world for eighteenth-century American college students. Francis Bacon (1561–1626) outlined in the *Novum Organon* (1620) a new logic that challenged that of the Old Learning and its reliance on "abstract first principles," such as the eternal existence of God or the divine inspiration of the Bible. In his new method, Bacon insisted that arguments must proceed from "the concrete data of experience rather than *a priori* speculation." His system "proceeded inductively, scrutinizing physical phenomena, inferring probabilistic generalizations, experimentally testing and retesting these inferences against physical data, and then mathematically formulating the generalizations that held up as expressions of natural law." Bacon claimed that his was a method by which human beings could gain much more than abstract thought; they could "manipulate and control nature."[13]

Isaac Newton (1642–1727) gave Bacon's method its greatest endorsement through his observations and calculations that resulted in a systematic model for physical reality. Rejecting a priori notions of how the universe operated, Newton conducted an empirical investigation of the physical world, which "showed the material order to be explicable in terms of insurmountable and uniform natural laws." Rather than being locked in supernatural mysteries, the universe, according to Newton, was "eminently knowable because [it was] completely rational." Through his own observation, Newton had discovered the laws, such as gravity, by which nature operated, and he had expressed those laws mathematically. A religious man, Newton did not see his new science as supplanting God. Rather, he concluded that behind such a "clockwork universe" there had to be an "intelligent and powerful Being." Nevertheless, Newton grounded his cosmological argument for the existence of God, unlike those that had preceded him, on "a scientific foundation which the New Learning's adherents took to be as forceful as it was irrefutably clear."[14] Yet for many of Newton's followers, this bred a greater fascination with the architecture than with the "primordial Architect."

While Newton mapped nature's laws, John Locke (1632–1704) examined the power of human reason to understand those laws. His *Essay Concerning Human Understanding* (1690) began with the Baconian rejection of innate ideas, arguing instead that the human mind is a tabula rasa (a blank tablet) that absorbs information derived from the senses. It is from these simple impressions that all human knowledge is constructed and all generalizations made. Thus Locke concluded that human reason created knowledge out of the world itself, and that people should be wary of claims to sacred truths implanted on the human heart. However, like Newton, Locke was an orthodox member of the Church of England and, also like Newton, tried to fit Christian belief into his new system of thinking. He said that there were "genuine" instances of revelation, and that those revelations were "above" human reason. Nonetheless, in the hands of eighteenth-century students, the New Learning initiated by Bacon, Newton, and Locke constituted a "new standard of investigation" that rejected traditional methods and their conclusions, including many of Christianity's most treasured beliefs.

Almost without exception, the Founding Fathers were educated in the New Learning. This does not mean that they embraced an anti-Christian worldview, but it does mean that they analyzed political and religious questions using methods other than those taught by the church and based on the authority of Scripture. For example, James Otis, John Hancock, Joseph Warren, and John and Samuel Adams, leading radicals in the American Revolution, studied the political theory of Jean-Jacques Burlamaqui at Harvard. His *Principles of Natural Law* was the standard text when they were students. Burlamaqui defined what he meant by natural law: a law that God imposes on all men, and which they are able to discover and know by the sole light of reason. While God is the author of natural law, it is up to human beings to use their reason to study nature, including their own human nature, to discern it. Burlamaqui believed that reason was sufficient to enable human beings to infer from nature the existence and nature of God.[15] God then becomes "Nature's God," as Jefferson termed the deity in the Declaration of Independence, not the New Testament God. And natural law constituted the foundation of a just republic, defining individual rights and the limits of government.

SCIENCE AND RELIGION

Natural phenomena represented something very different to Puritan minister Increase Mather from what they represented to Benjamin Franklin. When lightning from a thunderstorm ignited fires that burned houses in seventeenth-century Boston, as it often did, the explanation was theological: indeed, God used "all nature for His own purposes." In one sense, Increase Mather had a scientific curiosity about the natural world that extended over a variety of events: "sea deliverances, preservations, thunder and lightning, magnetic variations, witchcraft, demonology, storms, earthquakes." His examination of such occurrences reflected two intentions: "to offer one level of explanation in terms of second causes, but also to insist that the Providence of God whether working through nature or outside its confines is ultimately inexplicable in this world." Stated differently, in all cases, Mather sought to "undermine the authority of scientific explanation of natural phenomena and to substitute the ancient sense of divine mystery in life."[16] Lightning was an awesome and frightful act of God whose devastation could be measured in terms of buildings burned and lives lost, but whose true purposes remained hidden in the divine Will. Good Puritans like Mather were far more concerned about the latter than the former. God could be sending a warning or meting out punishment through the frightful fire from heaven, and believers should pay heed to that message and probe its meaning through prayer and fasting.

But for Benjamin Franklin, lightning was a natural phenomenon that was worth studying for its own sake. When storm clouds gathered over eighteenth-century Philadelphia, Benjamin Franklin welcomed the opportunity to test his theory about the nature of lightning, namely, that bolts of lightning behaved the same as electrical currents. To test his theory, he proposed an experiment that would prove the identity of electricity and lightning. He constructed a kite by attaching silk onto a cedar frame, and at the top of the upright stick he placed a "very sharp pointed Wire, rising a Foot or more above the Wood." Then near the end of the string, close to the kite flyer's hand, he tied a metal key with a silk ribbon. He flew his kite when a "Thunder Gust" came on, standing in a doorway so that the silk ribbon stayed dry. Franklin described what would happen when the first thunderclouds came over the kite. "The pointed Wire will draw the Electric Fire from them," he reported, "and the Kite, with all the Twine, will be electrified." The wet kite and twine conducted the electricity. At the key, "Electric Fire" could be obtained and "all the other Electric Experiments be obtained . . . ; and thereby the *Sameness* of the Electric Matter with that of Lightning completely demonstrated." With that experiment, Franklin gained an international reputation; Joseph Priestley called his finding the greatest scientific discovery since the time of Newton.[17]

Franklin's experiment had immediate practical and theological implications. He had discovered a way to protect people from one of nature's greatest scourges: fires, caused by lightning, that destroyed homes and lives. His simple lightning rod, attached to the highest points of a house and grounded, attracted electrical charges during thunderstorms and conducted them through wires so that they passed harmlessly into the ground. Some persons around the world hailed Franklin as "a sort of demigod who had invaded the supernatural realm and by harnessing lightning had exercised a huge liberating control over nature." Franklin chose to interpret his discovery less dramatically. "It has pleased God in his Goodness to Mankind," he wrote, "at length to discover to them the Means of securing their Habitations and other Buildings from Mischief by Thunder and Lightning."[18] Thus, from his perspective, he had merely discovered the laws governing lightning and used them to benefit people.

Puritan divines had a very different interpretation, as John Adams reported from Boston shortly after graduating from Harvard in 1755. Born into the Puritan world but educated in that of the Enlightenment, Adams could assess both theological and scientific reactions. He applauded Franklin's experiments and viewed lightning rods as an important example of how scientific knowledge could benefit people. But many other Bostonians thought Franklin had interfered with God's own uses of nature. Many in the province, Adams wrote, "consider Thunder, and Lightning as well as Earthquakes, only as Judgments, Punishments, Warnings &c. and have no Conception of any Uses they can serve in Nature." He continued, "I have heard some Persons of the highest Rank among us, say, that they really thought the Erection of Iron Points, was an impious attempt to robb the almighty of his Thunder, to wrest the Bolt of Vengeance out of his Hand." Others maintained that Franklin's rods were foolish as well as impious. Adams added that no manner of evidence could convince those persons that lightning could indeed be controlled. In Adams's view, the opposition to the new scientific breakthrough came from "the superstition, affectation of Piety, and Jealousy of new Inventions, that Inoculation to prevent the Danger of the Small Pox, and all other usefull Discoveries, have met with in all ages of the World."[19] What the young graduate was trying to understand was nothing short of an intellectual upheaval, as two very different intellectual outlooks clashed over the biggest questions of the day, including those of God, nature, and humanity.

John Adams was a Harvard sophomore when he first encountered the excitement and tension that science created in Puritan New England. Science and theology offered two different explanations of the world and two different modes of understanding in the mid–eighteenth century, and John Adams discovered those differences under the tutelage of Edward

Wigglesworth, professor of divinity, and John Winthrop, professor of natural philosophy. Wigglesworth told his students that the new Newtonian math and science were all well and good, but the young men should remember that "God in His infinite wisdom had opened more than one road to knowledge." Specifically, he taught, one could learn through logic and through observation and experimentation. Logic, particularly Ramist logic, was the way that Christians extracted doctrine from Scripture. God revealed his great truths in the Bible, and he called certain people to unlock those truths through logic. Professor Winthrop, on the other hand, reminded Adams and his classmates that in the "apparatus chamber," or laboratory, doctrine or a priori propositions counted for naught: nothing was to be accepted on faith; all must be proven.[20] Winthrop would exercise the greater sway. Adams had entered Harvard with the intention of studying theology and becoming a minister, but, as James Madison would later discover at Princeton, the new possibilities for making the world a better place held greater appeal.

In the spring of his sophomore year, Adams encountered Locke as well as Newton. When he studied Locke's *Essay Concerning Human Understanding*, the book confirmed for him the truths he had discovered in Winthrop's apparatus room. While Newton insisted that one understands matter through observation and experimentation, Locke extended that notion to the human mind. Ideas, he argued, did not originate as inborn notions. Rather, they entered through the individual's experiences as sensory perceptions gathered from the world through observation. That notion changed Adams's intellectual world. From Locke, he learned that truth, including religious truth, was not defined by how passionately one held onto preconceived ideas or those handed down by authorities; it must be tested by experience and reason. For John Adams, such thinking contradicted what he had been taught back in his hometown of Braintree. His uncle Ebenezer, elder in the local congregation, was certain in his beliefs, but he did not base his theological notions on experience or reason; he simply accepted them as they had been handed down, and he insisted that his nephew do the same. But when John returned to Braintree, he and his uncle, for the first time ever, took opposite positions on an important religious matter. John learned that his uncle had led a movement to oust the local minister, Lemuel Briant, for preaching free will instead of determinism. In what amounted to an intellectual declaration of independence, John told his uncle and his father, who also opposed Briant, that he supported the minister and agreed with his opposition to Calvinism.[21] No longer was he willing to accept as truth the assertions of others, including family elders and religious leaders. Adams would determine truth through his own experience and reason.

For Adams and other Founders, the Enlightenment offered optimistic possibilities. While Calvinism and most Christian dogma split intellectual hairs over unimportant issues such as predestination and sanctification, the Enlightenment buoyed the Founders' beliefs that human beings had the means and power to shape their own futures. Franklin could barely contain his delight in present and anticipated scientific discoveries. "The rapid Progress *true* Science now makes," he wrote, "occasions my regretting sometimes that I was born too soon." He envisioned a bright future:

> It is impossible to imagine the Height to which may be carried, in a thousand years, the Power of Man over Matter. We may perhaps learn to deprive large Masses of their Gravity, and give them absolute Levity, for the sake of easy Transport. Agriculture may diminish its Labor and double its Produce; all Diseases may by sure means be prevented or cured, not excepting even that of Old Age, and our Lives lengthened at pleasure even beyond the antediluvian Standard.

He added his hope that "moral Science" could improve in a similar fashion, that "Men would cease to be Wolves to one another, and that human Beings would at length learn what they now improperly call Humanity!"[22]

Like Franklin, Jefferson was buoyed by the prospects of science. By the end of the eighteenth century, Jefferson had concluded that the human mind was "perfectible to a degree of which we cannot as yet form any conception." As he contemplated the future, he could only imagine the "immensity in every branch of science" that would be discovered. The key for advances depended upon a free society: "for as long as we may think as we will and speak as we think, the condition of man will proceed in improvement." He warned against those "despots" in religion and politics who want to preserve tradition, who believe that "it is not probable that anything better will be discovered than what was known to our fathers."[23] To Jefferson, the past was the past, and history's heavy hand, whether that of the Puritan Fathers or the Hanover monarchy, should not restrain the present and the future.

The unintended consequence of Isaac Newton's investigation of natural laws was the questioning of faith in revealed religion in general and Christianity in particular. The challenge came in the form of natural religion and moral rationalism. The former emanated from the idea that written into the laws of nature are laws governing human conduct that are discernible through right reasoning. While insisting that a Supreme Being created the world and the laws by which it operates, devotees of natural religion denied a personal God who interfered with those laws in order to alter the course of human history. According to the English minister William Wollaston, whose works gained favor at Harvard, God created things, including human nature, *"to be as they are,"* and the moral person orders his life in accordance with "the law of Reason." That law, not divine revelation, is the sure guide to moral conduct. In *The Religion of Nature Delineated* (1722), he concluded that *"If there be moral good and evil, distinguished as before, there is religion; and such as may most properly be styled natural."* He clarified what he meant by "religion." It was no more or less than to do "what ought not to be omitted, and to *forbear* what ought not to be done."[24]

While natural religion was theistic, clearly the focus was on human beings. Even the existence of God was a reasonable proposition rather than a revealed truth. In Wollaston's understanding, "Reason discovers that this visible world must owe its existence to some invisible Almighty being." God, then, is a necessary cause, *"for the universe could not produce itself."*[25] While God is the First Cause, man is responsible for and capable of finding his true happiness. True to Newtonian science, the search for individual happiness begins with observation and experimentation. That is, each person discovers through reflection and experience "what his own abilities, passions, &c. truly are." He alone "has the *internal* knowledge of himself" sufficient to bring his conduct into conformity with his true nature.[26] In short, humans save themselves.

At the center of natural religion then was moral rationalism, or ethics. The concern was not dogma or right belief or scriptural tenets, but behavior. And it was the shift from theology to ethics that would make the New Learning most threatening to orthodox Christianity, certainly that held by eighteenth-century Calvinists. At the heart of Calvinism was the notion that God's grace, not good works, was the means of salvation. Now the Enlightenment boldly put the focus on human acts and dismissed as abstractions or superstitions ideas that God somehow "saved" people. In constructing their "Christian Common-wealth," the Puritan Fathers had been guided by Christian principles, more specifically, those of the Calvinist turn. Now many of the most influential men who would become the Founding Fathers became severe critics of the Puritans' most cherished beliefs, including that of God's central role in shaping the course of human existence.

FOUNDERS AND "TRUE" RELIGION

As a young man, Benjamin Franklin had become disenchanted with the church. Religiously educated as a Presbyterian, he found "some of the Dogmas of that Persuasion" to be geared more toward keeping clergy-men in power than toward helping their parishioners become better moral creatures. Accordingly, he "early absented [himself] from the Public Assemblies of the Sect," but he did not ignore religion. Indeed, through-out his life, he considered himself to be a person with "religious Princi-ples," although they were those of his choosing, not those of any particu-lar religion, including Christianity. He approached religion and morality with the same empirical methodology that he followed in his scientific experiments. In his well-known quest for "moral perfection," he identified thirteen virtues that he determined to make habitual in his life through a systematic, disciplined approach. Though he was tripped up by his at-tempts to master the virtue of "order," Franklin said that he was a better person for having pursued the scheme. Later, when he drafted his reli-gious creed, he made morality, not theology, the centerpiece of a good life. Indeed, he could not embrace the central Christian tenet of Jesus' divinity. He stated his position in a reply to Ezra Stiles's request for his religious views:

> As to Jesus of Nazareth, my Opinion of whom you particularly de-sire, I think the System of Morals and his Religion, as he left them to us, the best the World ever saw or is likely to see; but I apprehend it has received various corrupting Changes, and I have, with most of the present Dissenters in England, some Doubts as to his Divinity; tho' it is a question I do not dogmatize upon, having never studied

it, and think it needless to busy myself with it now, when I expect soon an Opportunity of knowing the Truth with less Trouble.[27]

Similarly, Thomas Jefferson questioned many of Christianity's central beliefs and became a Deist, and he differentiated between what he considered to be the moral teachings of Jesus and Christians' corruptions of those teachings. In response to Benjamin Rush's inquiry regarding his religious principles, Jefferson responded, "I am a Christian, in the only sense in which [Jesus] wished any one to be; sincerely attached to his doctrines, in preference to all others; ascribing to himself every *human* excellence; and believing he never claimed any other." But because Jesus wrote nothing himself, his teachings, like those of Socrates, have been corrupted by his followers. The Bible, then, far from containing divine truth, is a mixture of sound moral instruction and errors and superstitions, and one must discard everything in Scripture that does not conform to reason and natural law. When he was president, Jefferson "edited" the Bible to rid it of all corruptions. He discarded the entire Old Testament because much of it reflected a supernaturalism that mocked the laws of nature, and because the god it revealed was an angry, spiteful, vengeful deity: just the opposite of the rational being displayed by nature. Similarly, he stripped the New Testament of all accounts of miracles and supernatural tales, leaving only the moral teachings attributed to Jesus. Jefferson's "Bible" reflected his confidence in his own reason and his belief that nature pointed to divine truth.[28] Further, like Franklin, Jefferson denied the divinity of Jesus, maintaining that zealous disciples, not Jesus, made that claim.[29]

Influenced by the New Learning, Franklin and Jefferson refused to accept religious truth, including that of orthodox Christianity, as handed down by divines or as trumpeted in Scripture. They insisted on determining with the aid of their own reason what was true. John Adams remembered clearly the moment of his declaration of religious independence from his Puritan family. Writing in the early nineteenth century, to illustrate his opposition to blind faith, Adams recalled the day he broke with his father and his uncle over Lemuel Briant. He remembered Briant as a "jolly jocular and liberal Schollar and Divine," one whose mind was open and supple, ready to accept the reasonable and to reject whatever was unreasonable regardless of its authoritative standing within Christendom. Adams contrasted Briant with his Latin schoolmaster, Joseph Cleverly, who accepted Puritan precepts as timeless truth and was guided by doctrinal purity. Adams remembered that Briant and Cleverly often disputed issues of religion and government. In one such debate, when Cleverly had been "more than commonly fanatical," the teacher declared that "if he were a Monark, He *would have but one Religion in his Dominions.*" The parson replied, "Cleverly! You would be the best Man in the World, if You had no Religion."[30] Adams's point was that there were many Christians like Cleverly, whose blind acceptance of religion resulted in dogmatism and bigotry.

Of the Founders whose pens advanced the cause of independence and freedom, none embraced a Deism as radical as Thomas Paine's. He had grown up in the Quaker faith, but by the time of the American Revolution, he had begun to question all authority, whether civil or religious. It was he who had made the case in *Common Sense* that the American colonists suffered oppression, not just because George III was a bad king, but because a monarch governed them at all. While such a radical political idea made him a champion of civil liberty, his later work *The Age of Reason* made him for many the spokesman for atheism. In fact, though very critical of Christianity and the author of an extreme expression of Deism, Paine was not an atheist. He began his profession of faith by averring, "I believe in one God, and no more." While declaring himself a theist, he refused to accept the teachings of any religion: "I do not believe in the creed professed by the Jewish church, by the Roman church, by the Greek church, by the Turkish church, by the Protestant church, nor by any church that I know of. My own mind is my own church." He thought that all religions, including Christianity, called on individuals to suspend their rational powers and accept on faith what leaders insisted were divine revelations. Paine wrote that "Each of those churches shows certain books, which they call revelation, or the Word of God. The Jews say that their Word of God was given by God to Moses face to face; the Christians say, that their Word of God came by divine inspiration; and the Turks say, that their Word of God (the Koran) was brought by an angel from heaven. Each of those churches accuses the others of unbelief; and, for my own part, I disbelieve them all."[31]

Certainly not all of the Founding Fathers became Deists, and fewer still were as radical as Paine. Most did not even publicize their views. Many, if not most, found it easy to integrate their "New Learning" and their confidence in scientific inquiry with Christianity. They believed that the Creator was benevolent, and that science confirmed their faith in his goodness by elucidating more about nature's marvels. To Orthodox Calvinists, however, the encroachment of the New Learning was insidious. Evangelicals during the Great Awakening singled out Deism, a term that contemporaries identified with a host of attacks on orthodoxy, as a dangerous set of propositions circulating in the eighteenth-century marketplace of ideas. Relying on human reason's direct grasp of "natural religion," Deists conceived of God as a "Creator or First Cause who subsequently stood aside from his creation to allow it to run according to its own rules."[32] But to evangelicals, a far more insidious enemy of Reformed theology came in the cloak of moderate Churchmen like Archbishop John Tillotson. One of the most often cited indications of Tillotson's place in the colonies is Virginia planter William Byrd's comment that he often read one of the archbishop's sermons in lieu of attending services at the parish church.[33] In emphasizing the reasonableness of Christianity, he and other latitudinarians, according to their critics, "at least played into the hands of the Deists."[34] Tillotson's printed sermons circulated widely in eighteenth-century America, especially among the "better sorts" in colonial society.

To his critics, Tillotson's latitudinarian and reasonable approach to Christianity enervated Calvinist theology. Stressing God's mercy rather than his wrath, Tillotson conceived of the deity in natural terms, viewing his connection with humanity as akin to a father's love for his children. From that perspective the archbishop found no place for such doctrines as that of predestination, whereby some were relegated to hell by a whimsical god:

> I am as certain that this doctrine cannot be of God as I am sure that God is good and just, because this [doctrine] grates upon the notion that mankind have of goodness and justice. This is that which no man would do, and therefore cannot be believed of infinite Goodness. If an apostle, or an angel from heaven, teach any doctrine which plainly overthrows the goodness and justice of God, let him be accursed. For every man hath a greater assurance that God is good and just than he can have of any subtle speculations about predestination and the decrees of God.[35]

Many Orthodox Calvinists feared that such soothing notions of God's goodness lulled sinners into a false sense of security. Awakeners charged Tillotson with making hell seem benign, and with emphasizing good works instead of God's grace.

Thomas Jefferson also thought that good behavior was more important than right belief. To him, morality was paramount to doctrine, and he thought that a moral society need not be a Christian one. He argued that morality was the essential mortar that bound people together and separated civilized peoples from barbarians, and that there were many sources of morality, including an innate moral sense. David Hume, one of the leading philosophers of the Scottish Enlightenment, shaped Jefferson's and Madison's understanding of how people of many faiths, as well as those unaffiliated with any religious tradition, could find a moral center. Jefferson believed that the Creator had endowed all persons with a moral compass, with a "sense of right and wrong." Moreover, he regarded this sense as being as "much a part of his nature as the sense of hearing, seeing, feeling, it is the true foundation of morality." Such a perspective placed Jefferson and those who shared his viewpoint at odds with orthodox Christianity, which held that divine revelation, correctly interpreted, not human conscience, was the only sure moral guide. According to most Christian ministers of the day, original sin rendered the conscience unreliable. Jefferson contended that the conscience, or moral sense, was not only intact; it was as "much a part of man as his leg or arm." He did think that, like the mind, the moral sense "may be strengthened by exercise, as may any particular limb of the body." However, he believed that while the moral sense was guided by reason, very little thought was required to guide it aright. "State a moral case to a ploughman and a professor," he reasoned, and "the former will decide it as well, and often better than the latter, because he has not been led astray by artificial rules."[36]

Jefferson believed that reason, not revelation, was the path to true religion. He warned his nephew Peter Carr to beware of sectarian claims that a particular group had discovered the one teaching that set them apart from all others as the one true faith. He also urged Carr to "shake off all the fears and servile prejudices under which weak minds are servilely crouched." In other words, do not let fear cloud independent judgment in the search for religious truth; conduct your own investigation.

He urged Carr to "fix reason firmly in her seat, and call to her tribunal every fact, every opinion." Do not depend upon the bible, upon the church, upon ministers. All of those are filled with a mixture of superstition and truth, prejudice and perspicacity. He counseled his nephew to question every religious claim, including the existence of God and the veracity of the Bible. Indeed, he should read the Bible as he would any other book, subjecting it to a rigorous assessment: "those facts in the bible which contradict the laws of nature, must be examined with more care, and under a variety of faces." Always consider the author and his motives: "here you must recur to the pretensions of the writer to inspiration from god. Examine upon what evidence his pretensions are founded, and whether that evidence is so strong as that it's [sic] falshood would be more improbable than a change of the laws of nature in the case he relates." His final advice was that his nephew base religious belief on observation, not popularity, using his own knowledge to test biblical claims instead of assuming that something is true because millions accept it.[37]

The Enlightenment and Deism did not make the Founders irreligious, nor did it make most of them anti-Christian. But the new ideas caused them to question much of orthodox Christianity, especially in colonies that had established a particular church. Certainly Franklin, Adams, Jefferson, Paine, Madison, Hamilton, and Jay were unwilling to submit to the authority of any church's clergy, nor were they willing to accept uncritically the Bible as God's word. They treasured religious liberty more than they valued any religious view because they believed that if minds were free, then the truth would eventually surface.

It was at that point that the interests of the Founding Fathers converged with those of evangelicals. Though guided by different lights, followers of the Enlightenment and the New Light insisted that the individual must be free in matters of faith. George Whitefield never accepted Benjamin Franklin's rationalist ideas about religion, nor did Franklin embrace Whitefield's claim that only God's grace could "save" him. But for all their differences, devotees of the Great Awakening and the Enlightenment had much in common, and both played important roles in transforming religion in colonial America. Each emphasized the individual as a maker of religious choices. For evangelicals, it was individual experience, not church doctrine or tradition, that mattered most in the drama of salvation. For Enlightenment devotees, it was individual reason that discovered the laws of nature and society, thus giving humans control over their own destinies, perhaps to the point of attaining moral perfection. Both revivalists and rationalists opposed church-state arrangements that promoted religious uniformity, on the grounds that religious truth transcended official pronouncements. Their converging interests played an important role in moving America from the "City upon a Hill" to separation of church and state. In the second half of the eighteenth century, these strange bedfellows would cooperate in the quest for unfettered religious liberty. And both came to see civil liberty as essential to religious freedom.

CHAPTER

❖ 7 ❖

Whigs and Dissenters Fight
Religious Regulation

THE VAST MAJORITY of Americans transformed by the Great Awakening and the Enlightenment agreed on one thing: religious tyranny and priestcraft must be rooted out of church and state. They believed that the individual, not the state or the church, should decide matters of faith. New Lights from the Great Awakening challenged religious authority of churches and pastors by insisting that a personal conversion experience, not subscription to creeds and hierarchies, was the path to salvation. Many of those New Lights lived in colonies with establishment churches, and they resented state-enforced religious regulation; by their practices of ignoring parish boundaries and taking their message directly to the people, they weakened the grip of official religions. The Enlightenment also shed new light on church-state relations. Armed solely with the light of their own reason, those who subscribed to its tenets questioned the authority of churches and their leaders, and, going beyond the awakeners, some challenged core beliefs of Christianity itself.

One of the many ironies of the struggle for religious liberty in colonial America is that the religious toleration that Americans already enjoyed surpassed that of most other people in the world. Even in Puritan Massachusetts, by the early eighteenth century, Quakers and Baptists were exempted from paying taxes to support the established churches. Perhaps because they enjoyed a great deal of freedom, dissidents wanted more. They were close enough to a complete freedom of conscience that any regulation, no matter how mild, rankled and rekindled a desire for unfet-tered liberty. Thus when the established church, or the Church of En-gland, sought to expand its influence to even those areas where it was not established, Dissenters reacted swiftly and vociferously.

In several instances during the 1750s and 1760s, American Whigs and Dissenters rose up against local threats to religious freedom. Dissenters had long resented paying taxes to support churches whose beliefs and practices they found repugnant. And they had chafed under restrictions imposed by establishment laws, such as those licensing preachers. At mid-century, new expressions of power raised the specter of even greater con-trol for the established church at the expense of Dissenters' freedom. In New York, Anglican leaders tried to put the new King's College under the sole governance of the Church of England despite the fact that the school would be supported by public funds. In Virginia, Anglican clergy-men petitioned George II's Privy Council to set aside a measure passed by the House of Burgesses regulating clerical salaries, drawing from ves-trymen charges of religious and political tyranny. And in Massachusetts, ministers of the established Congregational churches, also known as the Standing Order, found themselves facing an aggressive Anglican invasion that threatened to install the Church of England as the new established church in New England. After successfully fending off that attack, the Standing Order faced a new threat as Separate Baptists opposed an estab-lished church of any sort.

In resisting these threats to religious freedom, Americans embraced a radical political ideology that had existed in England for more than a hundred years and in the colonies for about fifty. At the core of Radical Whig ideology was the call for unfettered freedom—freedom of the press, religious freedom, political freedom, and the like—and a belief that the surest way to guarantee freedom was for virtuous citizens to check power concentrated in the court and church. These republican notions provided a framework for Americans to interpret what they perceived to be encroachments on their liberties, especially religious freedom. By invoking Whig ideas, American Dissenters tied religious freedom to civil liberty, viewing establishment laws and the official churches they created and protected as abridgments of natural rights.

New Light evangelicals and rationalist proponents of the Enlighten-ment could not have been further apart in their views of religious truth, but their common passion for freedom of conscience brought them to-gether as allies in the struggle for religious freedom. The former believed that God revealed himself most fully in the New Testament, and that the Almighty was a personal God who continued to redeem individuals through Jesus' salvific sacrifice. The latter believed that God revealed him-self most fully in nature, and that people ought to use their reason to discover the truths of natural religion. Where the two converged was at the point of religious liberty. Both insisted that all persons should be free to follow their religious beliefs wherever they led with no outside interference.

Whig and Dissenting Traditions

During and immediately after the English civil war, fought in the middle of the seventeenth century, there emerged a radical political perspective that called for an extension of political liberty far beyond anything envi-sioned by the Puritan Parliament that had challenged Charles I. Men like Algernon Sidney, James Harrington, and John Milton urged in their extensive writings that the civil war be a true revolution to rid En-glishmen of all artificial restraints imposed by church and state. No one made the case for freedom more eloquently than did Milton, whose 1644 *Areopagitica* remains a classic in defense of liberty of the press. A Puritan, he wrote it to protest a 1643 parliamentary order requiring government approval and licensure of published books; the order was aimed especially at religious views that questioned the authority of the Church of England. Milton argued for the free circulation of ideas, including religious notions currently deemed heretical, and opposed censorship that would place government officials in the position to "make 'em and cut 'em out what religion ye please." Besides, he claimed, censorship would not stop the flow of ideas; it would just send them underground. Better to allow a free, unregulated public exchange through which the truth would win out. "What can be more fair than when a man judicious, learned, and of a conscience, for aught we know, as good as theirs that taught us what we know," he asked, shall "publish to the world what his opinion is, what his reasons [are], and . . . [demonstrate] wherefore that which is now thought cannot be sound?"[1] In such an atmosphere, one does not worry about error and blasphemy because these will be exposed, challenged, and eliminated forthwith in the unhindered jostle of ideas.

Milton envisioned a free marketplace of ideas with the entire nation involved in the unregulated production and consumption of knowledge. Such a place would be a beehive of truth seeking where reason, not coercion, would prevail:

> Behold now this vast City: a city of refuge, the mansion house of liberty, encompassed and surrounded with His protection; the shop of war hath not there more anvils and hammers waking [i.e., making noise], to fashion out the plates and instruments of armed Justice in defence of beleaguered Truth, than there be pens and heads there, sitting by their studious lamps, musing, searching, revolving new notions and ideas wherewith to present, as with their homage and their fealty, the approaching Reformation: others as fast reading, trying all things, assenting to the force of reason and convincement. What could a man require more from a Nation so pliant and so prone to seek after knowledge? What wants there to such a towardly and pregnant soil, but wise and faithful labourers, to make a knowing people, a Nation of Prophets of Sages, and of Worthies?[2]

Milton called on his countrymen to "join, and unite in one general and brotherly search after Truth" and to "forego this prelatical tradition of crowding free consciences and Christian liberties into canons and precepts of men." Truth needed no state protection: "For who knows not that Truth is strong, next to the Almighty? She needs no policies, nor stratagems, nor licensings to make her victorious; those are the shifts and the defences that error uses against her power. Give her but room."[3]

But alas, with the Restoration of the Stuarts in 1660, the crown, not a Miltonian free marketplace of ideas, defined religious "truth" in England. The year before, Milton had published his plea for Parliament to recognize religious freedom for all English men and women. His title encapsulated his argument: *A Treatise on Civil Power in Ecclesiastical Causes Shewing That it is not Lawfull for any Power on Earth to Compell in Matters of Religion.*[4] The Restoration Parliament, however, wasted no time in compelling in matters of religion, imposing such measures as the Test Act and the Conventicle Act to restrict Dissenters' freedom of worship. Once again, religion followed the crown, and with the accession of the Catholic James II in 1685, that entailed the prospect of England's reverting to Catholicism.

It was that grave threat that inspired a new generation of writers to recast the ideas of Milton and other champions of religious and civil liberty. No one was more persuasive than John Locke, whose 1785 treatise, *A Letter Concerning Toleration*, a radical call for religious freedom, was aimed at church leaders as well as state officials. He realized that church and state maintained an unholy alliance, with each side seeking advantage from the association. Backed by state coercion, the Church of England kept Dissenters out of places of influence including the faculties of Oxford and Cambridge. And by defending the church, the crown secured the support of powerful clergy and the landed gentry, who were predominantly Churchmen. Locke opened his treatise by addressing the clergy, declaring toleration the "chief characteristic of the true Church." The business of religion, he argued, was not obtaining "ecclesiastical dominion, nor . . . exercising . . . compulsive force, but . . . regulating men's lives, according to the rules of virtue and piety."[5]

Turning to civil magistrates, Locke argued that church and state are wholly separate. He wrote, "all the power of civil government relates only to men's civil interests, is confined to the care of the things of this world, and hath nothing to do with the world to come." That means, he added, that neither the state nor any person therein can deprive another of "his civil enjoyments because he is of another church or religion." Here Locke made the case for the broadest toleration, one that extends to all persons, including those outside the Christian faith. Neither church nor state has the right "to invade the civil rights and worldly goods of each other upon pretence of religion"; or, stated more bluntly, "no violence or injury is to be offered him, whether he be Christian or Pagan."[6] Though too radical for the crown in seventeenth-century England, Locke's ideas would find a warm reception in eighteenth-century America, where religious pluralism and weak establishment laws stimulated the growth of a free marketplace of religious ideas, where persuasion, not power, would reign.

Though a Whig triumph, the Glorious Revolution of 1689 did not result in complete religious freedom for all Englishmen. While Parliament granted broad religious toleration, this did not mean freedom from state regulation. And as long as the state retained a voice in religious matters, Dissenters faced the prospect of persecution at the hands of an unsympathetic court. That continued threat prompted yet another generation of Radical Whigs to speak out against concentrated power that endangered English civil and religious freedoms. Most English politicians at the time considered themselves to be Whigs in that they supported parliamentary supremacy and religious toleration. But some, like John Trenchard and Thomas Gordon, believed that parliamentary supremacy itself did not safeguard liberty, especially when Robert Walpole, George II's prime minister from 1721 to 1742, used patronage as a tool for building a powerful political machine. Trenchard and Gordon sympathized with the Opposition, who charged the ministry and its hordes of placemen with being far more concerned with maintaining their own power than with protecting the liberties of English citizens. The Opposition claimed that the engines of power—high taxes and a standing army—undermined property, the foundation of independence and liberty. A featured theme in the Radical Whig critique was a demand for religious freedom, especially from state-imposed regulations that restricted Dissenters' activities.

Between 1720 and 1723, Trenchard and Gordon published weekly essays that would have enormous influence on America's Founding Fathers. Soon after appearing in a London newspaper, the essays were collected and published as a single volume entitled *Cato's Letters*, perhaps the greatest distillation of Radical Whig ideas. Like Milton and Locke, Trenchard and Gordon argued that religious liberty rested on separation of church and state. Their underlying premise was that where government was a man-made institution, religion was "a Relation between God and our own Souls only." No state currently in existence, they maintained, owed its "Formation or Beginning to the immediate Revelation of God, or can derive its Existence from such Revelation." Quite to the contrary, all governments were "established by the Wisdom and Force of mere Men, and by the Concurrence of Means and Causes evidently human." Therefore, states have power only over what "Men can give"; they have no jurisdiction over matters pertaining to God. "Every Man's Religion is his own," they wrote, "nor can the Religion of any Man ... be the Religion of another Man, unless he also chooses it." In other words, like Locke, they argued that religion is voluntary, not compulsory, and therefore "excludes all Force, Power, or Government." Further, "Religion can never come without Conviction, nor can Conviction come from Civil Authority; Religion, which is the Fear of God, cannot be subject to Power, which is the Fear of Man." The conclusion, then, according to Trenchard and Gordon, was self-evident: "Religion . . . can never be subject to the Jurisdiction of another," including, and especially, the state.[7]

Works of the Radical Whigs quickly found their way to the American colonies and, in the words of historian Bernard Bailyn, "from the earliest years of the [eighteenth] century . . . nourished [the colonists'] political thought and sensibilities."[8] Eleven months after the first of *Cato's Letters* appeared in London, colonial newspapermen began reprinting them. James Franklin published excerpts of the letters in his *New England Courant* before the end of 1722, and his brother Benjamin worked them into his *Silence Dogood* papers of 1722 and 1723. In *Silence Dogood*, No. 9, of July 23, 1722, Franklin addressed the question of whether religion makes officeholders more or less effective in executing their duties. At either end of a spectrum, he considered on the one hand "hypocritical Pretenders to Religion" and on the other the "openly Profane." Franklin considered the hypocrite to be the more dangerous in public office. First, he argued, the hypocrite was able through a "few savoury Expressions" of his religious beliefs and moral concerns to obtain among the voters an "Opinion of his Goodness," especially in a land "noted for the Purity of Religion." By satisfying those who put him in office with a steady stream of pious words, the hypocrite "every day deceives his betters, and makes them the Ignorant Trumpeters of his supposed Godliness: They take him for a Saint, and pass him for one, without considering that they are . . . the Instruments of publick Mischief out of Conscience, and ruin their Country for God's sake."[9] While Franklin's argument was consistent with that often expressed in Puritan New England—a godly country must have godly rulers—it went beyond the customary warning to suggest that religious talk itself was grounds for voters' suspicion.

Franklin warned that power corrupts the religious officeholder just as it does the irreligious. Further, he argued that when combined at court, religion and politics represented a particularly insidious danger to liberty. He noted that "*a little Religion, and a little Honesty, goes a great way in Courts*," meaning that they win enough confidence to mask the evil designs of a "Religious Man in Power." Franklin cautioned New Englanders to judge office-seekers, not by their pious words, but by their honest behavior, lest they be deceived. To support his contention that some politicians used religion to gain and wield power, Franklin cited one of Gordon and Trenchard's "Cato" entries in the *London Journal* that had appeared just ten months earlier. In that issue, Cato had addressed the question of religion as a guise of designing politicians, noting how many "set up for wonderful pious Persons, while they were defying Almighty God, and plundering Men." The occasion for their outrage was the notorious South Sea Bubble, a securities fraud wherein a group of stockjobbers, with the backing of some unscrupulous members of Parliament, won the public trust and promoted a highly speculative venture that promised great wealth to those who bought shares in the South Seas Company. After fostering a mania that rocketed the shares' price to dizzying heights, the insiders, who knew the venture was more hype than substance, dumped their holdings at a profit, leaving the unsuspecting public with stock that plummeted when the "bubble" burst. Gordon and Trenchard pointed out that the public had trusted the members of Parliament who had backed the scheme and had thought the company's directors to be *"great and worthy Persons,"* an evaluation based in part on an assessment of their religious reputations. The conclusion that Gordon and Trenchard drew, and Franklin echoed, was that in determining who should run government, persons should keep religion and politics separate. Voters should not entrust political power to persons professing certain religious beliefs; rather, they urged, "we must judge of Men by the whole of their Conduct, and the Effects of it."[10]

WARNING AGAINST "SPIRITUAL DIRECTORS"

Events in the middle decades of the eighteenth century gave poignancy to Radical Whig ideas for many Americans who believed that their religious freedom was threatened. In a series of local, scattered, and uncoordinated instances, Anglican clergymen sought to extend their power and influence. These episodes exposed and strengthened a virulent anticlericalism, no doubt heightened by the Great Awakening's attack on "unconverted Ministers" and the Enlightenment's charge that the clergy had corrupted Christian principles by violating both reason and Scripture. When the clergy were Anglicans, the protests took on political as well as religious hues, especially when the clergy appealed to Whitehall for royal support. In defending their religious liberty against overreaching clergy, Americans in all regions found that Radical Whig ideas best framed their argument that state-supported clergy undermined liberty of conscience and should be opposed.

In New York the issue that evoked protest was religious instruction. Anglican leaders proposed the establishment of a college whose governing board would consist solely of members of the Church of England, whose professor of divinity would be Anglican, and whose religious services would subscribe to the Book of Common Prayer. In other words, the new King's College would look very much like the other colleges in colonial America in that it would be affiliated with one particular Protestant church: Harvard and Yale were Congregational institutions, William and Mary was Anglican, and Princeton was Presbyterian. New York, however, was a much more pluralistic colony, with Dutch Reformed, Presbyterians, Huguenots, Baptists, Quakers, Catholics, and Jews living and worshiping alongside Anglicans. Thus when the organizers petitioned the New York Assembly to support the college with public funds, they set off a wave of protests that opposed not only the college's religious slant but the establishment of religion itself. Leading the opposition was William Livingston (1723–1790), a lawyer and a member of one of the dominant political families of New York. The Yale graduate published his views in a newspaper he founded, *The Independent Reflector or Weekly Essays on Sundry Important Subjects More particularly adapted to the Province of New-York*. The title itself suggests that Livingston was greatly influenced by the *Independent Whig*, a work by John Trenchard and Thomas Gordon dedicated to exposing violations of civil and religious liberty. Published throughout 1752 and 1753, the *Independent Reflector* raised the ire of those defending religious establishment while boosting the confidence of those seeking true religious liberty.

In the first issue, published on November 30, 1752, Livingston stated his intentions. He vowed to vindicate the *"civil and religious RIGHTS"* of all people and to expose the various corruptions and oppressions that threatened those rights. He said that "the Espousing of any polemic Debate between different Sects of Christians, shall be the last Charge against him; tho' he shall be ever ready to deliver his Sentiments on the Abuses and Encroachments of any, with the Freedom and Unconcerned-ness becoming Truth and Independency."[11] Though nominally a Presbyterian, Livingston viewed himself as an independent Christian who was not wed to any creed other than his own. To declare his independence from "our spiritual Directors," as he termed the clergy, Livingston published his creed, expressing his belief in the Old and New Testaments, but "without any foreign Comments, or human Explications but my own." He believed that the clergy through the years and in the present obscured biblical truths, and he roundly criticized ministers and those who blindly followed them. "I believe," he wrote, "there is no Merit in pretending to believe what is impossible to be believed; and that Mysteries, tho' not incredible, are incomprehensible, and that whoever attempts to explain or illustrate them, proves himself an illustrious Blockhead." He believed that Christianity was not the church, and that "a Man may be a good Christian, tho' he be of no Sect in Christendom." And he believed that religion was voluntary and, as such, should be advanced solely by reasonable persuasion without the state's having any power or voice in religious matters: "I Believe, that to defend the Christian Religion is one Thing, and to knock a Man in the Head for being of a different, is another Thing."[12]

Given those views, it is not surprising that Livingston led the opposition against putting King's College on an Anglican footing. Having criticized the organizers in several essays for their proposal, he set forth his own plan on April 19, 1753. He held that "no Person of any Protestant Denomination be, on Account of his religious Persuasion, disqualified for sustaining any Office in the College." He believed that students ought to attend daily prayer services because such exercises "will have a strong Tendency to preserve a due Decorum, Good Manners and Virtue amongst them," and besides, "they will be thereby forced from the Bed of Sloth." However, he opposed any set prayer that "would be a discrimination Badge," reflecting his fear that prayers offered under the guise of a "Christian" prayer would in fact be one favoring a particular church or sect. Lest professors stamp their own theological biases on the "tender Minds" of the students, he further proposed that "Divinity be no Part of the public Exercises of the College," and that the corporation be prohibited from hiring a divinity professor. The college ought to exist only to confer degrees in "the Arts, Physic, and the Civil Law." If a student wished to prepare for the ministry, he could do so "by a Study of the Scriptures, and the best Divinity Books in the College Library, as well without as with the Aid of a Professor." He concluded by warning that if the college became a seminary of the Church of England, then it would be the "Nursery of Bigotry and Superstition.—An Engine of Persecution, Slavery and Oppression.—A Fountain whose putrid and infectious Streams will overflow the Land, and poison all our Enjoyments."[13] Livingston's challenge was the first in American history to call for public colleges and schools to be "if not secular at least nondenominational."[14]

For Livingston, the question of public support of religion, especially a particular church, raised the issue of whether religious establishment of any sort had a place in a free society. He made his position clear in a two-part essay entitled "The Absurdity of the civil Magistrate's interfering in Matters of Religion." His opening sentence declared that "Mankind being naturally free, and with respect to a Right of Dominion, upon a perfect Equality; it is absurd to suppose, that any Man, or Body of Men, would ever have consented to resign and Controul of another, but for some Advantages they expected from such Submission." Government, Livingston contended, "was instituted for the Establishment and Preservation of our civil Interests" and possesses no "Right to interfere in Matters of Religious Belief." He argued that when government does interfere through any sort of religious establishment, then learning and reason suffer. "The Advancement of Learning," he declared, "depends upon the free Exercise of Thought." He concluded by appealing to history: "whenever Men have suffered their Consciences to be enslaved by their Superiors, and taken their Religion upon Trust, the World has been over-run with Superstition, and held in Fetters by a tyrannizing Juncto of civil and ecclesiastical Plunderers."[15]

Livingston's attacks on religious establishment and the clergy prompted a spirited counterattack from Anglican sponsors of the college. Led by Samuel Johnson, who would become the institution's first president, Anglican clergymen charged Livingston with proposing to make the New York college "a sort of free-thinking latitudinarian seminary."[16] They insisted on the necessity of a "Church-college," while at the same time assuring Dissenters that their religious freedom was not endangered—an assurance that had a hollow ring when the clergymen implied the Church of England's superiority by denying that any "perfect Equality" existed among religious sects. And thus the battle lines were drawn. On the one hand, the Anglicans wished to perpetuate higher education as it had been long practiced, instituted under the authority and governance of one branch of the Christian church and dedicated to teaching the principles of that church. On the other hand, Livingston and his supporters wished to make colleges secular institutions. He wrote, "a public Academy is, or ought to be a mere civil Institution, and cannot with any tolerable Propriety be monopolized by any religious Sect." Further, he added, public colleges ought to be "entirely political, and calculated for the Benefit of Society, as a Society, without any Intention to teach Religion, which is the Province of the Pulpit."[17]

As with many of the Founding Fathers, Livingston's religious views were tinged with a strong anticlericalism. In particular, he opposed the clergy on two grounds: first, that they represented as truth their own inventions, and second, that they acted more out of self-interest than from concern for the truth. Livingston maintained that clergymen in every branch of the church engaged in "ecclesiastical Trumpery." That is, "They all claim to be orthodox, and yet all differ from one another, and each is ready to damn all the Rest." In his opinion, an independent thinker would not find among the ministers of any of the Christian denominations "a candid Inquirer after Truth."[18] By placing sectarian doctrine above the search for truth, the clergy acted out of self-interest rather than the common good, thus violating the Radical Whig understanding of virtue.

In the end, the New York Assembly decided that King's College should be chartered as a nonsectarian institution, but under Anglican control. The colony's pluralism as well as Livingston's arguments no doubt influenced the legislators to stop short of making the college a thoroughgoing "Church-school" in the Church of England mold. By the end of the American Revolution, the college, renamed Columbia College, had almost completely severed ties with its Anglican origins.

Shortly after Livingston challenged the Anglican clergymen's complete control over King's College, Patrick Henry, another figure who would play a prominent role in the American Revolution, dramatically confronted the Virginia clergy. The issues were money and power, specifically clerical salaries and who had the right to determine them. From Virginia's settlement, the Church of England had been the established church, and the provincial government had levied taxes to support its clergy. Because of a shortage in specie, payment had been made in tobacco, and from 1662 until 1755, clerical salaries had varied with market prices. Then, in 1755, the legislature passed the so-called Two-Penny Act, fixing the clergy's income on the basis of a twopence-per-pound tobacco rate. Though the Assembly reenacted the measure in 1758, the Privy Council disallowed the act the following year. As a result, the clergy initiated lawsuits against their respective vestries demanding back salaries, thus beginning what was known as the Parsons Cause, which divided the clergy and laity. For their part, clergymen believed that their appeal to the Privy Council was a legitimate plea for justice. The vestrymen, however, viewed the matter as the crown's unwarranted intrusion into Virginia's church-state relations. If the monarch could arbitrarily set aside measures Virginians deemed necessary for their church, then there was no freedom of religion. And, by voiding their legislation, Whitehall weakened the burgesses' ability to lead, thus lessening their political influence with their constituents. In a hierarchical society, those at the top could not afford to be made to look weak.

The most celebrated case in the Parsons Cause transformed the dispute over the Two-Penny Act into one of the opening salvos in the American Revolution. Reverend James Maury of Louisa County, the same person who had protested the "invasion" of evangelical itinerants, brought suit in the county court against the tax collectors. In hopes of improving his chances, Maury had his case heard in nearby Hanover County, where the Louisa vestry's political influence was weaker, but the change of venue also meant that the jury would likely include more Dissenters: Hanover was the center of Virginia's Great Awakening. The case was heard in November 1763 by the presiding judge, Colonel John Henry, who ruled that the Two-Penny Act was null and void from its enactment. This meant that the only question for the jury to decide was the amount of back salary due Maury, supposedly the difference between the market price of his tobacco allotment and the twopence per pound he had actually received.[19]

Representing the vestry was a young lawyer, Patrick Henry, whose fiery defense sounded very much like the evangelists of the Great Awakening. Henry was from a prominent Anglican family in Hanover County; his father, the judge, was a vestryman at the Hanover Church, and his uncle, the Reverend Patrick Henry, was rector at Saint Paul's Church in

Hanover County. This case, then, was very much an affair played out within a family with close ties to the church. Jury selection was the first order of business and perhaps the most important. Young Patrick succeeded in placing on the jury at least three "New Lights," Dissenters who had left his uncle's church in pursuit of a more evangelical, experiential faith. Maury later described the men as part of the "vulgar herd" rather than people of wealth and social position. He also thought that they were anything but impartial, desiring nothing so much as to undermine the Anglican establishment by attacking the clergy.[20]

Patrick Henry's performance was dramatic and brilliant. He appealed to the jurors much as the itinerant Samuel Davies attracted them, with his fiery sermons that stressed individual freedom. Davies had assured Virginia New Lights that salvation came from God's free grace, not from a church or clergy more interested in maintaining their own position than in saving souls. Henry sounded a similar theme, but this time representing the king as the one subverting Virginians' freedom by disallowing an act passed by the people's own representatives. Henry asked, "Who was the ruler in the great Colony of Virginia? Was it the King, an alien across the seas, whose dominion too often was only misrule? Or was it the Burgesses, the direct representatives of the people of Virginia?" He then chose the metaphor of king-as-father to make his point: "If the King was the father of his subjects, what sort of father was this who denounced a law so needful to the welfare of the common man? If a father betray his children, they owe him no allegiance, and no obedience if he be a tyrant." With that, Maury's counsel, Peter Lyons, sprang to his feet shouting, "This man has spoken treason!"[21] Treason or not, Henry had transformed what had begun as a matter between a clergyman and his vestry into the classic Whig confrontation of power and liberty.

But Henry was not finished. He next linked the clergy with the king, tarring them both with the same brush of greed and corruption. "We have heard a great deal about the benevolence and holy zeal of our reverend Clergy," he told the jury, "but how is this manifested? Do they manifest their zeal in the cause of religion and humanity by practicing the mild and benevolent precepts of the Gospel of Jesus? Do they feed the hungry and clothe the naked? Oh, no, gentlemen. Instead of feeding the hungry and clothing the naked, these rapacious harpies would, were their power equal to their will, snatch from the hearth of the honest parishioner his last hoe-cake, from the widow and her orphan children her last milch-cow, the last bed—nay, the last blanket, from the lying-in woman!" With that, Henry made himself champion of the Dissenters. He appealed to the jury to take a stand for freedom against tyranny from a distant king and from the established clergy. The jurors got the message and awarded Maury a settlement of one penny.[22] As Livingston had done in New York, Patrick Henry had successfully linked the assertion of clerical power with religious tyranny. The verdict indicated that the jury shared his concern that the Anglican rectors had improperly manipulated political power by appealing to the crown and convincing the Privy Council to set aside a Virginia legislative proposal.

While the episodes in New York and Virginia were separate, local affairs and did not coalesce into a concerted fight for religious liberty, they did reflect important commonalities. First, they were both sparked by real or perceived attempts by the Church of England to exercise greater power in the colonies. In New York, the church sought sole control of King's College; in Virginia, the church's clergy enlisted royal power to loosen the laity's control of religious affairs. Second, in each instance, Livingston and Henry invoked the same Whig principles in checking the church, casting the contests in terms of concentrated power versus individual liberty. Considered by themselves, these events did not ignite revolution, but they provided important dress rehearsals. When the British provided the colonies with a set of common grievances following the French and Indian War, these local fights for religious freedom would fuse, and revolutionary leaders would discover to their delight that they had been reading the same Whig writers and thus spoke the same language in fighting for civil and religious liberty.

Dissent against the Standing Order

Anticlericalism was important to the way Americans would eventually determine church-state relations. Individuals emboldened by the Great Awakening and the Enlightenment were no longer willing to defer to ministers in religious matters. Moreover, growing pluralism meant that no one church could possibly speak for all Protestants. But even more significant for the place of religion in America than anticlericalism was disestablishmentarianism. Although establishment laws rested lightly on Americans' shoulders, in comparison to those in Europe, increasingly colonists grew restive under religious establishment. In the mid-1700s, two dramatic confrontations between different Protestant groups revealed the difficulties established churches faced and the value outsiders placed on religious liberty.

In the early 1760s, a print war in New England pitted advocates of England's established church, the Church of England, against supporters of New England's establishment, the Congregational churches. The background to the war was an Anglican challenge to the Congregational establishment that proceeded from the assumption that no such establishment existed, because Massachusetts and Connecticut were royal colonies, and the royal establishment was the Church of England. Through an aggressive missionary offensive, Anglicans sought to extend the church's influence where Dissenters, which was the Anglican designation for all Protestants outside the Church of England, had dominated from early settlement. To strengthen their position, the missionaries called on the king and the archbishop of Canterbury to appoint a resident bishop for America, a move many New Englanders interpreted as an exercise in tyranny, a bold first step in supplanting Congregational churches with the Church of England.

Reverend East Apthorp, the SPG missionary at Cambridge, Massachusetts, fired the opening salvo by publishing a pamphlet declaring that the society's primary mission was to provide spiritual nourishment for English citizens of New England, not to evangelize Indians as the Congregationalists had thought. Before the ensuing war ended, almost a dozen authors had joined the fray. To Jonathan Mayhew, the leader who first responded to Apthorp's expansive view of the SPG's mission, the issue at stake was nothing less than religious liberty. If allowed to alter its charter at will, invade parishes of the established Congregational churches, and woo disaffected persons to their churches, then the society could, with help from the archbishop and the crown, succeed in their long-standing goal of securing the appointment of an American bishop who would preside over an Anglican religious uniformity.

Pastor of the West-Church in Boston, Mayhew insisted that the controversy was not about religious liberty, if that term was defined as "the natural and legal right which protestants of all denominations have, in any part of His Majesty's dominions, to worship God in their own way respectively, without molestation." Because New England Puritans had been accused of denying religious freedom to those dissenting from the Congregational churches, Mayhew wanted to emphasize that the current debate was not about *individual* liberty of conscience. Nor, he added, was it about "whether any person . . . have a right, considered in their private capacity, if they think it expedient, to encourage and propagate episcopacy in America, by transmitting money to build churches here, to support missions and schools, or the like. Whatever our sentiments may be about the church of England, we are not so vain as to assume a right of dictating to them the manner in which they shall, or shall not bestow their charity; or in any sort to controul." In short, *private* religious beliefs and practices were not at issue. The question as Mayhew saw it was "Whether the planting Episcopal churches, supporting missions and schools, &c. in certain parts of America, particularly in New-England, in the manner, and under the circumstances in which this has been, and still is done by the Society, is conformable to the true design of their institution, according to their charter; or a deviation therefrom, and consequently a misapplication of their fund."[23] The actions that concerned him were not those of conscientious individuals who believed differently from him, but those of an ambitious, even parasitic, well-financed organization that had the backing of the Church of England and the British monarchy.

To demonstrate that the SPG was in fact moving beyond the authority granted it by its charter, Mayhew first reviewed the history of religion in New England. His purpose was to show that the Congregational churches had always provided orthodox instruction in the Protestant faith, and, therefore, there was no need for Anglican missionaries to work in their midst. It was well known, he asserted, that "the first settlers of New-England were such as came hither chiefly on account of their sufferings for non-conformity to the church of England. They fled hither as to an asylum from Episcopal persecution, seconded by royal power." Second, he declared that "It is no less certain that these refugees were very far from being persons of a loose, irreligious character"; they had suffered much for their religious principles at the hands of the church sponsoring the SPG. And, he added, "It is well known that they very early made provision for the public worship of God, and founded a seminary of learning, which has been encreasing and flourishing to the present time." He concluded by noting that in the established churches of Massachusetts and Connecticut, "the doctrines almost universally professed . . . are and ever have been, very agreeable to the doctrinal articles of the church of England."[24] In light of the past and present state of religion in New England, Mayhew saw no grounds for the SPG to invade Congregational church parishes other than to establish a religious beachhead from which they intended to impose their own religious uniformity.

Underlying Mayhew's argument was the assumption that orthodox Protestant Christianity was already established in New England, and that the presence of the Anglicans was unnecessary and, therefore, signaled something sinister. He claimed that "the people of New-England, particularly in those two principal governments of it [Massachusetts and Connecticut], are all in general professed Christians." He added that "there is no such monster as an *Atheist* known amongst us; hardly any such person as a *Deist*. And as to the superstitions and idolatries of the church of Rome, there neither is, nor has been the least danger of their gaining ground in New-England. The Congregationalists and Presbyterians are known to hold them *at least* in as great abhorrence as the Episcopalians do." In other words, the existing establishment was as effective in keeping out heretics as the Church of England could be. And, contrary to what Apthorp suggested about irreligious conduct, Mayhew averred, "as to practical religion tho' we have no cause for boasting, yet, to say the least, we have no cause for blushing on a comparison of our morals with those of the people in England, in the communion of that church."[25] Protestant faith and piety thrived in New England, and, Mayhew concluded, the Anglicans could add nothing but confusion through competition.

Of course, denominational differences did matter, and that is why Apthorp and Mayhew contested the issue of establishment so hotly. Each believed that his church represented orthodoxy, and that the other's embraced heterodoxy. In his polemic, Mayhew indicated that the invading Anglicans were not agents of the "true" church, a claim that he made for the Congregationalists: "When we consider the real constitution of the church of England; and how aliene her mode of worship is from the simplicity of the gospel, and the apostolic times: When we consider her enormous hierarchy, ascending by various gradations from the dirt to the skies. . . ." By contrast, the purpose of the Puritans from the initial settlement of Massachusetts Bay had been "that of serving the cause of truth and righteousness, of pure and undefiled religion in America; in distinction from all private party-opinions whatsoever."[26] Apthorp countered by asserting that because of the SPG's efforts, "in many respects the Religious State of it [this Country] is manifestly improved." Moreover, he added, the Anglican missionaries had begun to reverse the ill effects of Puritanism: "Religion no longer wears among us that savage and gloomy appearance, with which Superstition had terribly arrayed her: its speculative doctrines are freed from those senseless horrors with which Fanaticism had perverted them; Hypocrisy has worn off in proportion as men have seen the *beauty of Holiness*."[27] Neither Mayhew nor Apthorp was willing to concede that the other's faith expressed "true" Christianity and could thus be trusted as an established church.

Beyond exchanging polemics, Apthorp and Mayhew agreed that the underlying issue in their debate was, despite protestations to the contrary, religious liberty. Apthorp maintained that his purpose was to protect freedom of conscience by exterminating that "monster Persecution" which in Puritan New England had been "the temper and practice of the age."[28] The Church of England, unlike the Congregational churches, would put in place an establishment that would guarantee the rights of all dissenting groups. On the other hand, Mayhew charged that the SPG pursued a plan designed "to promote, as much as possible an agreement [uniformity] in faith and worship." He said that only such a goal "fully and clearly accounts for their being so ready to encourage small Episcopal parties all over New-England, by sending them missionaries." From those cells, Mayhew concluded, the Anglicans hope in time to become numerous enough to "absorb all our churches."[29]

Mayhew's principal weapon against Apthorp and the society was history. The first settlers came to New England, he asserted, seeking not only religious freedom but safe haven from "Episcopal persecution, seconded by royal power; which often condescended to be subservient to the views of domineering prelates, before the glorious revolution."[30] Make no mistake, he warned, it was the same church-state power structure in England that now supported the SPG's current efforts to subvert religious liberty. Knowing that such an argument would score points among New England Congregationalists, John Apling, a gentleman from Rhode Island and sympathizer with Apthorp, responded that Mayhew was raising past horrors as a scare tactic. "The Doctor seems resolved, at all Events," he wrote, "to render the church of England, odious and terrible to his Majesty Subjects of New-England, and so is not content with publishing Slander, by Wholesale, against her Guardians of the present Age, but goes on to deal out, by retail, the Scandal of two Ages past; and brings up to view, Oppressions suffere'd scepter'd Tyrants, as he calls them." He urged readers to focus on the present, when "his Majesty's mild and gracious Government" guaranteed the "Security of Dissenters by the Toleration."[31] Apthorp and his allies were bound to lose the historical argument in a land where "the Toleration" meant that religious liberty was something both granted and potentially removed by the crown. Mayhew wanted something more fundamental: liberty of conscience and freedom for New Englanders to decide religious matters for themselves. Writing to a sympathetic audience whose ancestors had fled Anglican oppression, Mayhew, and the Congregationalists he represented, emerged the victor.

However, within a few years, the Congregational churches, or the Standing Churches, as they were known at the time, faced a new threat, this time from those who had split from them for reasons of conscience. These new religious protests were more antiestablishment than anticlerical, as Dissenters, especially Separates, charged that the Standing Churches, backed by government coercion, made a mockery of religious freedom. One of the hot spots was along the Connecticut border with Rhode Island, where Separate Baptists resented regulations imposed by the Standing Order. Inspired by the Great Awakening, Separate Baptists were evangelicals who had separated themselves from their congregations, sometimes because they believed that the pastor was unconverted, or because they wished to form their own church consisting of only those who had experienced the New Birth. Opposing the Separates were the Standing Churches, the designation given to the Congregational churches duly constituted under the Saybrook Platform. Stonington, Connecticut, was the epicenter of the clash between Separates and the Standing Order. There the Separates had made deep inroads in the Congregationalist parish, luring away as many as two-thirds of the Stonington congregation. In two scathing publications, the pastor, Joseph Fish, accused the Separate "fanatics" of a number of errors in practice and doctrine, which, under the Saybrook Platform, made them heretics and schismatics. A Baptist itinerant, Isaac Backus, who preached in the area and knew the Separates in question, defended them in a reply entitled *A Fish Caught in His Own Net* (1768). In the course of his defense, Backus argued for complete liberty of conscience based on separation of church and state.

Backus began by reviewing New England's religious history and, unlike Mayhew, considered the Congregationalists, not the Anglicans, as the oppressors, claiming that the Standing Order represented a departure from the forefathers' intentions. Fish had contended that the Standing Churches were the "true churches of Jesus Christ," noting that they were "for mutual benefit, *consociated* or united together by agreement, yet they remain congregational." Backus countered that the Cambridge Platform (1648) had declared that the "the church since the coming of Christ is 'only congregational, therefore neither national, provincial nor classical [i.e., Presbyterian].'" That view of the church was biblical, Backus argued, adding that the Saybrook Platform in effect constituted a national church by giving power to a group of "consociated" ministers to decide, for example, whether or not an individual was qualified to be minister of a church in Connecticut. Backus viewed that power as a violation of religious liberty. He held that each congregation was a voluntary association of believers who alone decided all matters relating to that church, including calling and removing ministers, drawing up articles of faith, and exercising discipline over its members.[32]

Fish had made the "Standing Churches" the centerpiece of his argument, asserting that they represented the standard of orthodoxy and the guardian of church order, so Backus focused on that claim and the authority that supported it. He explained that one of his purposes was to "show what [the Standing Churches] *stand upon*; even the same that other *national* or *provincial* churches do—*civil authority.*" Backus said that Fish and others often conceded, "if it were not for the support of the civil powers their churches would soon be broken up." Drawing upon Governor Thomas Hutchinson's history of Massachusetts, Backus cited a passage on the Standing Churches: "After all that may be said in favor of the *constitution* [i.e., the Saybrook Platform], the *strength* of it lay in the union declared with the civil authority."[33] To Backus, that union represented religious tyranny.

Having exposed the Standing Churches as a national church that relied on state coercion rather than persuasive biblical argument, Backus made clear his opposition to all national churches and all religious establishments. He reasoned that civil rulers and gospel ministers engage in totally different enterprises and employ very different means for pursuing their separate missions. Magistrates are charged with the responsibility of promoting "order and peace among men in their moral behavior towards each other," and they possess sufficient power "that all contrary behavior may be restrained or forcibly punished." They govern people of "all denominations," and they punish all offenders regardless of religious affiliation. On the other hand, ministers strive to show people the truth by laboring "to *open* men's *eyes* and to *turn them from darkness unto light, and from the power of Satan unto God.*" They do that through persuasion alone, "as any kind of *force* tends to shut the eyes rather than open them." Backus concluded that because "there is a great difference between the nature of their work," magistrates and ministers "never ought to have *such a union* together" as existed between the Standing Churches and the Connecticut Assembly.[34]

For those who doubted that the Standing Churches actually violated anybody's religious rights, Backus cited numerous examples. He showed how the Saybrook Platform created what were in effect ecclesiastical courts by investing the Standing Churches with the power of "*licensing of candidates for the ministry* and so *limiting* the churches to such in their choice of pastors." His grandfather Joseph Backus had been part of a congregation in Norwich, Connecticut, who, rather than submit to the Standing Order, left the church and held a separate meeting. In 1752, Isaac's mother, Elizabeth, and ten other Separates in Norwich spent time in jail for refusing to pay taxes to support the minister of the Standing Church. As a member of the Separate congregation, Mrs. Backus "did her part towards the support of divine worship according to her conscience," and, therefore, she thought it unfair that she must also contribute to the upkeep of the parish minister whose religion she opposed. Because she remained steadfast in her convictions, "she was taken and, though a weakly woman was carried to prison in a dark rainy night." Though the Standing Order prevailed through force, Isaac Backus concluded that his mother's "Christian character" and "Christian temper," along with the resolve that "she and others then discovered, greatly weakened" the Standing Order.[35]

Backus concluded his response to Fish by returning to his argument that the Standing Churches violated the faith of the Puritan Fathers.

Those divines had been convinced, he contended, that truth needed no coercion, and certainly God's word depended on no external power. Further, he pointed out that good people, including good Christians, have differences concerning religious beliefs and practices. Even among the earliest Dissenters who left England for New England in the seventeenth century, there were disagreements, most notably those between the Separatists who settled at Plymouth and the Puritans who founded Massachusetts. New England's spiritual fathers, Backus maintained, guaranteed liberty of conscience by separating church and state. He quoted Cotton Mather's sermon to the first general assembly after Plymouth and Massachusetts united. Concerning the civil magistrate, Mather declared, "He is most properly the officer of *human society*, and that a Christian by nonconformity to this or that imposed way of worship does not break the terms on which he is to enjoy the benefit of *human society*." For Mather, one's religious preference in no way affects one's civil rights and civil liberties. Mather added that even nonbelievers do not forfeit civil rights in not subscribing to the Christian faith. If magistrates prosecute those who do not follow prescribed religious views and practices, they may through force coerce men and women to comply, thus making them "*hypocrites*, but they will never make them to be *believers*."[36] Backus agreed with Mather: church and state are separate by nature, and they must be kept separate in fact.

Writing after the War of Independence, John Adams declared that the first clash of ideas, if not arms, in the American Revolution had occurred in American minds. He explained that long before the first shots were fired, Americans had embraced a Radical Whig understanding of liberty and the threats to liberty posed by English tyranny. When the Patriots began to protest the new imperial measures Parliament imposed after the French and Indian War, they were well armed with revolutionary ideas to challenge British authority. Similarly, seeds of an American religious revolution germinated in the minds of colonists decades before the Founders constitutionally separated church and state in 1787. To combat religious as well as political tyranny, Dissenters marshaled the ideas of the Great Awakening, the Enlightenment, and Radical Whiggism—all of which insisted on the individual's right to determine his or her own beliefs and practices without any involvement from the state. By the time the drama of the American Revolution opened, Americans were far along in their conception of the most radical expression of religious liberty, one that regarded unfettered religious freedom as the best means of pursuing truth in a free society. Unlike the colonizers, who emphasized the need to plant religious "truth" in the American wilderness, the Founding Fathers focused on religious freedom. Though the British had rejected it, Americans meant to adopt a Miltonian free marketplace of ideas.

PART THREE

Religious Freedom

❖

T
HE FOUNDING FATHERS' religious settlement, embodied in the
First Amendment to the United States Constitution, gave legal
sanction to an American revolution of religion that redefined the
place of religion in America. With the exception of William Penn and
Roger Williams, the planters had organized church-state relations around
the central idea of religious uniformity, the notion that the established
church within a colony represented the one true religion that all should
be compelled to support. Whether Puritans or Anglicans, the planters
of a given colony shared a common faith, believed that their particular
formulation of Protestantism was the correct one, and accepted the responsibility of ensuring its purity within their jurisdiction. The Founders,
on the other hand, made religious freedom the cornerstone of faith in
the new republic. Representing thirteen states and scores of sects, delegates to the Constitutional Convention refused to establish any single
religion as an official church; instead, they guaranteed the free exercise
of all. Some critics of the Constitution found the failure to establish an
official church disturbing, suggesting that the Founders disregarded the
importance of religion in fostering public virtue. But the central question
for the Founders had not been religion's role; indeed, most were convinced that Christianity was the surest foundation of a moral society.
Rather, they worried about religion's place, deciding in the end that it

would flourish more through persuasion in a free religious marketplace than through government coercion.

Religious settlements occur within specific moments of time and must be considered within historical context. The sixteenth-century Elizabethan Settlement reflected the queen's concern for bringing peace to a kingdom that had made martyrs of Catholics and Protestants. While she made no new martyrs, Elizabeth did create dissenters who wanted a purified Church of England. The seventeenth-century planters of English colonies in North America were either loyal sons of the church or persecuted dissenters, and they expressed their faith in the colonies they established. America's eighteenth-century Founders defined their religious settlement in the birth of a republic conceived in liberty. In 1776, Americans had announced to the world that they were a "free and independent" nation, and in 1787 they framed a constitution "to secure the blessings of liberty." In addition to political freedom, they embraced economic freedom, the idea that self-interested individuals offering their goods and services in a free, competitive market would bring greater benefit to society than could government trade regulations and monopolies. Similarly, many Americans rejected state regulation of religion, insisting on complete religious freedom with no one regarded as a dissenter, where all could pursue truth as they saw it. With almost unanimous consent, the Founders agreed, going beyond the planters' notion of religious liberty: the "Protestant sense of liberation from the shackles of Rome (or in the case of an independent America, Canterbury)." Rather, they embraced the "liberal idea of free competition among a variety of sects . . . qualified by concern lest liberty degenerate into license."[1]

Before the War of Independence, predictions abounded on both sides of the Atlantic that Americans could not form a lasting union. Among the reasons for the gloomy prognosis was the region's religious diversity. The centrifugal force of myriad sectarian interests, it was feared, would render futile any attempt at defining a common faith. The Founders were more optimistic, believing that a free, competitive religious market would both ensure religious vitality and prevent religious wars. In other words, they believed that religious liberty, not religious regulation, was the more effective bond in a pluralistic society.

❖ 8 ❖

The American Revolution of Religion

T HE WAR of Independence was part of a radical revolution in which Americans dissolved their bonds with the British monarchy and created a new republic. The revolutionary rhetoric of 1776 announced to the world that Patriots were seeking liberty over entrenched power, and in the Declaration of Independence, the Continental Congress cited a long train of abuses of power by which the king had undermined the colonists' freedoms.[1] At the same time, Adam Smith called for free trade through the removal of government-granted monopolies that favored certain groups and individuals. American merchants had long chafed under the Navigation Acts that had restricted manufacturing and markets. Everywhere, it seems, free Americans seized the revolutionary moment to throw off traditional shackles that thwarted their desire for self-determination, whether in political or in economic endeavors.

Americans also sought a revolution in religion. In 1776, as delegates met in the thirteen states to draft new constitutions that would safeguard their liberties, dissenters led the fight for complete religious freedom. Their arguments had a decided republican ring as they listed the abuses they had suffered, from payment of taxes to support ministers of the established church with whom they disagreed, to persecution for following the dictates of their consciences. Advocates of establishment tried to mollify dissenters by promising liberal religious toleration for nonconformists. But dissenters wanted more, something as radical as the political revolution; they wanted religious freedom, not mere toleration. Baptist minister John Leland explained the difference. First, he wrote, "Government has no more to do with the religious opinions of men than it has with the principles of mathematics." Second, he continued, "Let every man speak freely without fear, maintain the principles that he believes, worship according to his own faith, either one God, three Gods, no God, or twenty Gods." And, third, he concluded, "let government protect him in so doing."[2]

The American revolution of religion actually began forty years before the Declaration of Independence.[3] During the Great Awakening, evangelical revivalists defied civil and ecclesiastical authority to preach the message of the New Birth without regard to existing institutions and laws. They ignored parish boundaries, preaching wherever people gathered. They allowed lay exhorters to preach, bypassing church boards that licensed ministers. And they continued to dispatch unlicensed itinerants on preaching tours after legislatures passed regulations to curb such activity. Empowered by their New Birth experiences, many laypersons rejected the authority of pastors they deemed to be "unconverted," removed themselves from established congregations, and formed their own Separate churches. Some further exercised religious choice by deciding to affiliate their new congregations with one of the dissenting sects, such as the Baptists. Church and state leaders attempted to stop what they considered to be "confusion and disorder" spread by the evangelicals, but to little effect. Despite their efforts, a de facto free marketplace of religion emerged, characterized by competition and choice. Moreover, the New Lights, especially those identifying with the Baptists, Methodists, and Presbyterians, grew at a much greater rate than did the state churches—the Congregational churches of New England and the Anglican churches in the southern colonies. In 1760, more than 60 percent of the congregations in America were Congregational or Anglican, but by 1790 the proportion had dropped below 30 percent.[4] The relative decline in state churches reflects a shift away from the regulated religious economy that prevailed in most colonies to an emerging free marketplace of religion. In 1776, the fast-growing population of dissenters lobbied legislators to bring laws into conformity with the new religious economy, by disestablishing state churches and guaranteeing complete religious freedom.

Whether Churchmen or Dissenters, all Patriots united in resisting British attempts to curb their religious freedom. The threat that a resident bishop of the Church of England might be installed was not new to colonists, but in the broader context of Britain's new imperial policies of the 1760s and 1770s, it took on a much more sinister character. If Parliament insisted on exercising legislative sovereignty, bypassing the colonial assemblies, could not the archbishop claim ecclesiastical supremacy and ignore the rights of dissenting congregations? The Quebec Act of 1774 presented an even greater threat to the colonists' religious freedom by giving parliamentary sanction to the Catholic Church in neighboring Canada. Though no credible evidence suggests that Parliament intended to impose Catholicism on the thirteen colonies, the act was one more element in a growing conspiracy theory that allowed for such an unthinkable assault on American religious sensibilities.

Though united in resisting British threats to religious freedom, Americans were deeply divided over the place of religion in the new state governments instituted in 1776. Some thought that a state religion, albeit one with no ties to England, was essential for the adequate support of religious instruction, and they deemed religious instruction necessary for a virtuous citizenry. While agreeing on the importance of religion in society, dissenters disagreed with the notion of a state church. They argued that true Christianity was voluntary, not coercive, and, therefore, society was best served through free and independent churches preaching the gospel.

The best-known contest occurred in Virginia, where a decade-long struggle culminated in the Virginia Statute for Religious Freedom (1785).[5] With Jefferson and Madison leading the legislative fight, most historians have credited them with winning the battle for religious freedom. However, they themselves recognized that their success would have been impossible without the thousands of Dissenters who over the previous forty years had poured into the state, many of them emigrating from Pennsylvania. Jefferson noted that by 1776 a majority of Virginians were Dissenters. Settling primarily along the frontier, where the presence of the established church was weakest, they operated within a relatively free marketplace of religion that provided men and women choice among competing sects. Reflecting on the triumph of religious liberty, Madison explained how the measure passed in a legislature dominated by Episcopalians favoring establishment. "It is well known," he wrote in 1788, "that a religious establishment would have taken place in that State, if the legislative majority had found as they expected, a majority of the people in favor of the measure; and I am persuaded that if a majority of the people were now of one sect, the measure would still take place and on narrower ground than was then proposed."[6] As Madison's observation illustrates, the American revolution of religion was more than the design of a few revered Founders; it was the insistence of masses of men and women that they had an unfettered right to make their religious choices. Religious freedom came about, then, when the interests of dissenters coincided with the convictions of radical Whigs. While some states retained established churches until well into the nineteenth century, Americans in 1776 took the revolutionary step of ensuring that no one is a "dissenter," and that all can pursue their beliefs and practices as they wish.[7]

RELIGION AND INDEPENDENCE

The controversy following the French and Indian War, between the British who wanted to exert more control over the colonies and the Americans who wanted to return to the status quo, was primarily a constitutional struggle. Lawyers, not clergymen, took the lead in challenging Parliament's new imperial policies and gave the colonists' resistance movement "consistent intellectual goals." The eighteenth century had witnessed a dramatic increase in the number of lawyers, especially in New England, as well as their professionalization after the English model. By 1774, eighty to ninety lawyers practiced in Massachusetts, compared with about four hundred Congregational clergymen. According to historian John Murrin, who studied the rise of the American bar and its relation to the American Revolution, "the legal profession had grown to a fifth the size of the established ministry, whereas even a generation earlier any comparison between the two would have been ludicrous." When Parliament passed the Stamp Act in 1765, lawyers such as James Otis of Massachusetts, Patrick Henry of Virginia, John Dickinson of Pennsylvania, and Daniel Dulany of Maryland emerged to make the constitutional case against the measure. With a "thorough knowledge of the English constitution and English law," lawyers "provided the colonists with an intellectual basis for unity until they could manufacture their own nationalism to take its place." Almost one-half of the fifty-six signers of the

Declaration of Independence were lawyers, as were about 60 percent of the delegates to the Constitutional Convention.[8]

Led by lawyers, Patriots framed their resistance to the new British imperial measures primarily in terms of Enlightenment principles and Radical Whig ideology, but they also responded through the language of Protestant Dissent, which had exerted a powerful influence from the colonies' original settlement. As the English philosopher and pro-American member of Parliament Edmund Burke noted, "The religion most prevalent in our northern colonies is a refinement of the principle of resistance: it is the dissidence of dissent, and the protestantism of the Protestant religion."[9] Agreeing with Burke, one British historian claims that at bottom the American Revolution was about religious differences, and "with an emphasis on the heterodoxy of Dissent, the war was truly a war of religion."[10] Protestants had fled religious and political oppression in the early seventeenth century, and they had a long history of rising up against arbitrary government that threatened their most cherished rights. Thus, in the 1760s and 1770s, it was out of a long tradition of dissent that they once again cried out against what they considered to be tyranny.

Dissenting clergymen and Whig lawyers were ready allies because they shared a common intellectual heritage and viewed civil and religious oppression as inextricably linked. Both were strongly influenced by the writings of the Commonwealthmen, including John Milton, James Harrington, and Algernon Sydney.[11] In 1765, John Adams connected the tyrannies of church and state as evils of the same order and, worse still, evils that were often conjoined in history by rulers and bishops eager to use one another in extending their respective power. Adams argued that "since the promulgation of Christianity, the two greatest systems of tyranny that have sprung from this original, are the canon and the feudal law." His opposition to those two systems was not to power per se but to unchecked power. He contended that when "restraints are taken off, it becomes an encroaching, grasping, restless, and ungovernable power." Under the canon law, one order of men devised a means of subjecting the masses. Adams wrote that "the most refined, sublime, extensive, and astonishing constitution of policy that ever was conceived by the mind of man was framed by the Romish clergy for the aggrandisement of their own order." Similarly, the feudal law concentrated power in the hands of the few. Under it, "the common people were held together in herds and clans in a state of servile dependence on their lords, bound, even by the tenure of their lands, to follow them, whenever they commanded, to their wars, and in a state of total ignorance of every thing divine and human, excepting the use of arms and the culture of their lands."[12]

As oppressive as the canon and feudal laws were in their separate jurisdictions, they became unbearable when united under the same regime, what Adams called "a wicked confederacy between the two systems of tyranny." He explained how spiritual and temporal lords conspired to subdue and exploit the people: "it seems to have been even stipulated between them, that the temporal grandees should contribute every thing in their power to maintain the ascendency of the priesthood, and that the spiritual grandees in their turn, should employ their ascendency over the consciences of the people, in impressing on their minds a blind, implicit obedience to civil magistracy."[13] Adams warned Americans that if they were not vigilant, the British church and state would combine to take away their civil and religious rights. At the same time, he assured Patriots that knowledge was power, and that if Americans understood how tyranny worked, they could instantly recognize its threat and meet its challenge.

Ministers also viewed civil and religious freedom as bound together. In a typical discourse on the subject, Boston pastor Isaac Skillman preached a 1772 sermon reminding his audience that their forefathers had fled tyranny to worship as they thought right, and that they must not succumb to evil ministers who threatened that liberty. Freedom was a precious legacy that must be protected from power-hungry placemen:

> Liberty, my lord, is the native right of the Americans; it is the blood-bought treasure of their Forefathers; and they have the same essential right to their native laws as they have to the air they breathe in, or to the light of the morning when the sun rises: And therefore they who oppress the Americans must be as great enemies to the law of nature, as they who would, if it were in their power, vail the light of the sun from the universe. My Lord, the Americans have a privilege [to] boast of above all the world: they never were in bondage to any man, therefore it is more for them to give up their Rights, than it would be for all Europe to give up their Liberties into the hands of the Turks. Consider what English tyranny their Forefathers

fled from; what seas of distress they met with; what savages they fought with; what blood-bought treasures, as the dear inheritance of their lives, they have left to their children, and without any aid from the King of England; and yet after this, these free-born people must be counted Rebels, if they will not loose every right to Liberty, which their Venerable ancestors purchased at so great expence as to lose their lives in accomplishing; and shall not their descendants be strenuous to maintain inviolate those sacred Rights, which God and Nature have given them, to the latest posterity. O America! America let it never be said that you deserted the Grand Cause, and submitted to English ministerial tyranny.[14]

Dissenters were vigilant, and when the British threatened to install a bishop in America and extend the boundaries of Catholic Quebec so that they abutted the thirteen colonies, they joined Whigs in exposing and denouncing royal oppression. Though Anglicans had long called for a resident bishop, their pleas in the midst of the constitutional crisis convinced Patriots that the church was a coconspirator in subjecting the Americans. Then with the passage of the Quebec Act in 1774, many American Dissenters were convinced that Parliament would stop at nothing in subjugating them, even to the extent of encouraging the spread of Catholicism in neighboring Canada. To the colonists, the message was clear: the king in Parliament can and will use religion as an instrument of tyranny. The First Continental Congress charged that the Quebec Act disposed Canadian Catholics "to act with hostility against the free Protestant colonies, whenever a wicked Ministry shall choose to direct them."[15] In protesting threats to undermine their religious as well as civil liberties, Whig lawyers mounted a natural rights defense, while Dissenting clergymen preferred biblical arguments.

One genre that Protestant ministers used to good advantage was that of biblical parody. They knew that the Bible was the most familiar book to many Americans, so ministers could effectively make parallels between the sufferings of the ancient Hebrews as God's Chosen People and those of Americans, considered by many to be a new Chosen People. Following the 1774 Coercive Acts that Parliament passed in retaliation against the Boston Tea Party, *The First Book of the American Chronicles of the Times* recast the measures in biblical language. Patterned after the Old Testament Book of Chronicles, the parody was organized into chapters and verses and was written in the language of the King James Version of the Bible. Its opening verse makes the parallel clear: "And behold! When the tidings came to the great city that is afar off, the city that is in the land of Britain, how the men of Boston, even the Bostonites, had arose, a great multitude, and destroyed the TEA, the abominable merchandize of the east, and cast it into the midst of the sea." The work appeared in several editions, with each new issue introducing an additional chapter that elaborated on the theme of oppressive ministers' deceiving the king into believing that his Chosen People were faithless. A typical warning captures the message: "Thy throne, O King, is encompassed about with lies, and thy servants, the Bernardites and the Hutchinsonians, are full of deceit, for be it known unto thee, O King, they hide the truth from thee, and wrongfully accuse the men of Boston, for behold, these letters in mine hand witnesseth sore against them, O King, if thou art wise, thou understand these things."[16]

In 1775, Oliver Noble, pastor at Newbury, Massachusetts, published a biblical parody whose lengthy title suggests the parallel between ancient and current events: *Some Strictures upon the Sacred Story recorded in the book of Esther, shewing The Power and Oppression of state Ministers tending to the Ruin and Destruction of God's People:—And the remarkable Interpositions of Divine Providence in favour of the Oppressed.* The story of Esther had all the elements necessary for a dramatic parallel between the ancient Hebrews and the present-day Americans: a wise and good king, the Persian Ahasuerus; a wicked prime minister, Haman; an oppressed people, the Jews; and faithful subjects, Esther and Mordecai. Jealous of Mordecai, who had won royal favor for warning the king of a treasonous plot, Haman sought his destruction by convincing the king that the Jews in his kingdom were preparing for a rebellion. After Haman secured the king's approval for a preemptive strike against the Jews, Esther, who had become queen, convinced Ahasuerus that it was Haman, not Mordecai and the Jews, who was the enemy. In the end, justice was served as Ahasuerus ordered Haman to be executed on the very gallows the minister had erected for Mordecai's demise. Noble made Haman's evil ministry sound like Whitehall: "Haman, the Premier, and his junto of court favorites, flatterers, and dependents in the royal city, together with governors of provinces, councilors, boards of trade, commissioners and their creatures, officers and collectors of REVENUE. . . ." He explained his parallel between the ancient Persian and modern British monarchies: "Not that I am certain the Persian state had all these officers. . . . But as the Persian monarchy was despotic . . . it is highly probable." Haman's wicked plot to kill the Jews failed because "a merciful God heard the cries of this oppressed people."[17] Noble assured his audience that if they remained faithful to God, Divine Providence would deliver them from ministerial wickedness.

Throughout the War of Independence, ministers preached against religious tyranny, weaving biblical, dissenting, and Whig themes into a condemnation of British attempts to enslave them.[18] Loyalists noted their effectiveness. According to Loyalist Peter Oliver, the Massachusetts councillor and chief justice of the Supreme Court, religion was both a long-term and an immediate cause of the American Revolution. Oliver described in his account of what he termed the "American Rebellion" how the Puritan settlers, upon arriving in New England, "soon forgot their *dear Mother, the Church of England*," and "formed themselves into independent & congregational Churches." Further, they set up their own religion and gave the right to vote only to members of "their Church, hereby excluding all of the established Church from this so natural Priviledge." Though voting qualifications were eventually severed from church membership, the early practice and "prejudice [were] so strongly riveted in their Successors" that members of the Church of England for a hundred years thereafter were effectively barred from holding high office. To Oliver, New Englanders represented three levels of rebellion: first, Protestants who had rebelled against the Church of Rome; then, Dissenters who had rebelled against the established Protestant Church of England; and, finally, Puritan emigrants who rebelled against England itself by establishing their own sect and excluding from it members of the Church of England.[19]

Turning to more proximate causes of the American Rebellion, Oliver again cited religion as a major factor, singling out activities of the Dissenting ministers or, as he called them, the "Black Regiment." To illustrate how effective the Dissenting ministers were in preaching civil rebellion from their pulpits, Oliver focused on Jonathan Mayhew. He described Mayhew's sermonic delivery style as "unharmonious and discordant," more akin to the "Water of a River dashing over the Rocks that impeded its Course, than to the smooth flowing Current." But he conceded that Mayhew "showed Strength of Reason." In the Stamp Act crisis of 1765, Mayhew "gave a loose to his Passions & commenced a partisan in Politicks." "It was remarked," Oliver wrote, "that on the day preceeding the Destruction of [Governor] Hutchinson's House, he preached so seditious a Sermon, that some of his Auditors, who were of the Mob, declared, whilst the Doctor was delivering it they could scarce contain themselves from going out of the Assembly & beginning their Work."[20] There was direct evidence supporting Oliver's account. On August 5, 1765, Mayhew preached a "fiery sermon on the text: 'I would they were even cut off which trouble you.' " When arrested for his part in destroying Hutchinson's house, one of the leaders explained his behavior on the grounds that he was excited by the sermon "and thought he was doing God service."[21]

Mayhew and the Boston clergy were not alone in using the pulpit to air grievances against the British oppressors and to call on "virtuous republicans" to resist. The Black Regiment operated in the South as well, where ministers preached on the same themes as their northern counterparts. One example will suffice to illustrate the similarities. William Tennent, pastor of the Independent congregation in Charleston, South Carolina, addressed Britain's "invasion" of American liberties in the Coercive Acts of 1774. He began his discourse by stating that "Political Subjects do not belong to the Pulpit." Behind that assertion was the widely shared belief that there existed two powers, ecclesiastical and civil, and that ministers' authority emanated from the former and should be exercised in pursuit of spiritual matters. Nonetheless, Tennent justified his "political" sermon on the grounds that history was filled with moral lessons, and every moment, no matter how political, held spiritual truths for those who could read them aright.[22]

In supreme irony, Tennent told his South Carolina audience, many of whom were slaveholders, that Parliament was engaged in nothing less than the enslavement of the colonies. He declared slavery to be a "general and perpetual Evil" and acknowledged that the first inclination of the colonists was to seek revenge against those trying to reduce them to it. But, Tennent added, "it should be an invariable Rule with *Christians* to regard the Hand of God in every Thing which happens, but especially in public Calamities." God, not Parliament, was directing events, and Americans should seek to understand what God was saying to them through the evils Parliament visited upon them. Rather than focus on the Coercive Acts, Tennent turned his attention to the moral character of the colonists to understand why they deserved God's wrath. "Nations," he explained, "like Individuals, have their Vices, which call for Punishment." He reminded his listeners of Sodom's fate when the inhabitants of that ancient city-state gave themselves over to immorality and licentiousness. Similarly, he warned, the moral character of the colonists gave every indication that "a Time of general Correction is not far from us."[23]

Tennent listed the religious and moral defects that he believed angered God and invited divine retribution. He described the current age as one of "universal Prevalence of Infidelity." Infidelity had "infected not only our recluse Philosphers, but every Rank and Profession." Tennent declared that "even the Coxcomb and Petit Maitre affect to treat the Christian Revelation with Ridicule." His comparison of the present age with that of the colonists' spiritual forefathers revealed the extent of decline in Christian faith and practice:

> What strange Heresies prevail in our National Churches! What a general Defection from Articles and Confessions of Faith! What insidious Interpretations of the Word of God! There cannot be a more awful sign of our general Corruption than this Treachery in the Ministers of the Gospel! How little do we find even of the *Form* of Religion among us! I do not mean here that there are few who go to Church, or have their Children baptized, or call themselves Christians. There was a Time indeed when these Things were considered as true Badges of the Christian Profession, but in our wiser Age the very Ideas of these Things are changed. They are now considered only as Matters of Custom, and in some Cases are complied with only to secure a Title to an Estate or as legal Qualifications for holding civil Offices.[24]

America was once a Christian land in truth, but if it could be called a Christian land now, it could only be regarded as such in form.

Having decried the religious decline, Tennent shifted his examination to that of the *"moral* Character of our Nation and Country." He singled out two vices for condemnation: swearing and profanation of the Sabbath. Considering both to be universal, Tennent thought that the latter deserved special attention. He said that "the universal Profanation of the

Sabbath Day" was a mark of "National Impiety." Then, placing that observation within the context of the imperial crisis, he averred, "We have more to dread from our Iniquities than our Enemies."[25]

Tennent's evangelical ideas were compatible with politicians' republican notions. At the center of the latter was the idea of virtue, whereby individuals brought their particular wills or interests into conformity with the general will or public good. The French *philosophe* Jean-Jacques Rousseau's views on the moral basis of a free society summed up the beliefs of most American leaders calling for a moral reformation in the face of the crisis with Britain. While arguing that "it is to law alone that men owe justice and liberty," Rousseau insisted that "the greatest support of public authority lies in the hearts of the citizens, and . . . nothing can take the place of morality in the maintenance of government." He concluded that "it is not only upright men who know how to administer the laws; but at bottom only good men know how to obey them."[26] When Whig leaders called on Americans to resist political oppression, they struck a theme familiar to Protestants.

Perhaps the most influential sermon during the period came from outside the pulpit, not delivered by a minister but published by the Radical Whig Thomas Paine. Though he would later dismiss biblical revelation as hearsay, Paine appealed to the Old Testament in urging Americans to separate themselves from Britain. His argument in *Common Sense*, which appeared in January 1776 and immediately became a best-seller, was that the engine of American oppression was not corrupt ministers or a bad king but monarchy itself. Knowing that most Americans were far more familiar with the Bible than with Enlightenment tomes, Paine explained the origins of monarchy by restating the biblical account. "Government by kings," he wrote, "was first introduced into the world by the Heathens, from whom the children of Israel copied the custom." Jealous of their neighbors who had kings arrayed in splendor, the ancient Hebrews clamored for a king of their own by appealing to the prophet Samuel. Through Samuel, God disapproved, reminding the Hebrews that he was their sovereign. When the Jews persisted, God relented and let his rebellious people have a king, a decision that resulted in endless wars and oppression. Paine concluded that "monarchy is ranked in scripture as one of the sins of the Jews."[27] The message to his readers was clear: by denouncing King George III and his rule, the colonists were placing their trust in the Sovereign God.

On July 2, 1776, the Continental Congress voted for independence and sent thousands of Americans into battle to make good on that historic declaration. Soldiers of the Continental Army represented a religious cross section of Americans. After the war, John Adams reflected on the army's religious diversity: "There were among them, Roman Catholics, English Episcopalians, Scotch and American Presbyterians, Methodists, Moravians, Anabaptists, German Lutherans, German Calvinists, Universalists, Arians, Priestleyans, Socinians, Independents, Congregationalists, Horse Protestants and House Protestants, Deists and Atheists; and 'Protestants que ne croyent rien ['Protestants who believe nothing'].' "[28] While that pluralistic army fought for independence, lawmakers in the various states began the initial attempts to define "who shall rule at home," including relations between church and state.

OPPOSING MASSACHUSETTS'S
"OPPRESSIVE ESTABLISHMENT OF RELIGION"

While Patriots were united in advocating religious liberty, they were deeply divided over relations between church and state, especially the desirability of an established church. Consequently, debates in state constitutional conventions were particularly contentious when delegates sought to define the place of religion under the new republican governments. Indeed, it might be said that the American revolution of religion began in the battle over religious clauses in the state constitutions. As the Continental Congress debated independence, the individual states began drafting constitutions based on republican principles. Accordingly, delegates elected to special conventions drafted constitutions that were then submitted to the freemen or citizens for ratification. Two major positions regarding church-state relations emerged. The first, the more conservative proposal, was to continue the status quo. Accordingly, in states that had had some sort of establishment clause, there were strong movements to go forward with an established church, albeit a new episcopal church where the Church of England had reigned. Proponents of that perspective argued that religious uniformity was important for an orderly, peaceful society. and that sectarianism led to chaos. Though dissenters would be required to support the official church, they would enjoy a liberal religious toleration enabling them to worship according to the dictates of their consciences. The second position rejected toleration in favor of complete religious liberty. Its proponents believed that religion was a matter of the individual's relation to God, and they found the notion that the state could "establish" or "tolerate" religion to be tyrannical. Even if the state should at one moment support what they believed, these Dissenters knew that a future administration could withdraw that support and favor another sect. What the state had the power to grant, it had the power to withdraw. These radicals, therefore, advocated complete religious freedom based on the separation of church and state.

In the early rounds of constitution making, conservatives and moderates prevailed in maintaining state regulation of religion, with radicals registering a very vocal protest. In revisions that followed the first drafts, the radical position gained favor. Several common themes reflected a strong move toward greater religious freedom. First, the seven states where the Church of England was established disestablished the church.[29] The Anglican clergy were staunch Loyalists, as were many of their parishioners in the northern colonies. In Virginia, where laymen had exercised great control over ecclesiastical affairs, the overwhelming majority of parishioners were Patriots. Second, delegates in the New England conventions where the Congregational churches were established greatly weakened ties between church and state, allowing Dissenters, for example, to earmark their taxes for churches of their own choosing. Third, religious tests for officeholding remained in place, although they were relaxed in many states. Maryland and Massachusetts insisted that office-seekers declare a Christian faith; New Jersey and North and South Carolina held that office-holders must be Protestant; and Delaware barred anti-Trinitarians.

The Revolutionary generation clearly viewed church-state relations very differently from those who first planted religion in America in the seventeenth century. First, such factors as immigration, the Great Awakening, and the Enlightenment changed the religious landscape dramatically in most colonies, in a movement away from a monolithic to a pluralistic religious society. The Congregational churches in early Massachusetts and the Church of England in early Virginia had not only established themselves as *the* "true" church in their respective colonies;

they had barred competitors through laws that punished "heretics." Now, in Revolutionary America, both states boasted large numbers of "dissenters," which made religious uniformity impossible. Second, religion had become voluntary as opposed to state-supported. Whig ideas of civil and religious freedom pervaded the country, and Americans jealously guarded their natural or God-given rights against all forms of oppression, whether that tyranny originated in the British Parliament or in the individual statehouses. Third, the fastest-growing Protestant sects included those evangelicals who insisted on a complete freedom of religion as opposed to religious toleration, no matter how liberal that toleration might be. Indeed, as the state constitutions reflected greater toleration, the cries for unrestricted freedom grew louder. Finally, many Americans, including the most influential Revolutionary leaders and members of the fastest-growing sects, called for a complete separation of church and state as the only sure safeguard of religious liberty.

While they agreed on the principle of separation of church and state, there was much disagreement between political and church leaders who fought for religious freedom. The former embraced the Lockean notions of natural rights and the social contract. Their point of departure was man in a state of nature with no government restraints whatsoever. Then, because of their desire to live in peace, free from the more rapacious and powerful among them, people gave up part of their individual freedom and placed themselves under a government of their own choosing, instituted to protect personal and property rights. However, men and women surrendered to that government only specific powers; they did not turn over such fundamental natural rights as freedom of conscience. Thus, according to this view, governments have no voice in religious matters other than to protect the rights of people in their free exercise of it. Church leaders reached the same conclusion but by way of a very different argument. They started with the idea that there are two distinct powers. In the words of Isaac Backus, the Baptist champion of religious freedom, "All acts of executive power in the civil state are to be performed in the name of the king or state they belong to, while all our religious acts are to be done in the *name of the Lord Jesus* and so are to be performed *heartily as to the Lord and not unto men.*" Just as the theory of natural rights recognized limits on government power in regard to religion, the Calvinist argument insisted that God did not surrender his sovereignty

to the state. "In all civil governments," Backus explained, "some are appointed to judge for others and have power to compel others to submit
to their judgment, but our Lord has most plainly forbidden us either to
assume or submit to any such thing in religion."[30]

Backus and other radicals faced powerful resistance to the notion of
complete religious freedom for all. In Massachusetts, the debate clearly
exposed the division between those who insisted that because morality
was the bedrock of a free society, the state must promote religion, and
those who agreed that morality was essential but thought that free, voluntary churches, not the state, were the best vehicles for attaining the
goal. Adherents of the latter view reminded their opponents that history
was replete with examples of how church-state alliances had been engines
of oppression. For the most recent example, they pointed to the threat
of a resident Anglican bishop and the toleration of Catholicism under the
Quebec Act.

It took the people of Massachusetts two years to ratify a constitution,
in large part because of disagreements over religious clauses. The General
Court adopted a draft in 1778, but the people rejected it. After a more
liberal religious toleration was granted, a revised version was ratified in
1780, though not without considerable protest from the growing number
of Separate Baptists and other Dissenters in the state. Writing from a
Lockean natural rights' perspective, John Adams composed Article 2 of
the Declaration of Rights, which affirmed that

> It is the right as well as the duty of all men in society, publicly and
> at stated seasons, to worship the Supreme Being, the great Creator
> and Preserver of the universe. And no subject shall be hurt, mo-
> lested, or restrained, in his person, liberty, or estate, for worshipping
> God in the manner and season most agreeable to the dictates of
> his own conscience, or for his religious profession or sentiments,
> provided he doth not disturb the public peace or obstruct others in
> their religious worship.[31]

Adams endorsed the belief that religion was fundamental in society, affirmed its voluntary nature, and embraced the free exercise of religion as
long as it did not disturb someone else's free expression. If that had been
the only statement on religion, Backus and the Separate Baptists would
have been satisfied.

However, Article 3 of the Declaration of Rights gave the government a substantial role in religious affairs, and that provision touched off a very heated and protracted debate that extended well beyond ratification, not totally subsiding until Massachusetts discontinued tax support for religion in 1833. To understand what the Dissenters found objectionable, we must examine a substantial portion of Article 3:

> As the happiness of a people and the good order and preservation of civil government essentially depend upon piety, religion, and morality, and as these cannot be generally diffused through a community but by the institution of the public worship of God and of public instructions in piety, religion, and morality: Therefore, To promote their happiness and to secure the good order and preservation of their government, the people of this commonwealth have a right to invest their legislature with power to authorize and require, and the legislature shall, from time to time, authorize and require, the several towns, parishes, precincts, and other bodies-politic or religious societies to make suitable provision, at their own expense, for the institution of public worship and for the support and maintenance of public Protestant teachers of piety, religion, and morality in all cases where such provisions shall not be made voluntarily.[32]

The contradictory articles 2 and 3 represented the two sides of debates waged in several states about the role of religion in society and church-state relations. Adams's wording in Article 2, similar to Jefferson's in Virginia, acknowledged the importance of religion and religious instruction in society. The best way to provide such instruction was through voluntary religious bodies that are guaranteed the free exercise of religion. The underlying assumption was that if it were free to spread its message, true religion would prevail and needed no assistance from government. Article 3 expresses the view that if people in local communities do not provide for the instruction of "true" religion, then it is the duty of the state to use its powers of coercion and taxation to ensure its promotion.

In making the case against Article 3, Isaac Backus turned to history, especially the history of Christianity. He began with the birth of the faith, in particular the attitudes and actions of Christ toward the state and religious affairs. Backus wrote, "Now 'tis well known that this glorious Head made no use of secular force in the first setting up of the Gospel-Church, when it might seem to be peculiarly needful if ever." But unlike Christ, who depended wholly upon God, some of his followers relied on the state to protect and promote their faith. "First," Backus explained, "they moved Constantine, a secular prince, to draw his sword against heretics." The problem, he continued, was that "earthly states are changeable, [and, alas,] the same sword that Constantine drew against heretics, Julian turned against the orthodox."[33] Backus's message was clear: if Christians acknowledge that government has any role in religious affairs, the day may come when that government imposes unacceptable demands on them. Better to trust God, not changeable men.

Beyond citing historical instances of secular control of or interference with Christianity, Backus made his fight for complete religious freedom a part of the current struggle to throw off British political oppression. To his opponents in Massachusetts who argued that the Massachusetts Constitution gave Baptists tax relief by allowing them to apply taxes to the church of their choice, Backus replied with a reference to Parliament's repealing the Townshend taxes. "If we ask why have you not been easy and thankful since the Parliament has taken off so many of the taxes that they had laid upon us," he reminded his opponents, "you answer that they still claim a power to tax us when and as much as they please." He asked, "is not that the very difficulty before us?"[34] Another Baptist minister, John Allen, in his address to the Massachusetts General Court, drew the connection between political and religious oppression even tighter in his protest over religious taxes:

> You tell your governor that the Parliament of England have no right to tax the Americans . . . because they are not the representatives of America; and will you dare to tax the Baptists for a religion they deny? Are you gentlemen their representatives before GOD, to answer for their souls and consciences any more than the representatives of England are the representatives of America? . . . if it be just in the General Court to take away my sacred and spiritual rights and liberties of conscience and my property with it, then it is surely right and just in the British Parliament to take away by power and force my civil rights and property without my consent; this reasoning, gentlemen, I think is plain.[35]

In October 1774, a group of Baptists went before the Continental Congress in Philadelphia to draw the parallel between civil and religious freedom. On the evening of October 14, a group of Philadelphia Dissenters invited the Massachusetts delegates to Carpenter's Hall to conduct "a little business." There the New Englanders found themselves facing a group of Quakers and Baptists who assembled to "confront the Massachusetts delegates with the discrepancy between the way 'in which liberty in general is now beheld' and the way the Baptists were treated in Massachusetts." At what John Adams called "a self-created tribunal," the Reverend James Manning, president of the Baptist College of Rhode Island (later Brown University) read a lengthy condemnation of Massachusetts for "retaining, inconsistently with her professed desire for civil liberty, an oppressive establishment of religion." The protesters closed by urging the repeal of "offensive laws" like those in Massachusetts in favor of Pennsylvania's endorsement of religious freedom.[36]

Backus and his followers lost the battle for complete religious freedom in Massachusetts. A majority supported the continued establishment of the Congregational churches while granting toleration to dissenters. Indeed, the old Puritan strongholds in New England proved to be the most resistant to disestablishment. New Hampshire continued to provide tax support for its churches until 1817, Connecticut until 1818, Maine until 1820, and Massachusetts until 1833. Ironically, it was in the South, where the Church of England had long circumvented their rights, that Dissenters first toppled establishments and guaranteed religious freedom for all.

TRIUMPH OF RELIGIOUS FREEDOM IN VIRGINIA

In Virginia a powerful combination of Dissenting ministers and Whig politicians combined to sever all state ties to religion and provide a truly revolutionary religious freedom. That freedom was not won without a struggle, however, as powerful lay leaders fought mightily for religious uniformity, a policy that had prevailed in Virginia since its founding in 1607. Opposing disestablishment were proponents of a continued episcopal establishment, albeit one with no ties to England. In a heated debate that lasted throughout the War of Independence, the result was as revolutionary as the political settlement it accompanied. In 1785, the Virginia

Statute for Religious Freedom declared religion to be a free and voluntary pursuit by individuals and forbade any government involvement whatever.

The groundwork for such a radical shift began in the 1740s and 1750s when large numbers of Virginians embraced the evangelical movement sparked by the Great Awakening. Thousands joined the Baptists, Presbyterians, and Methodists, fracturing the religious uniformity that the planters had cherished. On the eve of the Revolution, as many as one out of every five Virginians considered himself or herself a Dissenter to the established Church of England; Jefferson put the percentage much higher, suggesting that "two-thirds of the people had become dissenters at the commencement of the present revolution."[37] Whatever their numbers were in fact, the evangelicals were a bold and vocal lot, challenging the social mores of the planters as well as the establishment laws that supported the church. Because the evangelical revival coincided with the revolutionary movement, the Patriot planters faced the need of wooing the very evangelicals who were challenging their religious convictions. Consequently, Patriot rhetoric took on an evangelical tone as political leaders appealed to Dissenters to join in fighting the common enemy. In their written arguments, Virginia's Patriot leaders wrote primarily in the language of classical republicanism, but in orations to the people, they invoked devotional piety or appealed to the Scriptures.

Though they closed ranks against the British threat, Churchmen and Dissenters clashed in Virginia over the state's proposed constitution. While willing to extend a liberal religious toleration to Dissenters, some former members of the Church of England sought to maintain an establishment of episcopacy, evoking an immediate and spirited opposition from those who sought an absolute liberty of conscience. On November 8, 1776, the clergy of the established church—that is, the Church of England—presented a memorial to the Virginia Assembly calling for a constitutional establishment. Like supporters of Massachusetts's Standing Order, the clergy promised that such an establishment would not encroach upon "the religious rights of any sect or denomination of men." They argued that a "religious establishment in a State is conducive to its peace and happiness," and "it, therefore, cannot be improper for the legislative body of a State to consider how such opinions as are most consonant to reason and of the best efficacy in human affairs may be propagated and supported." They added that "the doctrines of Christianity have a greater tendency to produce virtue amongst men than any human laws or institutions," and that "these can be best taught and preserved in their purity in an established church." They pointed to the 150-year establishment in colonial Virginia as proof of its efficacy, arguing that, under the established church, "order and internal tranquility, true piety and virtue have more prevailed than in most other parts of the world." They warned that if the Dissenters prevailed in abolishing establishment, and "all denominations of Christians be placed upon a level," the resulting competition among sects would produce "much confusion, [and] probably civil commotions will attend the contest."[38]

Thomas Jefferson replied that establishment was not necessary for religion to flourish. He invoked Pennsylvania, where competing sects existed solely through the voluntary financial support of their members, where religion had "long subsisted without any establishment at all." Further, he added, the absence of state regulation there did not result in the triumph of religious enthusiasm or other dangerous fanatical expressions. In Pennsylvania, he wrote, "Religion is well supported; of various kinds, indeed, but all good enough; all sufficient to preserve peace and order; or if a sect arises, whose tenets would subvert morals, good sense has fair play, and reasons and laughs it out of doors, without suffering the State to be troubled with it."[39] What Jefferson described was a free marketplace of religion that was self-regulating, as multiple, competing sects checked each other.

Virginia Methodists, however, were not swayed by Pennsylvania's example and weighed in on the side of establishment. Their petition stated that though they might be regarded as Dissenters, they considered themselves to be "in communion with the Church of England" and were opposed to disestablishment. Without being specific, the petitioners warned that disestablishment would result in "very bad consequences."[40]

Most Dissenters disagreed with the Methodists, and they flooded the Assembly with petitions calling for the abolition of establishment. Presbyterian, Lutheran, and Baptist congregations and associations called for liberty of conscience. In a typical plea, a group of inhabitants from Prince Edward County called Virginia's establishment a "long night of ecclesiastical bondage." They hoped that "all church establishments might be pulled down, and every tax upon conscience and private judgment abolished, and each individual left to rise or sink by his own merit and the general laws of the land." In other words, they called for a secular state where citizens could worship as their consciences directed them without suffering any civil penalty. Such religious freedom, they promised, would make Virginia "an asylum for free inquiry, knowledge, and the virtuous of every denomination."[41]

A petition from the presbytery of Hanover County called for a complete separation of church and state. First, they argued that America was fighting for freedom, and that establishment is antithetical to freedom. "In this enlightened age and in a land where all of every denomination are united in the most strenuous efforts to be free," the petitioners reminded the legislature, "we hope and expect that our representatives will cheerfully concur in removing every species of religious, as well as civil, bondage." Second, they argued that *any* establishment, including that of the "Christian religion"—that is, Christianity itself and not that of a single sect—would amount to surrendering liberty of conscience to the state. They explained, "There is no argument in favor of establishing the Christian religion but what may be pleaded, with equal propriety, for establishing the tenets of Mohammed by those who believe the Alcoran; or if this be not true, it is at least impossible for the magistrate to adjudge the right of preference among the various sects that profess the Christian faith, without erecting a chair of infallibility, which would lead us back to the Church of Rome."[42] The message was clear: religion is a matter of conscience between God and individuals, and the state should have no role whatever in religious affairs.

Faced with petitions both defending and attacking establishment, the Virginia legislature in the fall of 1776 engaged in heated debate. Thomas Jefferson called it "the severest contest in which I have ever been engaged." Leading the proponents of establishment were Edmund Pendleton and Robert Carter Nicholas, "honest men, but zealous churchmen," according to Jefferson. While a majority of Virginians were dissenters, a majority of the legislators were Churchmen. However, many of them were "reasonable, and liberal men" who tried to safeguard religious liberty within an establishment bill. The bill that passed did in fact make some strides toward religious liberty. Most significantly, it repealed the laws that "rendered criminal the maintenance of any religious opinions (other than those of the Episcopalians)." But it also declared that "religious assemblies ought to be regulated, and that provision ought to be made for continuing the succession of the clergy and superintending their conduct." However, the thorniest problem, that of tax support for religion, remained unresolved and would continue to be debated from 1776 to 1779. The question was "whether a general assessment should not be established by law on every one to the support of the pastor of his choice; or whether all should be left to voluntary contributions."[43]

With the cry for freedom growing louder during the Revolution, the Virginia legislative session of 1779 brought the downfall of establishment in Virginia but failed to enact Thomas Jefferson's bill for religious freedom. In June, governor-elect Jefferson's bill for complete religious freedom was reported to the House. Again petitions poured into the Assembly supporting and attacking the bill. Some wanted to abolish establishment altogether, including public support of the clergy, while others wished to retain "an establishment . . . under certain regulations" that allowed for considerable freedom. After much debate, the lawmakers ended the establishment to the extent that the "clergy could no longer look for support to taxation." However, they retained possession of their glebes and kept a near monopoly of marriage fees. As to Jefferson's bill on religious liberty, a majority found it too radical, preferring instead Patrick Henry's "liberal Establishment," which granted toleration to Dissenters.[44]

After the War of Independence, Virginians again took up the issue of the place of religion in the state. Dissenters and Churchmen had staked out clear and opposing positions. The former wanted absolute religious freedom—that is, no state support or regulation of religion whatever. The latter, reconstituted in 1783 as the Protestant Episcopal Church, advocated a new and more liberal establishment. In late 1784, legislators favoring establishment put forth the "Bill Establishing a Provision for Teachers of Religion," widely known as the "General Assessment Bill." Supporters justified public support of religion in the preamble:

Whereas the general diffusion of Christian knowledge hath a natural tendency to correct the morals of men, restrain their vices, and preserve the peace of society, which cannot be effected without a competent provision for learned teachers, who may be thereby enabled to devote their time and attention to the duty of instructing such citizens as from their circumstances and want of education cannot otherwise attain such knowledge; and it is judged such provision may be made by the Legislature, without counteracting the liberal principle heretofore adopted and intended to be preserved, by abolishing all distinctions of pre-eminence among the different societies or communities of Christians.[45]

Jefferson opposed the bill and argued that Virginia should adopt religious competition as the best way to check religious extremism, and he expressed his hope that Virginians would learn from Pennsylvania. "Let us too give this experiment fair play," he wrote, "and get rid, while we may, of those tyrannical laws." He conceded that the revolutionary era itself had created an atmosphere that alerted Americans to tyranny, civil or ecclesiastical. "It is true," he conceded, "we are as yet secured against them by the spirit of the times. I doubt whether the people of this country would suffer an execution for heresy, or a three years imprisonment for not comprehending the mysteries of the Trinity." But he worried about the time to come. He feared the rise of future religious enthusiasts who might find allies in politicians eager to win popular support. He declared, "the spirit of the times may alter, will alter. Our rulers will become corrupt, our people careless. A single zealot may commence persecutor, and better men be his victims." He argued that "the time for fixing every essential right on a legal basis is while our rulers are honest, and ourselves united." In regard to the protection of individual rights, he warned that "from the conclusion of this war we shall be going down hill. It will not then be necessary to resort every moment to the people for support. They will be forgotten, therefore, and their rights disregarded." Worse, he added, "they will forget themselves, but in the sole faculty of making money, and will never think of uniting to effect a due respect for their rights. The shackles, therefore, which shall not be knocked off at the conclusion of this war, will remain on us long, will be made heavier and heavier, till our rights shall revive or expire in a convulsion."[46]

Jefferson's call for complete religious freedom worried many who believed that a state religion was essential to social cohesion. While the Jeffersonian free market of religion represented freedom *from* religion, others wanted a more positive arrangement, guaranteeing freedom *of* religion. Anglican minister Jonathan Boucher feared that if the practice of religion were voluntary and liberty of conscience meant that individuals could choose what religion to follow and whether or not to attend public worship, the result would be chaos. Societies made a fetish of freedom at their own peril; freedom must be linked with obedience. Boucher believed that social cohesion depended upon obedience and conformity, and that conscience must be linked with obedience. He thought that "the numerous sects into which the Christian world has been divided, is one of the greatest calamities with which mankind has ever been visited." He noted that there were "no less than sixty-four different sects" in the British provinces. Boucher rejected the sectarian notion of freedom of conscience, calling instead for "obedience for conscience' sake." Society depended upon the principle of obedience to bind the different classes and generations together into an organic whole. To him, the "manners of a community may be regarded as one great chain." He thought that individual liberty must be balanced with social cohesion, and in regard to religion that meant conformity to a common faith.[47]

James Madison agreed with Jefferson that the bill represented "a dangerous abuse of power," and wrote a remonstrance summarizing the arguments of English republican theorists from Milton to Locke to Trenchard. First, he held it as a "fundamental and undeniable truth, 'that Religion or the duty which we owe to our Creator and the manner of discharging it, can be directed only by reason and conviction, not by force or violence.' " The religion of each person is solely a matter of that person's conscience, and he or she has the right to exercise that right as he or she thinks fit. This right is "unalienable," because "the opinions of men, depending only on the evidence contemplated by their own minds cannot follow the dictates of other men: It is unalienable also, because what is here a right towards men, is a duty toward the Creator." Moreover, this right and duty take precedence over those imposed by civil society. "Before any man can be considered as a member of Civil Society, he must be considered as a subject of the Governour of the Universe." Thus citizens' allegiance must be first to God and then to society. In Madison's argument, "in matters of Religion, no mans right is abridged by the institution of Civil Society and . . . Religion is wholly exempt from its cognizance." Society's "will of the majority" cannot "trespass on the rights of the minority," and religion is one of those rights.[48]

Having argued that religion is exempt from the authority of society, Madison then turned to the role of government in matters of religion. He started by reminding his readers that the legislature is but a creature of society, and that its jurisdiction is derivative and limited. Therefore, he reasoned, lawmakers, like the society that created the state, cannot infringe upon the individual's right and duty to worship the Governor of the Universe in the way his conscience dictates. Americans who fled to the New World to escape religious persecution should never forget the principle that if people allow a government any say over religion, even if a given government may support one's own religion or sect, then there can be no assurance of religious liberty. "The same authority which can establish Christianity, in exclusion of all other Religions," Madison reasoned, "may establish with the same ease any particular sect of Christians" or, for that matter, any other religion. He concluded by restating that religion according to the dictates of one's conscience is "the gift of nature," and not of government.[49] Therefore, governments have no authority over the free exercise of religion.

Dissenters agreed with that analysis. A convention of Presbyterian lay and ministerial leaders petitioned the legislators to oppose the general assessment as an abuse of state power and a violation of individual liberty. First, they based their case on the idea of limited government and the notion of separate spheres for the spiritual and temporal. They argued, "The end of civil government is security to the temporal liberty and property of mankind, and to protect them in the free exercise of religion." They added, "legislators are invested with powers from their constituents for this purpose only; and their duty extends no further." Second, they took the position that the exercise of religion was a natural right belonging to the individual. They contended, "Religion is altogether personal, and the right of exercising it unalienable; and it is not, cannot, and ought not to be, resigned to the will of the society at large; and much less to the Legislature." The petitioners feared that if Virginians gave the state a voice in religious matters, no matter how benign, they would jeopardize future generations' freedom as well as their own. "It establishes a precedent for further encroachments by making the Legislature judges of religious truth," they wrote. "If the Assembly have a right to determine the preference between Christianity and the other systems of religion that prevail in the world, they may also, at a convenient time, give a preference to some favored sect among Christians."[50] If lawmakers are enabled to become "judges of religious truth" in one instance that may favor a particular group, future legislators may exercise that power in ways that are unfavorable.

Baptists also weighed in against establishment. They had historically championed the notion of religious freedom by insisting on the separation of church and state. The Baptists of the Ketocton Association were typical of Baptists in general in opposing the bill. They argued that "the distinction between civil and ecclesiastical governments ought to be kept up without blending them together." Christ, not the government, "hath given laws for his kingdom and direction of his subjects." Further, they warned, religious freedom is like freedom of the press; "if government limits the press, and says this shall be printed and that shall not, in the event it will destroy the freedom of the press; so when legislatures undertake to pass laws about religion, religion loses its form, and Christianity is reduced to a system of worldly policy." Finally, religious freedom is not a matter of majority opinion and majority rule. If it were, then it "would give an opportunity to the party that were numerous (and, of course, possessed the ruling power) to use their influence and exercise their art and cunning, and multiply signers to their own favorite party."[51] In that case, politics, not truth, would determine the place of religion.

With scores of petitions and memorials registering opposition to the assessment bill, the Assembly, deliberating as a "Committee of the Whole," failed to muster a majority vote to pass the measure. Madison's notion that religious freedom was more important than orthodoxy, and that it was best safeguarded by a complete separation of church and state, had prevailed over Patrick Henry's belief that religious liberty was peripheral to religious orthodoxy, which was best protected by the establishment of a state-sponsored church. By burying the assessment bill, Madison and his dissenting allies were able to bring forward Thomas Jefferson's Statute for Religious Freedom, which he had drafted in 1777 and introduced in the House in 1779, where it was debated and tabled while the issue of establishment took center stage.

"Almighty God hath created the mind free," Jefferson wrote, "and manifested his supreme will that free it shall remain by making it altogether insusceptible of restraint; that all attempts to influence it by temporal punishments, or burthens, or by civil incapacitations, tend only to beget habits of hypocrisy and meanness, and are a departure from the plan of the holy author of our religion." History, he then argued, bears witness to a long chain of abuses as church and state leaders have tried to impose their religious wills on people by force. To Jefferson it was the height of arrogance; "impious presumption of legislators and rulers, civil as well as ecclesiastical, who, being themselves but fallible and uninspired men, have assumed dominion over the faith of others, setting up their own opinions and modes of thinking as the only true and infallible, and as such endeavoring to impose them on others, hath established and maintained false religions over the greatest part of the world and through all time." To hold religious beliefs solely according to one's conscience is a natural right, and those beliefs should have no bearing upon one's civil liberties: "our civil rights have no dependance on our religious opinions, any more than our opinions in physics or geometry; that therefore the proscribing any citizen as unworthy the public confidence by laying upon him an incapacity of being called to offices of trust and emolument, unless he profess or renounce this or that religious opinion, is depriving him injuriously of those privileges and advantages to which, in common with his fellow citizens, he has a natural right."[52]

Anticipating Henry's objection that the state must support religion in order to prevent dangerous heresies from disrupting public order, Jefferson set forth his notions on how a free marketplace of ideas would sift out the truth and expose lies and errors. He distinguished between "truth" and "orthodoxy." The former needed no external power to uphold it; the latter depended on ecclesiastical and civil power to enforce it. Jefferson held "that truth is great and will prevail if left to herself; that she is the proper and sufficient antagonist to error, and has nothing to fear from the conflict unless by human interposition disarmed of her natural weapons, free argument and debate; errors ceasing to be dangerous when it is permitted freely to contradict them." Having completed his argument, Jefferson then set forth the heart of the bill: "no man shall be compelled to frequent or support any religious worship, place, or ministry whatsoever, nor shall be enforced, restrained, molested, or burthened in his body or goods, nor shall otherwise suffer, on account of his religious opinions or belief; but that all men shall be free to profess, and by argument to maintain, their opinions in matters of religion, and that the same shall in no wise diminish, enlarge, or affect their civil capacities."

While he believed that "the land belongs to the living," and that one generation could not bind subsequent ones, Jefferson maintained that the rights stated in the act were "of the natural rights of mankind, and that if any act shall be hereafter passed to repeal the present or to narrow its operation, such act will be an infringement of natural right."[53] On December 17, 1785, the House, dominated by Churchmen, voted to make Jefferson's bill law by a margin of 67 to 20. And with its passage, the law signaled one of the most revolutionary moments in the entire American Revolution.

When David Ramsay published his history of the American Revolution in 1789, he considered the separation of church and state to be among its most revolutionary legacies. He proclaimed categorically, "all religious establishments were abolished." About the various states, he added, "Some retained a constitutional distinction between Christians and others, with respect to eligibility to office, but the idea of supporting one denomination at the expence of others, or of raising any one sect of Protestants to a legal pre-eminence, was universally reprobated." What Ramsay found truly remarkable was that "the alliance between church and state was completely broken," and that thenceforth "each was left to support itself, independent of the other."[54] He knew that his readers would agree that such a separation represented a radical departure from traditional practice.

In 1787, the Founding Fathers faced questions concerning what sort of church-state relations should prevail at the federal government level. Many of them had participated in state constitutional conventions and were well aware of the various religious settlements. They could adopt some sort of establishment, perhaps not that of a single sect but one broad enough to include all Christians. They could safeguard the rights of those who fell outside that definition by enacting a liberal law of religious toleration. Or they could adopt the Virginia model and choose religious freedom. The former would place the United States alongside other enlightened nations, such as England and the Low Countries. The latter would make America's religious settlement truly revolutionary.

❖ 9 ❖

Constitutional Recognition of a
Free Religious Market

W HEN he first read a draft of the proposed new federal constitution in 1787, William Williams of Connecticut was dismayed. Nowhere did the document affirm faith in God. Not only did this New Light merchant call for the omission of the sentence categorically debarring a federally mandated religious test for officeholders; he wanted a religious test for officeholders that would "require an explicit acknowledgment of the being of a God, his perfections and his providence." Indeed, what Williams desired was a strong affirmation of religious beliefs to introduce the entire document. He proposed a preamble that began: "*We the people of the United States, in a firm belief of the being and perfections of the one living and true God, the creator and supreme Governour of the world, in his universal providence and the authority of his laws; that he will require of all moral agents an account of their conduct; that all rightful powers among men are ordained of, and mediately derived from God. . . .*"[1] Citizens of a Christian nation, Williams believed, should not allow the historic moment of constitution making to pass without acknowledging their faith in God.

In Williams's opinion, the framers of the Constitution, the Founding Fathers, had betrayed their forebears, especially the Puritan Fathers. Those earlier divines had brought to New England a determination to establish not only a Christian nation but one whose beliefs and practices would so conform to Scripture that future generations would look on it as a "City upon a Hill." The most cursory comparison between the Constitution's preamble and John Winthrop's *Model of Christian Charity* reveals the fundamentally different orientations between the two blueprints. First, the Constitution took its authority from "the People," whereas the *Model* rested on a "special overruling Providence" and the "Churches of Christ." Second, the Constitution pursued secular goals: "to form a more perfect union, establish justice, insure domestic tranquility, provide for the common defense, promote the general welfare, and secure the blessings of liberty to ourselves and our posterity." Winthrop's goals were sacred, his concern less about this world than about preparing for the next. The Puritans of Massachusetts sought to "improve our lives to do more service to the Lord and to comfort and increase the body of Christ of which we are members, so that ourselves and our posterity may be better preserved from the common corruptions of this evil world in order to serve the Lord and work out our salvation under the power and purity of His holy ordinances."

Relations between religious and civil duties were also very different. In the state the Puritan Fathers erected, freemen took an oath as Christians, swearing by "the great and dreadful name of the ever-living God that I will be true and faithful to the same. . . . So help me God, in the Lord Jesus Christ." Now, 150 years later, the Constitution fashioned by the Founding Fathers made no mention of God or Christ. And one's religious persuasions had nothing to do with citizenship and officeholding. In its only reference to religion, the Constitution declared that "no religious test shall ever be required as a qualification to any office or public trust under the United States." Moreover, according to Luther Martin, one of the few delegates who favored a religious test, the clause had occasioned little debate or dissension. Indeed, only North Carolina voted against the ban, and Martin's Maryland delegation split on the issue.

The pacific atmosphere in Philadelphia stands in sharp contrast to the rancor that had characterized the debate over religious freedom in Virginia two years earlier. In that historic moment, Baptist and Presbyterian Dissenters fought Episcopalians who insisted on continuing their colonial tradition of an established religion. Recognizing that the state was too pluralistic to make the Episcopal Church the official body, some delegates suggested that Christianity in general be established. Thomas Jefferson described what happened when someone moved to add Christ's name to

237

the law's preamble, so that it would read "a departure from the plan of Jesus Christ, the holy author of our religion." He said that "the insertion was rejected by a great majority, in proof that they meant to comprehend within the mantle of its protection the Jew and the Gentile, the Christian and Mahometan, the Hindoo and infidel of every denomination."[2] Like Virginia's constitution, the United States Constitution created the framework for a secular state open to all persons regardless of religion.

Rather than viewing religion as an integrative force, the Founding Fathers considered it to be divisive, threatening their desire to form a "more perfect union."[3] American society had grown more pluralistic and sectarian from the Great Awakening to the Revolution. As dissenters grew in numbers and confidence, they became bolder in defying authority, in both church and state. Some splintered from existing denominations and went their separate ways. Then, at the state constitutional conventions, they agitated for disestablishment in bitter battles pitting Protestant sects against each other. Religious passions were intense, and they emphasized sectarian differences rather than Christian unity. Indeed, Madison cited "a zeal for different opinions concerning religion" as one of the powerful passions that have "inflamed [men and women] with mutual animosity, and rendered them much more disposed to vex and oppress each other, than co-operate for their common good."[4]

The Founders' solution to the problem of how to keep religion from undermining union was to ignore it. That is, they gave it no place in the Constitution. They delegated to the federal government no power whatever over religion, leaving matters of faith and practice in the hands of the people and the states. Such separation represented a radical departure from other governments around the world, where the state promoted and defended an official religion. The creation of a secular state resulted from the enlightened conviction of many leading Founders who thought that, by natural right, church and state ought to be separate. But the framers were also practical politicians who, recognizing the growing numbers and influence of dissenters, decided to put contending sectarians on equal footing by giving special status to none.

Just how radical the Founders' religious settlement was became apparent in 1797 when the United States declared emphatically to the world that it was not a "Christian" state. On Monday, June 26, the lead story in the *Boston Price-Current and Marine Intelligencer* was that of the "Treaty

With Tripoli," running under the heading "Important State Papers" and prominently located at the head of the first column of the front page. Because many of the paper's subscribers were involved in Boston's shipping industry, which sent vessels to the Mediterranean, any news about that region was of interest, especially matters bearing on the pirates from the Barbary States. Indeed, since losing the protection of the British navy following the American War of Independence, American ships were regularly seized and tribute demanded of their owners. Thus, with more than a little attention, Boston's merchants and investors read the "Treaty of Peace and Friendship Between the United States of America and the Bey and Subjects of Tripoli of Barbary." The second of the twelve articles told the good news: "If any goods belonging to any nation with which either of the parties is at war shall be loaded on board of vessels belonging to the other party they shall pass free, and no attempt shall be made to take or detain them." Article 11, however, told news of a different sort. It contained a pledge from the United States that must have brought up short some readers whose forefathers had planted the "City upon a Hill":

> As the government of the United States of America is not in any sense founded on the Christian Religion,—as it has in itself no character of enmity against the laws, religion or tranquility of Musselmen,—and as the said States never have entered into any war or act of hostility against any Mehomitan nation, it is declared by the parties that no pretext arising from religious opinions ever produce an interruption of the harmony existing between the two countries.[5]

Boldly stated for all Americans and the world to see, "the government of the United States of America is not in any sense founded on the Christian Religion." Moreover, this was no declaration uttered by one of the radical Deists such as Thomas Paine or Ethan Allen who regularly attacked Christianity and its leaders. This was a treaty negotiated by an agent of the federal government, presented by the president of the United States to the Senate, which, after due deliberation, had ratified it with a two-thirds vote. And the government had been at pains to make the treaty known. Philadelphia's *Porcupine Gazette* explained the route that the treaty took in reaching the newspapers: "Now be it known, That I John Adams, President of the United States of America, having seen and considered the said treaty do, by and with the advice and consent of the senate accept, ratify, and confirm the same, and every clause and article thereof. And to the end that the said treaty, may be observed and performed with good faith on the part of the United States, I have ordered it to be made public."[6]

Reprinted and prominently displayed throughout the United States, the treaty, and in particular its remarkable Article 11, elicited almost no public comment. William Cobbett, editor of the *Porcupine*, was an exception. Following the reprint of the treaty, Cobbett editorialized within brackets as follows:

> The 11th article of this treaty certainly wants some explanation. That "the government of the United States of America is not in any sense founded on the Christian Religion," is a declaration that one might have expected from Soliman Kaya, Hassan Bashaw, or the sans-culotte Joel Barlow; but it sounds rather oddly from the President and the Senate. If it will admit of satisfactory explanation, it ought to receive it, for it certainly looks a little like trampling upon the cross.[7]

Taken aback, Cobbett first tried to pass the statement off as the creation of the Muslim negotiators or perhaps the insertion of Joel Barlow. Barlow was a republican ally of Thomas Jefferson, and Cobbett viewed him as a Deist at best and a pro-French infidel at worst. But the editor finally acknowledged that Article 11 was no private statement. It came from the "President and the Senate." It was the deliberate product of discussion that allowed ample opportunity for objections and time to remove objectionable clauses. The editor was stunned by the statement's bold and public nature.

Upon close analysis, however, the clause is entirely consistent with the Constitution. Ten years earlier, the delegates to the Constitutional Convention had crafted a secular state, one that established, supported, and defended no religion. Indeed, the end result of the Founding Fathers' deliberations was the acknowledgment that religion was not under government jurisdiction, remaining one of those natural rights that the people retained for themselves. Article 11 of the 1797 treaty affirmed that the *"government* [my emphasis] of the United States of America is not in any sense founded on the Christian Religion." Under the Constitution, church and state were separate. But the Founders differentiated between the state and the nation. The former was the political power that bound the people together, and the latter was their cultural unity, including their common beliefs, aspirations, and principles. By no means did the separation of church and state mean that Americans were not a religious people. Nor did it preclude the possibility that the nation was already or could become a Christian nation; that would be determined by the voluntary decisions of men and women in a free religious market, not by government coercion.

Religious Factions and the Threat to Union

James Madison has with good reason been called the Father of the Constitution. Introduced in the opening days of the convention, it was his Virginia Plan that provided the framework for debate, and after four months of line-by-line scrutiny and a couple of major compromises, his draft held up. Underlying the diminutive Virginian's plan was his concern that the United States under the Articles of Confederation was weak and therefore subject to internal rebellion and external invasion. Shays's Rebellion in Massachusetts in 1786 fueled fears of the former, while British trade wars against the new republic and the continued presence of British troops in frontier forts fed anxieties about the latter. Like George Washington, Madison believed that as long as states controlled the central government, the country was at the mercy of the special interests that dominated them. As commander of the Continental Army, Washington had seen firsthand the reluctance of some states to supply their share of men and money for the war effort. After the war, states continued to hold the national Congress hostage under the Articles of Confederation, which called for the unanimous consent of all the states for passage of any tax measure. When Rhode Island refused to agree to an excise tax to keep the new republic afloat, the United States faced bankruptcy.

As he contemplated a new and stronger national government, Madison was therefore most concerned about special interests and "factions," among which he numbered the nation's many religious groups. By faction, Madison meant "a majority or minority of the whole, who are united and actuated by some common impulse of passion, or of interest, adverse to the rights of other citizens, or to the permanent and aggregate interests of the community." Along with politics and property, he considered religion to be among the greatest sources of factions. As a participant in Virginia's struggle over the place of religion, Madison had witnessed firsthand the passions religious differences inflamed. And he knew that delegates from other states, such as Massachusetts, had faced similarly emotional battles. Madison knew that factional conflict could not be avoided at Philadelphia; indeed, he believed that factions resulted from human nature and therefore could never be eliminated. People would always divide into contending parties and sects. He concluded, then, that factions must be controlled so that no one interest group could impose its will on all of society, so that an emergent majority could not oppress others.[8] How to do that was the biggest question facing the Founders in Philadelphia during the summer of 1787. How can a society of great diversity and pluralism govern itself so that the public interest is optimally served while the rights and property of private citizens are protected?

At first, Madison thought that the enormous size of the republic made representative government unworkable. Historically, he knew, the republics that worked best were those in small territories where representatives were close to those they represented and shared their interests. Inspired by reading David Hume, Madison eventually concluded that a large area could actually promote republican government by preventing factions from dominating the whole. "Extend the sphere," he wrote in *Federalist* No. 10, "and you take in a greater variety of parties and interests; you make it less probable that a majority of the whole will have a common motive to invade the rights of other citizens."[9] He reasoned that America's factionalism and pluralism were assets in securing liberty. Throughout the whole republic there would be "so many parts, interests and classes of citizens, that the rights of individuals or of the minority, will be in little danger from interested combinations of the majority." He concluded that "in a free government, the security for civil rights must be the same as for religious rights. It consists in the one case in the multiplicity of interests, and in the other, in the multiplicity of sects. The degree of security in both cases will depend on the number of interests and sects; and this may be presumed to depend on the extent of country and number of people comprehended under the same government."[10] Religious pluralism in fact promised religious freedom. Thus Madison, like Adam Smith, realized that with no single religion able to impose its views on the whole, all religious sects must compete in a free marketplace of ideas, therein providing a check against religious tyranny.

Madison's strong convictions against civil and religious tyranny date from his college days. In 1769, he left Virginia, electing to attend the College of New Jersey (later Princeton University), known for its hostility to episcopacy, over the Anglican-controlled College of William and Mary. The year before Madison arrived at Princeton, John Witherspoon had become the college's president, bringing with him a passion for the Enlightenment and a firm opposition to Parliament's oppression of the colonies. Under his leadership, Princeton became more than a college to train Presbyterian ministers. He expanded the curriculum, offering students a much more liberal education with a focus on the arts and sciences. Then, protest against the Stamp Act converted Princeton into a "cradle of liberty." A decade before Madison's arrival, "religion held the dominant place in the minds and hearts of faculty and students," but political protest changed the atmosphere. Groups of undergraduates discussed the "injustice of the Stamp Act . . . in the refectory, on the campus, and in the chambers of Nassau Hall." Moreover, beginning in the mid-1760s, commencements became occasions "for harangues on patriotism, or debates on the thesis that 'all men are free by the law of nature.' " In September 1765, the assembled graduating class "were attired in cloth of American manufacture, an act of patriotism which brought forth warm praise from the public and the press."[11] President Witherspoon added his fervor to the Patriot cause when he arrived in 1768.

As a delegate to the Second Continental Congress, John Witherspoon expressed views that James Madison would echo a dozen years later at the Constitutional Convention. Witherspoon was the only minister to sign the Declaration of Independence, in part because he understood that the issue of independence was a political, not a religious, matter. Another Presbyterian minister, John Zubly of Georgia, had preceded him at the congress. Noting that Zubly was the "first Gentleman of the Cloth who has appeared in Congress," John Adams quickly added that "I can not but wish he may be the last."[12] Zubly wanted to make the question of American independence a theological, not a political, issue. Out of step with his fellow delegates, he wanted the congress to focus on making America a "Christian" nation rather than an independent state. A staunch Calvinist, he believed that God's grace, not human laws, was of ultimate importance. In fact, he considered it an "extreme absurdity" to struggle for "civil liberty, yet continue slaves to sin and lust." Through his other-worldly preachments, Zubly made himself irrelevant at the congress; he simply was not a factor in the proceedings. Far more influential was Witherspoon, who, though a Calvinist, understood that the issue before the Congress was that of civil liberty. Furthermore, he knew that civil liberty and religious liberty were connected. "There is not a single in-stance in history," he noted, "in which civil liberty was lost, and religious liberty preserved entire."[13] Witherspoon and his fellow delegates believed that they, and not Parliament, were the proper guardians of American liberties, civil and religious.

In 1787, Madison brought to Philadelphia a strong conviction as to how religious freedom would best be protected: church and state must be separate. He arrived at that position in part through his understanding of natural rights, in part through the Enlightenment ideas he learned at Princeton, and in part through his role in the struggle for religious liberty in Virginia. In arguing for the adoption of Jefferson's Statute for Religious Freedom (1785), Madison had premised his remarks on the "undeniable truth, 'that religion or the duty which we owe to our Creator and the manner of discharging it, can be directed only by reason and conviction, not by force or violence.' " He therefore opposed on principle any kind of religious establishment, no matter how mild it might be. In an obvious reference to the current political tyranny, he warned "that the same au-thority which can force a citizen to contribute threepence only of his property for the support of any one establishment may force him to conform to any other establishment in all cases whatsoever." To him, religious establishments were like parliamentary taxes: they were uncon-stitutional powers imposed on free citizens without consent. He denied that a civil magistrate was a "competent judge of religious truths," and he feared that magistrates would "employ religion as an engine of civil policy." Further, he thought that government support of religion belittled the Christian faith. He reminded his fellow Virginians that for centuries Christianity "both existed and flourished, not only without the support of human laws but in spite of every opposition from them."[14]

In 1785, the same year Madison and Jefferson fought for separation of church and state in Virginia, the issue of religious liberty confronted the national Congress. The question surfaced in the debate over the Land

Ordinance, a measure setting forth a system for surveying the land between the Appalachians and the Mississippi River known as the Northwest Territory. A group of Massachusetts land speculators had urged Congress to make federal land available to them at low prices for the purpose of developing the region. Reflecting the sponsors' Puritan backgrounds, the proposed bill contained a provision for federally supported religion in the territory: "There shall be reserved the Central section of every township for the maintenance of public schools and the [section] immediately to the Northward for the support of religion, the profits arising therefrom in both instances to be applied for ever according to the will of the majority of male residents of full age within the same." The clause for the support of religion touched off in Congress a debate over church and state. Charles Pinckney of South Carolina moved that the paragraph be amended by the deletion of the words "for the support of religion" and the insertion of "for religious and charitable uses." But, wishing to expunge any mention of religion whatever, William Ellery of Rhode Island moved that the lawmakers amend the amendment by striking out the words "religious and," so that it read "for charitable uses." Ellery's motion passed, thereby expressing the principle of separation of church and state for the first time at the federal level.[15]

Locked in Virginia's battle for religious liberty, Madison was delighted to learn about Congress's stand. In a letter to his friend James Monroe, Madison wrote, "It gives me much pleasure to observe by 2 printed reports sent me by Col. Grayson that, in the latter Congress had expunged a clause contained in the first for setting apart a district of land in each Township for supporting the Religion of the majority of inhabitants." He expressed his strong opposition to any government support of religion, even if it were the religion of the majority of citizens: "How a regulation so unjust in itself, foreign to the Authority of Congress, so hurtful to the sale of the public land, and smelling so strongly of an antiquated Bigotry, could have received the countenance of a Committee is truly a matter of astonishment." He concluded with the hope that the ringing victory of separation of church and state at the federal level would influence lawmakers in Virginia to embrace the same principle to guarantee religious freedom in the state.[16]

Thus when the Constitutional Convention convened on May 14, 1787, James Madison was well prepared to take the lead in proposing a totally new framework for government. Like George Washington, Madison had been an outspoken critic of the Articles of Confederation, which rendered the country weak by granting sovereignty to thirteen jealous states that were often more concerned about local than about national interests. In Madison's view, the states, controlled by powerful interest groups, were not the best guardians of civil and religious freedom. Determined to transfer power from the states to the federal government, he brought with him a plan designed to protect individual liberty by dividing power.

THE "GODLESS" CONSTITUTION[17]

In designing a frame of government, the delegates to the Constitutional Convention in Philadelphia appealed primarily to secular, not sacred, authority. An analysis of citations in American political pamphlets and treatises in the late eighteenth century indicates that almost 90 percent of the references are to European writers who wrote on Enlightenment or Whig themes or who commented on the English common law. Only about 10 percent of the citations were biblical, with most of those coming from writings attributed to Saint Paul. Framers of the United States Constitution were steeped in political theory and history, and they had seen firsthand how unchecked power undermined freedom. Because of the abuse of constitutional power by the king and Parliament, Americans sought to preclude future tyranny by making a "fixed Constitution" the supreme law against which no civil or religious authority could transgress. The task for American lawmakers was one of law, not theology, and raised two fundamental questions: "First, what shall the form of government be? And Secondly, What shall be its power?"[18]

Unlike the Puritan Fathers, the Founding Fathers gave Christianity no privileged place of authority in their deliberations regarding a frame of government. While religion offered insights into the means and ends of human fulfillment, no single sect possessed exclusive insights. "All sober inquirers after truth," wrote John Adams in 1776, "ancient and modern, pagan and Christian, have declared that the happiness of man, as well as his dignity, consists in virtue. Confucius, Zoroaster, Socrates, Mahomet, not to mention authorities really sacred, have agreed in this." But when considering how government should be structured to provide for the greatest human happiness, Adams appealed not to truths lodged in various documents claiming divine revelation but to "the minds of people." For principles of republican government, he recommended not Jesus, Saint Paul, Augustine, Luther, Calvin, Wesley, the Mathers, or Edwards, but "Sidney, Harrington, Locke, Milton, Nedham, Neville, Burnet, and Hoadly."[19]

Though relying on secular authorities to structure the Constitution, many of the Founders did believe that religion, particularly Protestant Christianity, was essential for a law-abiding nation. During the Revolution, Whig spokesmen frequently linked Christianity and citizenship. In a typical sermon, the congressional chaplain Jacob Duche reminded the legislators that American freedom rested on twin foundations: "the charter of TEMPORAL FREEDOM, and the records of ETERNAL TRUTH." One could not separate the civil from the religious liberty of a people where the "banners of CHRISTIAN and BRITISH Liberty were at once unfolded." In a 1776 review of the colonists' "present calamities," Duche blamed Britain, whose "merciless and unhallowed hands" had choked her colonists, but he also reminded his constituents that the "present chastisements have . . . been drawn down upon us by a gross neglect of our SPIRITUAL PRIVILEGES." The only solution was "the revival of every private and public virtue, which can adorn and dignify the citizen and the christian."[20]

Delegates to the Constitutional Convention were concerned primarily with "temporal freedom"—specifically, the problem of how to allocate and restrain power in a way that best assured liberty. The pursuit of "eternal truth" they left to individuals and churches. The delegates wrestled with mundane but important questions, like that of sovereignty, or whether the states or the national government should have ultimate authority. In the end they decided on a strong central government organized on federalist principles whereby sovereignty was split between the national and state governments. Delegates also debated the vexing issue of representation, determining that for the House of Representatives "the people" should elect their own representatives, the number to be proportionate to each state's population, and in the Senate the states should have equal representation. And they argued over which powers should be assigned to each branch of the federal government, and which powers should remain with the states. During four months of deliberation, those big structural and functional issues concerning the distribution and balance of power predominated. Within the context of those broader discussions, religion rarely surfaced. As historian John Murrin concluded, while the delegates were not antireligion, they were humanists determined to create a secular state based on sound constitutional principles, such as the separation of powers and "checks and balances," designed to provide a republicanism that optimally protected citizens' property and rights.[21]

The delegates knew that social concord in a republic depended on a virtuous citizenry, but the question was how to ensure public virtue. The Puritan Fathers had believed that God through divine Election produced men who could be trusted with the franchise and officeholding. Leaders of the Great Awakening had agreed, emphasizing the necessity of a spiritual conversion to transform willful, selfish people into obedient servants of God and man. Though many delegates expressed their belief that religious instruction promotes morality and thus good citizenship, few had faith that religion alone would produce virtuous citizens. Ancient and recent history testified to the fact that religious people sometimes engaged in irreligious behavior. And with so many different sects in America insisting that they represented the one true religion, no delegate proposed establishing any one of them as the nation's official religion. Followers of the Enlightenment thought that the ideal social order was one where reason prevailed and rational men discerned and obeyed the "laws of nature and nature's God." The problem was that too many Americans allowed tradition and superstition, rather than informed reason, to guide them. Some followers of the Scottish Enlightenment, like Jefferson, believed that all people possessed a "moral sense," an inner compass that could be relied upon for virtuous behavior.

In the end, the delegates agreed with Madison that men and women could not be relied upon to act always as virtuous citizens. But they could be relied upon to act out of self-interest, and the great diversity of competing interests presented a fair prospect of preventing any one interest from oppressing the others. By framing a constitution that divided power and checked its abuse, self-interested people could pursue their own ends without turning the republic into an engine of tyranny. Rather than relying upon virtuous people to pursue the common weal, the delegates hoped that they could construct a constitution that would promote virtue.

Though religion was not at the center of the delegates' deliberations, it nevertheless had to be considered. Like their counterparts at the various state constitutional conventions, the men who gathered in Philadelphia faced two issues regarding religion. First, they had to define church-state relations as they pertained to the federal government. They could follow Massachusetts's model, establishing religion in the sense of insisting that every person must have the benefit of religious instruction by a "Protestant" minister, appointed and remunerated by the government if the people in a specific location did not undertake this responsibility. Such an arrangement would ensure that all citizens received public religious and moral instruction deemed by many to be the cornerstone of a peaceful, law-abiding society. And they could protect the rights of dissenters by guaranteeing the free exercise of religion according to the dictates of each person's conscience. The delegates to the federal convention knew, however, that the Massachusetts religious clause had touched off heated controversy in that state. As dissenters in Massachusetts pointed out, the state constitution imposed a narrow establishment whereby the Congregational churches were deemed to be the orthodox and privileged churches and all others were subject to government restrictions.

If delegates to the Philadelphia convention opposed such a narrow establishment, they could have adopted the more expansive provision in the South Carolina Constitution. After much wrangling over whether a single denomination should be preferred above all others, the South Carolina delegates affirmed that "the Christian Protestant religion shall be deemed, and is hereby constituted and declared to be, the established religion of this State." They then defined a set of beliefs that any religious group must subscribe to in order to be "incorporated and esteemed as a church of the established religion of this State":

1st. That there is one eternal God, and a future state of rewards and punishments.
2nd. That God is publicly to be worshipped.
3nd. That the Christian religion is the true religion.
4th. That the holy scriptures of the Old and New Testaments are of divine inspiration, and are the rule of faith and practice.
5th. That it is lawful and the duty of every man being thereunto called by those that govern, to bear witness to the truth.[22]

The delegates at Philadelphia in fact chose, or at least endorsed, the Virginia model of a free marketplace of religion, refusing to grant any power whatever to the federal government concerning religion, thereby leaving religion as a voluntary pursuit of individuals and their churches. While some embraced the view out of conviction, the prevailing sentiment was a desire to avoid dissension that would undermine union. To these delegates, religion was a divisive, not a unifying, force in pluralistic America. Any hope of obtaining ratification would be dashed if the new constitution attempted to define or support religion, because one or more sects would construe any formulation as violating their freedom of conscience. Better to make no mention of religion at all. Thus the enumerated powers of the federal government set out in the Constitution omitted any discussion of religion. During the ratification debates, many people in fact feared that the Constitution's silence on religion opened the door for the federal government at some future point to establish religion or otherwise interfere in its free exercise. But as Madison argued, that was not the case. The Constitution delegated specific powers to the federal government, prohibiting all others, including that of religious establishment.[23]

The second issue the delegates faced with regard to religion was that of a religious test for officeholders.[24] Again, the state constitutions offered several models. The idea behind a religious test was that government officials ought to be men of high moral stature, and that sound religion—namely, Protestant Christianity—was the foundation of that morality. The Massachusetts Constitution required the governor and legislators to swear that they believed the "Christian religion, and have a firm persuasion of its truth." Maryland officeholders were required to make "a declaration of a belief in the Christian religion." The New Hampshire Constitution declared that "no person shall be capable of being elected a senator, who is not of the protestant religion." Delaware's oath of office was even more restrictive, reading like a Christian creed: "I, . . . , do profess faith in God the Father, and in Jesus Christ His only Son, and in the Holy Ghost, one God, blessed for evermore; and I do acknowledge the holy scriptures of the Old and New Testament to be given by divine inspiration." Similarly, North Carolina's constitution held "That no person, who shall deny the being of God or the truth of the Protestant religion, or the divine authority of either of the Old or New Testaments, or who shall hold religious principles incompatible with the freedom and safety of the State, shall be capable of holding any office or place of trust or profit in the civil department within this State."[25] In light of diverse formulations, the delegates at Philadelphia were well aware of the many distinctions Americans made regarding religious faith and the potential that religious questions posed for contentious debate.

On Tuesday, May 29, 1787, the Constitutional Convention began its substantive work by hearing two proposed drafts of constitutions that would replace the Articles of Confederation. Edmund Randolph of Virginia introduced Madison's Virginia Plan, which was heard and referred to the Committee of the Whole House for consideration of its specific provisions. That draft was silent on religious matters, reflecting Madison's views of religion's place in society. He contended that government is a compact between the governed and their governors, and that the former retain all rights that they do not explicitly grant to the latter. He considered religion to be a natural right that the governed did not cede to the government; it remained secure with the people themselves. Delegates would not have been surprised at the silence, because the Articles of Confederation were also mute on the subject. Charles Cotesworth Pinckney of South Carolina also offered a proposed constitution that day, similar in structure to the Virginia Plan, but his was explicit in prohibiting the federal government from having any positive role concerning religious matters, stating, "The legislature of the United States shall pass no law on the subject of religion."[26] At least on this point the delegates in Philadelphia apparently agreed. There is no record of any delegate's proposing a positive role for government in supporting religion.

The only mention of religion at all was in the negative, the prohibition against religious tests. On August 20, Pinckney proposed that "no religious test or qualification shall ever be annexed to any oath of office under the authority of the U.S." Ten days later the measure was brought before the convention for debate and a vote. Madison's notes suggest that the debate was limited. Roger Sherman of Connecticut thought that the proscription was unnecessary, with "the prevailing liberality being a sufficient security agst such tests." A majority of his fellow delegates had less faith than he that such liberality could be counted on in succeeding decades, and voted to include the clause. Only North Carolina opposed.[27]

Several possibilities explain the exclusion of positive language regarding religion. First, the delegates could have subscribed to the view that religion was beyond the purview of government because it was a natural right, the Madisonian position. Second, others could have placed it outside the state's jurisdiction by viewing religion as a spiritual matter whose authority rests with God and not with man at all. Third, some no doubt considered religion to be under state, not federal, control. This meant that if the people in any given state desired some sort of religious establishment, they were free to secure it within their own constitution. Fourth, some were confident that the establishment of Christianity was unnecessary because most Americans were Christians, and Christianity, by virtue of its own perceived superiority, would always prevail in the marketplace of ideas. Many, Deists as well as Christians, expressed confidence that "true religion" needed no coercive support from the government and would emerge victorious because of the force of its tenets. A final explanation for the absence of any federal government role in supporting religion was the pluralistic nature of religion in America. Scores of sects existed in the new republic, each claiming that its teachings and practices represented "true" Christianity. To many of these competing groups, any establishment, no matter how broadly conceived, was offensive. They were unwilling for any government, comprising unholy as well as holy men, to make any binding statements regarding religion. Given these reasons against the inclusion of a positive statement regarding religion, the delegates, more interested in union than uniformity, took the path least likely to offend any sect or church and said nothing at all.

The Founders' religious settlement thus stood in sharp contrast to the Elizabethan Settlement, which had since the sixteenth century maintained a "national church under royal and parliamentary authority." Instead of a national state church like the Church of England, wherein all English inhabitants were regarded as being members, America would have voluntary churches gathered by individuals subscribing to similar beliefs and practices and joined by those who shared those views. And while the Church of England received "financial support, the right to hold ecclesiastical courts, and political privileges secured by the Test and Corporation Acts," American churches would receive only the right to worship freely and to use all legal means of persuasion to maintain themselves and woo new members.[28]

On Monday, September 17, the delegates completed their work. Benjamin Franklin, who had said little during the deliberations, rose with a speech endorsing the Constitution. He acknowledged that there were parts of the draft that he did not approve, but that he consented because "I expect no better, and because I am not sure, that it is not the best." Franklin warned against the delegates' insisting on a constitution that conformed in every part to their own individual preferences and biases. In seeking compromise and agreement, he turned to religion for an instructive analogy.

> Most men indeed as well as most sects in Religion, think themselves in possession of all truth, and that wherever others differ from them it is so far error. Steele a Protestant in a Dedication tells the Pope, that the only difference between our Churches in their opinions of the certainty of their doctrines is, the Church of Rome is infallible and the Church of England is never in the wrong. But though many private persons think almost as highly of their own infallibility as of that of their sect, few express it so naturally as a certain french lady, who in a dispute with her sister, said "I don't know how it happens, Sister, but I meet with no body but myself, that's always in the right."[29]

Franklin no doubt anticipated the heated debates that would rage in the various state ratifying conventions as individuals and groups tore the Constitution apart. He certainly knew that people would view the document through lenses tinted by self-interest as well as high principle. Indeed, every aspect came under intense scrutiny, including the Constitution's silence on religion and its ban on religious tests.

RATIFICATION CONTINGENT UPON RELIGIOUS FREEDOM

The debate over church-state questions begun by the delegates to the Constitutional Convention reached the states even before the document proposed for ratification did. Those voicing concerns fell into two categories. Some hoped that the federal Constitution would reflect the faith of the Puritan Fathers. That meant some level of government support for the Christian religion and the assurance that only Christians would hold offices in the new government. Others, including the Constitution's principal architects, envisioned a secular state built on Enlightenment and Whig principles. They feared that a powerful, unchecked federal government would do as monarchies had done through the centuries: establish an official religion for political purposes, one that could become powerful enough to demand special governmental favor and so threaten liberty of conscience.

Once the Constitution became public, its silence on religion became a matter of public debate. An Anti-Federalist, the designation by which Madison and others referred to those who opposed the Constitution, warned in a Boston newspaper on January 10, 1788, that because God was absent from the Constitution, Americans would suffer the fate that the prophet Samuel foretold to Saul: "because thou hast rejected the word of the Lord, he hath also rejected thee."[30] Another letter-writer argued that civic virtue depended upon governmental encouragement of the Christian faith. He compared Massachusetts's constitutional provision requiring public officials to be Protestants with the federal Constitution's "public inattention" to religion and found the latter flawed. He charged the framers with "leaving religion to shift wholly for itself," and he predicted that the new nation was headed toward disaster, for "it is more difficult to build an elegant house without tools to work with, than it is to establish a durable government without the publick protection of religion."[31] A delegate to the Massachusetts ratifying convention, Amos Singletary, voiced his objection to the absence of a religious test. Upset that the Constitution did not require men in power to be religious, he noted that "though he hoped to see Christians [in office], yet by the Constitution, a papist, or an infidel was as eligible as they."[32] All of these protesters proceeded from the same assumption: America was a Christian nation and its constitution must reflect that fact by supporting the "true faith."

No one voiced that position more eloquently than did Ezra Stiles, the president of Yale, who from the beginning of the Revolution envisioned the United States as "God's American Israel." Stiles, like John Adams and others, believed that the American Revolution was as much about religion as it was about politics. Indeed, he thought that the new republic's unprecedented religious freedom would become a model for all nations, inspiring other countries to rid themselves of persecution. Writing in

1783, Stiles looked back to his Puritan Fathers and hailed John Winthrop as an "American Nehemiah" who had established the importance of founding a society on the principles of "true religion."[33] As Winthrop had deemed Massachusetts a "City upon a Hill," a beacon for future generations, Stiles saw the United States as a land of the "most ample *religious liberty*," which, he ventured, "will also be the basis for making America a new Israel." He acknowledged that the new republic started with natural advantages, especially its vast stretches of productive land and a growing population. But, he warned, those assets alone were insufficient to guarantee happiness. He claimed that "our system of dominion and CIVIL POLITY would be imperfect, without the TRUE RELIGION." Indeed, Stiles argued, "Holiness ought to be the end of all civil government." But "true religion" and "holiness" must come from the people; they cannot be imposed by any government. Of all polities, he favored the one he considered to be best suited to the "nature of man" and that which withstood the "comparison of ages": a "well-ordered DEMOCRATICAL ARISTOCRACY standing upon the annual elections of the people, . . . revocable at pleasure." Predicting that that polity would "approve itself the most equitable, liberal, and perfect," Stiles argued that the acid test of its liberality would be in how it handled religious differences.[34] European countries had long histories of religious oppression whereby the monarch or ruling oligarchy favored one religion in order to secure the political support of its adherents. Stiles envisioned a very different America, a Christian nation that guaranteed religious freedom for all.

In the republic Stiles envisioned, no religious group would be excluded, nor would one body be favored over another. Rather, "the united states will embosom all the religious sects or denominations in Christendom. Here they may all enjoy their whole respective systems of worship and church government, complete." Further, he added, "all religious denominations will be independent of one another . . . , and having, on account of religion, no superiority as to secular powers and civil immunities, they will cohabit together in harmony." The absence of a state religion would create an atmosphere for a "candid and liberal disquisition" of religious ideas and issues that Stiles maintained would set America apart from all other nations. "Removed from the embarrassment of corrupt systems, and the dignities and blinding obedience connected with them," he explained, "the unfettered mind can think with a noble enlargement, and with an unbounded freedom, go wherever the light of truth directs." Unlike in other nations, "here will be no bloody tribunals, no cardinals inquisitors-general, to bend the human mind, foreceably to control the understanding, and put out the light of reason, the candle of the Lord, in man; . . . Religion may here receive its last, most liberal, and impartial examination."[35]

An unfettered search for the truth, Stiles believed, would demonstrate that Protestant Christianity was the "true religion." Moreover, he foresaw the day when the United States was "increased to 40 or 50 millions": then, "while we see all the religious sects increased into respectable bodies, we shall doubtless find the united body of the *congregational* and *consociated* and *presbyterian* churches, making an equal figure with any of them." By that prediction he meant that denominations with hierarchical structures—such as the Church of England—which had done well during the colonial period, would not fare as well after the War of Independence. Stiles was also projecting his New England bias and expressing his hope that the rest of the American religious landscape would soon look like that in the northernmost states. While admitting that there had been imperfections and controversies, nonetheless, in his mind, New Englanders had indeed created a spiritual "City upon a Hill" that the new republic should view as a model.[36]

As Stiles contemplated what kind of nation the United States might become, he thought it would be well served if led by men like the Founding Fathers of Puritan New England. In his mind, they had returned Christianity to its primitive, unadulterated form, without the "mutilated artificial forms of the pontifical or patriarchal constitutions, of the middle and present ages." He had little hope that such leaders would emerge from the present generation, which he characterized as "the present period of deism and sceptical indifferentism in religion, of timidity and irresolution in the cause of the great *Emmanuel*." But perhaps in the future "there may arise a succession of civil magistrates, who will not be ashamed of the cross of Christ, nor of patronizing his holy religion." In that day, Stiles, exclaimed, "the *religious* as well as the *civil* patriot will shine in the faces of the future *Moses's* and *Joshuas* of the land."[37]

Stiles summed up his review of idolatry, Deism, and Christianity by asking which would "most contribute to the secular welfare," and which would be "most subservient to eternity and its momentous concerns."

He then guaranteed the right response by asking, "Which of these empires would be the favorite of Jesus? Or is he indeed an unconcerned spectator of human affairs? If not, why should we doubt or hesitate to give the preference to the *christian republic?*"

While Stiles wished the Founders had constructed a *"christian republic,"* other Christians applauded their work.[38] While they agreed with Stiles on the superiority of Christianity to all other religions, they disagreed with his belief that the new republic would be best served by its being framed on the Massachusetts model. Dissenters, a broad category that included all American Christians who did not subscribe to an established religion, believed that Stiles's representation of Massachusetts's church-state relations was grossly distorted. Isaac Backus, a delegate to the Massachusetts ratifying convention, expressed the sentiments of Dissenters everywhere when he rose to defend the framers' exclusion of religious tests:

> Many appear to be much concerned about it; but nothing is more evident, both in reason and the Holy Scriptures, than that religion is ever a matter between God and individuals; and, therefore, no man or men can impose any *religious test*, without invading the essential prerogatives of our God Jesus Christ. Ministers first assumed this power under the Christian name; and then Constantine approved of the practice, when he adopted the profession of Christianity, as an engine of state policy. And let the history of all nations be searched from that day to this, and it will appear that the imposing of *religious tests* hath been the: greatest engine of tyranny in the world. And I rejoice to see so many gentlemen, who are now giving in their rights of conscience in this great and important matter. Some serious minds discover a concern lest, if all *religious tests* should be excluded, the Congress would hereafter establish Popery, or some other tyrannical way of worship. But it is most certain that no such way of worship can he established without any *religious test*.[39]

Supporters of a constitutional religious test raised the specter of all sorts of undesirables being elected to the highest offices. Some couched their objections in general terms. Patrick Calhoun told his fellow delegates to the South Carolina convention that "too great latitude [was] allowed in religion."[40] Others were more specific. Reverend David Cald-

257

well of North Carolina feared that the open "invitation to Jews and pagans" carried political as well as religious dangers. In supporting Caldwell's position, a like-minded delegate expanded the list of undesirables. The failure to exclude non-Christians, which he defined more narrowly as non-Protestant Christians, meant that it "is most certain, that Papists may occupy that chair [i.e., the presidency], and Mahometans may take it."[41]

One pamphleteer attempted to allay such concerns by expressing his confidence that voters would impose their own tests and consequently never elect persons other than Christians. Samuel Langdon, pastor at Hampton Falls, New Hampshire, called on his readers to select for their officials "men who fear God, and hate covetousness; who love truth and righteousness." He claimed that only men who fear God could rule well. Moreover, "will not the example of their impiety and immorality defeat the efficacy of the best laws which can be made in favour of religion and virtue?" Langdon warned voters against being seduced by sectarians, saying, "regard not men who are continually crying up their own sect, and employing their utmost zeal and art to proselyte men to their party: they aim to strengthen themselves by your numbers and purses, more than to save your souls." He also warned against "imbibing the licentious principles of men who affect to render all religion doubtful, by persuading you that every kind of religion is equally acceptable to God if a man is but sincere in it."[42] Langdon urged citizens to impose their own religious test on officeholders and select only those whose beliefs and practices met the electors' standards.

While some expressed support for religious tests, many others voiced concern over the lack of a Bill of Rights that would safeguard the individual's rights of conscience from federal government coercion. It became apparent in some of the largest states' conventions, including those of Massachusetts and Virginia, that the Constitution would not be ratified without amendments guaranteeing certain rights. Religious freedom was one of the rights that delegates were uneasy about, fearing that the Constitution's silence on religion was insufficient protection against government "mischief" in religious affairs. Dissenters in particular were concerned that future governments might establish an official religion and thereby interfere with the free exercise of religion according to one's conscience. Accordingly, delegates drafted bills of rights, or lists of expressed rights that individuals held without interference from the federal government. The Virginia convention approved the following amendment regarding religion:

> That religion, or the duty which we owe to our Creator, and the manner of discharging it, can be directed only by reason and conviction, not by force or violence; and therefore all men have an equal, natural, and unalienable right to the free exercise of religion, according to the dictates of conscience, and that no particular religious sect or society ought to be forced or established, by law, in preference to others.[43]

James Madison opposed the measure because he feared that any constitutional or legislative attempt to define religious freedom would result in narrowing its scope. In a letter to Jefferson, who was in Paris as minister to France, Madison expressed his concern: "I am sure that the rights of conscience in particular, if submitted to public definition would be narrowed much more than they are ever to be by an assumed power." As an example, he noted that New Englanders opposed the Constitution's prohibition of religious tests because it "opened a door for Jews Turks and infidels."[44] Liberty of conscience was a natural right that all should enjoy, not a grant of positive law.

Madison was a practical politician, and he recognized that to win ratification, he must support a Bill of Rights. Therefore, he pledged his support in getting the amendments passed in the first Congress. While Madison may have been satisfied with the absence of an explicit guarantee of religious liberty, dissenters were not. Several groups appealed to George Washington, already regarded as father of his country and protector of citizen rights.[45]

In May 1789, the General Assembly of Presbyterian Churches sought assurance from Washington that their religious rights would be honored. In his reply, Washington first reiterated his belief that the pious practice of sound religion was essential to good citizenship. He opined that "the general prevalence of piety, philanthropy, honesty, industry, and oeconomy seems, in the ordinary course of human affairs, particularly necessary for advancing and conforming the happiness of our country." He expressed his hope that civic responsibility would accompany religious freedom in the new republic. "While all men within our territories are protected in worshipping the Deity according to the dictates of their consciences," he wrote, "it is rationally to be expected from them in return, that they will be emulous of evincing the sanctity of their professions by the innocence of their lives and the beneficence of their actions; for no man, who is profligate in his morals, or a bad member of the civil community, can possibly be a true Christian, or a credit to his own religious society." He concluded by asserting that churches, though separated from government, played an important role in promoting republican virtue. He asked the Presbyterians to accept his gratitude for their "laudable endeavors to render men sober, honest, and good Citizens, and the obedient subjects of a lawful government."[46] In short, churches were to provide the moral foundation necessary for good government.

Virginia Baptists expressed to Washington their lingering concern that without an explicit prohibition against religious establishment in a Bill of Rights, the government could erect and maintain an official church, thereby undermining religious liberty. He replied that he was convinced that the Constitution, even without a Bill of Rights, barred any religious establishment. He explained, "if I could have entertained the slightest apprehension that the Constitution framed in the Convention, where I had the honor to preside, might possibly endanger the religious rights of any ecclesiastical society, certainly I would never have placed my signature to it." He added that "if I could now conceive that the general government might ever be so administered as to render the liberty of conscience insecure, I beg you will be persuaded that no one would be more zealous than myself to establish effectual barriers against the horrors of spiritual tyranny, and every species of religious persecution." He repeated his oft-stated sentiment "that every man, conducting himself as a good citizen, and being accountable to God alone for his religious opinions, ought to be protected in worshipping the Deity according to the dictates of his own conscience."[47] He extended that same idea to Catholics, wishing them "every temporal and spiritual felicity" in a liberal republic where all "are equally entitled to the protection of civil government."[48]

In addition to Christians, Jews viewed Washington as a champion of freedom, and they, too, sought his assurances that all people, non-Christians as well as Christians, would enjoy complete religious freedom. He responded by declaring America's revolution in religion to be an example for the rest of the world. "The citizens of the United States of America," he wrote, "have a right to applaud themselves for having given to mankind examples of an enlarged and liberal policy—a policy worthy of imitation. All possess alike liberty of conscience and immunities of citizenship." He made clear that religious liberty in the United States was not mere toleration; the government simply had no positive role in religion. In a commentary on what the Founders had done in Philadelphia, Washington declared, "It is now no more that toleration is spoken of as if it were the indulgence of one class of people that another enjoyed the exercise of their inherent natural rights, for, happily, the Government of the United States, which gives to bigotry no sanction, to persecution no assistance, requires only that they who live under its protection should demean themselves as good citizens in giving it on all occasions their effectual support."[49]

True to his word, Madison provided leadership in the passage of a Bill of Rights. In a speech to the House of Representatives on June 8, 1789, Madison enunciated the amendments that he would like to see made to the Constitution. Rather than grouping them as a Bill of Rights, he advocated incorporating the changes within the text of the main body. Regarding the place of religion in the republic, he made two proposals. First, he recommended the insertion of the following clause in Article 1, section 9, which prohibited specific measures that Congress could pass:

> The civil rights of none shall be abridged on account of religious belief or worship, nor shall any national religion be established, nor shall the full and equal rights of conscience be in any manner, or on any pretext infringed.

In his analysis of the text, Chief Justice William Rehnquist attempts to draw Madison into the accommodationist interpretation. First, he views Madison as preeminent in defining church-state relations, not Jefferson, whose metaphor of a "wall" separating church and state lies at the center of the separationist perspective. "On the basis of the record of these proceedings in the House of Representatives," Rehnquist wrote in *Wallace v. Jaffree*, "James Madison was undoubtedly the most important architect among the Members of the House of the Amendments which became the Bill of Rights." But, he adds, "it was James Madison speaking as an advocate of sensible legislative compromise, not as an advocate of incorporating the Virginia Statute for Religious Freedom into the U.S. Constitution."[50] Rehnquist fails to note, however, that Madison also proposed language that would, in fact, prohibit the states from interfering with individuals' rights of free exercise. Madison's preference was indeed to extend Virginia's guarantee of complete religious freedom to all states, including those in New England that continued to restrict dissenters' rights. He therefore proposed inserting the following clause in Article 1, Section 10, which placed certain prohibitions on the states:

> No state shall violate the equal rights of conscience, or the freedom of the press, or the trial by jury in criminal cases.[51]

Had they been passed, Madison's measures would have banned religious regulation by any government act—state or federal.

After considerable debate, the House rejected Madison's format and his proposals. On August 24, 1789, the representatives passed a series of constitutional amendments that would stand as a Bill of Rights as opposed to being incorporated into the Constitution's body. The third article dealt with religion, and stated that

> Congress shall make no law establishing religion or prohibiting the free exercise thereof, nor shall the rights of Conscience be infringed.[52]

Though a categorical prohibition against religious establishment by the federal government, the wording was silent regarding the states. The Senate debated the House proposal and proposed a change in the wording. The senators sent the following version to the House:

> Congress shall make no laws establishing articles of faith, or a mode of worship, or prohibiting the free exercise of religion.[53]

A narrow reading of the first two clauses could give Congress some role in establishing religion. As one historian has noted, there was the suggestion that "Congress was barred only from enacting laws supporting particular points of doctrine (for example, belief in the Holy Trinity or the divinity of Jesus or the reality of transubstantiation) or requiring certain forms of worship. Legislation supporting (or establishing) religion in other ways would presumably be acceptable." In the conference committee appointed to resolve differences between the House and Senate versions, Madison succeeded in reinstating language that "flatly commanded Congress to 'make no law respecting an establishment of religion.' "[54]

Religious freedom resulted from an alliance of unlikely partners. New Light evangelicals such as Isaac Backus and John Leland joined forces with Deists and skeptics such as James Madison and Thomas Jefferson to fight for a complete separation of church and state. Influenced by the Great Awakening, the former believed that individuals were free to make religious choices among competing claims to truth. God alone was governor of the conscience, and only he could judge the choices individuals made. Moreover, they believed that Christianity had stood on its own without government assistance in the past and would do so in the future. Indeed, they pointed to the historical evils resulting from a union of church and state. The latter argued from Whig and Enlightenment principles but came to the same end. They held that reason, not force, should determine religious beliefs and practices. And they thought that religion was a voluntary matter and should be sustained by voluntary means.

For Madison and his supporters, the Constitution's guarantee of religious freedom represented a triumph of the spirit of 1776. The Declaration of Independence had upheld the great principles of natural and "unalienable" rights, and the Founders numbered religion among those. In 1787, they explicitly barred the federal government from violating that sacred freedom. The Constitution also reflected Adam Smith's notions that religion should operate within a free marketplace of ideas, notions set forth in his *Wealth of Nations*, published in 1776. The idea was that if left free to operate without governmental establishment or restraint, numerous competing sects would be placed on an equal footing such that they could woo followers on the strength of their respective beliefs and practices. The Founders, then, crafted a constitutional solution that gave the fullest expression to the expansive dreams of freedom set forth in 1776. America would have a secular state wherein all persons would be free to pursue their religious preferences in open competition.

Both Jefferson and Madison lived long enough to observe how well the Founders' religious settlement worked in practice. Adhering to the Constitution's proscription of an establishment, Jefferson instituted a competitive religious marketplace at the University of Virginia. He rejected the traditional practice of appointing a professor of divinity from a particular church, yet he believed that religious instruction was an important part of a young person's education and vital to the nation's good order. His solution was to open the campus to all sects, thereby offering the students choice. In 1822, he and the Board of Visitors encouraged "the different religious sects to establish, each for itself a professorship of their own tenets, on the confines of the university, so near as that their students may attend the lectures there." He expressed his confidence that the plan would promote "peace, reason, and morality."[55]

Throughout their deliberations, the Founders indicated that they were thinking about future generations. They acknowledged that their generation was a particularly liberal one, meaning that it was attuned to the dangers of any form of tyranny including that of a majority. But they knew that if proper constitutional safeguards were not in place, an imaginable political tyrant of the future could make a play for power by giving a popular religious group a position of favor in the eyes of the state. They also knew that without the separation of church and state, religious leaders would do as they had in the past and try to promise political support to the regime that would grant them privileges. They could not have foreseen, however, that the very first time candidates of opposing parties vied for the presidency, the combustible question of religion and politics would once again be kindled.

❖ 10 ❖

Religion and Politics in the Presidential Campaign of 1800

IN THE CAMPAIGN of 1800, William Linn of New York praised Thomas Jefferson as a public servant of extraordinary talents but urged voters to reject the Republican's presidential bid because of his religious beliefs. In a pamphlet, the Dutch Reformed minister stated that "my objection to his being promoted to the Presidency is founded singly upon his disbelief of the Holy Scriptures; or, in other words, his rejection of the Christian Religion and open profession of Deism." To Linn, the connection between Jefferson's religious views and his fitness for office was clear: "No professed deist, be his talents and achievements what they may, ought to be promoted to this place by the suffrages of a Christian nation." Having made the assertion that America was a Christian nation, Linn found it preposterous that voters would consider allowing a non-Christian to occupy the top political position. "Would Jews or Mahometans, consistently with their belief, elect a Christian?" he asked. Certain that his readers saw the absurdity of such a prospect, he then asked: "shall Christians be less zealous and active than they?"[1]

"Though neither the constitution, nor any law forbids his election," Linn acknowledged, "yet the public opinion ought to disqualify him. On account of his disbelief of the Holy Scriptures, and his attempts to discredit them, he ought to be rejected from the Presidency." To underscore his position, Linn repeated his argument a few pages later: "Though there is nothing in our constitution to restrict our choice, yet the open and warm preference of a manifest enemy to the religion of Christianity, in a Christian nation, would be an awful symptom of the degeneracy of that nation, and . . . a rebellion against God." Having twice noted the constitutional ban on religious tests, Linn stated his unequivocal support of an amendment instating religious tests, arguing that "a provision that the supreme magistrate should be a professor of Christianity would show the temper of the nation more clearly."[2] The supreme law of the land, in other words, should reflect the religious character of the nation.

Linn's call for a religious test echoed a similar debate held at the constitutional and ratifying conventions of 1787–1789.[3] Opposing each other then were delegates holding fundamentally different conceptions of religion's proper place in American public life. On one side were those stressing that America was a Christian nation and should be led by Christians. On the other were those emphasizing that the nation was a haven of religious freedom and should separate matters of state and issues of faith. The latter argument prevailed and resulted in a constitutional ban against religious tests. But while the Constitution guaranteed a secular state, to many Americans who considered religion central in their lives, especially defenders of Protestant orthodoxy, the issue was not settled. They discovered during the presidential campaign of 1800 the means and a forum for attaining their goal: a voter-imposed religious test to be applied in the arena of public opinion. Religion could be ignored by the Constitution, but it could not be removed from politics.

For the orthodox ministers who led the fight, the year 1800 represented their best opportunity since 1787 to argue that a Christian nation must have Christian leaders.[4] The French Revolution was to them a case study of what happens when infidels gain control: churches ransacked, divine revelation ridiculed, and Christ mocked by a "goddess of Reason." Moreover, the bribes and insults American emissaries encountered in France, culminating in the recent XYZ Affair, had created widespread anti-French sentiment among outraged Americans. The Federalist-dominated congress capitalized on the outsize fear of foreign intrigue and restricted the free speech provisions of the First Amendment by passing the Sedition Act, aimed squarely at Jeffersonian newspaper editors. Some hoped that the current atmosphere would permit a similar curb on freedom of religion. While a few people pondered ways to either amend or circumvent constitutional safeguards protecting religion from state interference, most opted to take their case directly to the people and seek a voter-imposed religious test that would bar Jefferson from the White House.

Historians have analyzed the religious question in 1800 from several perspectives. One scholar viewed it as a profound "political struggle between rationalist Christianity and Protestant orthodoxy." In this interpretation, the combatants fought over what was "true" faith, and which expression would best provide American society with a firm moral base.[5] Another interpretation defined the opponents as, on the one hand, "secular humanists" who wanted no discussion of religion at all in matters of state, but were not necessarily antireligious, and, on the other, those religious leaders who wished to present the campaign as one for the survival of orthodox Christianity in the republic.[6] And yet another, borrowing from Jefferson's own analysis of the campaign, conceived of the fight over religion as narrow-minded sectarian bigotry.[7]

What has received inadequate attention is the fundamental debate over where and how religious issues should be discussed in a secular state, a struggle first joined at the constitutional and ratifying conventions. This chapter focuses on that debate and the arena in which it occurred: a competitive marketplace of ideas. In 1787, Americans adopted a constitution embodying the principle that the state "is neutral on questions of religion . . . [and] maintains . . . religious liberty for all, special privileges for none." But that did not settle the issue. For many persons, religion remained in 1800, as it had been in 1787, "their most cherished source of comfort and absolutely central to their identity."[8] Indeed, as the presidential campaign progressed, an evangelical revival known as the Second Great Awakening was gaining thousands of converts to the Christian faith in churches and camp meetings from New England to the Kentucky and Tennessee frontier. Moreover, the rise of political parties provided an organized structure for the mobilization of public opinion, and in 1800, no issue was more hotly contested than that of religion. With evangelistic zeal partisans sought voter support for their respective positions regarding the proper relation of church and state.

"... GOVERN ... IN THE NAME OF THE Lo: JESUS CHRIST"

At the Constitutional Convention, the ban against a federally imposed religious test passed with little debate. But in state conventions, especially those of New England, delegates were determined that officeholders be also Christians. To them their pious Puritan Fathers cast a much more influential shadow than did the secular Founding Fathers. Thus all of the New England constitutions with the exception of Rhode Island's contained religious tests reflecting the deeply held conviction that at least that part of America was a Christian nation. Connecticut's religious test summed up the views of those who still wished to create a "City upon a Hill." There, the governor had to swear that he would govern "according to the rule of God's word ... in the name of the Lo: Jesus Christ."[9]

New England Federalists knew that many persons in the country agreed that the constitutional proscription against religious tests was a mistake. Many citizens had been appalled that Christ was not mentioned in the Declaration of Independence or in the United States Constitution, an unthinkable omission in a Christian land. Though disappointed in the Constitution's religious provisions, those wanting closer church-state relations sought remedy through legislation. Federalist lawmakers during the Washington and Adams administrations succeeded on several fronts in gaining government support for religious interests. They lobbied for and got presidential decrees for days of thanksgiving and prayer, a Puritan tradition that recognized God's hand in all human affairs. They secured tax exemptions for church property, thereby obtaining a form of government financial aid for churches and seminaries. And they got chaplains appointed for the Congress and for the armed forces. Supporters of these measures lauded them as evidence that Deists such as Thomas Jefferson and James Madison were out of step with their fellow citizens, who indeed constituted a Christian people.

For their part, Madison and Jefferson believed that one of the most original and significant achievements of the Founders was the separation of church and state. It had been under their leadership that Virginians had guaranteed religious freedom for all by removing the government entirely from religious matters. Reflecting on the first state constitutions, Madison observed, "they have the noble merit of first unshackling the conscience from persecuting laws, and of establishing among religious Sects a legal equality." No doubt thinking of the religious tests and establishment clauses in New England constitutions, he hastened to add that not all the states had fully embraced the "Christian principle" of freedom of conscience, but said that "all of them present examples by which the most enlightened States of the old world may be instructed; and there is one State at least, Virginia, where religious liberty is placed on its true foundation and is defined in its full latitude."[10] Thus, in his mind, what Americans had done in safeguarding religious liberty was an example to the rest of the world.

Accordingly, he called on states "which retain in your Constitutions or Codes, any aberration from the sacred principle of religious liberty, by giving to Caesar what belongs to God, or joining together what God has put asunder, [to] hasten to revise & purify your systems, and make the example of your Country as pure & compleat, in what relates to the freedom of the mind and its allegiance to its maker, as in what belongs to the legitimate objects of political & civil institutions." He also warned that there would always be those who would try to commingle church and state, and that freedom-loving Americans must be ever vigilant. Similarly, Madison expressed concern that religious liberty could be frittered away at the federal level. "Strongly guarded as is the separation between Religion & Govt in the Constitution of the United States," he warned, "the danger of encroachment by Ecclesiastical Bodies, may be illustrated by precedents already furnished in their short history." Already, he noted, in small ways the wall between church and state had been breached, and religious freedom thereby weakened. Before listing examples of "a direct mixture of Religion & civil Government," Madison explained that there are indirect and subtle ways that churches can undermine the principle of religious liberty.[11]

One was by taking advantage of laws that would enable them to accumulate property. He explained the evils in a brief review of how property owning had corrupted church and state in Europe:

The excessive wealth of ecclesiastical Corporations and the misuse of it in many Countries of Europe has Long been a topic of complaint. In some of them the Church has amassed half perhaps the property of the nation. When the reformation took place, an event promoted if not caused, by that disordered state of things, how enormous were the treasures of religious societies, and how gross the corruptions engendered by them; so enormous & so gross as to produce in the Cabinets & Councils of the Protestant states a disregard, of all the pleas of the interested party drawn from the sanctions of the law, and the sacredness of property held in religious trust. The history of England during the period of the reformation offers a sufficient illustration for the present purpose.

Madison then asked, "Are the U. S. duly awake to the tendency of the precedents they are establishing, in the multiplied incorporations of Religious Congregations with the faculty of acquiring & holding property real as well as personal!" Further, " Are there not already examples in the U. S. of ecclesiastical wealth equally beyond its object and the foresight of those who laid the foundation of it!" Lest people think him an alarmist exaggerating a small issue, Madison observed that "the people of the U. S. owe their Independence &. their liberty, to the wisdom of descrying in the minute tax of 3 pence on tea, the magnitude of the evil comprized in the precedent. Let them exert the same wisdom, in watching agst every evil lurking under plausible disguises, and growing up from small beginnings."[12]

Madison pointed out other violations of church-state separation that he regarded as threats to religious liberty. He cited the appointment of chaplains to serve the two houses of Congress as being inconsistent with the Constitution and with the "pure principle of religious freedom." He reminded readers that the "Constitution of the U. S. forbids everything like an establishment of a national religion." In his view, the law appointing chaplains "establishes a religious worship for the national representatives, to be performed by Ministers of religion, elected by a majority of them; and these are to be paid out of the national taxes." He asked, "Does not this involve the principle of a national establishment, applicable to a provision for a religious worship for the Constituent as well as of the representative Body, approved by the majority, and conducted by Ministers of religion paid by the entire nation?" In addition to violating the establishment clause, the appointment of congressional chaplains was, Madison argued, a "palpable violation of equal rights, as well as of Constitutional principles: The tenets of the chaplains elected by the majority shut the door of worship agst the members whose creeds & consciences forbid a participation in that of the majority." He singled out Roman Catholics and Quakers as groups that had always had members in one or both of the legislative branches. To emphasize his point, Madison asked, "Could a Catholic clergyman ever hope to be appointed a Chaplain!"[13]

Madison's stance was not antireligious in any respect. He did not even object to chaplains in Congress. What he did oppose was public support of those chaplains. His solution supported the congressmen's free exercise of religion but without violating the Constitution. He reasoned

If Religion consist in voluntary acts of individuals, singly, or voluntarily associated, and it be proper that public functionaries, as well as their Constituents shd discharge their religious duties, let them like their Constituents, do so at their own expense. How small a contribution from each member of Cong wd suffice for the purpose! How just wd it be in its principle! How noble in its exemplary sacrifice to the genius of the Constitution; and the divine right of conscience! Why should the expence of a religious worship be allowed for the Legislature, be paid by the public, more than that for the Ex. or Judiciary branch of the Gov?

Madison also opposed public support of chaplains for the military branches. In addition to objecting on grounds similar to those outlined in his argument against chaplains in Congress, he questioned the efficacy of religious instruction for military morale and performance. If soldiers and sailors do not possess a zeal and devout spirit for their cause, "the official services of their Teachers are not likely to produce it." Madison pointed to the armies of the seventeenth-century Puritans in England, who had "their appointed Chaplains; but without these there would have been no lack of public devotion in that devout age."[14]

Finally, Madison denounced government proclamations for thanksgivings and fasts because they had religious overtones. Although such proclamations are recommendations only, he contended that they "imply a religious agency, making no part of the trust delegated to political rulers." Madison repeated his oft-stated position that the government had no say whatever in citizens' religious views. "The members of a Govt as such can in no sense," he wrote, "be regarded as possessing an advisory trust from their Constituents in their religious capacities. They cannot form an ecclesiastical Assembly, Convocation, Council, or Synod, and as such issue decrees or injunctions addressed to the faith or the Consciences of the people." Madison thought that government officials "in their individual capacities, as distinct from their official station, . . . might unite in recommendations of any sort whatever, in the same manner as any other individuals might do."[15] As individuals, presidents and congressmen and judges may express their religious views, but they should be represented as such and should be accorded no more weight than any other American's sentiments regarding personal belief.

Thus, in the early republic, Americans were divided over questions of church and state, with sons and daughters of New England Puritans on one end of the spectrum and humanists such as James Madison and Thomas Jefferson on the other. The latter had powerful allies among many of the evangelical groups in the nation, including Baptists, Methodists, Presbyterians, and Disciples of Christ. These sects were doing very well in the marketplace of religious ideas, winning thousands of converts through revivals and other evangelizing initiatives. They wanted no government interference with the free practice of religion.

The question of religious tests, specifically, and religion and politics, generally, did not enter presidential politics during the Washington and Adams administrations. In fact, by electing George Washington as the first president, voters rendered moot for a time the constitutional argument over religious tests. While historians point out that Washington was a moderate Deist, the popular culture of the day transformed him into a model Christian, indeed an orthodox believer. In 1800, Federalists held up Washington's Christian beliefs and behavior as a standard against which Jefferson's religion should be measured. When Washington died early in the year, scores of eulogies extolled his piety and reminded voters in that election year that Christian America had had, and should always have, a Christian president. In a typical sermon preached at Haverhill, Massachusetts, Congregationalist minister Abiel Abbot presented Washington as an instrument of God's providence to deliver his people. The former president took his place alongside Noah, Moses, and Joshua as a deliverer of God's people from the hands of degeneracy and oppression. While Americans should remember Washington's military feats with pride and gratitude, they should also reflect with reverence on his deep faith. "Ardent and intrepid as Caesar in the field," Abbot wrote, "in the tent [Washington] is kneeled a humble suppliant to the God of armies." Moreover, the general wove morality and religion into his system of military discipline, forbidding his soldiers to swear and gamble. To Abbot, such rectitude presented American mourners a choice: to admire "the sound policy of the GENERAL, or the incorruptible integrity of the CHRISTIAN." He concluded with the wish that all succeeding presidents also be men of faith.[16]

According to the Federalists, however, Thomas Jefferson could not be so easily baptized into the Christian faith, certainly not in its orthodox expression. First, his outspoken political opposition to administrations that he had served called his loyalty into question. Second, his stated admiration for the French Revolution caused some to identify him as a radical freethinker. And, third, his widely known philosophic musings were seen by many as deistic and Unitarian at best and blasphemous and anti-Christian at worst.

Nevertheless, Jefferson's religious beliefs were not a central focus during his unsuccessful bid for the presidency in 1796. Instead Federalists then depicted the Virginian as a shrinking coward and an impractical philosopher. They pointed out that in 1776 Jefferson had refused to accept the dangerous but important congressional assignment of traveling to Europe to solicit foreign alliances. His opponents charged him with cowardice, saying that fear of an "ocean filled with British cruisers" prompted him to stay at home. They added that he resigned as Virginia's governor in 1781 when the British invaded the state, thus abandoning "the trust at the moment when he was bound by every principle of virtue and patriotism to act the man, and wait the issue."[17] Federalists also cast him as an amateur philosopher who conjured up impractical schemes ill-suited for sound government, such as his "extravagant project of emancipating all the slaves in Virginia."[18] With charges like that at hand, Jefferson's religion need not be made an issue. However, the narrow margin of Adams's victory meant that the Federalists would need more anti-Jefferson ammunition if they were to maintain control of the presidency.

In 1800, Federalist clergymen appealed to voters to impose their own religious test. The constitutional ban meant that voters alone would decide whether a candidate's beliefs were important, and, if so, would pronounce judgment on them. With no state protection of a specific creed or sect, those wishing to make religion an issue must make their case in a free marketplace of ideas, a public sphere beyond the control of any private religious or other interest group and outside the jurisdiction of the government. Jefferson had long advocated such an arena for the voicing of personal religious views, believing that only through free debate would the truth be winnowed from false notions. There, competing claims would be voiced, and voters would decide according to criteria of their own choosing. Central to the public sphere was a free press where all ideas could be aired, and readers, free of coercion, could decide which ideas to embrace.[19] The quadrupling (from 90 to 370) of newspapers in circulation over the period 1790–1810 gives some idea of just how competitive the information market had become.[20] It was in that arena that the Federalist clergy launched a vigorous and extensive effort to secure a voter-imposed religious test against Jefferson. Through scores of pamphlets and hundreds of speeches, they made their case that Jefferson was an infidel, and that his election would undermine the nation's Christian foundation just as French revolutionaries had desecrated their country's religious heritage.

Jefferson had often voiced his belief that religious discussions belonged in a free marketplace of ideas. By that concept he meant a forum where persuasion, not coercion, was the means of gaining converts to one's viewpoint. With numerous sects competing for the hearts and minds of individuals, America was perfectly suited for free choice in religious matters, provided the state did not interfere. In the clash of ideas, Jefferson believed, truth would prevail as persons freely chose the group to which they wished to conform. He recognized that choice must extend to everyone: "if we chuse for ourselves," he wrote, "we must allow others to chuse also. . . . This establishes religious toleration."[21] In drawing up Virginia's Statute for Religious Freedom, he opposed the state's granting "a monopoly of worldly honors and emoluments [to] those who will externally profess and conform to" an established religion.[22]

To some orthodox Protestants, the presidential campaign of 1800 was a propitious moment to reopen the debate over religious tests. While many of the arguments for and against such tests had been raised in 1787, the historical context had changed dramatically. At the constitutional and ratifying conventions, most examples concerning church-state issues had been taken from the remote past, often from ancient Greece and Rome; in 1800, current events gave Americans a fresh, poignant illustration. To many, the French republic represented a frightening contemporary example of what happened when infidels controlled a state. Jefferson's long-time adversary, Alexander Hamilton, was a leader in making religion a central issue in the campaign of 1800. Shortly after word of the XYZ Affair reached America, Hamilton sought to exploit the spreading anti-French sentiment. In a series of articles published in the *[New York] Commercial Advertiser*, he attacked the French revolutionary leaders, especially their attempt "to destroy all religious opinion, and to pervert a whole people to Atheism." He demonstrated their animosity to Christianity by claiming that they altered the Christian calendar for the express purpose of "supplanting the Christian Sabbath." He added that the Jacobin-controlled National Convention had openly avowed atheism and had sought to install that view in French culture by publishing a book "professing to prove the *nothingness* of religion" and instituting the "GODDESS OF REASON" as the object of public worship. To demonstrate the depths of Jacobin hatred toward Christianity, Hamilton said that revolutionary leaders congratulated children who appeared in the convention hall "to lisp blasphemy against the King of Kings."[23]

Hamilton and other Federalists insisted that what happened in France had significance in the campaign of 1800 because of Thomas Jefferson's strong ties to the French Revolution. He charged Jefferson with being an atheist and argued that his election would impose on America the same sort of infidelity as that witnessed in France. Though an ardent defender of the Constitution, Hamilton felt so strongly about Jefferson's unfitness for office that he floated a strategy to circumvent the Constitution in order to deny the presidency to his political enemy. In a May 7 letter to John Jay, governor of New York, Hamilton expressed his profound disappointment at learning that the Anti-Federalists, or Jeffersonians, had won a majority in the New York legislature, and the "very high probability . . . that this will bring *Jefferson* into the Chief Magistracy." He knew that if Jefferson won New York, he would probably win the necessary majority in the electoral college. To prevent "an *Atheist* in Religion and a *Fanatic* in politics from getting possession of the helm of the State," Hamilton proposed a measure of dubious constitutional legitimacy. He wanted Jay to call a special session of the current Federalist-dominated legislature to alter the rules for selecting electors in order to deny the election to Jefferson. Hamilton explained that the possibility of an atheist in the highest office dictated extraordinary measures. "It will not do to

be overscrupulous," he wrote, adding that "it is easy to sacrifice the substantial interests of society by a strict adherence to ordinary rules." Jay, a
coauthor with Hamilton and James Madison of the *Federalist Papers*,
would not agree to such partisan constitutional manipulation. He wrote
at the bottom of the letter: "Proposing a measure for party purposes wh.
I think it wd. not become me to adopt."[24]

Jefferson saw a sinister link between the XYZ plot and attacks against
his religious views. He believed that Federalists intended to exploit anti-
French sentiments to restrict constitutional protections of religious freedom. He pointed out that Federalists had already succeeded in undermining the Constitution's free speech guarantee in order to silence Jeffersonian critics of the Adams administration. Jefferson responded to the
Sedition Act through the Kentucky Resolutions. In that document, he
tied together the themes of free speech, free press, and free exercise of
religion.[25] He feared that the Sedition Act's attack on political expression
was only the first subversion of civil liberties, and predicted that Federalists aimed to curb religious liberty as well. He charged that the successful
assaults against free speech "had given to the clergy a very favorable hope
of obtaining an establishment of a particular form of Christianity thro'
the U.S."[26] What proponents of religious tests had failed to attain in 1787,
they hoped to achieve at the dawning of the nineteenth century, but they
faced the formidable challenge of having to persuade voters in the arena
of public opinion. Thus a Federalist idea—religious tests—would be debated and decided in a Jeffersonian forum: a free marketplace.

"JEFFERSON—AND NO GOD"

Knowing that a narrowly defined religious test would fail in pluralistic
America, Federalist strategists framed the question in the broadest possible terms, asking voters whether they wanted a religious president or a
non- or even antireligious leader. To make their case that Jefferson would
be the latter, they seized upon his statement in the *Notes on the State of
Virginia* that whether his neighbor believed in twenty gods or no god was
of no concern to him. Extrapolating from that comment that Jefferson
was at least open to infidelity, one Federalist writer declared that voters
had a clear choice: "GOD—AND A RELIGIOUS PRESIDENT . . . [or] JEFFERSON—

AND NO GOD." To opt for the impious Jefferson, with his "disbelief of the Holy Scriptures" and his "rejection of the Christian Religion," was to vote to "destroy religion, introduce immorality, and loosen all the bonds of society." By replying with their own religious comparison of the candidates, Republicans implicitly validated the idea of a voter-imposed test. They countered that voters indeed had a clear choice: one side representing "religious liberty, the rights of conscience, no priesthood, truth and Jefferson"; the other, Adams and "an established church, a religious test, and an order of Priesthood."[27]

The heart of the orthodox Protestant argument was that Jefferson was an infidel, and pamphleteers argued that his own words proved it. William Linn was just one of many who combed *Notes on the State of Virginia* to prove that Jefferson not only was not Christian but ridiculed divine revelation. Linn cited four indicting passages. First, Jefferson rejected the idea of the great biblical flood, noting that if the entire contents of the atmosphere emptied onto earth, they would reach only a little over fifty feet, hardly the Genesis deluge that covered mountains. Second, Jefferson insinuated that Native Americans constituted a "distinct race of men originally created and placed in America, contrary to the sacred history that all mankind have descended from a single pair." Third, Jefferson slighted the Bible by suggesting that young students whose "judgments [were] not mature enough for religious inquiry" would profit more by reading Greek, Roman, European, and American history. Linn called the proposal a "deistical education." Fourth, and most damning, Linn cited Jefferson's remark that it did not matter to him whether his neighbor believed in twenty gods or no god.[28] Linn called on Christian voters to reject one who had so little regard for Christianity and the Bible.

Some who opposed Jefferson constricted the meaning of religion to matters of the church. Ignoring his public professions of faith, David Daggett, a New Haven lawyer and Federalist, attacked Jefferson for not being a good church member. "It is a well established fact," Daggett wrote in 1800, "that Mr. Jefferson never has attended public worship during a residence of several years in New York and Philadelphia." The writer was unimpressed by reports that Jefferson had provided financial support for a minister; Daggett was willing to give the presidential candidate credit for such an act only if *"he would attend* [the preacher's] ministrations and not confine them to servants."[29]

To other detractors, it was not good enough that Jefferson declared his support for religion; they insisted that he stand for *true* religion. They interpreted his statement concerning the number of gods his neighbor worshiped as proof of his religious indifference. Daggett conceded that the remark was an attempt to show "the impropriety of legislative interference in matters of religion." But Daggett read much more into Jefferson's thoughts underlying the statement: "he unquestionably means that it is not injurious to individuals or society for a man to *declare* that there are twenty Gods, or that there is no God, and consequently that there should be no law against blasphemy and therefore *clearly,* none against profanity of any kind." Thus Jefferson's affirmation of religious liberty became a testament of sacrilege. "Alas! the religion of the bible," Daggett concluded, "the Saviour of sinners, the God of the universe, may be prophaned, derided or blasphemed, with impunity."[30]

In sum, Jefferson's much vaunted toleration of all religion proved that he was no true Christian. Again, Daggett used one of Jefferson's statements supporting religious liberty to indict him for blasphemy. Of New York and Pennsylvania, Jefferson had written that in those two states, "religion is well supported, of *various kinds* indeed; but ALL GOOD ENOUGH; all sufficient to preserve peace and order." From that comment, Daggett deduced that Jefferson held that "the only benefit of religion to society is preservation of peace and order . . . [and] for that purpose all the various religions are *equally good.*" Of such a comment, Daggett insisted, "no Christian, unless deluded, could say it."[31] True Christians knew that their faith was the only true one, and would never present it as one of many others equally valid.

Although the orthodox clergy wanted a religious test that would exclude all but professing Christians, they attempted to persuade Jewish voters that a Christian president was far preferable to an atheist. Writing as a "follower of Moses and the Old Testament," one contributor to the *Philadelphia Gazette* invited his fellow Jews to make "COMMON CAUSE" with Christians to defeat Jefferson. Signed by "Moses S. Solomons," the article evoked a congratulatory letter signed by "A Christian" that appeared in the same newspaper. The author said that Solomons's testimonial was "the more valuable because he is a Jew." Any advantage the Federalists hoped to realize disappeared a few days later when the Philadelphia synagogue published a statement that "no such man as Moses S. Solomons has *ever been*, or is now a member of the Hebrew congregation in this city."[32] In their zeal to garner Jewish votes, the Federalists violated a cardinal rule of the marketplace of ideas: "that truth is great and will prevail if left to herself."[33]

Jefferson and his supporters defended the Republican candidate's religious beliefs, but in doing so, they entered a debate whose terms the Federalists had set. Jefferson considered himself to be a Christian, a position he had reached as "the result of a life of inquiry and reflection." In a letter to Benjamin Rush three years after the 1800 election, he declared, "I am a Christian, in the only sense [Jesus] wished anyone to be; sincerely attached to his doctrines, in preference to all others." If he had allowed that simple statement to stand without explanation, perhaps he would have escaped the scurrilous attacks he endured. But he continued, denying the divinity of Jesus and thus violating a central tenet of all confessions and creeds of orthodox Christianity. He ascribed to Jesus "every *human* excellence" and expressed the belief that "he never claimed any other."[34]

Jefferson professed to be a Christian, but according to most Protestant confessions of faith he was not. Indeed, as John Murrin has noted, Jefferson and many of the other prominent Founding Fathers were what some today call secular humanists. The modern definition of that term includes three components: (1) elevation of human reason above divine revelation, (2) reliance on human solutions for human problems, and (3) ethical relativism.[35] Clearly, Jefferson qualified on all three counts, but especially on the first. Jefferson did indeed give precedence to reason over revelation in determining truth. In his oft-quoted advice to Peter Carr, he urged his nephew to "Fix reason firmly in her seat, and call to her tribunal every fact, every opinion. Question with boldness even the existence of God; because if there be one, he must approve of the homage of reason, than that of blindfolded fear." Jefferson believed that nothing, including biblical teachings and clerical pronouncements, should be accepted as authoritative without being subjected to reason and the laws of nature. He insisted that the Bible be read as one would read any other book. And when scriptural passages "contradict the laws of nature," they should be treated as similar claims would be if encountered in "Livy or Tacitus." Citing an example in a letter to Carr, Jefferson suggested that if one read in the Latin histories Joshua's claim that the sun stood still, it would be classified as myth, and so it should be in the Old Testament.[36]

Some Jeffersonians countered the Federalists' insistence on imposing a religious test by devising one of their own to be applied to the incumbent and his running mate, Charles Cotesworth Pinckney. The October 14 edition of the Republican newspaper *Aurora* presented voters with a clear choice. They could vote for "Things As They Have Been" under the Federalists: "Priests and Judges incorporated with the Government for political purposes, and equally polluting the holy altars of religion, and the seats of Justice." Or they could opt for "Things As They Will Be" under the Republicans: "Good government without the aid of priestcraft, or religious politics."[37]

Republicans made their barbs personal when they attacked Pinckney's religious views and moral behavior in a scurrilous campaign whose calumny matched the venom, if not the volume, of that leveled at Jefferson's. One newspaper reprinted a 1788 poem attributed to Timothy Dwight that referred to the Federalist vice presidential nominee's "profligate character." In the verse entitled "The Triumph of Infidelity," Pinckney is made to speak these lines:

> I am the first of men in the ways of evil,
> The truest, thriftiest servant of the Devil;
> Born, educated, glory to engross
> And shine confess'd the Devil's Man of Ross.
> Here's three to one I beat even him in pride;
> Two whores already in my chariot ride.

The behavior that inspired the assault was Pinckney's seduction of a Parisian "female of a respectable family" whom the American had impregnated and abandoned "without . . . compensation for the loss of her virtue."[38] The message was clear to Federalists attacking Jefferson: if you hurl stones at our candidate, you can expect similar missiles to rain upon your ticket.

"ONE GOD, THREE GODS, NO GOD, OR TWENTY GODS"

The Federalists failed in their attempt to secure a voter-imposed religious test that would ensure a Christian president (as they defined "Christian"). Voters insisted that any religious test they might impose should be of their own choosing. While many Baptists and other dissenters embraced the idea of America as a Christian nation and believed that it should be governed by a Christian president, they voted Republican because they rejected the Federalist attempt to paint Jefferson as something other than a Christian. Furthermore, they concluded that Jefferson would be a better defender than the Federalists of the place of religious minorities within the nation. Moreover, the great diversity of religious opinion among voters meant that no single formulation of a test, however broadly framed, would meet with universal, or even majoritarian, approval. The election's outcome indicated that many Federalist assumptions about voters were flawed. First, a large number of Americans were indifferent about religious matters, and they, therefore, cast their votes on issues other than Jefferson's beliefs. Second, those professing Christianity disagreed among themselves over essential beliefs and practices, as evidenced by increased competition among a growing number of sects and denominations. Third, and most important in the election of 1800, a majority of voters held religion to be a matter beyond the federal government's jurisdiction.

John Adams credited widespread antiestablishment sentiment for his defeat. He described the choice facing voters as one of religious orthodoxy versus religious liberty. His opponents were able to link orthodoxy with establishment, suggesting that if the Federalists won the election, some sort of Christian establishment would be the result. In a nation characterized by pluralism, such a prospect sent many voters running to the Jeffersonian standard. Adams believed that the Jeffersonians had been successful in scaring people into believing that the Federalists threatened religious liberty. He wrote, "With the Baptists, Quakers, Methodists, and Moravians, as well as the Dutch and German Lutherans and Calvinists, it had an immense effect, and turned them in such numbers as decided the election. They said, let us have an Atheist or Deist or any thing rather than an establishment of Presbyterianism."[39] Ironically, the Federalist accusation that Jefferson was "indifferent" about religion hurt Adams more than it did his opponent. When Jefferson, quoting from John Leland, said that it mattered not to him if someone believed in one, three, twenty, or no gods, he struck a responsive chord with evangelical voters. They had much rather see government protecting freedom of conscience than establishing religion, no matter how orthodox that religion might be.

To the extent that church adherence measures religiosity, statistics for 1800 suggest that organized religion had little influence on most Americans. According to one recent estimate, only 17 percent of Americans claimed to be church members in 1776, and, though it showed remarkable growth over the first half of the nineteenth century, membership reached only 34 percent by 1850.[40] Even if those figures are low, a considerable number of voters paid little attention to clergymen's political views, and others voiced outright hostility.

Many other Americans professed Christianity but, like Jefferson, embraced a civil religion that excluded or ignored many tenets central to Christian orthodoxy. Jefferson, Adams, Washington, Franklin, and Hamilton all expressed some version of what Rousseau called "civil religion": a belief in "the existence of a powerful, intelligent, beneficent, foresighted, and providential divinity; the afterlife; the happiness of the just; the punishment of the wicked; [and] the sanctity of the social contract."[41] But beyond those general sentiments, the Founding Fathers in their public utterances said almost nothing that could be construed as specifically Christian. In the Declaration of Independence, Jefferson referred to "Nature's God," and in his first inaugural address, Washington spoke of the "smiles of Heaven." But neither mentioned Christ or made any other Christian reference. They differentiated between civil religion and Christianity. The former was general: it applied to persons of all religious persuasions and had a place in public comments. The latter came in many denominations and was best discussed and observed within churches over which the state exercised no control.[42]

The fastest-growing religious groups opposed religious tests of any stripe. Indeed, the campaign of 1800 coincided with a burgeoning religious revival in which certain evangelical sects aggressively sought new members and challenged the Standing Order's legal establishment in Massachusetts and Connecticut, where the Congregational churches continued to enjoy state preference. Groups such as Baptists and Methodists, still considered outsiders by the older denominations, "had little sense of their limitations" and took their message to men and women "flushed with confidence about their prospects."[43] These groups advocated voluntarism instead of establishmentarianism and, therefore, applauded Jefferson's fight for religious freedom while tolerating his unorthodox theology. In a sense, they did not care whether he believed in twenty gods or no god if he protected their freedom to proclaim their beliefs—their freedom to, among other things, attempt to convince Jefferson that his religious views were wrong.

There is little evidence that Jefferson's rationalist, Unitarian religious views found any more favor with voters than did the self-styled orthodoxy posited by the Federalists. However, when Jeffersonians shifted the debate's focus from religious beliefs to religious freedom, their candidate represented a position favored by many in the nation's marketplace of ideas at the turn of the century. Under the new terms of debate, Jefferson appeared as the champion of religious liberty, and his supporters cited his long and distinguished record in fighting bigotry while promoting liberty of conscience. They also put on the defensive those Federalists who had made religion an issue. Republicans reminded voters that Connecticut and Massachusetts, the home states of many of Jefferson's attackers, still had religious tests in their constitutions, and suggested that they would like to impose similar restrictions on all Americans. Connecticut's Abraham Bishop charged the Federalists with politicizing religion. The New Haven lawyer and Republican partisan dismissed the charge that Jefferson "wished to destroy all religion" as being absurd on its face. What Jefferson did wish to destroy, Bishop contended, was "that kind of religion, which is made a foot-ball or stalking-horse and which operates only to dishonor God and ruin man."[44] Bishop quoted from Jefferson to make his point: "Can the liberties of a nation be thought secure when we have removed their only firm basis, a conviction in the minds of the people, that these liberties are of *the gift of God?*—That they are to be violated but with his wrath? Indeed I tremble for my country, when I reflect that *God is just*, that his justice cannot sleep forever." Bishop asked, "Is this the language of an atheist?"[45]

In an address delivered late in the campaign at New Haven, Bishop stepped up his attack on the anti-Jeffersonian clergy, linking them with "Romish" priests in Catholic countries who have employed "test-acts, oaths and inquisitions . . . [as] so many state-engines to subordinate mankind to the great and little tyrants." He expressed his hope that "the good sense of Americans is ready to repel the first attempts to bind us with ecclesiastical fetter, and to say to the clergy 'your business is to teach the gospel.' " He chastised them for preaching sermons aimed at political instead of spiritual ends. "How much," he asked, "has religion been benefited by sermons, intended to show that Satan and Cain were jacobins? How much by sermons in which every deistical argument has been presented with its greatest force as being a part of the republican creed?" He predicted that the political sermons might backfire as voters considered that those clergy spreading alarm "lest religion should suffer under a new administration" were in fact the ones "using it as a state engine."[46]

Bishop argued that religion has always been ill-served when the state has intervened, and, moreover, true religion needs no state protection or support. He asked his listeners, "Have you not read that the head of the church will sustain his own cause, and that this cause will never be perfected, till wars and rumours of war shall cease from under the whole heaven?" He added that "the Captain of salvation is not so weak as to need an army and navy and a majority in Congress to support his cause." Not only does Christ need no government help; the state undermines his work.

After his election, Jefferson received many letters from evangelicals expressing their appreciation for his firm support of religious liberty. It was in response to one of those letters that he used the metaphor of a "wall of separation between church and state."[47] Many accommodationists and conservatives on the "religious right" have made much of the point that only Jefferson imposed a "wall," and that he did so only once, in response to the Danbury Baptist Association of Connecticut. Applying the same sort of literal reading of historical documents as that they give Scripture, people like Pat Robertson note that the metaphor does not appear in the Constitution or elsewhere, and, therefore, the Jeffersonian interpretation must be idiosyncratic. They fail, however, to note that while the word "wall" is unique, the sentiment that it expresses was widespread among Americans, especially within evangelical groups.

Indeed, when one examines the Danbury Baptists' letter, one sees that Jefferson's response simply echoed many of their strong statements against any government voice regarding religion. First, the Baptists expressed their views on religious freedom:

Our Sentiments are uniformly on the side of Religious Liberty— That Religion is at all times and places a matter between God and individuals—That no man ought to suffer in name, person, or effects on account of his religious Opinions—That the legitimate Power of civil government extends no further than to punish the man who works *ill to his neighbor.*

Having stated their position, the Baptists then complained of their lack of religious liberty in Connecticut, one of the states that retained a religious establishment. Noting that the state's constitution continued to reflect the "Laws & usages" of its "ancient" charter, they described religion's place in that state:

Religion is considered as the first object of Legislation; and therefore what religious privileges we enjoy (as a minor part of the State) we enjoy as favors granted, and not as inalienable rights: and these favors we receive at the expense of such degrading acknowledgements, as are inconsistent with the rights of freemen.

They concluded by asserting that the government "dare not assume the prerogatives of Jehovah and make Laws to govern the Kingdom of Christ."[48] In other words, church and state are separate, with God as head of the former and a magistrate as head of the latter.

The Danbury Baptists closed the letter by expressing their hope that the religious liberty enjoyed at the federal level would soon prevail in Connecticut. They acknowledged that "the national government cannot destroy the Laws of each State," but they hoped that "the sentiments of our beloved President, . . . like radiant beams of the Sun, will shine and prevail through all these States and all the world till Hierarchy and Tyranny be destroyed from the Earth." In part because of the Baptists' agitation, the people of Connecticut disestablished the Congregational churches in 1818 by a vote of 13,918 to 12,361, applying federal ideas of religious freedom and separation of church and state to their state.[49]

Jefferson also echoed the sentiments of the Baptist minister John Leland, who based his views of religious liberty on biblical principles and the Lockean idea of the social compact. Thus he framed the question: "Does a man, upon entering into social compact, surrender his conscience to that society, to be controlled by the laws thereof; or can he, in justice, assist in making laws to bind his children's consciences before they are born?" His answer in the negative contained the heart of his argument: "Every man must give an account of himself to God, and therefore every man ought to be at liberty to serve God in a way that he can best reconcile to his conscience. If government can answer for individuals at the day of judgment, let men be controlled by it in religious matters; otherwise, let men be free." He concluded with the statement that Jefferson had paraphrased in the campaign and the Federalists had singled out for attack: "Let every man speak freely without fear, maintain the principles that he believes, worship according to his own faith, either one God, three Gods, no God, or twenty Gods: and let government protect him in so doing."[50]

Also, like Jefferson and the Danbury Baptists, Leland and his cobelievers in Massachusetts considered the marketplace of ideas, not the government, to be the arena and arbiter of religious debate. Having lived under Virginia's and then Massachusetts's constitutions, which discouraged religious pluralism through "proscriptions, fines, [and] confiscations," Leland advocated a state that promoted free discussion wherein a "man [could] bring forth his arguments and maintain his points with all boldness; then, if his doctrine is false, it will be confuted, and if it is true, (though ever so novel,) let others credit it." Only religious error needs government protection. Leland wrote that "whenever men fly to the law or sword to protect their system of religion, and force it upon others, it is evident that they have something in their system that will not bear the light, and stand upon the basis of truth." He certainly did not want Massachusetts Congregationalists to define religious standards for officeholders.[51] Leland lived to see Massachusetts disestablish religion by constitutional amendment in 1833.

Though New England dissenters including Baptists supported Jefferson, many did so despite strong disagreement with many of his religious views. William McLoughlin's recent study of New England Baptists highlights some of those differences. He points out that "[m]any Baptists disagreed with Jefferson . . . that religious liberty should include the right to hold office even for Jews, Mohammedans, deists, atheists, and infidels." Moreover, unlike Jefferson, Baptists "believed that if [America] was not a Christian nation it should be." They supported state laws "against theatergoing, blasphemy, disturbing the Sabbath, card playing, and gambling."[52] Many New England Baptists did care very much whether Jefferson believed in twenty gods or no god.

Like the Baptists, Alexander Hamilton supported Jefferson's stance against government-imposed tests, although he disagreed with many of

Jefferson's religious views. While he had flirted with questionable tactics to deny Jefferson New York's electoral votes, Hamilton recognized that he had to defeat his opponent by persuading voters. Even as he failed in that effort, he devised a plan to ensure that in the future only Christians would occupy the presidency. After the election, Hamilton outlined in a letter to James Bayard his scheme for "The Christian Constitutional Society," whose twin objects were "the support of the Christian Religion" and "the support of the Constitution of the United States." It would be a national organization with councils in each state, facilitating "the diffusion of information" and a "lively correspondence" and employing "all lawful means in concert to promote the election of *fit men*." Though he believed that Christian Americans should choose Christian leaders, Hamilton rejected any state coercion. He agreed with the constitutional ban on religious tests, insisting that "the present Constitution is the standard to which we are to cling."[53] The significance of Hamilton's scheme is his recognition that his campaign to elect a Christian president should be waged in the marketplace of ideas, with a voluntary organization using all persuasive means to gain followers.

The fact that combatants in 1800 confined their heated debate to the marketplace of ideas underscores the importance of the victory secured in 1787–1789. By creating a secular state and regarding religion as a natural right beyond the state's jurisdiction, the Founders opted for persuasion rather than coercion. In the campaign of 1800, though some pined for a constitutional religious test and others flirted with notions of circumventing the proscription, differences were settled in a contest of appeals aimed at voters. Without official privilege protecting one religious expression above all others, debaters had no alternative but to gain adherents to their cause by swaying voters one at a time.

❖ Epilogue ❖

CONTRARY to the predictions of some defenders of an establishment, religion as well as religious freedom thrived in the early
republic. On several occasions after leaving the presidency in
1816, James Madison reflected on the Constitution's church-state settlement and argued that it had promoted religion. In an 1819 letter to his
friend Robert Walsh, Madison observed, "there has been an increase of
religious instruction since the Revolution." He noted that while old
churches, "built under the establishment at the public expense, have in
many instances gone to ruin," among the other sects "Meeting Houses
have multiplied and continue to multiply." He expressed his opinion that
"the number, the industry, and the morality of the priesthood and the
devotion of the people have been manifestly increased by the total separation of the Church from the State."[1] More than ten years later, Madison
again reported on the flourishing condition of religion in America. In an
1832 letter to a minister, he wrote, "the lapse of time now more than 50
years since the legal support of Religion was withdrawn sufficiently
proves that [religion] does not need the support of Govt and it will
scarcely be contended that Government has suffered by the exemption
of Religion from its cognizance." Religion had in fact grown, and social
order was intact.[2]

When Madison made his observations in 1832, not only was religion
growing, but religious freedom was expanding. Massachusetts was in the
process of disestablishment, making the support of religion "voluntary"
and guaranteeing "equal protection" to all. In 1818, Connecticut had removed all legal compulsion to support "any" religion and had rescinded
its religious test for officeholders. Beginning with Vermont's admission
to the union in 1786, all new states followed the federal Constitution and
erected no established churches, recognized religious freedom as a right
for all, and prohibited religious tests.

A free, expanding religious marketplace does not mean, however, that
religion was absent from the political arena. As the presidential election

of 1800 indicated, voters do not cease to be religious beings when they cast their ballots for candidates or lobby for public policies. Moreover, sometimes individuals and sects disapprove of ideas and behaviors that prevail in the religious marketplace, and on occasion they seek government support for their particular concerns. Times of national crisis, such as civil unrest or war, evoke calls for closer ties between church and state. Some people express the view that the country's woes are linked to spiritual decline, and advocate measures designed to reestablish the country's Christian foundation. One strategy has been to seek constitutional amendments that would affirm the nation's spiritual heritage and draw church and state closer together. A notable attempt occurred during the Civil War when a group of concerned Protestants sought to amend the Constitution to reflect the country's Christian heritage and culture. In 1862, when the United States' military fortunes were at their nadir, delegates from eleven Protestant denominations met in Xenia, Ohio, to offer a spiritual answer. Convinced that God was dissatisfied with the nation's secular Constitution, the group demanded that the "United States of America should place their allegiance to God on record in the Constitution." As an outgrowth of the Xenia meeting, the National Reform Association was formed in 1864 to lobby for some form of "Christian Amendment." In 1867, the organization's journal, *The Christian Statesman*, called for the following amendment to the preamble to the Constitution, reminiscent of that suggested by the Anti-Federalist William Williams in 1787:

> We, the people of the United States, acknowledging Almighty God as the source of all authority and power in civil government, the Lord Jesus Christ as the Ruler among the nations, and His Will, revealed in the Holy Scriptures, as of supreme authority, in order to constitute a Christian government, form a more perfect union, establish justice. . . .[3]

Though the amendment failed to get the requisite two-thirds vote in Congress, it gained enough support to encourage its sponsors to breach the constitutional line between church and state. In 1878, the National Reform Association proposed a bill that would violate the prohibition against use of public funds for sectarian purposes, allowing tax dollars to be appropriated for Bibles in public schools. The National Liberal League, a watchdog of civil liberties including that of religious freedom, protested. In a letter to Senator George F. Edmunds, chair of the committee debating the measure, league spokesman Francis Abbot expressed concerns similar to those voiced by Thomas Jefferson in the 1780s during the debate on religious liberty in Virginia. Abbot wrote, in part,

> The whole pith and purport of the movement I now represent is to establish equal rights in religion, so far as the laws under which all must live are concerned. Our government is not for Christians alone, but also for vast multitudes who are not covered by that name. If the government should allow partiality to Christianity, it would compel all to pay homage to a religion which is not the religion of all; for all are taxed for the government's support. Just as you, Sir, would feel yourself oppressed to be taxed for the support of Mohammedanism if you lived in Turkey, so would Jews and non-Christians feel oppressed to be taxed for the support of Christianity. Surely the Golden Rule itself should teach us how to deal with this question. I am not pleading for any privilege or advantage for non-Christians over Christians—far from it! I only plead for impartial justice towards both; I only beg you, who will be so influential in this matter, to rise above the partialities of your own individual faith, and throw your influence so as to help enact righteous, equal and impartial justice, towards those of all faiths, however unlike.[4]

Proposals to change the constitutional settlement on church-state relations failed, but the debate over the place of religion in America intensified during the second half of the nineteenth century. Many Protestants were deeply disturbed by the drift of the religious marketplace that seemed to be moving America ever further from the "City upon a Hill." Scientific discoveries and historical research challenged traditional ways of viewing space and time and, in the process, brought about "pervasive shifts in moral and religious attitudes." First, in the field of science, Charles Darwin's publication of *Origin of Species* was for the nineteenth century what Isaac Newton's *Principia Mathematica* had been for the eighteenth: the cardinal idea shaping how humans conceived of themselves and the natural processes over time that explained their evolution. In contrast to the Bible's supernatural explanation of the origin of life, natural selection elucidated the unfolding of life quite apart from miracle and myth. For some, science offered not only an alternative but a superior way of acquiring knowledge. Second, in historical analysis, Karl Marx's publication of *Das Kapital* offered a historicist view of human events, maintaining that nothing is self-evident, and "that all things human are inescapably historical." Such a view questioned claims to "absolute truth," suggesting instead that everything is relative and must be understood within the specific historical context that shaped it. Marx's dialectical materialism added to historicism a deterministic view of time, that history moves inexorably along a path not of human beings' choosing but according to deep-seated social and economic structures. For some, the new historical approach meant that "the Bible, the Christian faith, and the Church are to be understood as having their existence entirely within history." For others, it meant that religion itself was a human invention, an "opiate" concocted by the "haves" to keep the "have nots" contented.[5]

American Protestants were divided over these modern assertions of science and history and engaged in a lively debate about how traditional Christianity should respond. On the one hand, theological liberals sought to accommodate the new scientific and historical understandings to Christian teachings. They, like their Enlightenment forerunners, tended to be optimistic, viewing the entire evolutionary process as evidence of human progress and believing that history was ushering in a more democratic, just society. To them the Bible was predominantly a human story, a history of the Jewish people that culminated in the life and message of Christ. Moral teachings, not divine miracles, stood at the heart of the Bible's significance. Embracing a "benign naturalism," liberals considered Jesus' divinity to be rooted in his sublime teachings, not in his literally being the Son of God. In theology, liberal Christians stressed ethics over doctrine, regarding creeds as historically conditioned and therefore subject to human error. Thus, in light of new learning, liberals reconsidered both the nature of religious faith and the source of its authority. In doing so, they followed a rationalistic course that Jefferson would have applauded.[6]

On the other hand, groups of evangelicals in several denominations rejected the idea that the Christian faith must be adapted to accommodate new approaches in science and history. To them, truth was objective, absolute, and timeless. God revealed truth most fully in the Bible, and it was a message for all ages; they, like those who first planted Puritanism in New England soil, were unafraid to define the one true religion and demand that all who professed to be Christians be measured against an exact yardstick. Moreover, evangelical Protestants accommodated and supported within their system of beliefs what they considered to be core values of American life: "Patriotism, manifest destiny, Anglo-Saxon self-confidence, the common man's social and economic aspirations, peaceful community life, the Declaration of Independence, and the Constitution." Troubled by the decline in Puritan morality and the advance of liberal theology, one group of evangelicals drew up a list of "Fundamentals," doctrines that sharply defined "true" Christianity, including biblical inerrancy, the Virgin Birth, and Christ's Second Coming. They believed that "historical relativism and positivistic science threatened the heretofore unchallenged certainties of Scripture and dogma."[7]

The Modernist-Fundamentalist controversy raised anew questions about the place of religion. The Modernists saw faith as dynamic, changing with the new, secular currents of thought that altered the way people thought about space and time, science and history. Rejecting such a concept as relativistic and subjective, Fundamentalists maintained that the one true faith was timeless and objective, that God was the same today, yesterday, and forever. Differences in their understanding of faith led to distinctions over religious freedom. While Fundamentalists did not proclaim that Modernists were not Americans, they did question whether they were true Christians. In other words, Fundamentalists believed that the kind of religious freedom that had eroded the faith of the country's fathers had indeed degenerated into a secular license that led men and women away from true Christianity. Determined to defend America's Christian heritage, Fundamentalists sought to ban from public schools the teaching of what they deemed to be anti-Christian ideas, most notably, Darwinism. For a time, they succeeded, securing state legislation and winning judicial decisions sympathetic to their cause. However, though they won the celebrated Scopes Trial (July 10–21, 1925), the Fundamentalists fared less well in the religious marketplace, where Modernists portrayed them as benighted literalists.

The large numbers of Catholics who poured into America from eastern and southern Europe during the late nineteenth and early twentieth centuries gave rise to a new political battle over the place of religion in America. The central question was whether American Protestant voters would entrust the nation's highest office to a Catholic. For the Puritan Fathers,

Catholics had no place in the "City upon a Hill," an exclusion that many, if not most, Protestants continued to applaud. And while the Founding Fathers' ban on religious tests had made Catholics eligible for the presidency, only Protestants had been elected. Supported by growing numbers of their coreligionists, Catholics in the twentieth century made serious runs for the White House. Twice, Catholics won their party's nomination, and both times their religion became a central campaign issue. Opponents of the 1928 Democratic nominee helped defeat Alfred E. Smith by raising his Catholicism as a scare tactic, implying that his loyalty was to the pope, not to the people of America. Again, in 1960, John Kennedy faced virulent anti-Catholicism. Attacked by those who thought that his religion made him unfit for the nation's highest office, Kennedy decided to take the issue on in an address before a Protestant body in the Bible Belt, the Protestant Greater Houston Ministerial Association:

[B]ecause I am a Catholic, and no Catholic has ever been elected President, the real issues in this campaign have been obscured— perhaps deliberately, in some quarters less responsible than this. So it is apparently necessary for me to state once again—not what kind of church I believe in, for that should be important only to me— but what kind of America I believe in.

I believe in an America where the separation of church and state is absolute—where no Catholic prelate would tell the President (should he be Catholic) how to act, and no Protestant minister would tell his parishioners for whom to vote—where no church or church school is granted any public funds or political preference— and where no man is denied public office merely because his religion differs from the President who might appoint him or the people who might elect him.

I believe in an America that is officially neither Catholic, Protestant nor Jewish—where no public official either requests or accepts instructions on public policy from the Pope, the National Council of Churches or any other ecclesiastical source—where no religious body seeks to impose its will directly or indirectly upon the general populace or the public acts of its officials—and where religious liberty is so indivisible that an act against one church is treated as an act against all.[8]

Kennedy's victory in part overturned the unofficial voter religious test barring non-Protestants from the presidency. In the 2000 presidential campaign, Joseph Lieberman became the first Jew nominated by a major party as its candidate for the vice presidency.

One of the biggest changes in the religious marketplace has been the electronics revolution that has enabled religious groups to address national audiences. First television and then the Internet have provided new and expansive means for individuals and sects to seek converts and win support. More than any other religious group, conservative Protestants have made effective use of the electronics age to seek the election of candidates they favor and to place their social and cultural concerns on the national political agenda. Through their skillful exploitation of television to attract large national audiences, televangelists have developed enormous political clout as politicians curry their favor in order to reach their followers. Billy Graham's rise as the nation's best-known evangelist illustrates both the power of electronic media and the interaction of politics and religion. In September 1949, Graham began an evangelistic crusade in Los Angeles, preaching in the "Canvas Cathedral," a tent erected especially for the purpose. The early days of the crusade attracted little press coverage and modest crowds; empty sents were readily spotted throughout the arena. It looked as if Graham would join the ranks of other barnstorming preachers who crisscrossed the country preaching on the "Sawdust Trail" in tent after tent. But that changed when Graham caught the attention of William Randolph Hearst, who applauded the evangelist's blistering attacks on "godless Communism." Hearst sent a telegraph to his two Los Angeles–area newspapers instructing the editors to "puff Graham." When they "puffed Graham," crowds soon overflowed the tent, and Graham entered the national spotlight. From that beginning, he became adept in generating advance publicity for the crusades he organized across the country. Then when television arrived, he arranged for television coverage of his preaching services, which made him the most popular religious figure in America. His popularity attracted politicians, including presidents who sought opportunities to be photographed with him. Beginning with Dwight Eisenhower, presidents made him their informal spiritual counselor, inviting him to the White House during times of crisis, either personal or national.[9]

More recently, the Christian Coalition has emerged as a powerful political machine in the electronics age, through its effective use of the Internet as well as television. In 1989, Pat Robertson, televangelist and Republican presidential hopeful, organized the Christian Coalition to put conservative moral issues on the national political agenda and to elect conservative candidates to offices at every level, from local school boards to the presidency. Robertson blamed Christians for allowing the country to drift away from its moral foundation. "During the 20th Century," he wrote in a message posted on the coalition's website, "many Christians vanished from the public policy arena. Post World War II prosperity, along with a desire to avoid becoming 'worldly,' lured many Christians into political complacency. Unfortunately, the further Christians removed themselves from the political arena, the more our nation's institutions decayed. By the time the danger to our once-great institutions was recognized, the bright lights of the nation once known as the shining 'City on a Hill' began to dim." He reminded his followers that "our nation's founding fathers expected people of faith to participate in the political process."[10] Robertson and his followers charged that the "separation of church and state" was nothing more than "a lie of the left," and that true Christians ought to take back the country. Randall Terry, head of the antiabortion group Operation Rescue, denounced those who celebrated the nation's religious pluralism. "I want you to just let a wave of intolerance wash over you," he told his followers in 1993. "I want you to let a wave of hatred wash over you. Yes, hate is good. . . . Our goal is a Christian nation. We have a biblical duty, we are called by God, to conquer this country. We don't want equal time. We don't want pluralism."[11]

And that takes us back to where we began, to our dual religious heritage. John Winthrop's exclusive "City upon a Hill" rested on his firm conviction that it expressed the one true religion, and on his antipathy toward pluralism. As inspiring as that sentiment may have been to the Puritans settling the Massachusetts Bay Colony, it was hardly unique in the seventeenth-century Anglo-American world. Indeed, the Elizabethan Settlement had established the Church of England as the one true religion, a belief that Virginians carried with them to the Chesapeake. Further, Massachusetts Puritans and Virginia Anglicans had each derided the other as a defective branch of the Christian church. Nonetheless, Winthrop believed that the Puritans were a chosen people who had entered into a covenant that promised divine favor if they lived their lives according to scriptural teachings. Winthrop's hope that Massachusetts Bay would represent a model of faith that would inspire all Christians has found favor among groups such as the Christian Coalition, whose members insist that the country must return to its covenant faith if it is to receive God's blessings.

But the Founding Fathers rejected the Puritan model. Instead they ensured the free exchange of competing faiths without government support of or opposition to any faith. In the early twenty-first century, with religious fundamentalists around the world calling for the establishment of religious republics, Americans continue to enjoy religious freedom in a pluralistic society, a society that is often contentious and even strident, but free.

Symbolic of the contested nature of America's religious marketplace is the hymn "Faith of Our Fathers." For more than a hundred years, Americans have celebrated their religious heritage in song, singing lustily of their forefathers' steadfast faith in the face of persecution. The text conjures vivid scenes of the torture of faithful Christians suffering in "dungeon, fire, and sword." Though "chained in prisons dark," however, these martyrs "were still in heart and conscience free." Written by an Englishman, Frederick W. Faber, in 1849, the hymn has been adopted by Americans who cherish their religious liberty and wish to pay homage to those who suffered for their beliefs.[12] But exactly who are the forefathers referred to in the song? It would, no doubt, surprise most Protestants to learn that Faber was an English Catholic, and that he wrote "Faith of Our Fathers" as a tribute to the devotion of Catholic recusants who refused to shift their allegiance from the Church of Rome to the Church of England. But two versions of the hymn circulate in the American religious market, one being Faber's original text, the other a Protestant revision. The hymn, in its two arrangements, symbolizes our dual legacy of faith and freedom. Though the Catholic version would have had no place in the "City upon a Hill," it enjoys constitutional protection under the free exercise clause of the First Amendment. Because of the faith of our Founding Fathers, neither rendition of "Faith of Our Fathers" enjoys official status, and both are sung freely and openly with equal conviction that they represent the truth.

❖ *Notes* ❖

Introduction

1. The Fundamental Orders of Connecticut, January 14, 1639, in *Documents of American History*, ed. Henry S. Commager, 7th ed. (New York, 1963), 23–24.

2. John Winthrop, *A Modell of Christian Charity*, in [Massachusetts Historical Society], *Winthrop Papers*, 5 vols.(Boston, 1931), 2:284 ff.

3. Fundamental Orders, 23.

4. Constitution of the United States, in *Documents of American History*, 138–149.

5. For discussion of the congressional debate, see Jack Rakove, *Declaring Rights: A Brief History with Documents* (Boston, 1998), 173–174, 184–188.

6. Philip B. Kurland and Ralph Lerner, eds., *The Founders' Constitution*, 4 vols. (Chicago, 1987), 4:643.

7. Elizabeth Fleet, ed., "Madison's 'Detached Memoranda,' " *William and Mary Quarterly* 4 (October 1946): 556–557.

8. In the 1980s, three eminent scholars of American religious history investigated the assertion that America was indeed a Christian Nation that had declined largely because of the work of "secular humanists." They concluded that the country was not in its founding and colonial periods predominantly Christian, and that such a characterization does a disservice to true Christianity. They do, however, view the American character as profoundly religious. See Mark Noll, George Marsden, and Nathan Hatch, *The Search for Christian America* (Westchester, Ill., 1983).

9. See, for example, Pat Robertson, *The Turning Tide: The Fall of Liberalism and the Rise of Common Sense* (Dallas, 1993); Jerry Falwell, *Listen America!* (Garden City, N.Y., 1980); and Patrick Buchanan, *Right from the Beginning* (Boston, 1988).

10. Cited in John F. Wilson, "Religion, Government, and Power in the New American Nation," in *Religion and American Politics: From the Colonial Period to the 1980s*, ed. Mark Noll (New York, 1990), 78.

11. None more passionately than Leonard Levy, *The Establishment Clause: Religion and the First Amendment* (Chapel Hill, 1994).

12. For Jefferson's reference to a wall separating church and state, see his letter to the Danbury Baptist Association in Peter Onuf, ed., *Thomas Jefferson: An Anthology* (St. James, N.Y., 1999), 181–182.

13. Wilson, "Religion, Government, and Power," 79. Other notable works embracing the separationist position include James Wood, Jr., ed., *Religion and the State: Essays in Honor of Leo Pfeffer* (Waco, Tex., 1984); Frank Souraf, *The Wall of Separation: Constitutional Politics of Church and State* (Princeton, 1976); John Webb, *Religion, Politics, and Diversity: The Church-State Theme in New York History* (Ithaca, 1967); Leo Pfeffer, *Church, State, and Feedom* (Boston, 1967); Walter Berns, *The First Amendment and the Future of American Democracy* (New York, 1976); and Thomas Buckley, *Church and State in Revolutionary Virginia, 1776–1787* (Charlottesville, 1977).

14. Accommodationist interpretations may be found in Akhil Amar, *The Bill of Rights: Creation and Reconstruction* (New Haven, 1998); Richard McBrien, *Caesar's Coin: Religion and Politics in America* (New York, 1987); Michael McConnell, "Accommodation of Religion," in *The Supreme Court Review 1985*, ed. Philip Kurland et al. (Chicago, 1988), and "Religious Freedom at the Crossroads," in *The Bill of Rights*, ed. Geoffrey Stone et al. (Chicago, 1992); and James Reichley, *Religion in American Public Life* (Washington, D.C., 1985).

15. Cited in Wilson, "Religion, Government, and Power," 80.

16. Sociologists Roger Finke and Rodney Stark have given the idea of the religious marketplace and religious economy much of its theoretical form. They conceive of the flow of religious ideas as a series of transactions between suppliers of religion, churches and their representatives, and consumers, laymen and -women. They write, "Religious economies are like commercial economies in that they consist of a market made up of a set of current and potential customers and a set of firms seeking to serve that market. The fate of these firms will depend upon (1) aspects of their organizational structures, (2) their sales representatives, (3) their product, and (4) their marketing techniques." See Roger Finke and Rodney Stark, *The Churching of America, 1776–1990: Winners and Losers in Our Religious Economy* (New Brunswick, N.J., 1992), 17.

17. R. H. Campbell and A. S. Skinner, eds., *An Inquiry into the Nature and Causes of the Wealth of Nations* by Adam Smith, 2 vols. (Indianapolis, 1981), 2:797.

18. Paul Ford, ed., *The Works of Thomas Jefferson*, 12 vols. (New York, 1904), 1:61–62.

19. Smith, *Wealth of Nations*, 2:792–793.

20. Ibid.

21. *Boston Price-Current and Marine Intelligencer*, June 26, 1797.

22. The Treaty of Tripoli is discussed more fully in chapter 9.

23. Smith, *Wealth of Nations*, 2:796.

24. See Patricia Bonomi, "Religious Dissent and the Case for American Exceptionalism," in *Religion in a Revolutionary Age*, ed. Ronald Hoffman and Peter Albert (Charlottesville, 1994), 31–51.

25. See Elliott Barkan, *Edmund Burke: On the American Revolution, Selected Speeches and Letters* (New York, 1966), 84.

PART ONE

INTRODUCTION

1. Lacey Baldwin Smith, *Elizabeth Tudor: Portrait of a Queen* (Boston, 1975), 105–106.

2. Roland Bainton, *The Reformation of the Sixteenth Century* (Boston, 1952), 211.

CHAPTER 1

ENGLISH HERITAGE

1. Karen Kupperman, ed., *Captain John Smith: A Select Edition of His Writings* (Chapel Hill, 1988), 81.

2. *Memorial of Bishop [Thomas] Sherlock Reviewing History of Colonial Jurisdiction and Proposing Appointment of Colonial Bishop*, in the SPG Papers at Lambeth Palace, London. SPG, vol. 10: *American Colonies and USA General*, #107.

3. Kupperman, *Captain John Smith*, 40.

4. Ibid., 76–77.

5. Ibid., 270–271.

6. William Symonds, *Virginia: A Sermon Preached at White-Chappel* . . . (London, 1609).

7. See Matt. 22:21; 2 Cor. 10:3; Matt. 6:24; and Rom. 13:1.

8. R. W. Dyson, ed. and trans., *Augustine: The City of God against the Pagans* (Cambridge, Eng., 1998), 609.

9. Ibid., 228.

10. Ibid., 232–233.

11. Constantine convened the council to settle the Arian dispute, which threatened the peace of his empire. Arians held that Jesus was not consubstantial with the Father, that he was, instead, born of the Father and thus not one with the eternal god.

12. William G. McLoughlin, ed., *Isaac Backus on Church, State, and Calvinism: Pamphlets, 1754–1789* (Cambridge, Mass., 1968), 416.

13. Williston Walker, *A History of the Christian Church*, 3d ed. (New York, 1970), 187–188.

14. Ibid., 204.

15. Ibid., 204–205.

16. Ibid., 205.

17. Ibid., 208.

18. Ibid., 209.

19. Ibid., 212.

20. Thomas Jones, ed., *The Becket Controversy* (New York, 1970), 1–2.

21. Ibid., 2.

22. G. R. Elton, *England under the Tudors* (London, 1974), 14–15.

23. Jones, *The Becket Controversy*, 11–14.

24. Cited in J. R. Lander, *Government and Community: England, 1450–1509* (Cambridge, Mass., 1980), 117–118.

25. G. B. Harrison, ed., *The Letters of Queen Elizabeth* (London, 1935), 29–30.

26. Philip Schaff, ed., *The Creeds of the Evangelical Protestant Churches* (London, 1877), 512 and 652–653.

27. William Seiler, "The Anglican Parish in Virginia," in *Seventeenth-Century America: Essays in Colonial History*, ed. James Morton Smith (Chapel Hill, 1959), 122.

28. Walker, *A History of the Christian Church*, 247.

29. Henry Bettenson, ed., *Documents of the Christian Church*, 2d ed. (New York, 1970), 173–174.

30. For discussion of Lollards, see Elton, *England under the Tudors*, 104.

31. Bettenson, *Documents*, 182–187.

32. Elton, *England under the Tudors*, 105–106.

33. Ibid., 111–113.

34. Ibid., 218, 227.

35. Schaff, *Creeds*, 500 and 600–601.

36. Symonds, *Virginia*.

37. Josiah Pratt, ed., *The Acts and Monuments of John Foxe*, 8 vols., 4th ed. (1563; reprint, London, n.d.), 6:610–612.

38. Harrison, *Letters of Queen Elizabeth*, 29–30.

39. For fifteenth-century English religion and politics, see Christopher Haigh, *English Reformations: Religion, Politics, and Society under the Tudors* (Oxford, 1993).

40. Bettenson, *Documents*, 284–286.

41. Ibid., 235.

42. Samuel Hopkins, *The Puritans: The Church, Court, and Parliament of England, During the Reigns of Edward VI. and Queen Elizabeth*, 3 vols. (Boston, 1860), 2:486–489.

43. Schaff, *Creeds*, 643–644.

44. Bettenson, *Documents*, 282–284.

45. William Barlow, *The Summe and Substance of The Conference, which it pleased his Excellent Maiestie to have with the Lords Bishops, and other of his Clergie . . . at Hampton Court Ianuary 14. 1603* (London, 1625), 5, 36–38, 73, 76, and 85.

46. Though not a religious war, the English civil war had a religious dimension. Charles and his supporters favored uniformity centered on the Church of England, while Parliament, certainly by 1640, was dominated by those who embraced Presbyterian Puritanism.

47. Thomas Carlyle, *Oliver Cromwell's Letters and Speeches*, 2 vols. (New York, n.d.), 1:448. Presbyterianism and Independency constituted the two main divisions of mid-seventeenth-century Puritanism. Both opposed episcopacy as a form

of church government without biblical sanction. Presbyterians preferred governance based on a body of church elders, or presbyters, consisting of ministers and laymen who exercise administrative and judicial oversight over a number of churches. Independents insisted on the autonomy and self-government of each congregation.

48. Cited in Edmund Morgan, *The Puritan Dilemma: The Story of John Winthrop* (New York, 1958), 39 and 42.

49. Kupperman, *Captain John Smith*, 76–77.

50. Morgan, *The Puritan Dilemma*, 188.

CHAPTER 2

TRANSPLANTING THE CHURCH OF ENGLAND IN THE CHESAPEAKE

1. S. G. Cullifor, *William Strachey, 1572–1621* (Charlottesville, 1965), 127.

2. See Darrett Rutman, *American Puritanism: Faith and Practice* (New York, 1979), 4–5, 37–38.

3. For Virginia's early planters as individuals seeking easy profits, preferably through exploiting others, see, for example, Edmund Morgan, *American Slavery, American Freedom: The Ordeal of Colonial Virginia* (New York, 1975).

4. See Perry Miller, "The Religious Impulse in the Founding of Virginia: Religion and Society in the Early Literature," *William and Mary Quarterly*, 3d ser., 5 (October 1948): 493. His article continued under the same title in the next volume (6 [January 1949]: 24–41).

5. Edwin Arber and A. G. Bradley, eds., *Works* by John Smith (Edinburgh, 1910), 928.

6. Cited in Christine Heyrman, *Southern Cross: The Beginnings of the Bible Belt* (New York, 1997), 4, 8.

7. In his study of early Virginia literature, cited in n. 4 above, Perry Miller claims that the "planters and promoters present themselves as only secondarily merchants and exploiters, only secondarily Englishmen; in their own conception of themselves, they are first and foremost Christians, and above all militant Protestants."

8. Isa. 49:23.

9. John Jewel, *The Apologie of the Church of England* (London, 1562).

10. *Petition to the Virginia Assembly from Amherst County, Virginia, November 27, 1783*, 1. In Archives and Manuscripts Collection, The Library of Virginia, Richmond.

11. Alexander Whitaker, *Newes from Virginia. The Lost Flocke Triumphant* (1610), in Alexander Brown, *The Genesis of the United States* (Boston, 1890), 23; William Crashaw, *A Sermon Preached in London before the right honorable Lord La warre, Lord Gouernour and Captaine Generall of Virginea* (London, 1610), B2 recto.

12. Crashaw, *A Sermon*, B2 recto.

13. Cited in George M. Brydon, *Virginia's Mother Church and the Political Conditions under Which It Grew* (Richmond, 1947), 15–16.

14. Ibid.

15. Ibid., 16.

16. David Flaherty, ed., *For the Colony in Virginea Britannia: Lawes Divine, Morall and Martiall*, comp. William Strachey (1612; reprint, Charlottesville, 1969), 9.

17. Ibid., 10.

18. Ibid., 10–11.

19. Ibid., 11.

20. John Cushing, ed., *Colony Laws of Virginia*, 2 vols. (Wilmington, Del., 1978), 1:158, 181–182.

21. Edmund Morgan, "The First American Boom: Virginia, 1618 to 1630," *William and Mary Quarterly* 28 (April 1971): 178–183.

22. Cushing, *Colony Laws of Virginia*, 2:433.

23. See Kenneth Lockridge, *The Diary, and Life, of William Byrd II of Virginia, 1674–1744* (New York, 1987), 70.

24. Cushing, *Colony Laws of Virginia*, 2:434.

25. Ibid., 2:433.

26. *County Court Records of Accomack-Northampton, Virginia, 1632–1640* (Washington, D.C., 1954), 39.

27. Ibid., 10–11.

28. Ibid., 28.

29. Ibid., 86–87.

30. One has to be cautious in reading accounts on the state of religion because they often say more about the authors than about the subject addressed.

31. Brydon, *Virginia's Mother Church*, 486, 490.

32. Ibid., 493–494.

33. Ibid., 506.

34. Cited in Rhys Isaac, *The Transformation of Virginia, 1740–1790* (New York, 1982), 60.

35. Ibid., 60–65.

36. William James, *Varieties of Religious Experience: A Study in Human Nature* (1902; reprint, New York, 1982), 157–159.

37. Ibid., 80–83.

38. Richard Kroll, Richard Ashcraft, and Perez Zagorin, eds., *Philosophy, Science, and Religion in England, 1640–1700* (Cambridge, Eng., 1992), 258–259.

39. *Diary of Samuel Sewall, 1674–1729*, 3 vols. (New York, 1972), 1:46–47.

40. Ibid., 2:267.

41. Louis Wright and Marion Tinling, eds., *The Secret Diary of William Byrd of Westover, 1709–1712* (Richmond, 1941), 102–103.

42. *Diary of Samuel Sewall*, 3:144.

43. Richard Allestree, *The Whole Duty of Man: Laid Down In a plain and a familiar Way, for the Use of all, but especially the meanest Reader* (Williamsburg, Va., 1746), vii, xvii–xx. Cited in Byrd's diary on 581.

44. *Diary of Samuel Sewall*, 2:258–259.

45. *The Secret Diary of William Byrd*, 425, 442.

46. Brydon, *Virginia's Mother Church*, 507.

47. *Bishop of London's proposals for an American Suffragan*, December, 1707, in the SPG Papers at Lambeth Palace, London. SPG, vol. 10: *American Colonies and USA General*, #67.

48. Brydon, *Virginia's Mother Church*, 280, 286.

49. For transcript of Lambeth Conference, see William S. Perry, *Historical Collections Relating to the American Colonial Church*, 5 vols. (1870; reprint, New York, 1969), 1:36–65.

50. *Bishop of London's proposals for an American Suffragan*, December, 1707, in the SPG Papers at Lambeth Palace, London. SPG, vol. 10: *American Colonies and USA General*, #67.

51. Louis Wright, *The First Gentlemen of Virginia: Intellectual Qualities of the Early Ruling Class* (Charlottesville, 1964), 199.

52. Cushing, *Colony Laws of Virginia*, 1:180.

53. Ibid., 2:269.

54. Louis Wright, ed., *The History and Present State of Virginia* by Robert Beverley (Chapel Hill, 1947), 58.

55. Cushing, *Colony Laws of Virginia*, 2:532–533.

56. Brydon, *Virginia's Mother Church*, 120.

57. Wright, *The History and Present State of Virginia*, 38.

58. Perry, *Historical Collections*, 1:129.

59. Cushing, *Colony Laws of Virginia*, 2:263.

60. Brydon, *Virginia's Mother Church*, 470.

61. David Blight, *Narrative of the Life of Frederick Douglass, An American Slave, Written by Himself* (Boston, 1993), 105.

62. Milton Sernett, ed., *Afro-American Religious History: A Documentary Witness* (Durham, 1985), 27. Slaves constructed their own religious practices and beliefs. See Philip Morgan, *Slave Counterpoint: Black Culture in the Eighteenth-Century Chesapeake and Lowcountry* (Chapel Hill, 1998).

CHAPTER 3

PURITAN FATHERS AND THE "CHRISTIAN COMMON-WEALTH"

1. See Rutman, *American Puritanism*, 4–5, 37–38.

2. Cotton Mather, *Magnalia Christi Americana; or, The Ecclesiastical History of New England*, 2 vols. (1702; reprint, Hartford, 1853), 1:45.

3. Winthrop, *A Modell of Christian Charity*, 2:284, 293.

4. Ibid.

5. Nathaniel Ward, *The Simple Cobler of Aggawam in America*, ed. P. M. Zall (Lincoln, Neb., 1969), 6.

6. Conforming to the Puritans' notion of the "true" faith were those known as "visible saints." See Edmund Morgan, *Visible Saints: The History of a Puritan Idea* (New York, 1963).

7. Cited in Perry, *Historical Collections*, 3:51.

8. John White, *The Planting of Colonies in New England. From John White's "The Planter's Plea"* (Boston, 1904), 7.

9. Winthrop, *A Modell of Christian Charity.*

10. Cotton Mather, *Magnalia Christi Americana*, 1:16.

11. See Perry Miller's explanation of the federal covenant and the relation between grace and faith in *The New England Mind: The Seventeenth Century* (Cambridge, Mass., 1939), 376–377.

12. Ibid., 420.

13. Cotton Mather, *Magnalia Christi Americana*, 1:61.

14. The most celebrated case involving the moral economy in Massachusetts Bay was that of the merchant Robert Keayne. See Bernard Bailyn, *Apologia of Robert Keayne: the Last Will and Testimony of One, Robert Keayne . . .* (New York, 1965).

15. Kenneth Lockridge, *A New England Town: The First Hundred Years* (1970; exp. ed., New York, 1985), 16–17.

16. For insight into the tensions between generations over sons' desire for land, see Philip Greven, *Four Generations: Population, Land, and Family in Andover, Massachusetts* (Ithaca, 1970).

17. David Hall, ed., *The Antinomian Controversy, 1636–1638: A Documentary History* (Middletown, Conn., 1968), 341–342. See also Emery Battis, *Saints and Sectaries: Anne Hutchinson and the Antinomian Controversy in the Massachusetts Bay Colony* (Chapel Hill, 1962), and Amy Lang, *Prophetic Women: Anne Hutchinson and the Problem of Dissent in the Literature of New England* (Berkeley, 1987).

18. See Bailyn, *Apologia of Robert Keayne.*

19. For discussion of the Half-Way Covenant, see Robert Pope, *The Half-Way Covenant: Church Membership in Puritan New England* (Princeton, 1969).

20. Cotton Mather, *Magnalia Christi Americana*, 1:105.

21. Robert C. Winthrop, *Life and Letters of John Winthrop*, 2d ed. (Boston, 1869), 2:427–438.

22. Cited in Thomas Hutchinson, *The History of the Colony of Massachusett's Bay*, 2d ed. (London, 1765), 490–501.

23. Morgan, *The Puritan Dilemma*, 95–96.

24. Ibid., 163.

25. Cited in Hutchinson, *The History of the Colony of Massachusett's Bay*, 490–501.

26. "Cambridge Platform. August 26, 1648," in Commager, *Documents of American History,* 19–21.

27. Morgan, *The Puritan Dilemma,* 163.

28. John Davenport, *A Discourse About Civil Government in a New Plantation Whose Design is Religion* (Cambridge, Mass., 1663), 4–11. While the title page of the sermon indicates that John Cotton was the author, Cotton Mather insisted that that was a mistake. See Cotton Mather, *Magnalia Christi Americana,* 1:330.

29. Davenport, *A Discourse About Civil Government,* 24.

30. Thomas Walley, *Balm in Gilead to Heal Sions Wounds* . . . (Cambridge, Mass., 1669), 13.

31. Cited in Mortimer Adler, ed., *The Annals of America,* 18 vols. (Chicago, 1968–1973), 1:211–212.

32. Neal Salisbury, "Red Puritans: The 'Praying Indians' of Massachusetts Bay and John Eliot," *William and Mary Quarterly* 31 (January 1974): 29–32, 54.

33. Adler, *Annals of America,* 1:213.

34. Ibid., 213–215.

35. Roger Williams, *The Hireling Ministry None of Christs* (London, 1652), 3, 23.

36. Ibid., 24–26.

37. See Timothy Hall, *Separating Church and State: Roger Williams and Religious Liberty* (Champaign, Ill., 1998).

38. Cited in Benjamin Poore, ed., *The Federal and State Constitutions, Colonial Charters, and Other Organic Laws of the United States,* 2 vols. (Washington, D.C., 1878), 2:1594.

39. Ward, *Simple Cobler,* 7.

40. Ibid., 8.

41. Ibid., 12.

42. Walley, *Balm in Gilead,* 14.

43. Ibid., 14.

44. Increase Mather, *A Brief Discourse Concerning the Unlawfulness of the Common Prayer Worship* (Cambridge, Mass., 1686), 1–2, 4.

45. An excellent treatment of dissent in New England is found in William McLoughlin, *New England Dissent, 1630–1833: The Baptists and the Separation of Church and State,* 2 vols. (Cambridge, Mass., 1971).

46. John Norton, *The Heart of New-England rent at the Blasphemies of the Present Generation. A Brief Tractacte concerning the Doctrines of the Quakers, Demonstrating the destructive nature thereof to Religion, the Churches, and the State* . . . (Cambridge, Mass., 1659), 2, 25.

47. Ibid., 48–50.

48. Ibid., 50–51.

49. Ibid., 51–52.

50. Ibid., 53–54, 57.

51. J. Franklin Jameson, ed., *Edward Johnson's Wonder-Working Providence* (New York, 1910), 140, 144–145.

52. Ibid., 140.

53. Ibid., 146.

54. Ibid., 244–245.

55. Bernard Bailyn, *The New England Merchants in the Seventeenth Century* (1955; reprint, Cambridge, Mass., 1979), 105–106.

56. Michael Hall, *The Last American Puritan: The Life of Increase Mather, 1639–1723* (Middletown, Conn., 1988), 130.

57. David Brown, "The Forfeitures at Salem, 1692," *William and Mary Quarterly* 50 (1993): 85.

58. Ann Kibbey, "Mutations of the Supernatural: Witchcraft, Remarkable Providences, and the Power of Puritan Man," *American Quarterly* 34 (Summer 1982): 126.

59. Timothy Breen and Stephen Foster, "The Puritans' Greatest Achievement: A Study of Social Cohesion in Seventeenth-Century Massachusetts," *Journal of American History* 60 (June 1973): 20.

60. [Publications of the Prince Society], *Edward Randolph* (Boston, 1898), 318.

61. T. H. Breen, *The Character of the Good Ruler: Puritan Political Ideas in New England, 1630–1730* (New Haven, 1970), 136, 152–155.

CHAPTER 4
A "HOLY EXPERIMENT" IN RELIGIOUS PLURALISM

1. For an overview of religious freedom in colonial Pennsylvania, see William Frost, *A Perfect Freedom: Religious Liberty in Pennsylvania* (University Park, Pa., 1993).

2. Cited in Edwin Bronner, *William Penn's "Holy Experiment": The Founding of Pennsylvania, 1681–1701* (New York, 1962), 6.

3. For a nice social study comparing Puritan New England and Quaker Pennsylvania, see E. Digby Baltzell, *Puritan Boston and Quaker Philadelphia: Two Protestant Ethics and the Spirit of Class Authority and Leadership* (New York, 1979).

4. For an overview of the Quakers' early history, see H. Larry Ingle, *First among Friends: George Fox and the Creation of Quakerism* (Oxford, 1996).

5. Cited in Gary Nash, *Quakers and Politics: Pennsylvania, 1681–1726* (Princeton, 1968), 10.

6. A helpful study of the relation between the pursuits of profits and piety in Quaker Pennsylvania is Frederick Tolles, *Meeting House and Counting House: The Quaker Merchants of Colonial Philadelphia, 1682–1763* (Chapel Hill, 1948).

7. Edwin Bronner and David Fraser, eds., *William Penn's Published Writings, 1660–1726: An Interpretive Bibliography*, 5 vols. (Philadelphia, 1986), 5:90.

8. Ibid., 90–91.

9. Ibid., 105.

10. Ibid., 112–115.

11. Ibid.

12. Poore, *The Federal and State Constitutions*, 2:1518.

13. Ibid., 1519.

14. Ibid.

15. Ibid., 1519–1520.

16. Ibid., 1520.

17. Ibid., 1526.

18. Ibid.

19. Cited in Sally Schwartz's fine treatment of religious pluralism and toleration in early Pennsylvania, *"A Mixed Multitude": The Struggle for Toleration in Colonial Pennsylvania* (New York, 1987), 86.

20. Cited in ibid., 71.

21. Smith, *Wealth of Nations*, 2:793.

22. Gabriel Thomas, *An Historical and Geographical Account of the Province and Country of Pennsylvania* (London, 1698), 23–45.

23. Jon Butler, "The Records of the First 'American' Denomination: The Keithians of Pennsylvania, 1694–1700," *Pennsylvania Magazine of History and Biography* 120 (January/April 1996): 89–105.

24. Bronner, *William Penn's "Holy Experiment"*, 50–51, 148.

25. Ibid., 150–151.

26. Cited in Schwartz, *"A Mixed Multitude"*, 62–63.

27. Thomas Bray, *A Memorial Representing the State of Religion on the Continent of North-America* (London, 1700).

28. Cited in Schwartz, *"A Mixed Multitude"*, 71.

29. For a sustained analysis of the fractious politics of Pennsylvania, see Nash, *Quakers and Politics*.

30. Ibid., 34.

31. Ibid., 39.

32. Ibid., 39–40.

33. Ibid., 110, 114, 174.

34. Gary Nash, "Slaves and Slaveowners in Colonial Philadelphia," *William and Mary Quarterly* 30 (April 1973): 256.

35. Jean Soderlund, "Women's Authority in Pennsylvania and New Jersey Quaker Meetings, 1680–1760," *William and Mary Quarterly* 44 (October 1987): 582, 595–601.

36. Schwartz, *"A Mixed Multitude"*, 40–41.

37. Nash, *Quakers and Politics*, 205–207.

38. Joseph Illick, *William Penn the Politician: His Relations with the English Government* (Ithaca, [1965]), 175–176, 180.

39. Schwartz, *"A Mixed Multitude"*, 46–48.

40. Ibid., 48.

41. George Read, ed., *Pennsylvania Archives: Papers of the Governors, 1681–1747*, 4th ser., 12 vols. (Harrisburg, 1900), 1:696–702.

CHAPTER 5
"TRAFFICKING FOR THE LORD" AND THE EXPANSION OF RELIGIOUS CHOICE

1. Cited in Isaac, *Transformation of Virginia*, 152.

2. Gilbert Tennent, *The Danger of an Unconverted Ministry, Considered in a Sermon on Mark VI.34* (Boston, 1742), 14.

3. I have dealt more broadly with the Great Awakening in Frank Lambert, *Inventing the "Great Awakening"* (Princeton, 1999). An excellent treatment of the Great Awakening as part of the larger evangelical revival of the eighteenth-century Atlantic world is W. R. Ward, *The Protestant Evangelical Awakening* (Cambridge, Eng., 1992).

4. John Gillies, ed., *The Works of the Rev. George Whitefield*, 6 vols. (London, 1771), 2:134.

5. *Boston Weekly News-Letter*, April 22, 1742.

6. *Virginia Gazette*, October 31, 1745.

7. I am indebted to John J. Contreni of Purdue University for insight into the origin of the parish system. See his chapter, "From Polis to Parish," in *Religion, Culture and Society in the Early Middle Ages: Studies in Honor of Richard E. Sullivan*, ed. Thomas F. X. Noble and John J. Contreni (Kalamazoo, Mich., 1987), 155–164.

8. *Diary of Samuel Sewall*, 3:163.

9. *The Secret Diary of William Byrd*, 102.

10. Edward Elton, *An Exposition of the Epistle of Saint Paul to the Colossians*, 2d ed. (London, 1620), 8–9.

11. Smith, *Wealth of Nations*, 2:797.

12. See Boyd Stanley Schlenther, "Religious Faith and the Commercial Empire," in *The Eighteenth Century*, ed. P. J. Marshall, vol. 2 in *The Oxford History of the British Empire*, 5 vols., ed. William Roger Louis (Oxford, 1998), 128–150.

13. For the tension between merchants and ministers, see Bernard Bailyn, "The Apologia of Robert Keayne," *William and Mary Quarterly* 7 (October 1950): 568–587.

14. Jacob Marcus, *The Colonial American Jew, 1492–1776*, 3 vols. (Detroit, 1970), 1:232–233.

15. Ibid., 265.

16. Perry, *Historical Collections*, 3:96–98.

17. Ibid.

18. Cited in Edgar Pennington, *Apostle of New Jersey, John Talbot, 1645–1727* (Philadelphia, 1939), 129–131.

19. For the analogy likening the religious sect to a "brand" or "product," see Finke and Stark, *The Churching of America*, 17.

20. Cotton Mather, *Theopolis Americana*, 39–49.

21. Perry, *Historical Collections*, 1:372.

22. Cited in Karen Kupperman, ed., *Major Problems in American Colonial History* (Lexington, Mass., 1993), 374–375.

23. For discussion of "religious economy," see Finke and Stark, *The Churching of America*.

24. See Neil McKendrick, John Brewer, and J. H. Plumb, *The Birth of a Consumer Society: The Commercialization of Eighteenth-Century England* (Bloomington, Ind., 1982), 125.

25. Kupperman, *Major Problems*, 373.

26. Ibid., 373–375.

27. Timothy Hall, *Contested Boundaries: Itinerancy and the Reshaping of the Colonial American Religious World* (Durham, 1994), 83.

28. Ibid., 118.

29. Sydney Ahlstrom, *A Religious History of the American People* (New Haven, 1972), 163.

30. Ibid., 60–61.

31. Ahlstrom, *A Religious History*, 270.

32. Smith, *Wealth of Nations*, 2:789.

33. Kenneth Silverman, ed., *Benjamin Franklin: Autobiography and Other Writings* (New York, 1986), 120.

34. Richard Hooker, ed., *The Carolina Backcountry on the Eve of the Revolution: The Journal and Other Writings of Charles Woodmason, Anglican Itinerant* (Chapel Hill, 1953), 42–44.

35. Ibid., 43.

36. Ibid. 42–43, 111–113.

37. Ibid., 90.

38. Ford, *Works of Jefferson*, 1:62.

39. George Whitefield, *A Letter From Whitefield . . . Shewing the Fundamental Error of . . . The Whole Duty of Man* (Charles-Town, 1740), 4.

40. See Gordon Wood, *The Radicalism of the American Revolution* (New York, 1991), 145.

41. See *The Testimony of the Pastors of the Churches in the Province of the Massachusetts-Bay in New-England, at their Annual Convention in Boston, May 25, 1743. Against several Errors in Doctrine, and Disorders in Practice . . .* (Boston, 1743), 13. Eells was moderator of the convention and drafted the orthodox opposition to innovations introduced by the evangelical revival that swept New England in the early 1740s.

42. *Diary of Joshua Hempstead: A Record of Life in Colonial New London, Connecticut, 1711–1758* (New London, 1998), 375.

43. For the so-called Antinomian Controversy, see Michael Winship, *Making Heretics: Militant Protestantism and Free Grace in Massachusetts, 1636-1641* (Princeton, 2002).

44. *The Testimony of the Pastors of the Churches*, 1–3.

45. *Diary of Joshua Hempstead*, 375.

46. Ibid., 401.

47. Ibid., 396–397.

48. Cited from *The Spiritual Travels of Nathan Cole*, in *The Great Awakening: Documents on the Revival of Religion, 1740–1745*, ed. Richard Bushman (New York, 1970), 67–70.

49. Marilyn Westerkamp, *Triumph of the Laity: Scots-Irish and the Great Awakening, 1625–1760* (New York, 1988).

50. Catherine Brekus, *Strangers and Pilgrims: Female Preaching in America, 1740–1845* (Chapel Hill, 1998), 52.

51. Cited in Alan Heimert and Perry Miller, eds., *The Great Awakening: Documents Illustrating the Crisis and Its Consequences* (Indianapolis, 1967), 241.

52. Ibid., 453–454.

53. Hooker, *The Carolina Backcountry*, 101–102.

54. Ibid., 103

55. Ibid.

56. John Leland, *The Virginia Chronicle* (Norfolk, 1789), 3–4.

57. John Leland, *The Rights of Conscience Inalienable* (Richmond, 1793), 4.

58. Isaac, *Transformation of Virginia*, 238.

59. Ibid., 166.

60. Mechal Sobel, *Travelin' On: The Slave Journey to An Afro-American Faith* (Westport, Conn., 1979), 98. See also Mechal Sobel, *The World They Made Together: Black and White Values in Eighteenth-Century Virginia* (Princeton, 1987).

61. Heyrman, *Southern Cross*, 14.

62. For an insightful look at the Indians' Great Awakening, see Gregory Dowd, *A Spirited Resistance: The North American Indian Struggle for Unity, 1745–1815* (Baltimore, 1992).

63. Perry, *Historical Collections*, 3:418.

64. Ibid., 360.

65. Ibid., 376.

66. Ibid., 349–350.

67. Ibid., 351 and 418.

68. The best discussion of New Lights' political involvement is found in Richard Bushman, *From Puritan to Yankee: Character and the Social Order in Connecticut, 1690–1765* (Cambridge, Mass., 1967). See 221 ff.

69. Ibid., 223–224.

70. Ibid., 226–227.

71. Ibid., 229–231.

72. T. H. Breen and Timothy Hall, "Structuring Provincial Imagination: The Rhetoric and Experience of Social Change in Eighteenth-Century New England," *American Historical Review* 105 (December 1998): 1428.

CHAPTER 6
DEISTS ENTER THE RELIGIOUS MARKETPLACE

1. Silverman, *Benjamin Franklin*, 89 and 119.

2. Gillies, *Works of Whitefield*, 1:255–256.

3. Jonathan Edwards, *A History of the Work of Redemption* (Philadelphia, [1773]), 281–282.

4. Merrill Peterson, ed., *The Portable Thomas Jefferson* (New York, 1975), 434–435.

5. Edmund Morgan, *The Gentle Puritan: A Life of Ezra Stiles, 1727–1795* (New Haven, 1962), 48–49.

6. Young Ezra Stiles, as teenagers are wont to do, understated the presence of science in New England before his entering Yale. Fifty years before Ezra entered Yale, Cotton Mather studied Baconian scientific method at Harvard, and his father Increase enjoyed astronomical observations through the Harvard telescope. See Kenneth Silverman, *The Life and Times of Cotton Mather* (New York, 1985), 40.

7. Cited in Morgan, *The Gentle Puritan*, 3, 7.

8. Ibid., 48.

9. Lyman Beecher, *Autobiography and Correspondence*, ed. Charles Beecher, 2 vols. (New York, 1866), 1:43.

10. Cited in Miller, *The New England Mind*, 92–93.

11. Ibid., 93.

12. Ibid., 95–96.

13. Kerry Walters, *Rational Infidels: The American Deists* (Wakefield, N.H., 1991), 13–14.

14. Ibid., 15–17.

15. Jean-Jacques Burlamaqui, *The Principles of Natural and Political Law*, 3d ed., 2 vols. (London, 1784), 1:1–12. In part 1, chapter 1, Burlamaqui defines natural law and man's ability to understand it through reason.

16. Robert Middlekauff, *The Mathers: Three Generations of Puritan Intellectuals, 1596–1728* (New York, 1971), 142–144.

17. Silverman, *Benjamin Franklin*, 212–215.

18. Ibid., 212–213.

19. L. H. Butterfield, ed., *Diary and Autobiography of John Adams*, 4 vols. (Cambridge, Mass., 1961), 1:61–62.

20. Catherine Drinker Bowen, *John Adams and the American Revolution* (New York, 1949), 82–84.

21. Ibid., 92–93 and 97–101.

22. Silverman, *Benjamin Franklin*, 255.

23. Thomas Jefferson, "A Tribute to Philip May Hamer on the Completion of Ten Years as Executive Director, the National Historical Publications Commission," New York, December 29, 1960, in the *Annals of America*, 4:113–115.

24. William Wollaston, *The Religion of Nature Delineated* (1724; reprint, New York, 1974), 25.

25. Ibid., 68, 77.

26. Ibid., 167.

27. Benjamin Franklin, *The Autobiography and Other Writings* (New York: Viking Penguin, 1986), 89–99, 259–260.

28. For Jefferson's Bible, see *The Jefferson Bible: The Life and Morals of Jesus of Nazareth* (New York, 1995).

29. Peterson, *Thomas Jefferson*, 490–494.

30. Lester Cappon, ed., *The Adams-Jefferson Letters: The Complete Correspondence between Thomas Jefferson and Abigail and John Adams*, 2 vols. (New York, 1959), 2:509.

31. Thomas Paine, *The Age of Reason, Being an Investigation of True and Fabulous Theology* (1794; reprint, New York, n.d.), 6–8.

32. J.C.D. Clark, *English Society, 1688–1832: Ideology, Social Structure and Political Practice during the Ancien Regime* (Cambridge, Eng., 1985), 279–280.

33. See, for example, *The Secret Diary of William Byrd*, 16.

34. Ibid., 282.

35. For discussion of Tillotson's writings in colonies, see Norman Fiering, *Jonathan Edwards's Moral Thought and Its British Context* (Chapel Hill, 1981), 227 ff.

36. Peterson, *Thomas Jefferson*, 424–425.

37. Ibid., 425–426.

CHAPTER 7
WHIGS AND DISSENTERS FIGHT RELIGIOUS REGULATION

1. Edward Arber, ed., *John Milton. Areopagitica*, (1644; reprint, London, 1869), 64–65.

2. Ibid., 69.

3. Ibid., 74.

4. John Milton, *A Treatise on Civil Power in Ecclesiastical Causes Shewing That it is not Lawfull for any Power on Earth to Compell in Matters of Religion* (London, 1659).

5. John Locke, *Treatise of Civil Government and A Letter Concerning Toleration*, ed. Charles Sherman (New York, 1937), 167–169.

6. Ibid., 175, 180, and 183.

7. [John Trenchard and Thomas Gordon], *Cato's Letters: Essays on Liberty, Civil and Religious, and Other Important Subjects*, 4 vols. (1755, 6th ed.; reprint, New York, 1971), 2:226–227.

8. Bernard Bailyn, *The Ideological Origins of the American Revolution* (Cambridge, Mass., 1967), 43.

9. Leonard Labaree, ed., *The Papers of Benjamin Franklin* (New Haven 1959), 1:30.

10. Ibid., 32.

11. Milton Klein, ed., *The Independent Reflector or Weekly Essays on Sundry Important Subjects More particularly adapted to the Province of New-York By William Livingston and others* (Cambridge, Mass., 1963), 55–57.

12. Livingston's creed is in essay number 46, October 11, 1753, in ibid., 387–397.

13. Ibid., 199–204.

14. Bailyn, *Ideological Origins*, 250.

15. Klein, *Independent Reflector*, 306–316.

16. Ibid., 276.

17. Ibid., 182.

18. Ibid., 275–276.

19. Richard Beeman, *Patrick Henry: A Biography* (New York, 1974), 17.

20. Ibid., 17–18.

21. Jacob Axelrad, *Patrick Henry: The Voice of Freedom* (New York, 1947), 26.

22. Ibid., 27–28.

23. Jonathan Mayhew, *Observations on the Charter and Conduct of the Society For the Propagation of the Gospel in Foreign Parts* (Boston, 1763), 11–13.

24. Ibid., 39–41.

25. Ibid., 45.

26. Ibid, 155, 174.

27. East Apthorp, *Considerations on the Institution and Conduct of the society for the Propagation of the Gospel in Foreign Parts* (Boston, 1763), 17.

28. Ibid.

29. Mayhew, *Observations*, 107.

30. Ibid., 39.

31. John Aplin, *Verses on Doctor Mayhew's Book of Observations on the Charter and Conduct of the society for the Propagation of the Gospel in Foreign Parts* (Providence, 1763), 14.

32. McLoughlin, *Isaac Backus*, 183.

33. Ibid., 189.

34. Ibid., 190–191.

35. Ibid., 188–189, 196.

36. Ibid., 243.

PART THREE

INTRODUCTION

1. Colin Kidd, "Civil Theology and Church Establishments in Revolutionary America," *History Journal* 42 (1999): 1017.

CHAPTER 8

THE AMERICAN REVOLUTION OF RELIGION

1. For an argument that the American Revolution was radical, see Wood, *Radicalism of the American Revolution*.

2. L. F. Greene, ed., *The Writings of John Leland* (New York, 1969), 184.

3. For an insightful discussion of how the Great Awakening undermined traditional authority, see Gordon Wood, "Religion and the American Revolution," in *New Directions in American Religious History,* ed. Harry Stout and D. G. Hart (New York, 1997), 173–205.

4. See Stephen Marini, "Religion, Politics, and Ratification," in Hoffman and Albert, *Religion in a Revolutionary Age,* 190.

5. For insight into the formation and meaning of the statute, see the essays in Merrill Peterson and Robert Vaughn, eds., *The Virginia Statute for Religious Freedom: Its Evolution and Consequences in American History* (Cambridge, Eng., 1988).

6. Cited in Michael Kammen, ed., *The Origins of the American Constitution: A Documentary History* (New York, 1986), 369.

7. Patricia Bonomi argues that claims of American exceptionalism are most valid when applied to religion. She points out that unlike European countries, America was from the beginning a land of Dissenters. The Dissenting position prevailed in the fight over the place of religion in America. See Bonomi, "Religious Dissent and the Case for American Exceptionalism," 31–51.

8. John Murrin, "The Legal Transformation: The Bench and the Bar of Eighteenth-Century Massachusetts," in *Colonial America: Essays in Politics and Social Development,* ed. Stanley Katz and John Murrin, 3d ed. (New York, 1983), 565–568.

9. Edmund Burke, *Second Speech on Conciliation with America. The Thirteen Resolutions* (Philadelphia, 1775).

10. Cited in James Bradley, "The British Public and the American Revolution: Ideology, Interest, and Opinion," in *Britain and the American Revolution,* ed. H. T. Dickinson (London, 1998), 141. For full discussion of the American Revolution as a war of religion, see J.C.D. Clark, *The Language of Liberty, 1660–1832: Political Discourse and Social Dynamics in the Anglo-American World* (Cambridge, Eng., 1994); and "The American Revolution: A war of Religion?" *History Today* 39 (1989): 10–16.

11. On the ways that the seventeenth-century Commonwealthmen influenced Whigs and Dissenters in the eighteenth century, see Caroline Robbins, *The*

Eighteenth-Century Commonwealthmen (Cambridge, Mass., 1959). See also Bailyn, *Ideological Origins.*

12. John Adams, *A Dissertation on the Canon and Feudal Law,* in *The Works of John Adams,* ed. Charles Francis Adams, 10 vols. (Boston, 1851), 3:449–450.

13. Ibid., 450.

14. Isaac Skillman, *An Oration on the Beauties of LIBERTY; Of the Essential Rights of the AMERICANS* (Wilmington, 1775), viii. This sermon has also been attributed to John Allen, a Baptist minister.

15. [Library of Congress], *Journals of the Continental Congress, 1774–1789,* 34 vols. (Washington, D.C., 1904), 1:75–80.

16. *The First Book of the American Chronicles of the Times* (Philadelphia, 1774), 1–2.

17. Oliver Noble, *Some Strictures upon the Sacred Story recorded in the book of Esther, shewing The Power and Oppression of state Ministers tending to the Ruin and Destruction of God's People:—And the remarkable Interpositions of Divine Providence in favour of the Oppressed* (Newbury-port, Mass., 1775), 5 ff. and 18.

18. Ministers effectively interwove millennial and republican aspirations in their sermons. They moved easily between the sacred and the secular in espousing the virtues of republican defiance of British tyranny and those of pietistic acts of faith in preparation for Christ's spiritual reign on earth. See Ruth Bloch, *Visionary Republic: Millennial Themes in American Thought, 1756–1800* (Cambridge, Eng., 1985).

19. Douglass Adair and John Schutz, eds., *Peter Oliver's Origin and Progress of the American Rebellion: A Tory View* (Stanford, 1961), 19–20.

20. Ibid., 41–44.

21. Frank D. Gifford, "The Influence of the Clergy on American Politics from 1763 to 1776," *Historical Magazine of the Protestant Episcopal Church* 10 (1941): 108.

22. William Tennent, *An Address Occasioned by the Late Invasion of the Liberties of the American Colonies by the British Parliament* (Philadelphia, 1774), 6.

23. Ibid., 8–10.

24. Ibid., 12.

25. Ibid., 13–14, 16, 18.

26. G.D.H. Cole, ed., *The Social Contract and Discourses by Jean-Jacques Rousseau* (New York, 1950), 294, 298–299.

27. Isaac Kramnic, ed., *Thomas Paine: Common Sense* (New York, 1976), 72–73.

28. Cappon, *The Adams-Jefferson Letters,* 2:339.

29. The Church of England had been established in Virginia, Maryland, North Carolina, South Carolina, and Georgia. It also enjoyed a partial establishment in New York and New Jersey.

30. McLoughlin, *Isaac Backus,* 314.

31. Poore, *The Federal and State Constitutions,* 1:957.

32. Ibid.

33. McLoughlin, *Isaac Backus,* 315.

34. Ibid., 339.

35. Cited in Bailyn, *Ideological Origins*, 268.

36. Ibid., 268–269.

37. Thomas Jefferson, *Notes on the State of Virginia*, ed. William Peden (Chapel Hill, 1982), 158.

38. Charles James, ed., *Documentary History of the Struggle for Religious Liberty in Virginia* (New York, 1971), 76–77.

39. Jefferson, *Notes on the State of Virginia*, 160–161.

40. James, *Documentary History*, 75–76.

41. Ibid., 68–69.

42. William Henry Foote, *Sketches of Virginia, Historical and Biographical* (Philadelphia, 1850), 323–324.

43. James, *Documentary History*, 80–81.

44. Ibid., 92–94, 100.

45. Ibid., 129.

46. Jefferson, *Notes on the State of Virginia*, 161.

47. Jonathan Boucher, *Views of the Causes and Consequences of the American Revolution: in thirteen Discourses, preached in North America between the Years 1763 and 1775* (1797; reprint, New York, 1967), 66 and 306.

48. James Madison, *Writings* (New York, 1999), 29–30.

49. Ibid., 30–31, 35.

50. James, *Documentary History*, 237–238.

51. Ibid., 132–133.

52. "An Act for Establishing Religious Freedom," in *Cornerstones of Religious Freedom in America*, ed. Joseph Blau (Boston, 1949), 74–75.

53. Ibid.

54. David Ramsay, *The History of the American Revolution*, 2 vols. (1789; reprint, New York, 1968), 1:353.

CHAPTER 9
CONSTITUTIONAL RECOGNITION OF A FREE RELIGIOUS MARKET

1. Kurland and Lerner, *The Founders' Constitution*, 4:643.

2. Thomas Jefferson, *Autobiography*, in *The Writings of Thomas Jefferson*, ed. Andrew Lipscomb, 20 vols. (Washington, D.C., 1905), 1:67.

3. Wood, *Radicalism of the American Revolution*, 329–331, 443.

4. Madison made his remarks in *Federalist* No. 10. See Jacob Cooke, ed., *The Federalist* (Middletown, Conn., 1961), 56–65.

5. *The Boston Price-Current and Marine Intelligencer*, June 26, 1797.

6. *Porcupine Gazette*, June 23, 1797.

7. Ibid., 351–352.

8. Cooke, *The Federalist*, 56–65 and 347–353.

9. Ibid., 64.

10. Ibid., 351–352.

11. Thomas J. Wertenbaker, *Princeton, 1746–1890* (Princeton, 1946), 55–56.

12. Cited in Jim Schmidt, "The Reverend John Joachim Zubly's 'The Law of Liberty' Sermon: Calvinist Opposition to the American Revolution," *Georgia Historical Quarterly* 82 (Summer 1998): 354.

13. Cited in ibid., 368.

14. Gaillard Hunt, ed., *The Writings of James Madison*, 9 vols. (New York, 1901), 2:184, 186–187.

15. *Journals of the Continental Congress*, 28:291–296.

16. Hunt, *The Writings of James Madison*, 2:143–145.

17. See Isaac Kramnick and Laurence Moore, *The Godless Constitution: The Case against Religious Correctness* (New York, 1997).

18. See Donald Lutz, "The Relative Importance of European Writers on Late Eighteenth Century American Political Thought," *American Political Science Review* 189 (1984): 189–197.

19. John Adams, *Thoughts on Government* in Charles Francis Adams, *The Works of John Adams*, 4:193–194.

20. Jacob Duche, *The American Vine, A Sermon Preached in Christ-Church, Philadelphia, Before the Honourable Continental Congress, July 20, 1775* (Philadelphia, 1775), 18, 20–21.

21. John Murrin, "Religion and Politics in America from the First Settlements to the Civil War," in Noll, *Religion and American Politics*, 19–43.

22. Poore, *The Federal and State Constitutions*, 2:1626.

23. Studies of the Constitutional Convention include Derek Davis, *Religion and the Continental Congress, 1774–1789: Contributions to Original Intent* (New York, 2000), and Bette Evans, *Interpreting the Free Exercise of Religion: The Constitution and American Pluralism* (Chapel Hill, 1998).

24. On religious tests, see Edwin Gaustad, "Religious Tests, Constitutions, and 'Christian Nation,' " in Hoffman and Albert, *Religion in a Revolutionary Age*, 218–235.

25. Poore, *The Federal and State Constitutions*, 1:276, 1:828, 1:970, 2:1286, 2:1418.

26. Jonathan Elliot, ed., *The Debates in the Several State Conventions on the Adoption of the Federal Constitution*, 5 vols. (Philadelphia, 1888), 1:148.

27. *Notes of Debates in the Federal Convention of 1787, Reported by James Madison* (New York, 1987).

28. H. T. Dickinson, "Britain's Imperial Sovereignty: The Ideological Case against the Colonies," in Dickinson, *Britain and the American Revolution*, 92–93.

29. Ibid., 653.

30. Kramnick and Moore, *The Godless Constitution*, 34–35.

31. Ibid., 36.

32. Ibid., 32.

33. Ezra Stiles, *The United States Elevated to Glory and Honor. A Sermon Preached before His Excellency Jonathan Trumbull, Governor and Commander in Chief, And the honorable The General Assembly of the State of Connecticut Convened at Hartford at the Anniversary Election May 8*[th]*, 1783* (New Haven, 1783), 7, 53.

34. Ibid., 20–21.

35. Ibid., 56.

36. Ibid., 58.

37. Ibid., 67, 72.

38. Ibid., 79, 84.

39. Elliot, *Debates*, 2:148–149.

40. Ibid., 4:312.

41. Ibid., 199, 215.

42. Samuel Langdon, *The Republic of the Israelites* (Exeter, N.H., 1788), 35, 45.

43. Elliot, *Debates*, 3:659.

44. Cited in Kammen, *Origins of the American Constitution*, 369.

45. See Jay Fliegelman, *Prodigals and Pilgrims: The American Revolution against Patriarchal Authority, 1750–1800* (Cambridge, Eng., 1982).

46. George Washington, letter to the General Assembly of Presbyterian Churches, May 1789, in *The Writings of George Washington*, ed. Jared Sparks, 12 vols. (Boston, 1834–1837), 12:152–153.

47. Ibid., 154–155.

48. Ibid., 178–179.

49. George Washington, letter to the Hebrew Congregation in Newport, August 1790, in *The Papers of George Washington: Presidential Series*, ed. Dorothy Twohig, 9 vols. (Charlottesville, 1996), 6:284–285.

50. Terry Eastland, ed., *Religious Liberty in the Supreme Court: The Cases That Define the Debate over Church and State* (Washington, D.C., 1995), 356.

51. Jack Rakove, *Declaring Rights: A Brief History with Documents* (Boston, 1998), 173–174.

52. Ibid., 184. See Derek Davis, *Original Intent: Chief Justice Rehnquist and the Course of American Church-State Relations* (New York, 1991).

53. Ibid., 187.

54. Ibid., 187–188.

55. H. A. Washington, ed., *The Writings of Thomas Jefferson*, 9 vols. (New York, 1859), 7:267.

CHAPTER 10

RELIGION AND POLITICS IN THE PRESIDENTIAL CAMPAIGN OF 1800

1. William Linn, *Serious Considerations on the Election of a President: Addressed to the Citizens of the United States* (New York, 1800), 4, 20, 28.

2. Ibid., 20, 28.

3. For the debate over religious tests at the constitutional and ratifying conventions, see Daniel Dreisbach, "The Constitution's Forgotten Religion Clause: Reflections on the Article VI Religious Test Ban," *Journal of Church and State* 38 (1996): 261–295; Morton Borden, *Jews, Turks, and Infidels* (Chapel Hill, 1984); Murrin, "Religion and Politics in America," 19–43; Jackson Turner Main, *The Antifederalists: Critics of the Constitution, 1781–1788* (Chapel Hill, 1961); James H. Smylie, "Protestant Clergy, the First Amendment, and Beginnings of a Constitutional Debate, 1781–1791," in *The Religion of the Republic*, ed. Elwyn A. Smith (Philadelphia, 1971), 116–153; and Gaustad, "Religious Tests," 218–235.

4. On religion and the campaign of 1800, see Mark A. Noll, *One Nation under God?* (New York, 1988), 74–89; Charles F. O'Brien, "The Religious Issue in the Presidential Campaign of 1800," *Essex Institute Historical Collections* 107 (January 1971): 82–93; Constance B. Schulz, " 'Of Bigotry in Politics and Religion': Jefferson's Religion, the Federalist Press, and the Syllabus," *Virginia Magazine of Biography and History* 91 (January 1983): 73–91; Charles O. Lerche, Jr., "Jefferson and the Election of 1800: A Case Study in the Political Smear," *William and Mary Quarterly* 3d ser., 5 (October 1948): 467–491; Fred C. Luebke, "The Origins of Thomas Jefferson's Anti-Clericalism," *Church History* 32 (September 1963): 344–356; and L. H. Butterfield, "Elder John Leland, Jeffersonian Itinerant," *Proceedings of the American Antiquarian Society* 62 (October 1952): 214–229.

5. See O'Brien, "The Religious Issue in the Presidential Campaign of 1800."

6. Murrin, "Religion and Politics in America," 19–43.

7. Schulz, " 'Of Bigotry in Politics and Religion.' "

8. Cited in Susan Curtis, "The Sovereignty of the Secular and the Power of Religion," *American Literary History* 8 (Summer 1996): 332.

9. Connecticut adopted for its first state constitution the Fundamental Orders of Connecticut, 1638–1639. The oath is found in Poore, *The Federal and State Constitutions*, 1:251. The Massachusetts oaths are found in ibid., 1:964, 970.

10. Cited in Fleet, "Madison's 'Detached Memoranda,' " 555–562.

11. Ibid., 556–557.

12. Ibid., 558–559.

13. Ibid.

14. Ibid., 560–562.

15. Ibid.

16. Abiel Abbot, *An Eulogy on the Illustrious Life and Character of George Washington* (Haverhill, Mass., 1800), 9, 17–18, 26.

17. [John Gardner], *A Brief Consideration of the Important Services and Distinguished Virtues and Talents which Recommend Mr. Adams for the Presidency of the United States* (Boston, 1796), 27.

18. Tench Coxe, *The Federalist: Containing Some Strictures Upon a Pamphlet Entitled, "The Pretensions of Thomas Jefferson to the Presidency, examined, and the Charges against John Adams, refuted"* (Philadelphia, 1796), 13.

19. For discussion of the public sphere, see Jürgen Habermas, *The Structural Transformation of the Public Sphere: An Inquiry into a Category of Bourgeois Society,* trans. Thomas Bergen (Cambridge, Mass., 1989).

20. Nathan O. Hatch, *The Democratization of American Christianity* (New Haven, 1989), 25.

21. Cited in Charles B. Sanford, *The Religious Life of Thomas Jefferson* (Charlottesville, 1984), 26.

22. For "Virginia Statute for Religious Freedom," see *Annals of America,* 3:53–54.

23. Harold C. Syrett, ed., *The Papers of Alexander Hamilton,* 26 vols. (New York, 1977), 21:402–404.

24. Ibid., 464–467.

25. For Jefferson's draft of the Kentucky Resolution, see Ethelbert Warfield, *The Kentucky Resolutions of 1798: An Historical Study,* 2d ed. (Freeport, N.Y., 1969), 153.

26. Ford, *Works of Jefferson,* 9:148.

27. Noble E. Cunningham, Jr., "Election of 1800," in *History of American Presidential Elections, 1789–1968,* ed. Arthur M. Schlesinger, Jr., 4 vols. (New York, 1971), 1:124, 139.

28. Linn, *Serious Considerations,* 6, 10, 14–15, 17.

29. Connecticutensis, *Three Letters to Abraham Bishop* (Hartford, 1800), 28–29.

30. Ibid., 29–30.

31. Ibid., 31.

32. Cited in Borden, *Jews, Turks, and Infidels,* 26.

33. "Virginia Statute for Religious Freedom."

34. *Works of Jefferson,* 9:457.

35. Murrin, "Religion and Politics in America," 32–33.

36. *Works of Jefferson,* 5:324.

37. Ibid., 1:139.

38. Cited in Marvin Zahniser, *Charles Cotesworth Pinckney: Founding Father* (Chapel Hill, 1967), 240.

39. Cited in Henry May, *Enlightenment in America* (New York, 1976), 274.

40. See Finke and Stark, *The Churching of America,* 16.

41. For Rousseau's definition of civil religion, see Jean-Jacques Rousseau, *On the Social Contract,* ed. Roger D. Masters, trans. Judith R. Masters (New York, 1978), 131.

42. See Robert N. Bellah, "Civil Religion in America," in *American Civil Religion,* ed. Russell Richey and Donald Jones (New York, 1974), 26–29.

43. Hatch, *The Democratization of American Christianity,* 10.

44. Abraham Bishop, *Connecticut Republicanism: An Oration On the Extent and Power of Political Delusion* ([New Haven], 1800), 45.

45. Ibid. The quotation is on ix (appendix).

46. Ibid., 20.

47. Merrill Peterson, ed., *Thomas Jefferson, Writings* (New York, 1984), 510. For an insightful analysis of Jefferson's letter, see Daniel Dreisbach, " 'Sowing Usefule Truths and Principles': The Danbury Baptists, Thomas Jefferson, and the 'Wall of Separation,' " *Journal of Church and State* 39 (Summer 1997): 455–501.

48. Cited in McLoughlin, *New England Dissent*, 2:1005.

49. Poore, *Federal and State Constitutions*, 1:264.

50. Cited in Butterfield, "Elder John Leland," 198–199.

51. Ibid.

52. William G. McLoughlin, *Soul Liberty: The Baptists' Struggle in New England, 1630–1833* (Providence, 1991), 194–195, 267–268.

53. *The Papers of Alexander Hamilton*, 25:606–608. See also Henry S. Randall, *The Life of Thomas Jefferson*, 3 vols. (1858; reprint, New York, 1972), 3:10–12.

Epilogue

1. James Madison letter to Robert Walsh, March 2, 1819, in *Letters and Other Writings of James Madison*, 4 vols. (New York, 1884), 3:121–126.

2. James Madison to Rev. Adams, 1832, in Hunt, *The Writings of James Madison*, 9:48.

3. Cited in David McAllister, *Christian Civil Government in America* (Pittsburgh, 1927), 21.

4. Cited in Blau, *Cornerstones of Religious Freedom in America*, 230–232.

5. Ahlstrom, *A Religious History*, 763–764, 773.

6. Ibid., 779–780.

7. Ibid., 805–806.

8. "Remarks of Senator John F. Kennedy on Church and State; delivered to the Greater Houston Ministerial Association," in *The Kennedy Reader*, ed. Jay David (Indianapolis, 1967), 363–367.

9. Marshall Frady, *Billy Graham: A Parable of American Righteousness* (Boston, 1979), 199–202.

10. Christian Coalition website, January 26, 2001.

11. Randall Terry, *News Sentinel* (Ft. Wayne, Ind.), August 16, 1993.

12. For an exposition of the hymn and its historical context, see Albert Bailey, *The Gospel in Hymns* (New York, 1950), 202–204, and Paul Richardson, "Faith of Our Fathers," in *Handbook to the Baptist Hymnal* (Nashville, 1992), 119.

❖ Index ❖